Correctional Assessment, Casework, and Counseling

Anthony Walsh, Ph.D.
Boise State University

Helen G. Corrothers, President
James A. Gondles, Jr., Executive Director
Patricia L. Poupore, Director of Communications and Publications
Elizabeth Watts, Managing Editor
Anne R. Grant, Project Editor
Kristen M. Miller, Editorial Assistant
Ellen Cohen, Cover Design

This publication may be ordered from:

American Correctional Association
4380 Forbes Boulevard
Lanham, MD 20706
(800) ACA-JOIN

Credits

Appendix A, pages 253-277, "Client Management Classification Assessment Instrument," from "Client Management Classification: Strategies for Case Supervision," by K. Lerner, G. Arling, and C. Baird. Used with permission of the authors and the National Council on Crime and Delinquency.

Appendix A, pages 278-280, "Felony Sentencing Worksheet," copyright The Ohio State Bar Foundation, with permission.

Appendix C, pages 323-324, "The Michigan Alcoholism Screening Test," from "The Michigan Alcoholism Screening Test: The Quest for a New Diagnostic Instrument," by Melvin L. Seltzer. *American Journal of Psychiatry* (1971), vol. 127, pp. 1653-1658. Revised 1980. Reprinted by permission.

ISBN 0-929310-75-6

Printed in the United States of America by Graphic Communications, Inc., Upper Marlboro, Md.

Foreword

The roles of the probation officer and the parole officer are important ones in corrections—ones that are not well understood or appreciated outside the field. These roles require a variety of cultural and socioeconomic backgrounds, the ability to evaluate and assess clients' needs, and the ability to meet those needs using a variety of resources and the right level of supervision. These professionals are part counselor/therapist, part sociologist/investigator, and part parent.

All these roles are addressed in *Correctional Assessment, Casework, and Counseling*. The author, a former probation officer and now a professor of criminal justice, combines the theoretical with the practical to present a balanced view of the work of the probation or parole officer. Counselors and case managers working inside institutions will also find this book valuable for its coverage of basic interviewing and counseling techniques, assessment instruments, and special chapters on the older or female offender, the drug addict or alcoholic, and the mentally impaired. Students will find the book invaluable for its realistic picture of corrections work.

Speaking of students, it is hoped that those taking a course using this book as a text will continue their interest in corrections by pursuing a career in it. Corrections is a fascinating field often overlooked by those who want to go into helping professions. We need the best and brightest of the next generation to meet the challenges of the next century; please join us.

James A. Gondles, Jr.
Executive Director
American Correctional Association

Contents

Introduction

Most social work and psychology texts, to which we all must turn for guidance in interviewing and counseling, do not respond to the special needs of criminal justice clients. These works proceed on the assumption that clients are self-selected and motivated to explore their problems. Criminal justice clients, on the other hand, are usually extremely reluctant to be in any counseling relationship and frequently impervious to the problems that led them to it. This book assesses the special problems of interviewing and counseling under these conditions.

Any realistic assessment of clients must be based on an understanding of criminal behavior, both in general terms and in terms of specific offender types. I have therefore included two chapters on theoretical criminology from a practical point of view. Having worked as both police officer and probation officer, I am sensitive to the practitioner's distrust of theory. As an academic with practical experience, however, I am also sensitive to the links between theory and practice. In writing these chapters and others, I constantly kept before me the question: "How does this theoretical discussion enhance professional understanding of criminal behavior as it appears in practice?" It goes without saying that understanding is a requisite for proper assessment and that meaningful counseling has to proceed from proper assessment.

The chapters on interviewing and counseling are also geared exclusively to the criminal justice client. The chapter on interviewing contains a section on interrogation, and the various counseling chapters address individual and group counseling in both community and institutional settings. Unlike most counseling works, this one recognizes that proper assessment before counseling and other kinds of intervention is of the utmost importance. Therefore, I have included two chapters on assessment and classification in community and institutional corrections.

Also unlike other writers on counseling, I recognize that criminal justice clients need more than counseling to turn their lives around. The probation or parole officer is as much broker of community resources as a counselor and supervision agent. A chapter on the use of community resources is therefore included.

The professional assessment of criminal justice clients has been a central part of the courses I teach, and I have always found it helpful to use case studies. Examples are helpful at any stage in professional development. I have therefore included in this book material I accumulated in my days as a field practitioner—presentence reports, sentencing guidelines, classification scales, and risk and needs scales—to make the theoretical discussion more useful.

This book is an extensively revised and enlarged version of an earlier text published by Brooks/Cole entitled *Understanding, Assessing, and Counseling the Criminal Justice Client*. Statistics and research findings have been updated. In the original work, alcoholism and drug addiction were included in the same chapter; they are now separate. Likewise, the sex offender, formerly included with the schizophrenic and the mentally immature client, is now the subject of a separate chapter. There are also three new chapters—on female, juvenile, and elderly offenders, topics that reviewers of the earlier work felt were important omissions.

This book encompasses a tremendous amount of material, all of which is available in more detail elsewhere. As I point out in the chapter on presentence writing, the secret of professional report writing is the ability to glean from voluminous and diverse sources that which is necessary—not merely nice—to know. I hope that I have done this.

Anthony Walsh, Ph.D.
Professor of Criminal Justice
Boise State University

Chapter 1
Understanding the Need for Theory

There is nothing so practical as a good theory.
Kurt Lewin

The purpose of this book is to introduce criminal justice students and practitioners to the process of "correcting" the antisocial behavior of correctional clients. There is considerable skepticism and cynicism about this corrective process. Although these attitudes have some basis in reality, they are often not warranted. Those in the criminal justice field who believe that "nothing works" will operate consistently with this belief, and the outcome will justify their beliefs. If we believe that and act as if people can change and that many do so every day, we will also find that belief vindicated—prophecies tend to be self-fulfilling. Of course, there are some people for whom it is true that nothing works, and indeed no one thing works for everybody. But some things work for some people some of the time, and other things work for other people at other times.

Counseling and Criminal Justice

Counseling is a process in which clients are led to explore their feelings and concerns; in the case of criminal justice clients, many of those feelings and concerns have led them to behave irresponsibly. We hope that the counseling process will lead clients to an increased awareness of the self-destructive nature of their behavior and of alternative behavior choices. Counseling aims at removing barriers to personal growth and uncovering resources that clients can use to forge a prosocial lifestyle.

Criminal justice counseling is different from general counseling in three important ways: (1) because criminal justice clients do not generally seek counseling voluntarily, counselors are more likely to encounter reluctance and resistance; (2) criminal justice clients in general have fewer coping resources on which to draw than do other clients; and (3) criminal justice clients often have a psychological and economic investment in retaining their current lifestyle. Few general counseling texts address the special needs of criminal justice clients and the special problems of dealing with them.

Counselors in criminal justice settings do enjoy an advantage over counselors in other areas; we often possess a wealth of verified information about our clients' backgrounds and past behavior from a variety of sources, such as juvenile files, police reports, and social and psychological evaluations. This information makes it easier for us to assess our clients than for counselors in many other settings.

Assessment is the formal evaluation and analysis of a client's deficiencies and needs and the risks the client poses to the community, so that realistic counseling plans and strategies can be created. Assessment is accomplished with well-tested instruments, many of which are included in this book. For a counselor to attempt to supervise, counsel, and otherwise help a criminal justice client without a thorough assessment would be like a physician performing surgery without having done a thorough diagnostic workup of the patient.

But for effective diagnosis, the physician must have a grounding in the diseases that could account for the patient's complaint. Similarly, you should have a grounding in the causes of the kind of behavior you are trying to correct. With this analogy in mind, this book is structured around (1) *understanding* criminal behavior and its correlates, (2) *assessing* the problems and needs of individual clients, and (3) using that understanding and knowledge to effectively *counsel* clients. We begin with the need to understand criminal behavior.

Criminology is the study of the causes of crime. It is an interdisciplinary study, encompassing biology, physiology, psychology, economics, and sociology (Jeffery 1985). Yet much of what passes as criminology is limited to sociological analysis. Individual differences are often ignored, and the implication is that everything is responsible for crime except the criminal. It is true that sociological insights are of tremendous importance in understanding crime, but they do not exhaust the causal possibilities.

This is not a comprehensive textbook on criminological theory; the theories of criminology that are briefly presented are intended to help you to understand more fully the theories of counseling addressed later and to make your application of them in practice more effective. In other words, we are interested in criminological theories here only as a foundation on which counseling techniques can be grounded. The discussion of these theories centers around the unifying theme of this book: criminality, like most other forms of destructive behavior, can often be traced to deprivation of love. This idea derives from many of the giants of the human sciences (Comte, Marx, Sorokin, Maslow, Fromm, Montagu) as well as the originators of the counseling theories we will encounter (Freud, Rogers, Berne, Glasser). Thus, we begin with a discussion of the usefulness of theory in general, and then go on to examine five theories of the etiology (cause) of crime.

The Usefulness of Theory

Workers in any field must understand the phenomena with which they work. As a correctional practitioner, you must understand the phenomenon of crime and its causation so that you may more effectively deal with your clients. Theories of crime seek to offer plausible explanations of how the known correlates of crime are linked together. Facts are incoherent in themselves; only theories of their interrelationships give voice to what would otherwise be unintelligible static. A theory is an intellectual scaffold around which is constructed an edifice of useful knowledge. Empirical facts are the bricks of the edifice, each one slotted into its proper place to form a coherent whole.

Given the numerous competing theories of crime causation, you may be forgiven for asking which is "true." Physicians do not ask which theory of disease is the true one, because they know that there are many different kinds of disease for which there are many different causes. No physician ever treats a person for "illness," but for a specific disease. Like disease, crime is not explicable in terms of a single cause or set of causes. Yet when we treat all offenders for "criminality," we are thinking and acting as if it were. Even treatments for specific diseases often vary according to such things as age and gender and are differentially successful according to how cooperative patients are, their personality types, and the psychosocial support they enjoy. Why should it be any different for criminals in all their diversity?

Thus, theories about crime and criminality must be context-specific. But even then theories are not "true" in any absolute sense. Truth for the scientist is tentative, relative, and open to qualification and challenge. If a theory generates useful empirical research and provides consistency within the domain of interest, we are more faithful to the spirit of science to call it adequate than to call it true.

An adequate theory must conform to the pragmatic, correspondence, and coherence theories of truth as outlined by philosophers of science. That is, a theory is "true" to the extent that it (1) provides useful guidance for the further exploration of certain phenomena, (2) corresponds with the facts already known about those phenomena, and (3) fits those data into propositions to form a logical and coherent whole.

The usefulness of a given theory depends on the context. It would be of little help to a sociologist seeking to explain fluctuations in the crime rate, for instance, to learn that neurophysiologists have discovered that certain criminals have a higher-than-expected frequency of dysfunction in certain regions of the brain. Likewise, the neurophysiologist is little interested in the sociocultural variables alleged by the sociologists to account for differentials in the crime rate. The sociologists and the neurophysiologists are simply dealing with two different units of analysis: societies and brains. The criminologist and the criminal justice practitioner seeking to understand clients, however, must be sensitive to both the macro (large-scale) analyses of the sociologist and the micro (small-scale) analyses of the physiologist, as well as to all the other disciplines that attempt to understand the phenomena of crime.

Much of the heat generated by theorists of different persuasions seems to result from the failure to distinguish between *crime* and *criminality*. Crime is socially disapproved behavior, the rates of which fluctuate with social conditions over time. Given a chance permutation of factors, anyone can fall afoul of the law and commit an out-of-character crime. Criminality, on the other hand, refers to "stable differences across individuals in the propensity to commit criminal (or equivalent) acts" (Wilson & Herrnstein 1985:23). Sociologists tend to be more interested in crime, and other kinds of scientists are more interested in criminality. In the business of corrections, you will run into both out-of and in-character offenders.

As a correctional worker you will quite naturally find theories dealing with the behavior of individuals and their immediate environment most suitable for your purposes. After all, these are the areas most accessible to perception and most amenable to change within the context of the correctional worker/client relationship. Nevertheless, when you are interviewing, assessing, and counseling criminal clients, you will be able to perform the task more professionally if you understand crime causation at all levels of analysis. Therefore, we shall briefly examine five theories of criminality, ranging from the macrosociological to the psychophysiological.

Figure 1-1 represents the routes that may have led your clients to you. It begins with the forces in the larger sociocultural environment that are considered to be criminogenic (crime-generating). This aspect of crime causation is addressed in *anomie theory*. A "lower" level of analysis is the subcultural theory of *differential association;* all Americans share the larger sociocultural environment of the United States, but only a small group of us share in those subcultures declared criminogenic by differential association theory. Even within a criminogenic subculture family environments affect individuals differently, and the effects are the subject of *control theory*. Finally, it is widely recognized that similar environmental experiences can produce both saints and sinners. By nature, some individuals socialize more easily than others for a variety of complex reasons. (Chapter 3 addresses those reasons in the context of psychopathy and love deprivation.)

Please note that although the diagram implies intimate connections among all levels of analysis, each of the theories may stand alone as a plausible explanation of crime at a given level of analysis. Persons who commit crimes because they lack legitimate opportunity (as anomie theory sets forth) do not necessarily belong to gangs (as differential association theory describes) or lack family attachments (as control theory proposes). The diagram simply suggests that the

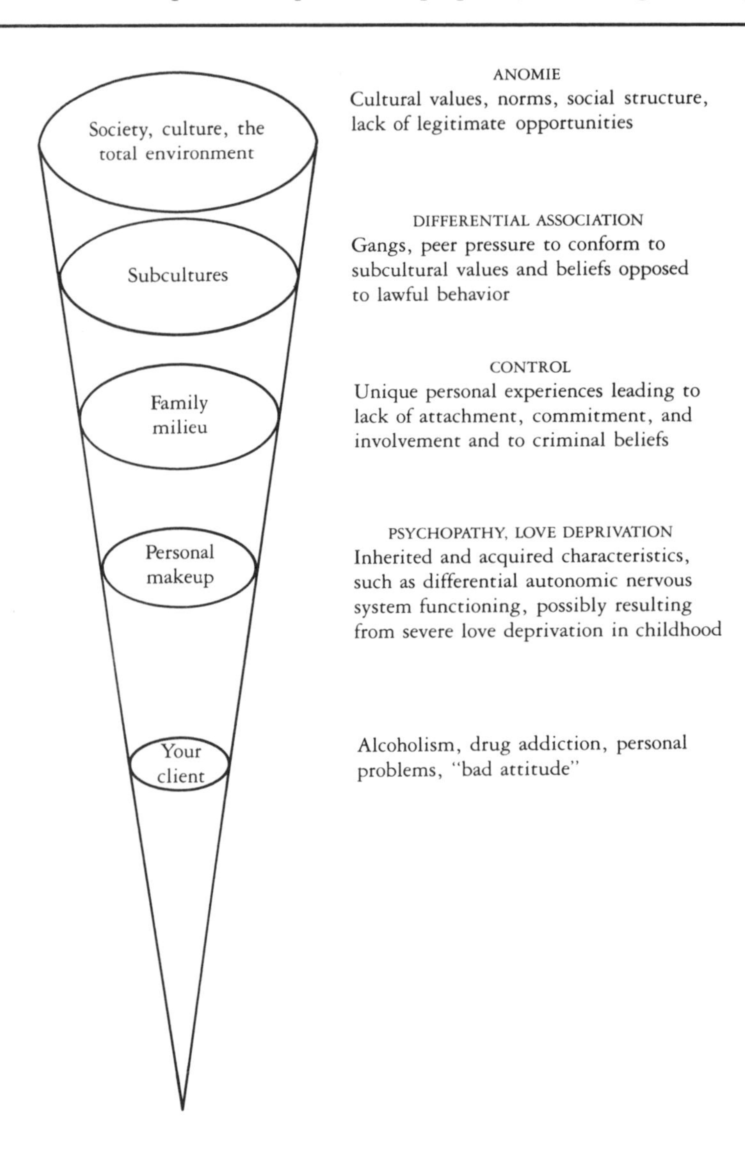

Figure 1-1 Criminal "causal" funnel and explanatory theories

development of individuals cannot be viewed in isolation from the micro or macro environments that constitute their reality. Nor can the effects of those environments be separated from the effects of the personal attributes and the unique experiences of individuals.

Summary

This chapter discusses operating assumptions and philosophy: rehabilitation is possible with a thoroughly professional approach to the business of correcting the criminal justice client's behavior. There are many negatives associated with counseling this type of client, foremost of which is the fact that the client/counselor relationship is not voluntary.

However, there are also certain advantages not found in other client/counselor relationships, such as the availability of information about the client, well-tested assessment tools, and the amount of control the counselor can exercise over clients' activities.

The usefulness of theory must be emphasized. Practitioners of any profession must be fully grounded in the knowledge available to that profession. You must not be afraid or suspicious of "mere" theory, for it is the jumping-off point for adequate practice. Without some theoretical understanding of the phenomena you are working with, you will be floundering around in the dark, making mistakes, and possibly thwarting your clients' chances of becoming useful citizens.

References and Suggested Readings

Jeffery, C. 1985. Criminology as an interdisciplinary behavioral science. In *Biology, crime and ethics,* edited by F. Marsh and J. Katz. Cincinnati: Anderson.

Wilson, J., and R. Herrnstein. 1985. *Crime and human nature*. New York: Simon & Schuster.

Chapter 2
Sociological and Psychological Theories

Criminological theories are often not so much proven wrong as simply pushed to one side in favor of newer interpretations. The hope of the social sciences, of course, is to achieve an elegant simplicity, and perhaps in time the explanation of crime will form a coherent whole.

Gresham Sykes

Anomie Theory

"Anomie" is a French term meaning "lacking in rules" or "normlessness." It is a relative term, for no society is completely lacking in rules for the regulation of social life. French sociologist Emile Durkheim first used this term in his book *The Division of Labor in Society* (1951). His basic idea was that as societies become increasingly complex, maintaining social cohesion becomes more problematic. Crime, like other forms of deviance, grows in proportion to the loss of social cohesion. A loss of social cohesion means that there will be ambiguity and contradictions in the rules and standards of moral behavior.

Durkheim did not, however, view crime as abnormal. He argued that because crime is found at all times and in all societies, it is normal and inevitable. What needs to be examined, Durkheim said, are the structural conditions and contradictions in society that result in different levels of criminal activity in different nations and at different times within the same nation (Durkheim 1950).

American sociologist Robert Merton expanded Durkheim's concept of anomie to develop a sociocultural explanation of crime. Like other macrosociological theories of crime, Merton's anomie theory uses a frame of reference that has three elements: social structure, social values, and social norms. His theory views crime not as a symptom of personal inadequacies but rather as a "normal" response to the ways these sociocultural elements impinge on and limit the responses of certain groups. Anomie theory ascribes the basic cause of crime not to individuals but to structural contradictions within society that place strain on individuals; the strain, in turn, may engender criminal behavior.

The structural contradiction identified by Merton as most important in generating criminal behavior is the disjunction between the cultural value of material success and the lack of access to legitimate means of achieving it:

> It is only when a system of cultural values extols, virtually above all else, certain common success goals for the population at large while the social structure rigorously restricts or completely closes access to approved modes of reaching these goals for a considerable part of the same population that deviant behavior ensues on a large scale (Merton 1957:146).

(Although the theories presented here were formulated by an American, they apply to other societies that to some degree share similar values and social arrangements.)

American society has taken what morality has traditionally considered to be base and evil—acquisitiveness—and elevated it to the status of a prescriptive (required or recommended) goal. In the American equation material things (two cars in the driveway, home entertainment centers, electric carving knives, mink belly-button brushes) equal happiness, prestige, and self-worth. If you do not possess visible trappings of self-worth, it is obvious to all that something is remiss in your character—you are not a participant in the "American Dream." Pause and reflect: is this not the constant message you receive from all quarters every day? Are not the most popular heroes of the "soaps" and the prime-time series on television rich and powerful men and women with many expensive toys?

To maintain a sense of self-worth, then, individuals are exhorted to strive to achieve culturally approved goals. However, certain groups are systematically denied access to the competition because of such structural impediments as race and class. In other words, we are all encouraged to develop champagne tastes, even if we have only beer budgets. It is not the beer budget per se that generates the dissatisfaction that may lead to crime, it is the size of that budget relative to the size of culturally defined wants and needs. It is difficult to be happy, as Eastern philosophers have long maintained, if expectations exceed accomplishments or if wants and needs are not proportionate to means. As Durkheim himself said (1951:246): "No living being can be happy or even exist unless his needs are sufficiently proportioned to his means."

Modes of Adaptation

Happiness, then, may be viewed as an equation:

$$\text{happiness} = \frac{\text{accomplishments}}{\text{expectations or goals}}$$

To bring this equation into balance, individuals have either to increase their accomplishments or to decrease their expectations. In other words, people have to adapt. Merton identifies five methods of adaptation to a social structure that exhorts us all to strive for accomplishments but that deny some persons legitimate access to the means by which they can be realized: conformity, ritualism, retreatism, rebellion, and innovation.

Conformists are individuals who accept the validity of cultural goals and socially approved methods of achieving them. Such people quietly live out their lives, probably never getting themselves into any serious trouble with the law. Most of us are conformists; if we were not, our society would be in serious trouble.

The *ritualist* is the nine-to-five slugger who has long given up on achieving the cultural goals but who nevertheless continues to work ritually within the boundaries set forth as legitimate. Although Merton considered the ritualist adaptation deviant because it rejects cultural goals, it is not a criminal adaptation. The ritualist, satisfied with the security of a job, is rarely in trouble with the police.

The *retreatist* rejects both cultural goals and institutionalized means of attaining them. People in this category drop out of society and often take refuge in drugs, alcohol, and transiency. They are often in trouble with the law because of crimes committed to support a drug or alcohol habit. This type of individual often presents the greatest challenge to the criminal justice worker.

The *rebel* rejects both the goals and the means of capitalist American society, but, unlike the retreatist, wishes to substitute alternative goals and means. He or she is committed to a sociopolitical ideal, such as socialism, that aims for a more just and equitable society. You will rarely have to deal with a rebel unless he or she becomes radicalized to the point of putting ideology into actions that break the law.

Finally, we have the *innovator*. This individual fully accepts the validity of the cultural goals of monetary success but rejects (possibly because of having been denied access to them) the legitimate means of attaining them. "The desire to make money without regard to the means in which one sets about doing it is symptomatic of the malintegration at the heart of American society" (Taylor, Walton & Young 1973:93). Innovators do not believe in working, stashing a few dollars in the bank, and then watching it slowly gather interest. That's for suckers. It is much faster, takes far less effort, and is far more exciting to rob the bank. In other words, crime is an innovative avenue to success—a method by which deprived people get what they have been taught by their culture to want.

Lessons and Concerns

Whether or not this theory is useful to the macrosociologist, it has little utility for the correctional worker dealing with individual retreatists or innovators. There are few, if any, policy recommendations logically derived from it that could be implemented by the corrections worker. This is partly why this and many other sociological theories are rejected by those in positions of power within the criminal justice system (Gilsinan 1990:103). The "cure" for crime that can be logically derived from anomie theory is the expansion of legitimate opportunities and the opening of equal access to them. All correctional workers can recount numerous instances in which they have shed blood, sweat, and tears to obtain employment for clients, only to see them "blow it" in short order. It is not enough simply to provide jobs for clients who may have come to prefer taking advantage of illegitimate opportunities. As a criminal justice worker, you must convince these clients of the ultimate futility of their short-run hedonism and the necessity of becoming responsible human beings. Clients have to be convinced to assess their situations realistically and to adjust their aspirations accordingly. Further, you must not be seduced into accepting the propositions of anomie theory as excuses for criminal behavior. The assertions of Merton notwithstanding, being a criminal does not necessarily mean that legitimate opportunities have not been available. In fact, one of the flaws in anomie theory is that it is tautologous (arguing circuitously): it poses a cause of crime (lack of legitimate opportunity) and then uses the alleged effects of that cause (crime) as a measure of the absence of opportunities (Nettler 1978:252).

But one lesson of anomie theory that is worth the attention of corrections workers is the notion that crime can be a highly rational response to social conditions as they are perceived by the offender. Here the term rational means having a logical fit between a desired goal and the means used to attain it.

Rational action in pursuit of a goal does not imply that the action is "right" or "moral." It merely means that the actors have sought a goal at a price they feel that they can afford. A criminal who risks life and limb in the illegitimate pursuit of legitimate cultural goals behaves irrationally from the point of view of a middle-class observer, but rationality must be defined in terms of the actor, not the observer. The innovator has more to gain and less to lose than does the middle-class observer. Perhaps realizing this will lead you to a deficiency definition rather than a pathological definition of criminal behavior: criminals may be deficient in the attributes that are productive of lawful behavior rather than being psychologically defective.

Differential Association Theory

Differential association theory, first formulated by sociologist Edwin Sutherland, focuses on elements in the subculture that may predispose an individual to one or another of Merton's adaptations. This theory stresses the potency of group pressures. It asserts that we all, like chameleons, take on the hues of our environment. We blend in, we conform. We tend to like baseball, hot dogs, apple pie, and Chevrolets rather than soccer, bratwurst, strudel, and Volkswagens, not because the former are superior to the latter but because we are born Americans and not Germans. We view the world differentially according to the attitudes, beliefs, and expectations of the groups around which our lives revolve.

Assumptions

There are nine propositions or components of differential association theory, but these may be compressed into four general principles:

1. Criminal behavior is learned in interaction with other people. Criminal behavior, therefore, is not biologically inherited, the result of psychological abnormalities, or invented anew by each criminal.
2. For the most part, people learn criminal behavior within intimate personal groups. This learning includes specific techniques, motives, rationalizations, justifications, and attitudes.
3. The cognitive components of learned criminal behavior are derived from definitions of the legal code (the law) as favorable or unfavorable to violations of the law. Thus, a person becomes a criminal because he or she holds an excess of definitions favorable to the violation of the law over definitions unfavorable to violations of the law.
4. Associations with others holding definitions favorable to violation of the law vary in frequency, duration, priority, and intensity. That is, the earlier in life and the more often one is exposed to criminal norms of conduct, the longer those exposures last, and the more strongly one is attached to those holding criminal norms, the more likely one is to become a criminal.

The general validity of this line of thinking has been supported by a number of empirical studies. (See Matsueda 1982 for a brief review.) The correlations between association with delinquent peers and delinquency are some of the strongest found in social science. But they should be, because such correlations are "built in" much as playing tennis is built in to association with tennis players. Association with delinquent peers tends to act more as a "releaser" of delinquent behavior than as a stimulator for otherwise prosocial individuals to engage in criminal activity. Reviews of friendship patterns (e.g., Berndt 1982) have shown that the propensity for a given pattern of activity (including criminal activity) precedes association with like-minded individuals and not the other way around (as this theory implies), though this is not to say that associations do not increase this propensity.

The theory has also been criticized by Nettler (1978:265), who described it as both "true and trivial," because it "reduces to the common-sense idea that people are apt to behave criminally when they do not respect the law." It can explain all sorts of values, attitudes, tastes, and behaviors as a general theory of socialization within subcultures. "Culture" explains everything in general, and therefore nothing in particular. Crime is a specific behavior engaged in by a few individuals within cultural settings with varying degrees of tolerance for antisocial behavior; in no sense is it a cultural *expectation.*

Differential association theory is a variation on the old social pathology theme: Criminal behavior is cooked up in the simmering caldron of pathological neighborhoods, stirred by morally bankrupt companions, spiced by trouble, toughness, and excitement, and dished up with a jungle philosophy of "do unto others as they would do unto you—but do it first!"

Lessons and Concerns

Although we cannot deny the cogency of the line of thought presented to us by differential association theory, it contains little practical leavening to lighten the dense dough of theory. As a correctional worker, you will be able to do nothing to mitigate the pernicious effects of poor neighborhoods. You can merely help clients to act responsibly within them. Nonetheless, you must be sensitive to the burden of peer pressure felt by criminal justice clients. An awareness of those pressures will enable you to formulate realistic goals for treatment rather than moralize with clients about the company they keep.

However, be aware that probation and parole have regulations regarding clients associating with other criminals. Differential association theory dictates that this is a plausible prohibition and that introducing clients to activities that lead them to associate with prosocial others is a reasonable treatment plan. But life in the steaming ghettoes of the United States often requires—literally requires—belonging to a gang and participating in its attitudes and behaviors for survival. Young men and sometimes young women living in a ghetto who do not take advantage of the comradeship and protection of the local gang are certainly not acting in their own best interests. Nonparticipation in such groups leaves them naked to the preying designs of those more in tune with the reality of their living conditions. Be aware of this distasteful fact, while taking some comfort that quite often simple acts like getting married or obtaining legitimate employment will distance clients from their former companions and place them in the company of others with more prosocial values.

One can take issue with the assumption of differential association theory that antisocial behavior is learned. Many critics of this theory stress that antisocial behavior comes naturally to the unsocialized individual: "What is there to be learned about simple lying, taking things that belong to another, fighting, and sex play?" asks an early critic (Glueck 1956:94). Assuredly, individuals learn to get better at doing these things because of their associations with other like-minded individuals, but they do not have to be taught such natural acts. What they have to be taught is how to curb them, what constitutes moral behavior, and how to consider the rights and feelings of others. We will now consider a theory that recognizes this simple fact.

Control Theory

Whereas anomie and differential association theories focus on causes said to propel people into crime, control theory focuses on conditions in the environment that restrain them. Control theory assumes that the criminological need is not so much to explain why some of us behave badly but rather why most of the time most of us behave well. Control theory implicitly agrees with the Freudians that self-interest is innate; that we are born antisocial (or perhaps, asocial); and that we must learn painful lessons. We must learn that civilization is bought at the cost of the repression of natural urges and that our wants and needs are inextricably linked to the wants and needs of others. Those who do not learn these lessons are heading for trouble.

Identifying the "Typical" Criminal

The version of control theory examined here (Hirschi 1977) is compelling. It is consistent with what we are reasonably certain we know about the personal and demographic characteristics of those who commit crimes, as well as with the perceptions of crime causation held by most workers in the field of criminal justice. Hirschi finds the "typical" criminal to be a young male who grew up in a fatherless home in an urban slum, who has a history of difficulty in school, and who is unemployed. Of course, there are also female criminals, but in the following discussion the masculine pronoun emphasizes that we are talking about Hirschi's typical criminal.

Having defined the typical criminal, Hirschi makes logical deductions flowing from the nature of crime. He first observes that criminal activity is contrary to the wishes and expectations of others. From this he deduces that those most likely to commit crimes are those least likely to be concerned with the wishes and expectations of others. Criminal activity is contrary to the law and involves the risk of punishment. Therefore, those who commit crimes are least likely to accept the moral beliefs underlying the law and are least likely to concern themselves with the risk of punishment. Finally, criminal acts take time and are, therefore, most likely to be engaged in by those who have the time that the act requires (they are unemployed).

What demands explanation are the conditions in the typical criminal's life that explain why he runs roughshod over the wishes and expectations of others, his lack of belief in the moral order, his relative lack of concern for punishment, and his possession of the time that criminal activity requires. To state the question in terms more consistent with the theory: What controls in the environments of noncriminals that restrain them from criminal activity are absent in the environments of criminals? These restraining controls are attachment, commitment, involvement, and belief.

The Four Controls

Attachment refers to one's psychological and emotional closeness to others. It implies a reciprocal love relationship in which one feels valued, respected, and admired and in which one values the favorable judgments of the person or persons to whom one is attached. Sociologists use the concept of "significant others" and "reference groups" to refer to the people we consider important to us and whose good opinions we value. Significant others are close family members and friends; reference groups are those groups of people we admire and seek to emulate. These are the people to whom we look for guidance in our behavior, values, and attitudes. Much of our behavior can be seen as attempts to gain favorable judgments from our reference groups and significant others. Parents are for many years the most important behavior-orienting significant others.

It follows that those who are most likely to behave in ways contrary to parental wishes are those who do not care about parental reactions. Risking the good opinion of another is of minor concern when that good opinion is not valued. Why that good opinion is not valued need not concern us at this point; in general, however, we may state that it is a function of the lack of a reciprocal love relationship between parent and child.

Lack of attachment to parents and the attending lack of respect for their wishes easily spills over into a lack of attachment and respect for the broader social groupings of which the child is a part. Much of the controlling power of others outside the immediate family lies in the threat of reporting juvenile misbehavior to parents. If the child has little fear of parental sanctions, the control exercised by others inevitably has limited effect. The family is the nursery of human nature. If the family is in disarray, if there is little love, concern, or attachment within it, then the product will be defective. The child of such a family will fail to form a conscience, will lack the ability to sympathize and empathize with others, will learn that the world for him is a cold and heartless place and will act toward it accordingly.

It would be naive to posit that all life's ills have their origins in the lack of early childhood attachment. After all, numerous other life events affect the probability of becoming criminal. Nevertheless, I am in deep agreement with Selma Fraiberg (1977:62), a psychiatrist who has spent a lifetime studying child development, when she writes:

> The condition of non-attachment leaves a void in the area of personality where the conscience should be. Where there are no human attachments there can be no conscience. As a consequence, the hollow men and women contribute largely to the criminal population. It is this group, too, that produces a particular kind of criminal, whose crimes, whether they be petty or atrocious, are always characterized by indifference. The potential for violence and destructive acts is far greater among the bondless men and women; the absence of human bonds leaves free "unbound" aggression to pursue its erratic course.

Commitment refers to a lifestyle in which one has invested considerable time and energy in the pursuit of a lawful career. The pursuit of such a lifestyle is highly rewarding to the individual, who, therefore, has a valuable stake in conforming to the moral standards of his society. The person who has made this considerable investment, or who aspires to, is not likely to risk it by engaging in criminal activity; the cost/benefit ratio (what the individual stands to benefit from crime contrasted with what he stands to lose if caught) renders the cost of crime prohibitive. However, the lower the stake with which one enters the criminal game, the more appealing are the possible prizes. The poor student, the truant, the dropout, the unemployed, has little invested in conventional behavior and risks less in the cost/benefit comparison. For example, although the bank president and the casual laborer may equally desire to engage the services of an underage prostitute, the bank president is more likely to restrain the urge because he stands to lose far more if caught and exposed.

The successful acquisition of a stake in prosocial conformity, of course, requires success in school. Success in school requires disciplined application to tasks that children do not particularly relish but that they nevertheless must complete in order to gain the valued approval significant others, especially parents. Again, if approval is not forthcoming or is not valued, children will busy themselves in tasks more congenial to their natural inclinations, inclinations that almost certainly do not include business math or the principles of grammar. Attachment, then, would appear to be an essential prerequisite to any genuine commitment to a prosocial lifestyle.

Involvement is a direct consequence of commitment, part of a conventional pattern of existence. Involvement is a matter of the time and energy constrictions placed on us by the demands of our commitments. Involvement in lawful activities reduces exposure to illegal activities. Conversely, the lack of involvement in lawful activities increases the possibility of exposure to illegal activities: "The devil finds work for idle hands." Puritanical considerations aside, it is a cogent statement.

Belief refers to the ready acceptance of social prescriptions and proscriptions. Those individuals who are free of the constraints on their behavior imposed by attachment, commitment, and involvement evolve a belief system shorn of conventional morality. It is a system of belief containing narrow images of self-interest and justified by a jungle philosophy.

Unlike differential association theory, control theory does not view the criminal belief system as causative in the sense that it generates criminal behavior. Rather, criminals act according to their urges and then justify or rationalize their behavior with a set of instrumental statements such as "Suckers deserve what they get," "Everybody does it—why not me?" and "Do unto others as they would do unto you—but do it first." These are the statements of alienated individuals—Merton's innovators—reflecting and rationalizing the lifestyle of the unattached. For the control theorist, the behavior gives birth to the belief rather than vice versa. Control theory agrees with differential association theory in that the beliefs of criminals are reinforced by the company of like-minded individuals. However, it strongly disagrees with the proposition that such peer groups are intimately connected, loyal to one another, and bound by a prescriptive code of conduct. Criminal ties reflect more the weakness of the bond criminals have with conventional society than the strength of their attraction to one another. Any worker in the criminal justice field will attest to the fact that criminals will trip over one another in the race to be the first to "cut a deal" favorable to themselves to the detriment of their "friends."

The following is a point of major importance to the criminal justice worker seeking to understand criminal behavior: The lack of attachment, commitment, and involvement with conventional others does not constitute a motive for crime; the lack of these controls represents social deficiencies that reduce the potential costs of engaging in criminal activity. Nor is a criminal belief system a motive for crime; it is merely a justification for antisocial behavior. The criminal justice worker must, of course, consider both the behavior and the alleged justification for it totally unacceptable.

Lessons and Concerns

The utility of control theory for the criminal justice worker is that it provides meaningful guidance in working with clients. Obviously, nothing can be done to make your clients more attached to their families. You cannot visit the past and clean up pathological family dynamics, unfortunate though that may be. But in your role as counselor and broker of community resources you *can* take steps to involve your client in a more conventional lifestyle. The criminal justice worker has considerable power over the activities of clients. That is to say, you cannot only lead the horse to water, with judicious use of your authority, you can also persuade your clients to sip a little. Perhaps they may even acquire a taste for it. Contrary to the currently fashionable nihilistic "nothing works" philosophy, I have witnessed many remarkable turnarounds by clients guided by caring criminal justice professionals, and many reviews of the rehabilitation literature (e.g., Gendreau & Ross 1987) substantiate this.

Although control theory has much in the way of practical guidance to commend it over the other two theories examined, it is certainly not the final word in the understanding of criminal behavior. It does not account for those who appear simply to prefer a criminal lifestyle despite numerous opportunities to forge a conventional lifestyle. It sees criminal activity as a poor second choice made by unhappy individuals whose socialization has rendered them largely unfit to pursue conventional avenues to success. In the vast majority of cases, this is an accurate assessment. Most individuals caught up in criminal activity might well prefer acceptance into the "moral community," $50,000 a year from a straight job, a house with a white picket fence, and membership at the country club. Unfortunately, their experiences during their formative years have not prepared them psychologically, emotionally, or intellectually to accept the possibility that such a lifestyle could be a reality for them. They have a stifling orientation to the here and now and a tremendous burden of inertia preventing them from taking that first step on the long journey to social respectability.

However, control theory does not address that small percentage of criminals who have genuine contempt for the "straight life," those who by nature find it extremely difficult to function in a conventionally acceptable way. These are the people who enjoy hurting people, who crave the danger, excitement, and adventure provided by a life of crime. Life without the opportunity to hurt and dominate others, without drugs and alcohol, without violence and predation, without fast cars and faster women, would be meaningless to them. We call such people psychopaths, sociopaths, or "antisocial personalities." Although they constitute a small minority of the criminal population with which you will have contact, it is important to understand them because they engage in criminal activity out of all proportion to their numbers. They will be discussed in Chapter 3.

Summary

The sociological theories outlined in this chapter, especially anomie and differential association, locate the causes of crime in the criminal's environment. Both of these theories support the proposition that societies get the kind of criminals they deserve. Anomie theorists believe we manufacture criminals by socioeconomic conditions that emphasize monetary success but at the same time deny a significant number of people access to legitimate avenues to this goal. The retreatist and innovator modes of adaptation to the social structure are the modes that generate criminal behavior. The conformist and the ritualist modes of adaptation produce individuals who are, in the main, law-abiding. Only under certain circumstances does the rebellious mode generate illegal behavior.

Differential association theory concentrates on specific subcultures that predispose individuals to specific modes of adaptation. This theory emphasizes that criminal behavior is learned within subcultures where criminal behavior is "normal" behavior. Differing levels of criminal behavior depend on the frequency, duration, priority, and intensity of association with criminals and criminal values and attitudes. Thus, for both these theories, criminal behavior can be a rational adaptation to environmental conditions. In short, theorists in both these camps tend to give the impression that everyone is guilty of crime—except the criminal.

Although these theories offer no policy recommendations that could be put into practice by the criminal justice worker, they do illuminate the relationship between criminality and the social arrangements in which it exists. Their main value is to lead you to a deficiency rather than a pathological interpretation of criminal behavior.

Control theory differs from the other two theories in that rather than looking at conditions that may lead people to commit crimes, it looks at conditions that isolate people from it. Those conditions, or controls, are attachment, commitment, involvement, and belief. The presence of the last three depends to a large extent on the initial presence of attachment. Criminal beliefs do not "cause" one to commit crimes; they merely provide rationalizations for those who do commit crimes.

Control theory fits well with most criminal justice practitioners' perceptions of why individuals commit crimes. It recognizes that lack of controls is not entirely the fault of the individual, but it does not attempt to justify irresponsible behavior by pointing to this lack as a cause. Control theory offers some useful practical guidance for criminal justice workers, both for understanding criminal behavior and for recognizing conditions that can be rectified in the counseling and supervision process.

References and Suggested Readings

Berndt, T. 1982. The features and effects of friendships in early adolescence. *Child Development* 53:1447-1460.

Durkheim, E. 1950. *The rules of the sociological method.* Glencoe, Ill.: Free Press.

Durkheim, E. 1951. *The division of labor in society.* Glencoe, Ill.: Free Press.

Durkheim, E. *1951. Suicide: A study in sociology.* Glencoe, Ill.: Free Press.

Fraiberg, S. 1977. *Every child's birthright: In defense of mothering.* New York: Basic Books.

Gendreau, P., and R. Ross. 1987. Revivification of rehabilitation: Evidence from the 1980s. *Justice Quarterly* 4:349-406.

Gilsinan, J. 1990. *Criminology and public policy: An introduction.* Englewood Cliffs, N.J.: Prentice Hall.

Glueck, S. 1956. Theory and fact in criminology: A criticism of differential association theory. *British Journal of Criminology* 7:92-109.

Hirschi, T. 1977. Causes and prevention of juvenile delinquency. *Sociological Inquiry* 47:322-341.

Matsueda, R. 1982. Testing control theory and differential association: A causal modeling approach. *American Sociological Review* 47:489-504.

Merton, R. 1957. *Social theory and social structure.* New York: Free Press.

Nettler, G. 1978. *Explaining crime.* New York: McGraw-Hill.

Reid, S. 1976. *Crime and criminology.* Hinsdale, Ill.: Dryden Press.

Sutherland, E., and D. Cressey. 1978. *Principles of criminology.* Philadelphia: Lippincott.

Taylor, I., P. Walton, and J. Young. 1973. *The new criminology.* New York: Harper & Row.

Wilson, J., and R. Herrnstein. 1985. *Crime and human nature.* New York: Simon & Schuster.

Chapter 3
Psychophysiological Theories

Two traits—lovelessness and guiltlessness—distinguish the psychopath from other human beings, for he is neither "normal," "neurotic," "psychotic," nor a usual criminal.
William McCord

Psychopathy

Ever since French psychiatrist Phillipe Pinel introduced the concept of psychopathy to the world in the eighteenth century, it has had a checkered career. Conceptual and ideological arguments associated with the psychopathic syndrome moved Gibbons (1973:171) to state: "We regard any attempt to proceed further with the psychopathy/criminality line of inquiry a futile business." Numerous studies before and since Gibbons' cavalier dismissal of the concept strongly suggest that his opinion was ill-considered. Such studies have shown convincingly that psychopaths can be distinguished from nonpsychopaths physiologically, psychologically, and sociologically (Allen, Linder, Goldman & Dinitz 1971; Goldman, Linder, Dinitz & Allen 1971; Walsh 1987). A similar claim cannot be made for the anomic, the alienated, or any other of the conceptual types (including race) said to be causally related to levels of criminal activity.

It is well known that a small number of recidivists account for the lion's share of all crime. Marvin Wolfgang's classic study (1972) of 10,000 males in Philadelphia over a period of twenty years found that 35 percent of them were arrested one or more times. However, a mere 6.3 percent of those arrested (2.2 percent of the total group) accounted for 52 percent of all offenses and 66 percent of all violent offenses attributable to all those arrested. Studies in other countries have shown essentially the same results; that is, approximately 6 to 8 percent of offenders are responsible for about 66 percent of all serious crimes. Although the studies were interested in identifying recidivists rather than psychopaths per se, it is reasonable to assume that many of those chronic and violent recidivists possessed the descriptive features of psychopaths. Interestingly, the percentages for chronic recidivists match almost exactly the percentages for those criminals diagnosed as psychopaths (7 to 10 percent) in a review of nine studies conducted since 1918 (Bennett, Rosenbaum & McCullough 1978:76).

Descriptive Features of Psychopaths

How can psychopaths be described? In an effort to find out, Gray and Hutchinson (1964) obtained data from 677 Canadian psychiatrists. The psychiatrists ranked ten descriptive items that they considered to be most characteristic of psychopaths. The results were as follows:

- unable to profit from experience
- lack of a sense of responsibility
- inability to form meaningful relationships
- lack of impulse control
- lack of moral sense
- consistently antisocial
- behavior unchanged by punishment
- emotionally immature
- unable to experience feelings of guilt
- extremely self-centered

The majority of these psychiatrists (43.9 percent) felt that psychopathy has its origins in an interplay of hereditary and environmental influences, 38.2 percent felt that the problem was mostly environmental, and 14.4 percent felt that it was mostly hereditary. We shall explore studies relevant to the majority view.

Psychopathy and the Autonomic Nervous System

On the premise that the primary defining characteristic of psychopaths is their inability to foresee the negative consequences of their behavior, a number of scholars have studied the autonomic nervous system (ANS). The ANS has two branches; the sympathetic and the parasympathetic. The sympathetic branch functions to increase the organism's potential for action. It prepares the body to react to fearful and stressful stimuli by pumping hormones into the bloodstream to make possible a more energetic response to threat (the "fight or flight" response). Individuals differ considerably in the reactivity of their ANSs. In general, the greater a person's reactivity to fear and anxiety-generating stimuli, the more likely the person is to avoid the stimuli that bring on the unpleasantness of autonomic upheaval. A person with a hyperreactive (overreactive) ANS is highly conditionable and compliant and has a strong fear of any sort of punishment or social displeasure.

Psychopaths appear to exhibit abnormally diminished ANS responses to stimuli that would be threatening to individuals with normal or hyperactive autonomic nervous systems. Hare and Quinn (1971) found significant differences between psychopaths and nonpsychopaths in such physical indicators of ANS arousal as electrodermal, cardiac, and vasomotor activity. Schalling (1978) found significantly lower levels of catecholamines in the urine of psychopaths awaiting criminal sentencing than in nonpsychopaths in the same anxiety-generating situation. (Catecholamines are stress-related hormones; their levels in the urine or bloodstream are a strong indicator of the level of stress being experienced.) Since psychopaths had significantly lower levels than nonpsychopaths, their ANSs were apparently not "turned on" or activated to pump catecholamines into the bloodstream. It follows that they were not unduly anxious or afraid about an impending event that might terrify most of us.

Similarly, Ferguson (1973) has reported that a number of different studies have found distinctly different brain wave patterns in psychopaths and nonpsychopaths in response to anticipation of an event. A normal subject's electroencephalogram (EEG) response to the anticipation of a stimulus, such as a flash of light, a noise, or a puff of air, is referred to as the contingency negative variation (CNV). Significantly, psychopaths show no CNV at all, indicating that they simply do not relate what went before to what will happen later. Such studies provide strong physiological explanations for the psychopath's inability to learn from experience and for the inability of punishment to alter his or her behavior. It is important to attribute this inability to learn from experience not to low intelligence, but to defective emotional controls.

Psychopathy and the Wechsler P/V Test

A marker of psychopathy that is readily available to the correctional worker is the Wechsler P/V (performance IQ greater than verbal IQ) test. In his studies of the sociopathic phenomenon, Wechsler (1958:176) noted: "The most outstanding feature of the sociopath's test profile is the systematic high score on the performance as compared with the verbal part of the scale." In a review of many studies of PV and antisocial behavior, Miller arrived at the same conclusion: "This PIQ/VIQ relationship was found across studies, despite variations in age, sex, race, setting, and form of Wechsler

Figure 3-1 Observed and expected numbers and percentages compared with Kaufman's normative sample P/V profiles

	Juvenile Delinquents				Prison Inmates			
	Observed		Expected		Observed		Expected	
P/V Level *	N	%	N	%	N	%	N	%
V > P	30	(05.8)	66.69	(13.0)	17	(00.9)	232.96	(13.0)
V = P	328	(63.9)	384.75	(75.0)	1307	(72.9)	1344.00	(75.0)
P > V	155	(30.2)	61.56	(12.0)	468	(26.1)	215.04	(12.0)
Totals	513	100.0	513	100.0	1792	100.0	1792	100.0

Juvenile Delinquents: Goodness-of-fit χ^2 = 170.42
df = 2, p. .000001

Prison Inmates: Goodness-of-fit χ^2 = 498.7
df = 2, p . 000001

* V > P = ≤ -15, V= P = -14 to 14; P > V = ≥ 15

The goodness-of-fit chi-square (χ^2) is a measure of how well the observed data "fit" expectations (in this case, how well the offender distribution fits the normative distribution). By comparing the observed numbers in each category with the expected numbers, we arrive at a value that informs us of the probability of finding such results by chance. The reported probability value ($p < .000001$) tells us that such results are likely to be obtained by pure chance less than one time in every one million samples of the same size and composition. Offenders and "normals" are therefore quite different with respect to P > V profiles.

Statistical analysis is original; data taken from Walsh and Beyer (1986) and Barnett, Zimmer & McCormack (1989).

scale administered, as well as differences in criteria for delinquency" (1987:120).

Let us test such statements using prison inmate data (Barnett et al. 1989) and data from a sample of 513 male juvenile delinquents (Walsh, Beyer & Petee 1987). We will compare the PIQ/VIQ profiles in inmate/delinquent samples with those in Kaufman's (1976) "normative" sample (a normative sample is one drawn from a "normal" population and used to generate norms or standards for scores on various tests and attributes that can be compared to "special" populations). Kaufman found a discrepancy of fifteen points between performance and verbal IQ was required for statistical significance at the .01 level of probability. Among his sample of 1,100 boys, he found that 13 percent had verbal IQs fifteen or more points greater than their performance IQs (V > P), 75 percent were "balanced," i.e., had discrepancy scores between -14 and +14 (V=P), and 12 percent had performance IQs fifteen or more points greater than their verbal IQs (P > V). If offending behavior is unrelated to P/V profile, offenders' profiles should not differ significantly from these normative profiles.

Figure 3-1 compares the number and percentage of cases in each P-V category in the delinquent and inmate samples with numbers and percentages expected on the basis of Kaufman's normative sample. It is obvious that neither sample fits normative expectations. V > P boys in the delinquent sample are underrepresented by a ratio of 2.24:1, and P > V boys are overrepresented by 2.5:1. In the inmate sample, V > P inmates are underrepresented by a ratio of 14.4:1, and P > V inmates are overrepresented by a ratio of 2.27:1. These findings indicate that P > V boys are 5.2 times more likely to be delinquent than are V > P boys and that P > V adult males are twenty-nine times more likely than VP adult males to be inmates.

The statistical analysis is original, based on data taken from Walsh and Beyer (1986) and Barnett, Zimmer, and McCormack (1989).

Using discrepancy scores less extreme than plus or minus fifteen, other studies have also discovered category percentages that noticeably depart from population norms. In a sample of seventy-four delinquents, Andrew (1977) found 11.3 percent in the V > P category, 55.6 percent in the P = V category, and 33.8 percent in the P > V category. The percentages in each category found in Tarter, Hegedus, Winsten, and Alterman's (1985) sample of 100 delinquents were 7.9, 63.4, and 28.7.

The evidence thus strongly indicates that a V > P profile can be considered predictive of good behavior in the general population and a P > V profile predictive of delinquent behavior in the general population. Further, it appears that the discriminating power of these intellectual profiles becomes greater as individuals get older, as evidenced by the extremely small number of V > P individuals in the inmate sample.

What are the possible mechanisms by which superior performance IQ relative to verbal IQ translates into antisocial behavior? The performance section of the WISC/WAIS tests short-term memory and is more productive of anxiety than the verbal section. We have already pointed out that psychopaths have low reactivity to anxiety-evoking stimuli; some authorities suggest that this functions to prevent the disruption of short-term memory (Mednick & Hutchings 1978; Andrew 1982; Mednick & Finello 1983). Keiser (1975:306) interprets the relationship between ANS hyporeactivity and memory disruption thus: "An interference hypothesis might suggest that when affective [emotional] processes are underreactive there will be less distortion of immediate memory traces within the same anatomical structures, for example, the hippocampal circuits that are thought to play a role in short-term memory systems." What this difficult sentence means is that a person who does not become nervous in a short-term-memory testing situation will tend to score much better than on tests of long-term memory, such as the verbal portion of the WISC or WAIS.

Psychopaths, then, tend to have higher performance IQ scores relative both to their own verbal IQ scores and to the performance/verbal discrepancy scores of nonpsychopaths. A recent study determined that this difference was not a function of either low verbal scores or lower overall intelligence; in fact, those subjects designated as psychopaths had significantly higher overall intelligence than nonpsychopaths on the full-scale IQ test and did not differ significantly on scores obtained on the verbal section (Walsh & Beyer 1986). This is a potentially useful piece of information in the assessment of your clients because substandard IQ scores are often reported in juvenile probation psychological reports. However, you should tread lightly and not be too anxious to pin the psychopathic label on a client based solely on a performance/verbal discrepancy score.

Psychopathy and the Reticular Activating System

Other investigators into the psychopathic syndrome have studied cortical arousal mechanisms to explore the possibility that psychopaths' apparent need for intense stimulation (a need that gets them into considerable trouble) could be a function of proneness to inhibition in their reticular activating systems (RAS). The RAS is a finger-sized network of cells located in the brain stem that regulates the brain's alertness. People with an RAS prone to inhibition (sluggishness) easily lose interest in people and things, leading them constantly to seek new excitement to alleviate their boredom. Their brains just seem to "turn off." Studies testing this proneness by such methods as noting electrically recorded involuntary pauses when subjects are asked to tap a metal stylus can be found in Hare (1970) and Eysenck (1970).

Stimulant drugs such as amphetamines increase cortical arousal, thus increasing responsiveness to environmental stimuli. The heavy use of psychoactive drugs, as well as a lack of protracted interest in hobbies, vocations, or other people may be valuable diagnostic clues in identifying possible psychopathy.

Lessons and Concerns

Psychopathy theories are more an interesting set of interrelated propositions drawn from many fields of inquiry than they are theories in the strict sense. The data presented here have not been formally linked into a fully coherent picture. This is a pity, because the data appear to be solidly grounded, unlike the strictly sociological theories. The challenge to society presented by psychopathic individuals makes understanding of them imperative. What follows is an attempt to link the empirical findings with the clinical insights provided by the major theories of counseling in a coherent theory of psychopathy.

Love Deprivation

What follows is my interpretation of the etiology of psychopathy, based on many years of experience dealing with loveless clients and on my own research on psychopathy and love deprivation. Like psychopathy "theory," love deprivation "theory" does not conform to the strict definition of theory, being an attempt to integrate data from a wide variety of disciplines. You may at times consider it difficult reading, but it will give you a firm foundation for understanding and applying the counseling theories you will encounter later. It will help you to see why love is emphasized so much in these theories, and you will have a firmer grasp of the underlying mechanisms.

Many giants of the human sciences have written eloquently of the ennobling power of love in human affairs (Comte 1896; Freud 1924; Sorokin 1954; Maslow 1953; Fromm 1965; Montagu 1978). To this list we add Marx and Engels (1956:119), who wrote, "Love not only makes the man an object, but love makes the object a man." (The term *object* is used here in the sociological sense; that is, the child has to develop the ability to "stand outside" and view itself through the eyes of others). If this is true, it would seem important to discover what kind of beings are created by the absence of love.

I use the following definition of love: "Love, then, can be defined as the satisfaction of our needs to receive and bestow affection and nurturance, to be given and to give assurances of value, respect, and appreciation, and to offer and accept the warm symbiosis that nature herself decrees" (Walsh 1981:96). Having perused thousands of criminal histories filed in juvenile and adult probation departments and at a state penitentiary, I am led to agree with Glasser (1976:187) that the vast majority (Glasser estimates about 85 percent) of those in constant and violent conflict with the law have not had these needs met.

Love Deprivation and the Brain

Love deprivation is a physical-emotional privation that begins in infancy and adversely effects the biochemical and neuronal (nerve-cell) structuring of the brain. It may also affect how the ANS responds to stimuli. The brain is a marvelously plastic organ, the functioning and even the structure of which are highly sensitive to early environmental input (Kalil 1989). The experiences that cultivate our beings are perceived, processed, and acted on via intricate electrochemical interactions among a conservatively estimated 100 billion brain cells (neurons). Our neurons are "wired" to each other via a maze of axons and dendrites, with the general structural pattern being contained in our genetic blueprints.

However, there simply are not enough DNA molecules in the blueprint to provide specific information about how two neurons are to be connected (Alexander 1984:29). The specific patterning and organization of the brain cells is a function of habituated synaptic connections (a synapse is the interface between neighboring neurons). Interneuronal connections are apparently made when neurons send axons snaking out to seek other neurons that are the sources of chemicals needed to make the synaptic connection. Interneuronal communication occurs more easily the more often the electrochemical synapses have been connected. Since the work of Bennett, Diamond, Kretch, and Rosenzwig (1964), it has been consistently shown that organisms raised in stimulus-enriched environments develop greater cortical density and greater quantities of essential neurotransmitter chemicals than organisms raised under less stimulating conditions.

The stimuli with which we are concerned are acts of cutaneous (skin) stimulation—affectionate touching, kissing, and cuddling—tactile assurances for the infant that it is loved and secure. The neural effects of a lack of tactile stimulation have been aptly described by Rutter (1972:57): "It has been well-shown that neural metabolism varies with the rate of stimulation, and recent work has demonstrated ganglionic atrophy and the reduction in dendritic growth following light privation during the stage of active cell growth." (Dendrites are short fibers that extend from neurons and receive the electronic impulses. Glial cells cover the dendrites, except at the synaptic terminals, and serve, it is thought, to amplify impulses.) The effects of tactile stimulation on the brain can be understood with the realization that the skin is almost an external extension of the brain, formed as it is from the same layer of embryonic tissue (Taylor 1979:136). In a quite literal sense, we are talking about the wiring of the neuronal circuits for love.

Experimental evidence for these effects includes the love deprivation studies with monkeys conducted by Harry Harlow and his colleagues (1958, 1962). Harlow raised monkeys in isolation from their mothers and other monkeys. These unfortunate simians, deprived of normal stimulation, especially of their mothers' tactile stimulation, never exhibited the normal behavior patterns of their nondeprived peers. Introduced to other monkeys, they responded either with fearful withdrawal or with excessive aggression—sometimes with both. The aggression was obviously not learned, since they had not had the opportunity to learn anything from other monkeys.

When female isolates were introduced to males raised normally, they insisted on remaining chaste. Harlow, however, devised "rape racks" in order that they might be impregnated. When the offspring of those rapacious unions were born, their mothers did not display normal maternal behavior, but rather ignored, attacked, and even killed them. We tend to call similar noncaring and violent behavior displayed by humans psychopathic. Subsequent deprivation experiments involved the sacrificing of deprived monkeys in order to examine their brains. Predictably, the brains of deprived monkeys showed abnormal dendritic wiring. It is important to note that the aberrant behavior observed was the direct result of abnormal brain structuring, which was in turn the direct result of deprivation of love (Suomi 1980).

A neurophysiological explanation for the behavior of Harlow's monkeys is that the circuits to the septum pellucidum (the brain's "pleasure center") had not been wired, thus allowing for the uninhibited expression of the impulses emanating from the primitive amygdala (the brain's "punishment center"). Both these neurological structures are part of the limbic system, the part of the brain that regulates emotional reactions. As Heath (cited in Restak 1979:150) has put it: "Aberrant electrophysiological activity occurs in deep cerebellar nuclei, as well as other deep-brain structures—most pronounced in the limbic system—in association with severely disturbed behavior resulting from maternal-social deprivation." Further, Mark and Ervin (1970) and Surwillo (1980) have demonstrated that violent criminals, many of whom were diagnosed as psychopathic, show abnormal brain waves from the limbic system on an EEG. Recent studies by Walsh and Petee (1987) and Walsh and Beyer (1986) have demonstrated a firm link between love deprivation, psychopathy, and violent crime among juvenile probationers in two different jurisdictions. Violent crime is the kind of crime that disturbs us most deeply. Although it must be said that the great majority of criminals are not psychopaths, psychopaths commit a disproportionate share of violent crime (Blair 1975; Andrew 1982).

The love deprivation-psychopathy-violence triangle appears to be a tight one, with evidence coming from a variety of sources. For instance, criminologist C. Ray Jeffery (1979:109) notes that psychopaths "come from homes without love or security, where beatings are everyday occurrences, where brutality is a way of life." Anthropologist Ashley Montagu (1978:178) writes: "Take any violent individual and inquire into his history as a child, and it can be predicted with confidence that he will be discovered to have had a lacklove childhood, to have suffered a failure of tender, loving care." Neuropsychologist James Prescott (1975:65) goes even further to state that deprivation of tactile manifestations of what he called "tender loving care," is responsible for "a number of emotional disturbances which include depressive and autistic behaviors, hyperactivity, sexual aberration, drug abuse, violence, and aggression." A more comprehensive review of the literature on this subject is to be found in Haynie (1978).

Love Deprivation and ANS Responsiveness

The ideas we have examined thus far would appear to indicate that neural dysfunction—specifically, limbic system dysfunction—mediates between love deprivation and violent behavior. That is, love deprivation adversely affects neural structure and function, and those effects lead to many of the aberrant behaviors displayed by the psychopath. The question we now ask ourselves is, could the hyporeactivity of the psychopath's ANS also be a function of love deprivation? Although the published research indicates a clear hereditary mechanism determining ANS response activity, the work of DiCara (1970), for one, has shown conclusively that ANS responses can be conditioned to an amazing degree.

An intriguing set of experiments by psychologist Richard Solomon (1980) showed that ANS adjustment to constant emotional arousal is necessary to prevent overtaxation and possible breakdown of physiological response mechanisms. These studies show that repeated aversive stimuli in the form of electric shocks given to laboratory dogs have a steadily decreasing effect on autonomic responses. Over time, the administration of these shocks has little or no effect on an animal's ANS responses.

The hardened criminal's ANS, like those of Solomon's unfortunate dogs, may be underresponsive to punishment or threats of punishment for the same reason: constant exposure to a cruel, brutal, and loveless environment. Criminologist Michael Wadsworth (1976:246) suggests that this is so: "Certainly from the published work it would be reasonable to speculate that children who in early life lived in surroundings of stress and emotional disturbance are more likely to develop some kind of mechanism for handling the effects of stress, and that may be reflected in later autonomic reactions to stressful situations." Wadsworth's own research cautiously supports his reasonable speculation, as do the findings of Buikhuisen (1982); Farrington (1987); and Walsh (1991).

The Violence-predictive Triad and Love Deprivation

A triad of early childhood and adolescent behaviors long considered to be predictive of violent behavior may also be examined in the light of physiology. These three behaviors—enuresis (bedwetting), fire-setting, and cruelty to animals—are often addressed in psychological reports. However, the reports do not explain exactly how this triad translates into violent behavior. The lack of connection confuses and frustrates judges and criminal justice workers who must act on the information. I have challenged examining psychiatrists and psychologists, without much success, to explain how the triad can be used predictively. The usual response is, "We don't know how or why; we only know that taken together they are a fairly reliable predictor." If any explanations do come forth, they are couched in misty psychoanalytic terms such as "urethral eroticism" for enuresis, "a destructive wish for close object relationships" for fire-setting, and "the acting out of aggressive sexual sadism with a non-threatening object" for cruelty to animals. While any or all of these unconscious sexual motivations may be true, such behaviors might be better explained with reference to physiological variables of the kind we have been discussing.

The response to the need to void the bladder during sleep usually results in the sleeper waking up and doing so, or holding the urine until time to get up. This response is under the control of the autonomic nervous system and has been conditioned by rewards and punishments. An ANS that conditions poorly may not alert us to void in the appropriate place. In the absence of any organic pathology, therefore, enuresis may be seen as a function of a hyporeactive ANS. Since a hyporeactive ANS is a defining characteristic of the psychopath, enuresis beyond early childhood—in conjunction with the other components of the triad—might also be viewed as a possible marker of psychopathy.

Setting fires and watching them burn is exciting. Most of us limit this kind of activity to burning leaves and garbage, but some find that setting fires to buildings to be intensely stimulating—a real "turn-on." Could this be a particularly destructive variation of the psychopath's need for intense emotional stimulation? Since psychopaths lack that attribute we call a conscience, there is little difficulty in accepting that they may have few qualms about sacrificing someone's home in the pursuit of the visceral excitement they crave. Recall that this need for excessive excitement has been viewed as a function of an overly sluggish reticular formation, which inclines the psychopath to consider what we find exciting to be eminently boring.

The third behavior in the triad, cruelty to animals, indicates the psychopath's lack of love and sympathy for other living things and their lack of empathy for the suffering of others. The violent adult psychopath would prefer torturing humans, but the child finds cats and hamsters a safe substitute. Not having had love, sympathy, and empathy wired into their neural circuits by their early experiences, psychopaths cannot be expected to display behavior for which they were not adequately programmed.

Any of these three behaviors taken alone could generate a variety of interpretations that do not concern us. Taken together, they give us an excellent diagnostic tool. The pertinent observation for us is that studies of individuals who have a history of such behavior have consistently unraveled histories of severe love deprivation (Hellman & Blackman 1966; Wax & Haddox 1972). It is important to emphasize that many other variables besides these three are predictive of violent behavior. This triad has been discussed because, unlike many other predictors, it is almost routinely included in the psychiatric/psychological reports that you will be reading as corrections practitioners.

Lessons and Concerns

What are the implications of love deprivation theory for you as a criminal justice worker—beyond an increased understanding of the problem of violence and the pernicious effect of deprivation of love? Certainly, you can do nothing about the early developmental history of your clients. The way to prevent that problem, if there is one, lies in social engineering of child-rearing practices on a massive scale. We have thus returned to sociology and to the same sort of practical difficulties we encountered when examining sociological theories. Canadian theorist Blaine Harvey suggests that we begin with hospital maternity practices (mother/infant bonding and tactile stimulation). He also suggests, citing recommendations made by a Canadian senate committee, that we offer family allowances and paid maternal leaves for women (1980:8). However, given the American ethic (the U.S. is one of the few industrial nations without such programs), these recommendations are not likely to be implemented. As corrections practitioners, we can say that it would be nice, but we have to adapt ourselves to conditions as they exist.

The psychopath is a particularly poor candidate for rehabilitation. Hare states (1970:113): "The psychopath is apparently incapable of the empathy, warmth, and sincerity needed to develop the type of emotional relationship required for effective therapy." Not only do psychopaths lack these attributes, they lack the anxiety that prods change and see nothing wrong with themselves. Hare does report on studies that have shown limited success with psychopaths when strict authoritarian methods were used (1970:113). Corrections worker who are to achieve any success at all with psychopaths must be prepared to set strict limits on their behavior and stand doggedly by them. They must be to some extent authority figures, albeit warm "parental" authority figures, with clients assumed to be psychopathic. Reality therapy (to be discussed later) may be the most effective method of dealing with the psychopath in a correctional setting.

Summary

From the two perspectives presented in this chapter, the tendency toward crime is located in the individual. This does not mean that people are born criminals or that crime is "in the genes." We have looked at psychopathy in terms of the functioning of the autonomic nervous system and the reticular activating system. A person with a hyporeactive ANS does not feel the same fear and anxiety as those people with more normal ANSs. Being little concerned with the punitive consequences of criminal activity, lacking a sense of guilt, and lacking sympathy for their victims, psychopathic persons tend to engage in crime with alarming frequency. We looked at the various physiological markers of psychopathy, with emphasis on the Wechsler P/V test. This is not necessarily the best marker, but it is usually readily available to the criminal justice worker.

A person with a sluggish RAS is prone to boredom, seeking higher levels of excitement than do most of us—a search that often ends in trouble. A person who is quickly bored is also not likely to spend much time in the academic pursuits that lead to a rewarding, legitimate career. Such a person is also likely to seek artificial stimulation through the use of drugs.

Deprivation of love was examined as an explanation for psychopathy. The experiences that we undergo during the phases of rapid brain cell growth influence the structure and function of our brains. Positive experiences in the form of plentiful stimuli, especially tactile stimuli, have the effect of wiring the brain for love. Negative early experiences have the opposite effect. Extremely negative experiences during infancy and childhood may lead to violent behavior of psychopathic proportions.

We looked at the possibilities that deprivation of love could result in later hyporeactive ANS functioning and that ANS functioning might be able to explain the triad of violence-predictive behavior: enuresis, fire-setting, and cruelty to animals. The chapter emphasizes the awesome importance of tender loving care for the development of wholesome individuals and points to the interaction of environmental influences and physiological functioning in the production of criminal behavior, especially violent criminal behavior.

References and Suggested Readings

Alexander, T. 1984. The new technology of the mind. In *Human development 84/85*, edited by H. Fitzgerald and M. Walragen. Sluice Dock, Conn.: Dushkin.

Allen, H., L. Linder, H. Goldman, and S. Dinitz. 1971. Hostile and simple sociopaths: An empirical typology. *Criminology* 6:27-47.

Perspectives from the Field

Interaction Between Criminology Theory and Practice in the Criminal Justice Field

Dr. Jane Foraker-Thompson

Dr. Foraker-Thompson is a professor of criminal justice at Boise State University. She has held a variety of positions in the field, including college teaching in Soledad and Deuel Prisons in California. She has been the chief planner for the New Mexico State Police, a correctional mental health liaison person, project director of a state-wide restitution project, and a prison reform worker. She has been actively involved in victims' rights issues since 1974.

Is theory useful in the CJ field? Definitely yes! It was my experience to work with offenders in two major prisons in California, one in New Mexico, and a well-rounded offender community treatment program before I got around to really studying criminology. When I finally began to study the theories seriously, I picked and chose among them for those that spoke to me in the sense that they described some of the hundreds of offenders that I had personally known and dealt with over the years. This is not the preferred or the normal way toward scholarship in this area. For me it was practice first and then meet the theories. However, it was a good way to test the theories for their reality value. I began in the criminal justice field as a practitioner with no thought of ever becoming a scholar.

My approach is eclectic. I don't believe that any one theory can explain all offenders, or even one offender. When one speaks of offenders as a category of people, one cannot classify them as a single type. All they have in common is that they have offended against the law. They have done so for a variety of personal, environmental, psychological, and sociological reasons. The mix is different for each person. I see merit and find help in Merton's theory of anomie, especially in his "retreatist " and "innovator" categories. The differential theory of Sutherland is also useful and contains some accurate descriptions of the experiences of some offenders in some circumstances, but by no means all offenders.

Judging by my interpretation of reality, Hirschi's control theory comes closer to being more specific and reality-based. As he puts it, the gathering of delinquents together is not a matter of "birds of a feather flocking together; the birds have already been flocked." That is, they have already been deprived by their early childhood and the ties of attachment, commitment, involvement, and belief. They are not part of the middle-class mainstream. So like seeks like for comfort and security, but not really friendship or caring.

The recent findings from a variety of fields regarding psychopathy bring together a fascinating combination of empirical data that the field has not yet dared to put together into a coherent theory. We (psychiatrists, psychologists, criminologists, social workers, and corrections personnel) have been talking about psychopaths for years, with some doubt that the category actually exists. But those of us who have personally dealt with hundreds of offenders over a number of years know that such a category exists. The psychopathy concept explains a group of people and their behaviors in a way that no other concept does. Certainly not all offenders are psychopaths, and not all psychopaths are offenders. Some are our neighbors, or our uncles or cousins, or a business person down the street. Whoever they may be, we do know that they exist.

Thanks to recent physiological studies, we now have indications that there are physical reasons for what otherwise seems to be the inexplicable, nonrational, and self-destructive behavior of people who may otherwise be intelligent, talented and often charming. We who are privileged to have been well-nurtured as children, to be trained and educated, and to have rational and responsible behavior patterns have difficulty understanding why some people do not turn out like us. This is especially true if such people are one of several children in a family and the other children seemed to "turn out okay." Perhaps their bodies do function differently, thereby causing criminal behavior.

Because the early biologically based writings of theorists such as Lombroso were found to be primitive and outrageous, we have been embarrassed ever since to return to the thought that there may be physiological explanations for some types of criminal behavior. Take the recent findings about the effects of nutrition as well as vitamin and mineral imbalances on the behavior of delinquents, for instance. These physiological variables are definitely worth exploring in an earnest, rigorous, and scientific manner. In fact, it is probably overdue that we make a serious attempt to weave the bits and pieces together to generate a respectable theory of psychopathy.

Walsh's love deprivation theory is an attempt to do just that. Given what we know about psychopaths and violent people in general, it makes sense. It is another piece of the puzzle in our attempts to figure out why some offenders behave the way they do. This knowledge can be used both by presentence investigators when making recommendations to the judge and by the judges themselves in their evaluations of the possible dangerousness of leaving certain offenders in society.

This theory also reinforces or explains the findings about victims of child abuse. When people are abused as children, they often grow up with deep psychological scars that impede both cognitive learning and the development of social/relational skills. Sometimes people suffer all their lives with these deprivations without dealing with the source of their anger, pain, and relational problems. In fact, they often are not aware that their childhood abuse is related to their dysfunctional behavior as an adult. The victims of child abuse who do get help in healing those emotional scars with some kind of counseling, group work, or psychotherapy are then able to experience more healthy relationships based on a more positive self-image and the hard work of unlearning destructive behavior patterns and replacing them with healthy ones.

We know now that an extremely high percentage of convicted offenders, both male and female, were abused as children. Often male children who were abused grow up and become aggressive and violent offenders, victimizers, carrying the abuse on to a new generation. Females who were abused as children usually grow up in a continuing cycle of victimization, often experiencing rape and domestic violence, and may unwittingly put themselves in relationships where their children will be abused. What male offenders (94 percent of all convicted offenders are male) have in common with female victims of personal violent crime (98 percent of known rape victims are female, as are 96 percent of domestic violence victims) is that 80 to 90 percent were abused as children, inadequately nurtured, and grew up with very low self-esteem.

Another step in the abuse cycle is that abused children often become substance abusers at an early age, sometimes enter into early inappropriate sexual behaviors or become promiscuous, and sometimes become socially isolated. They find it very difficult to fit into so-called "mainstream" activities for their age and often begin to participate in deviant behaviors in their preteen years. These sociopathic abused males and females, though often going in opposite directions, end up meeting each other in the middle of the circle where as victimizers and victims they feed on each other's unmet needs in a sick symbiotic relationship. The predator must have prey. Neither party is conscious of the drama the two are acting out. Very few people can scape this self-perpetuating cycle without intervention, therapy, discipline, and hard work.

All the theories addressed here provide useful information that can assist judges, presentence investigators, and correctional workers. The more they learn about and assimilate these theories, the more appropriate diagnoses and sentencing of offenders will be possible. The more thoroughly correctional workers incorporate these theories into their understanding of their clients and implement that understanding in their everyday operating practices, the more effective their work can be. More effective sanctions and treatment and a reduction in recidivism should be the ultimate pay-off for more accurate and enlightened criminological theory. As Lewin said, "There is nothing so practical as a good theory."

Andrew, J. 1977. Delinquency: Intellectual imbalance? *Criminal Justice and Behavior* 4:99-104.

Andrew, J. 1982. Memory and violent crime among delinquents. *Criminal Justice and Behavior* 9:364-371

Barnett, R., L. Zimmer, and J. McCormack. 1989. PV sign and personality profiles. *Journal of Correctional and Social Psychiatry and Offender Treatment and Therapy* 35:18-20.

Bennett, E., M. Diamond, D. Kretch, and M. Rosenzwig. 1964. Chemical and anatomical plasticity of the brain. *Science* 146:610-619.

Bennett, L., T. Rosenbaum, and W. McCullough. 1978. *Counseling in correctional environments.* New York: Human Sciences Press.

Blair, D. 1975. Medicolegal implications of the terms 'psychopath,' 'psychopathic,' and 'psychopathic disorder.' *Medicine and Science* 15:110-123.

Buikhuisen, W. 1982. Aggressive behavior and cognitive disorders. *International Journal of Law and Psychiatry* 5:205-217.

Comte, A. 1896. *The positive philosophy of Auguste Comte.* Translated and edited by H. Martinue. London: Bell.

DiCara, L. 1970. Learning in the autonomic nervous system. *Scientific American* 222:30-39.

Eysenck, H. 1970. Crime and personality. London: Palladin.

Farrington, D. 1987. Implications of biological findings for criminological research. In *The causes of crime: New biological approaches,* edited by S. Mednick, T. Moffit, and S. Stack. Cambridge, England: Cambridge University Press.

Ferguson, M. 1973. *The brain revolution.* New York: Bantam.

Freud, S. 1924. *A general introduction to psychoanalysis.* New York: Washington Square.

Gibbons, D. 1973. *Society, crime, and criminal careers.* Englewood Cliffs, N.J.: Prentice-Hall.

Glasser, W. 1976. *The identity society.* New York: Harper & Row.

Goldman, H., L. Linder, S. Dinitz, and H. Allen. 1971. The simple sociopath: Physiological and sociological characteristics. *Biological Psychiatry* 3:77-83.

Gray, K., and H. Hutchinson. 1964. The psychopathic personality: A survey of Canadian psychiatrists' opinions. *Canadian Psychiatric Association Journal* 9:452-461.

Hare, R. 1970. *Psychopathy.* New York: John Wiley.

Hare, R., and M. Quinn. 1971. Psychopathy and autonomic conditioning. *Journal of Abnormal Psychology* 77:223-235.

Harlow, H. 1958. The nature of love. *American Psychologist* 13:673-685.

Harlow, H. 1962. Social deprivation in monkeys. *Scientific American* 206:137-144.

Harvey, B. 1980. Searching for the roots of violence. *Liaison: A Monthly Journal for the Criminal Justice System* 6:3-8.

Haynie, R. 1978. Deprivation of body pleasure: Origin of violence? A survey of the literature. *Child Welfare* 59:287-297.

Hellman, D., and N. Blackman. 1966. Enuresis, firesetting, and cruelty to animals: A triad predictive of adult crime. *American Journal of Psychiatry* 132:1431-1435.

Jeffery, C. 1979. Punishment and deterrence: A psychobiological statement. In *Biology and crime,* edited by C. Jeffery. Beverly Hills, Cal.: Sage.

Kalil, R. 1989. Synapse formation in the developing brain. *Scientific American* 76:85.

Kaufman, A. 1976. Performance discrepancies on the WISC-R. *Journal of Consulting and Clinical Psychology* 5:739-744.

Keiser, T. 1975. Schizotype and the Wechsler digit span test. *Journal of Clinical Psychology* 31:303-306.

Mark, V., and F. Ervin. 1970. *Violence and the brain.* New York: Harper & Row.

Marx, K., and F. Engels. 1956. *The Holy Family, or critique of critical critique.* London: Foreign Language Publishing House.

Maslow, A. 1953. Love in healthy people. In *The meaning of love,* edited by A. Montagu. New York: Julian Press.

Mednick, S., and K. Finello. 1983. Biological factors and crime: Implications for forensic psychiatry. *International Journal of Law and Psychiatry* 6:1-15.

Mednick, S., and B. Hutchings. 1978. Genetic and psychophysiological factors in asocial behavior. *American Journal of Child Psychiatry* 17:209-223.

Miller, L. 1987. Neuropsychology of the aggressive psychopath: An integrative review. *Aggressive Behavior* 13:119-140.

Montagu, A. 1978. *Touching: The human significance of the skin.* New York: Harper & Row.

Prescott, J. 1975. Body pleasure and the origins of violence. *Bulletin of the Atomic Scientists* 31:10-20.

Restak, R. 1979. *The brain: The last frontier.* New York: Warner.

Rutter, M. 1972. *Maternal deprivation reassessed.* Middlesex, England: Penguin.

Schalling, D. 1978. Psychopathy-related personality variables and the psychophysiology of socialization. In *Psychopathic behavior,* edited by R. Hare and D. Schalling. New York: Wiley.

Solomon, R. 1980. The opponent-process theory of acquired motivation. *American Psychologist* 35:691-712.

Sorokin, P. 1954. *The ways and power of love.* Boston: Beacon Press.

Suomi, S. 1980. *A touch of sensitivity.* Boston: WGBH Foundation.

Surwillo, W. 1980. The electroencephalogram and childhood aggression. *Aggressive Behavior* 6:9-18.

Tarter, R., A. Hegedus, N. Winsten, and A. Alterman. 1985. Intellectual profiles and violent behavior in juvenile delinquents. *Journal of Psychology* 119:125-128.

Taylor, G. 1979. *The natural history of the mind.* New York: E.P. Dutton.

Wadsworth, M. 1976. Delinquency, pulse rates and early emotional deprivation. *British Journal of Criminology* 16:245-246.

Walsh, A. 1981. *Human nature and love: Biological, intrapsychic and social-behavioral perspectives.* Lanham, Md.: University Press of America.

Walsh, A. 1983. Neurophysiology, motherhood, and the growth of love. *Human Mosaic* 17:51-62.

Walsh, A. 1987. Distinguishing features of diagnosed psychopaths among convicted sex criminals. *Free Inquiry in Creative Sociology* 15:40-42.

Walsh, A. 1991. *Intellectual imbalance, love deprivation and violent delinquency: A biosocial perspective.* Springfield, Ill.: Charles C Thomas.

Walsh, A. and J. Beyer. 1986. Wechsler performance-verbal discrepancy and juvenile delinquency. *Journal of Social Psychology* 126:419-420.

Walsh, A., and T. Petee. 1987. Love deprivation and violent delinquency. *Journal of Crime and Justice* 10:45-61.

Walsh, A., J. Beyer, and T. Petee. 1987. Violent delinquency: An examination of psychopathic typologies. *Journal of Genetic Psychology* 148:385-392.

Wax, D., and V. Haddox. 1972. Enuresis, fire-setting and cruelty to animals in male adolescent delinquents: A triad predictive of violent behavior. *Journal of Psychiatry and Law* 2:45-71.

Wechsler, D. 1958. *The measurement and appraisal of adult intelligence.* Baltimore: Williams and Wilkins.

Wolfgang, M., and R. Figlio. 1972. *Delinquency in a birth cohort.* Chicago: University of Chicago Press.

Chapter 4

The Self: Principal Tool of the Criminal Justice Helper

The most important factor affecting behavior is the self-concept. . . . The self is the star of every performance, the central figure in every act. Persons engaging in the helping professions, therefore, need the broadest possible understanding of the nature, origins, and functions of the self-concept.

Arthur Combs, Donald Avilla, and William Purkey

As Garrett (1982:5) points out, it is important that professional interviewers have more than a casual knowledge of human behavior and motivation, and "They should apply this knowledge, not only to an understanding of their clients' personalities, needs, prejudices, and emotions, but also to an understanding of their own. The wise maxim of the ancient Greeks, 'Know thyself,' applies especially to interviewers."

Knowing Yourself

There are many tools available to CJ workers to modify the behavior of their clients, but the worker's self-concept is the most important. A person can decline the use of other tools, but corrections work demands the use of the self. Effective helping behavior involves interaction between two selves: The offender's self, almost by definition, is deficient in some important aspects. Involvement in the criminal justice system demonstrates difficulty in behaving in a responsible manner. In order to compensate for the deficiencies of one-half of the interacting dyad, the other half—the worker—must possess some extraordinary qualities if the relationship is to be effective. Before we discuss the interviewing process, then, let us examine briefly the primary tool used in that process.

The Self-concept

The importance of your self-concept in understanding your behavior and that of your clients is of the utmost importance. Your self-concept is who and what you believe that unique individual you refer to as "me" is all about. It is the central core of your existence, the focus of reality from which you experience, understand, and evaluate the world around you. The self-concept is not the "real self" (whatever that is), it is the picture you have of yourself in your head. Your self-concept is both product and producer of your experiences. If you are capable of giving and receiving love, if you consider yourself to be a worthwhile person, if you are confident in yourself, and if you behave responsibly, you will be able to bring positive feelings about yourself to the helping relationship.

You have developed these ideas about yourself through a lifetime of interacting with others and internalizing both their attitudes and feelings about you and their evaluations and expectations of you. This is what it means to say that your self-concept is the product of your experience. Once you have a positive self-concept derived from the positive beliefs about you held by significant others, your behavior will tend to confirm their belief—and your own—in a psychological version of the "rich get richer" spiral. Was it Nathaniel Hawthorne who said, "What a man thinks of himself contains his destiny"? This is what it means to say that your self-concept produces your behavior.

Now, consider individuals whose experiences have given them a negative self-concept. Their behavior, too, will tend to confirm the self-perceptions they have derived from those unhappy experiences. They are likely to view the world as an unfriendly place and to engage in behavior not likely to endear them to others. Such people may feel trapped in a way of life without much hope of improvement, becoming victims of their own self-perceptions. The psychological spiral now swirls in the opposite direction: "The poor get poorer." "I'm no good. I can't be—nobody loves me, wants me, or cares for me." "Who cares anyway? Not me; they can all go to hell!" "I can't get a job because I'm not very smart—everyone says so." "I'll just get what I need by taking it from all those suckers out there, and just let them try to stop me." This is the mind-set of many clients caught up in the criminal justice system. This is the mind-set that the CJ helper must wrestle with and overcome.

To accomplish this task, and it is an arduous and lengthy one, your own self-concept must be strong. As Combs, Avila, and Purkey (1971:56-57) so well put it:

> Since new concepts of self are learned as a consequence of interactions with the helper, effective helpers must be significant people. They cannot be nonentities. One cannot interact with a shadow. The helping relationship is an active one, and a passive helper is unlikely to teach his [or her] client anything but his [or her] own futility. The personality of the helper must play a vital part in any helping relationship. It is the helper's use of his [or her] self which makes the interaction whatever it is to become.

Self-esteem

The terms self-concept and self-esteem are not synonyms, though they are often thought to be. The self-concept has two separate motives: the motive to think well of the self—self-esteem—and the motive to protect the self from change—self-consistency (Rosenberg 1979:53). All counseling can be viewed as an effort to enhance clients' self-esteem and to get them to examine the self-consistency motive in order to change the image they have of themselves in desired directions.

The desire for self-approval—to think of oneself as worthy—is perhaps the dominant force in a person's motivational system (Kaplan 1982:139). Many theorists are convinced that self-esteem is rooted in the ability to give and receive love (e.g., Glasser 1975), an assertion that has received much empirical support (Buri, Kirchner & Walsh 1987; Walsh & Walsh 1989; Walsh & Balazs 1990). Because criminals do not usually feel worthy, their lack of self-esteem gets them into trouble with the law. They take drugs and alcohol in vain attempts to feel better and seek out other deviant ways to bolster this damaged self-esteem (Berman & Siegal 1976; Buikhuisen 1987). Yablonsky (1990:449) writes that violent youths (like adults) are "because of their low self-esteem, acting out self-destructive behavior; they have limited concern about whether they live or die." It is part of your job as a criminal justice worker to help your clients recognize their self-destructive behavior, to challenge their self-consistency motives, and to change the patterns of self-talk that contribute to their negative self-esteem. A tall order, but an exciting one for the dedicated and effective criminal justice worker.

Qualities of an Effective CJ Worker

CJ helpers must possess some extraordinary qualities if they are to be effective in changing the deficient self-concepts of so many of their clients. What are those qualities? What are some potential problems in a CJ worker's self-understanding that might detract from the helping process?

The criminal justice worker must have a thorough knowledge of criminal behavior and its correlates. You should develop the interest and the patience to be constantly studying the forces and events affecting the lives of your clients. Knowledge of criminological theories and theories about substance abuse and abnormal psychology enables you to see your clients' frame of reference more objectively and lessens any impulse to moralize about how their behavior differs from your own. The subject matter of your field is people with problems that cause them to act irresponsibly. Individuals who aspire to be professionals must know their subject matter.

No one expects you to be a specialist in all areas pertaining to criminal behavior. Like a physician in general practice, you must know something about a wide range of subjects, but you should be wise enough to know the limits of your knowledge and to refer your clients to someone more knowledgeable—a specialist—when those limits are reached.

The criminal justice worker must be realistic, neither a Pollyanna nor a Cassandra. A Pollyanna is one whose irrepressible optimism finds good in everything. Such a person often fails to see, or discounts, danger signals. Pollyannas avoid or discourage negative feedback and are extremely reluctant to confront resisting or reluctant clients. They allow manipulative clients to get away with too many minor infractions, believing that leniency marks them as nonauthoritarian and nondirective. They really are, however, individuals who lack the self-confidence needed to provide meaningful supervision to clients whose personal and legal needs require guidance.

The Cassandra sees negativism in everything. Cassandras feed their own sense of incompetence by discounting positive feedback. Cassandras do not trust their clients and try to avoid positive interactions with them. They also tend to set their expectations impossibly high, thus ensuring failure. Whereas Pollyannas tend to provide unwarranted positive feedback when confrontation is required, Cassandras will not reinforce positive behavior with positive feedback and give feedback only when the client has not lived up to expectations.

Both of these working styles are unrealistic and reflect attitudes about the worker's self as well as about clients. The Pollyanna sees corrections work solely as social work; the Cassandra views it as police work. The realistic corrections worker views it as both and has sufficient self-understanding and self-confidence to know when either role is appropriate.

The criminal justice helper does not use clients to satisfy his or her own needs. The counselor/client relationship is not the place to satisfy the criminal justice worker's own unresolved needs. The insecure worker who needs to feel powerful, for instance, will overcontrol interactions by dominating the direction of counseling sessions, posing as an expert, and trying to convert clients by preaching at them. Power-hungry counselors may feel safe in pursuing resolution of their needs in this way with a captive clientele, but it is a counterproductive misuse of authority.

Other criminal justice workers may attempt to satisfy their needs for warmth and acceptance by working to elicit cues from their clients that they are liked and accepted. When, like Pollyannas, they blind themselves to negative cues because they fear rejection, they are opening themselves to manipulation.

In contrast, there are those unresourceful counselors who are fearful of control or of closeness. Whereas the power-hungry and the acceptance-needers suffocate their clients with attention, the weak and the distance-needers avoid contact. Those counselors who fear control will neglect to offer clients needed advice and direction and will generally be passive onlookers. Those who fear closeness will be distant with their clients, will avoid addressing clients' positive feelings, and will not develop the involvement necessary to the helping process.

In other words, criminal justice workers must like people and enjoy frequent contact with them. They must like to solve different problems and must take pride in doing a job that many people cannot do.

The criminal justice worker inspires trust, confidence, and credibility in clients. If you are to be an effective helper, clients must feel confident that they can share themselves with you. If they are to share their feelings, hopes, fears, and concerns openly, they must first sense a nonjudgmental acceptance on your part. They must come to view you as a credible professional, have confidence in your abilities and motives, and trust you to accept their feelings and concerns without criticizing, shaming, or ridiculing them. To be perceived this way you must *be* this way. You cannot long feign openness, honesty, concern, and acceptance.

The criminal justice helper reaches inward as well as outward. To be good at your work, you will need a commitment to nondefensive self-examination and awareness: "Who am I, what am I like as a person? Am I almost always honest, trustworthy, likable, accepting? Am I the kind of person who inspires confidence and trust? Do I really make an effort to understand my clients and their environments? Am I a competent person? Do I find myself using people to satisfy my needs for power or for acceptance? Do I have the courage to change those aspects of myself that I don't like?"

As a criminal justice helper, you will often have clients who are different from you. What are your attitudes about people who are different? Do you harbor racist or sexist attitudes and stereotypes? Can you accept and interact with individuals of a different race, sex, or socioeconomic background as easily as with individuals with whom you share similar characteristics? Do you value, or are you fearful of, diversity of attitudes and values? Do you accept different religions, political ideologies, and sexual lifestyles as alternatives rather than as deviant?

The more you learn about the types of people with whom you will come into contact, and the more you explore your attitudes toward them and toward yourself with an open mind, the more you will become the sort of person who is an effective helper. Let us now examine the benefits of looking inward.

The Benefits of Self-disclosure

One of the most important qualities that criminal justice workers should possess is the willingness to share their selves with others, including their clients, through self-disclosure. In self-disclosure you communicate personal information to another who would not normally have that information. You may well ask what use it is for the CJ helper to communicate personal information to a client: is not the client's self the focus of the client/helper relationship—indeed, the reason for its existence? Yes, it is. Only with the advent of humanistic psychology did self-disclosure come to be considered appropriate and beneficial (Okun 1987:261;). Being willing to share your self in your CJ work serves some useful functions.

First, self-disclosure is a form of modeling behavior that encourages reluctant clients to reveal intimate facts about themselves. The difficulty that clients experience in revealing their most intimate feelings, thoughts, and valuations may well be lessened by the helper's example. Reciprocal self-disclosure is the basis of the success of such self-help groups as Alcoholics Anonymous. Confession is good for the soul, and it elicits an abundance of information for the assessment of the client to boot. Arcaya puts the self-disclosure process in a criminal justice context when he writes: "For the ex-offender forced to present himself [or herself] before a probation officer, rehabilitation counselor, or psychologist, no meaningful dialogue will occur unless the client can identify a glimmer of his [or her] own humanity in the individual with whom he [or she] deals" (1978:231).

Second, self-disclosure gives the client a new perspective on experiences similar to your own. Again, the sharing of personal experiences, the implanting of possibilities for alternative frames of reference in the minds of others, is part of the modus operandi of self-help groups in which clients come to see reflections of themselves in others. The process of self-disclosure should, of course, be free of value judgments, moral exhortations, and boastful exhibitionism. Besides being bad practice, it is not considered good taste to advertise what a great person you are. If the contrast between the client's experience and yours is too great, the client will not view your frame of reference as realistic. If you moralize and pass judgment, the client is not likely to reveal to you any further personal information that could invite further denigration.

You must always be aware of the feelings and the humanity of your clients. If, for example, Bob reveals that he has had great difficulty obtaining employment because of his lack of a high school diploma and the vagaries of his lower-class upbringing, you may reply with sensitivity, revealing your own class origins, the possibility of obtaining a general education diploma (GED), and how you managed to acquire an education despite acknowledged early deficiencies. Rendered in such a nonthreatening way, your experience may strike in Bob a responsive chord of the possible. If, instead, you use terms designed to emphasize your moral superiority ("I did it, why can't you?" "It takes guts, buddy." "You can get a job if you get off your lazy ass and start looking."), Bob is likely to react negatively to the assault on his self-concept, either by becoming hostile or by clamming up. Either way, you have lost the opportunity to further the meaningful interaction so necessary for adequate assessment of a client. You have also reinforced Bob's sense of hopelessness and his feeling that "nobody cares"—and revealed your own inadequacies as a helper. If such an exchange takes place during the initial interview, and if Bob is subsequently placed under your supervision, your efforts to counsel him will meet with resistance because you have already communicated to him that he is not worth much and that you are not really interested in him or his problems.

Some caveats about self-disclosure to a client are in order, though. The client's problems must be the focus of any interview or counseling session; your self-disclosure should therefore be infrequent, relevant, and focused and should not give the client the impression that you are working out your own problems in the session. Chatty, unstructured conversations are inappropriate in a session designed to gather information about the client, although they may have use in establishing a genuine atmosphere of informality in later sessions. Egan's advice (1986:231) is instructive here: "Helpers should be willing and able to disclose themselves, even deeply, in reasonable ways, but should do so only if it is clear that it will contribute to the client's progress."

Improving Your Self-concept Through Self-disclosure

Exercises in self-disclosure such as those given at the end of this chapter should be an integral part of the CJ helper's training. They are necessary for two reasons. First, they give you a gut-level understanding of the feelings of your clients as they are asked to reveal intimate information. Disclosing intimate information can be highly intimidating. Imagine the embarrassment of a fifty-five-year-old minister who has been found guilty of molesting a child when a probation officer young enough to be his son asks him to reveal details of his sex life. Only the probation officer who is highly sensitive to this embarrassment can conduct a successful interview and make an adequate assessment. One of the best ways to learn this sensitivity is to experience the same sort of discomfort by self-disclosure in the classroom.

However, the classroom setting will not be as threatening to the student as the real-life setting is for the client. Students can easily walk through the roles rather than dealing with real concerns; that is, they can manufacture fictitious problems that do not threaten them, rather than exploring their own real problems. Only by realistically exploring problems can you gain insight into what it is like to be a client. Remember that all prospective psychoanalysts have to undergo intensive psychoanalysis before they are allowed to practice their skills on others.

The second reason for engaging in realistic self-disclosure is to improve your greatest asset—your self-concept. People have a strong desire to preserve the picture they have of themselves—the self-consistency motive. If we protect the self from change, we cannot grow psychologically. Paradoxically, to preserve self-consistency, some people may retain low self-esteem. People who expect little of themselves cannot fail. If expectation are low, a weak performance will meet them (Rosenberg 1979:61). Psychological growth implies that we have the courage to test ourselves to our limits and to acknowledge the possibility of failure.

It is important for us to assess ourselves, to know what kind of people we are, to know our strengths, weaknesses, potential, and problem areas so that we can operate effectively. Some authorities consider wholesome self-disclosure to be as necessary for mental health as proper exercise and nutrition are for physical health. Fromm (1955) has written that in order to reduce our alienation from ourselves and from others we must open ourselves to ourselves by disclosing ourselves to others; and Mowrer (1964) says that an unwillingness to disclose oneself is a major factor in many areas of behavioral pathology. The more we know about ourselves, the better we will understand others. Self-knowledge is desirable for everyone; it is vital for those in the helping professions, because understanding others is a prerequisite to helping them. How can you help your clients resolve feelings that are hindering their functioning if you have not dealt with similar feelings in yourself?

If we harbor static images of ourselves, we will see the world and our relationship to it unrealistically. A static self-concept cuts us off from the fullness of the experiences that the world offers us, thus stunting our emotional and intellectual growth. Rather than building walls and defenses against life's fullness, let us accept all experiences and adopt them into our self-concepts.

We must adapt positively to the environment as it changes. To accomplish this successfully, we must acquire information about ourselves from concerned others and use it for positive change. To receive information about ourselves from others we must be strong enough to share ourselves with others. Both the receiving of information about ourselves and the sharing of ourselves with others is accomplished by meaningful self-disclosure. You will, after all, be asking your clients to do all these things: adapt positively to their environments, experience lifestyles different from the one they have grown accustomed to, share themselves through disclosure, and receive information from you that you will expect them to employ fruitfully. If this is not part of your own operating philosophy, you will not be successful in imparting it to your clients.

The Johari Window

An Aid to Self-understanding

A useful framework for understanding how self-disclosure is valuable in improving the self-concept is the Johari Window (Luft 1963). This device divides the self into four components or "cells" representing aspects of the self, ranging from those known to almost everyone to aspects of which you yourself are not aware. Positive self-disclosure should have the effect of enlarging Cell I (the public self) while shrinking the other three cells. The following is a general discussion of the principles of self-disclosure; it should not be viewed as part of the counselor/client relationship. You certainly will not be asking clients to help you to explore your intimate concerns.

The **public self** is the self as it is habitually shared with others. It is an area of self-knowledge that you have no qualms about revealing.

	Known to self	Unknown to self
Known to others	I Public self	II Blind self
Unknown to others	III Private self	IV Unknown self

Figure 4-1 The Johari Window (adapted from Luft 1983)

The **private self** obviously has relevance to self-disclosure. You need not, nor should you, burden others with excessive and exhibitionist disclosure of your private self: "If only you knew what I've accomplished in my life and against what odds, you too would realize what a great person I am." The idea is to disclose only those aspects of the private self that others can use to help you explore aspects that are of concern to you, such as values, weaknesses, and social and sexual identities.

The **blind self** is that part of ourselves that others see but we do not. It is involved in self-disclosure only if others bring their images of you to your attention and if you are willing to acknowledge the validity of those images. Another's image of you may not be an accurate assessment of you, but it may be beneficial for you to at least to recognize the possibility that it is. If the image is negative, do not retreat from it. Instead, work with that aspect of your self to see how it can be improved. Never ignore characteristics that others perceive; they may be negatively affecting your effectiveness as a helper—or as a person.

The **unknown self** is the area of latent, subconscious, and preconscious facets of the self. It is full of shadowy fears and weaknesses, but is also a reservoir of great potential and untapped talents for all of us. An unwillingness to explore unknown areas of the self is indicative of a frozen self-concept. As you explore the blind self, aspects of the unknown self may become accessible to you so that you can confront them, developing those that are desirable and dealing constructively with the others.

Although it is generally agreed that self-disclosure (moving information contained in cells II, III, and IV into cell I) facilitates personal growth, it may also inhibit growth. Whether self-disclosure is beneficial or harmful depends on the state of the receiver and the quality of the relationship the receiver shares with the transmitter. Inevitably, self-disclosure involves risk-taking. A turtle never moves forward until it sticks its neck out of its shell—neither will you.

Self-disclosure demands trust and an investment in the other person. As a professional criminal justice worker, you will be asking clients to trust and invest in you. If you are to work effectively and efficiently, you must prove yourself worthy of that trust and investment by responding to clients in a sensitive, empathetic, and fully involved way. You must also be secure enough in yourself to be completely honest with your client. Your honesty, openness, and acceptance do not guarantee similar behavior in your client, but they certainly make it more probable.

Application to the Client

Although the Johari Window was conceived as a strategy for self-exploration, it can be fruitfully adapted to be a model for the helper/client relationship. For instance, the immediate state of your "knowledge" of your clients on your first meeting with them is represented in Figure 4-2. The major difference between exercises in voluntary self-disclosure for the purpose of self-growth and the helper/client encounter is that the public self in the latter case is the self that the client chooses to present to you, not the public self he or she habitually shares with family, friends, and acquaintances. Your knowledge of his or her public self is, for the moment, limited to information in various official documents. Therefore, even getting to know the client as others know him or her may prove to be exacting. At this point you know only the **official** client. Your initial task is the melding of the two subsections of cell I to form a unified picture of how the client normally presents him or herself to others. Clients who have aspects of the public self that they are unwilling to share with you may erect barriers to protect those areas. The barriers can be scaled by an effective interview with the client and by collateral interviews with those who know the client.

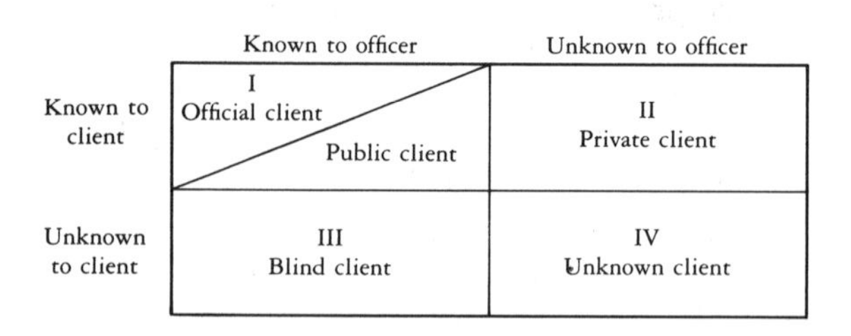

Figure 4-2 The Johari Window applied to the client

The Mask: Please Hear What I'm Not Saying

Author Unknown

This essay by an anonymous writer is an anguished cry for understanding and acceptance. It illustrates our discussion of self-disclosure, as well as the discussion of listening still to come. Notice how the writer has built a false self-image and barriers to protect it and how painful the writer finds that inauthenticity. We all want to be accepted and loved, but many of us fight against what we so desperately need. The writer wants to be authentic by disclosing his or her true self and true feeling, but is terribly afraid of rejection. This could have been written by any of your future clients, perhaps even by some of your classmates, or you. Remember it when you do your exercises in self-disclosure. Above all, remember it when you are working with real clients.

Don't be fooled by me. Don't be fooled by the face I wear. For I wear a mask. I wear a thousand masks, masks that I'm afraid to take off, and none of them are me. Pretending is an art that's second nature to me, but don't be fooled, for God's sake don't be fooled. I give you the impression that I'm secure, that all is sunny and unruffled with me, within as well as without. That confidence is my name and coolness is my game, and that I need no one.

But don't believe me. My surface is my mask. Beneath dwells the real me in confusion, in fear, in aloneness. But I hide this. I don't want anybody to know it. I panic at the thought of my weakness and fear being exposed. That's why I frantically create a mask to hide behind, to shield me from the glance that knows. But such a glance is precisely my salvation—that is, if it's followed by acceptance, by love. It's the only thing that can liberate me from my own self-built prison walls. It's the only thing that will assure me of what I can't assure myself of—that I'm really worth something.

But I'm afraid to tell you this; I'm afraid that your glance will not be followed by acceptance and love. I'm afraid you'll laugh, and that laugh will kill me. I idly chatter to you in the suave tones of surface talk. I tell you everything that's really nothing and nothing of what's everything, of what's crying within me.

Please listen carefully and try to hear what I'm not saying, what I'd like to be able to say, what for survival I need to say. I'd really like to be genuine and spontaneous, and me, but you've got to help me. You alone can release me from my shadow-world of panic and uncertainty, from my lonely prison. It will not be easy for you. A long conviction of worthlessness builds strong walls. The nearer you approach me, the blinder I may strike back. I am irrational—I fight against the very thing that I cry out for. But I am told that love is stronger than strong walls. Please try to beat down those walls with firm hands, but with gentle hands—for I am very sensitive. Who am I, you may wonder. I am someone you "know" very well. I am every man you meet and I am every woman you meet.

The **private client** is that part of the self that the client wishes to keep unscrutinized by others, especially the corrections worker. It represents the behaviors, feelings, and motivations that the client habitually hides but that may be revealed at will. These behaviors, feelings, and motivations, since the client is aware of them, will probably be the first areas targeted for mutual exploration. They are not necessarily problem areas; they may just as well be growth-promoting areas that, with a little support and encouragement, the client could actualize. When aspects of the private client are positive, the client may be more disposed to expose them to a relative stranger who is perceived as caring and accepting than to more familiar others who might respond with ridicule.

The **blind client** represents those aspects of the self of which the client is unaware but which the officer perceives and is sensitive to. Just as the corrections worker can enhance the self by feedback in an atmosphere of openness and trust, so can the client. The worker should first emphasize the positive aspects of the client's self of which the worker is aware, such as positive statements by others. If, for instance, school records indicate that the client scored well on IQ tests, a corrections officer might discuss the nature of IQ and the possibilities open to a person with such scores. This kind of welcome information, needless to say, tends to spill over into congenial discussions of other aspects of the client's blind self that the client might not be so ready to accept.

The **unknown client** represents those aspects of the client's self that are unknown to officer and client alike. Realistically, we know that many aspects will remain unknown. The initial interview, no matter what the reason for it, is not the place to probe the unknown client. Under supervision, however, the client should be encouraged to explore it in order to discover the potential that we surely all possess. You must have faith in this proposition if you are to be an effective correctional worker.

The Johari Window is, then, a useful framework for conceptualizing the process and purpose of interviewing. However, we should never forget that our criminal justice clients come to the interviewing process with vastly different biographies, motives, and attitudes. Each interview is a unique interaction between human beings who are far too individualized to be reduced to precise formulas. Interviewing is an art, not a science, but there are certain basic principles that enable the helper to conduct a successful interview. They are discussed in the next chapter.

Summary

This chapter emphasizes the primacy of the worker's self in the helping process. Nothing is more important to the success or failure of a counseling relationship than the quality of the helper's self. The self-concept is the product and producer of experience. Positive experiences lead to a positive self-concept, and a positive self-concept leads to further positive experiences. The opposite progression, often found in criminal justice clients, is also true.

We looked at the various attributes that characterize the professional criminal justice worker. Examine these attributes closely to determine how you measure up. Deficiencies and weaknesses in any area can be explored in the process of self-disclosure.

To improve the self-concept, a person must accept a wide variety of experiences and integrate. One way to do this is through meaningful self-disclosure. Self-disclosure helps us to gain knowledge about ourselves by receiving feedback about ourselves from others. Every prospective counselor should experience self-disclosure in a number of sessions before actually practicing counseling, not only to gain valuable self-insight but also to experience the process in which he or she will be asking clients to engage. The Johari Window is an excellent device for guiding self-disclosure. There are few pieces of advice more useful than the ancient injunction to "know thyself."

Exercises in Self-exploration Through Disclosure

The purpose of this activity is twofold: to facilitate self-exploration by disclosing to a partner various aspects of yourself; and to give you some experience of what it is like to reveal oneself to a relative stranger. During the initial session, you may, out of fear, anxiety, or embarrassment, decide upon some relativley nonthreatening topic. Or you may possess the self-assurance to pick a topic that is of real concern to you. It is preferable, of course, to choose aspects of the private self, especially those of an interpersonal nature, for exploration. The section asking you to explore values and attitudes toward various kinds of individuals will prove to be valuable in developing an empathetic understanding of them if both disclosure and feedback are open and honest.

Exercises should be done in pairs, with frequent changes of partner. If your instructor chooses not to assign partners, it is preferable that you do not sit with the same the same person too often. Make an effort to sit with someone of a different race, sex, or ethnic background. You will find this to be a good learning experience and very rewarding. Each student should take turns in disclosing the chosen issue to the other. Remember, you are not engaing in a conventional conversation. The disclosing person should have control of the conmunication. The listener should listen, paying attention to the techniques of active listening as outlined in the next chapter. The listener should speak only for the purposes of clarification and of prompting further disclosure by the use of probes. Each of the following suggested topics is suitable for a discussion of about five to ten minutes.

Topic 1: Generalities

The kinds of people I like best are________________

The kinds of people I like least are________________

I try to avoid thinking about____________________

I think that the most important thing in life is________

I feel most competent when I___________________

I feel least comptetent when I __________________

My career goals are_____________________________

I would really like to be able to__________________

Topic 2: Values and Attitudes

My values are important to me because____________

Here's how I *really* feel that the relationship between the sexes should be___________________________

Here's how I *really* feel about blacks/whites_________

Here's how I feel about alcoholics ________________

Here's how I feel about drug abusers_______________

Here's how I *really* feel about homosexuals _________

Here's how I *really* feel about criminals___________

An open mind is desirable because________________

Topic 3: Feelings

I am happiest when_____________________________

I get the most depressed when___________________

I get embarrassed when I get very angry when______

I feel guilty when I am sometimes ashamed of______

I feel very hurt when____________________________

I feel anxious when______________________________

Topic 4: Identity

Odds are that you have never really thought too much about your identity. Who are you? What kind of person are you? Try writing ten separate answers to the question "Who am I?" Next, eliminate those answers that signify only ascribed and achieved statuses, such as "American," "student," "female," or "twenty-nine years old." With your partners, explore those aspects of the self that are left on your lists. You may have written, for example, "I am a shy person." Explore this with your partner. Why do you think you are shy? What does your shyness do to your social life? How much more successful in life do you think you would be if you were not shy? How do you feel about your shyness? What do you think you can do about it?

Topic 5: Strengths and Weaknesses

List your five greatest strengths and five greatest weaknesses and discuss each with your partner. These strengths and weaknesses should be developmental "feeling" topics rather than statements like "I'm a good/poor tennis player." For instance, how do you relate to other people, especially those close to you? Are you secure in your sexual identity? Are you a leader or a follower? Do you respect the feelings of others? Are you an autonomous person? Can you take constructive criticism?

Topic 6: Effectiveness as a Criminal Justice Helper

Go back to the discussion of the qualities of an effective criminal justice helper and rate yourself according to those attributes. Where are you weak, and where are you strong? What attributes do you possess that will help you become a more effective helper? What attributes do you think will most detract from your becoming an effective helper? Discuss these strengths and weaknesses with a partner.

References and Suggested Readings

Arcaya, J. 1978. Coercive counseling and self-disclosure. *International Journal of Offender Therapy and Comparative Criminology* 22:231-237.

Buri, J., P. Kirchner, and J. Walsh. 1987. Familial correlates of self-esteem in young American adults. *Journal of Social Psychology* 127:583-588.

Combs, A., D. Avila, and W. Purkey. 1971. *Helping relationships: Basic concepts for the helping professions*. Boston: Allyn and Bacon.

Egan, G. 1982. *The skilled helper*. Monterey, Cal.: Brooks/Cole.

Fromm, E. 1982. *The sane society*. New York: Rinehart and Co.

Garrett, A. 1982. *Interviewing: Its principles and methods*. New York: Family Services Association of America.

Hartman, H. 1978. *Basic psychiatry for corrections workers*. Springfield, Ill.: Charles C Thomas.

Ivey, A. 1983. *Intentional interviewing and counseling*. Monterey, Cal.: Brooks/Cole.

Luft, J. 1963. *Group process: An introduction to group dynamics*. Palo Alto, Cal.: National Press.

Mowrer, O. 1964. *The new group theory*. Princeton, N.J.: Van Nostrand.

Okun, B. 1982. *Effective helping*. Monterey, Cal.: Brooks/Cole.

Rosenberg, M. 1979. *Conceiving the self*. New York: Basic Books.

Walsh, A., and P. Walsh. 1989. Love, self-esteem, and multiple sclerosis. *Social Science and Medicine* 29:793-798.

Walsh, A., and G. Balazs. 1990. Love, sex, and self-esteem. *Free Inquiry in Creative Sociology* 18:37-42.

Yablonsky, L. 1990. *Criminology: Crime and criminality*. New York: Harper & Row.

Chapter 5

Interviewing and Interrogating

It is not easy to achieve the ideal balance between relieving a client of the unbearable burden of what seem to be insurmountable difficulties and leaving him with essential responsibility for working out his own destiny. . . . One of the most important skills of the interviewer is a knowledge of his own limitations.

Annette Garrett

The interview is a focused process of communication by which you gather information in order to assess the interviewee. It is a structured, purposeful method of getting to know another person. Any interview, regardless of the context in which it takes place, is designed to help the interviewer make decisions, usually about the interviewee (Is this person suitable for the job? eligible for benefits? serious about this task? a good candidate for treatment? and so on). Corrections workers spend most of their time conducting interviews with clients, victims, police officers, and many other people involved in some way with their clients' activities. Thus, it is necessary that you become familiar with the basic principles of effective interviewing.

Interrogation may also be part of the corrections worker's task. Like interviewing, interrogation involves gathering information, but the focus is sharper. As Wicks (1974:133) defines it: "Interrogation is conducted either to get an admission of guilt from a person who has been involved in a crime or to obtain clarification and elaboration of certain facts from someone who is innocent." The ability to conduct an effective interrogation is a necessary part of your professional development.

Purpose of the Criminal Justice Interview

The Client

Applied to the criminal justice client, interviewing is a diagnostic tool that will enable you to arrive at a preliminary understanding of clients and their problems and to recommend and implement effective treatment. A well-conducted interview may also be the first step in the counseling process if it creates an arena in which clients can formulate a honest picture of their problems and if they gain an understanding of the motives and resources of the helping person. As criminologist and prominent correctional administrator Paul Keve put it: "The most important step in the investigation process is the first interview with the defendant, and if you handle it skillfully, you not only have the basis for a truly competent report, but you also have gone a long way toward launching the treatment job that must develop later" (quoted in Hartman 1978:309). The interview, then, can be the beginning of the rehabilitative process, or it can be merely a ritual in which demographic data are gathered and reported but not interpreted.

The principles of interviewing are the same whether the specific purpose of the interview is preparing a presentence investigation report (PSI), meeting a newly assigned probationer or parolee, or conducting an intake interview for a new arrival at an institution.

The Victim

A growing, long-overdue awareness of the victim as the forgotten party in the criminal justice system has prompted a number of states to require that victims have a more active part in the sentencing process. Ohio law, for instance, requires that a "victim impact statement" be included in each PSI and mandates that the judge consider the statement in sentencing. This requirement demands something more than the perfunctory telephone call to ascertain financial losses that used to be the norm. A telephone call will suffice, however, when the victim in a case of theft, burglary, or forgery is a business establishment, no one has been personally victimized, and you merely wish to determine restitution figures.

In the case of personal victimization, however, victims should be given the courtesy of a face-to-face meeting with you. Both you and the victim benefit from such an interview. You gather information that will help you to evaluate your client; the victim can be reassured that he or she is safe and has not been forgotten or ignored by the criminal justice system.

Techniques of Interviewing

The goal of interviewing is to gather information given voluntarily. It is not as difficult as you may think to obtain voluntary information from clients, even criminal justice clients. Most people like to talk about themselves; even reluctant, angry, or embarrassed clients will probably succumb to the temptation if they perceive that you are genuinely interested in them. This is why the development of genuine caring and empathy above technique is stressed in interviewing and counseling classes. Too much emphasis on technique detracts from the humanness of the interviewing process, and the lack of human concern can be painfully transparent.

Active Listening

This is not to say that techniques are not valuable; they are, extremely. The most valuable technique is active listening—the opposite of passive listening and the key to effective communication. The active listener pays complete attention to the information being offered by the client and conveys that attention to the client both verbally and nonverbally.

To communicate to the client that you are actively listening, maintain eye contact. In addition to conveying interest, eye contact enables you to observe your client's nonverbal responses to uncomfortable questions. When are the eyes averted? When does the client flush, smile, or sneer? You cannot know if you are not watching.

There are, however, certain subcultural differences attached to the meaning of eye contact. Middle-class people tend to view frequent eye contact as a sign of honesty and the averting of the eyes as indicating furtiveness. Inner-city residents, especially blacks, consider too much eye contact to be a nonverbal challenge, so it may provoke hostility. Be careful that your efforts to maintain eye contact do not turn into an attempt to stare the client down.

When you are listening to your client, sit about two arm-lengths apart, with no desk or other physical object between you, and lean forward slightly. Leaning forward at certain points during the interview conveys an intensification of interest. Do not get so close that the client feels uncomfortable—that is, that he or she feels an invasion of personal space. This is particularly important if the client is of the opposite sex; it is all too easy to convey unintended messages of a sexual nature. I once had a female client who started to cry during a PSI interview. I offered her a tissue and placed a comforting hand on hers. She took immediate advantage of this gesture of sympathy to grasp my hand and state: "I'll do anything to get out of this." This obvious sexual invitation was disquieting to me. Clients who make such offers expect something in return (a favorable sentencing recommendation, easy supervision conditions, a blind eye turned to certain violations). Had I accepted her invitation I might well have found myself paying the $700 in restitution she owed, violating my professional code of ethics, and, not least, opening myself up to a criminal charge. Be careful that your behavior is not open to misinterpretation.

Questioning and Probing

Although the purpose of the interview is to listen to what the client has to say, the communication must be guided toward relevant topics. You are seeking information about the client's background and lifestyle, attitudes towards the offense, and problems that may have led to it. To get this information you have to ask questions. We will discuss two types of questioning here: **open** and **closed**. "Open questions are those that can't be answered in a few short words. They encourage others to talk and provide you with maximum information. Closed questions can be answered in a few short words or sentences. They have the advantage of focusing the interview and obtaining information, but the burden of talk remains with the interviewer" (Ivey 1983:41). **Probes** are indirect open-ended questions that encourage the client to explore some point he or she has mentioned.

Criminal justice clients will often be unwilling to explore their personal lives and feelings with you. It is rare, however, that they will refuse outright to answer your questions. With reluctant clients, it is necessary to encourage sharing through the use of probes. Probes are verbal tactics for prompting clients to share specific thoughts, feelings, and concerns with you. For example, if Debbie hints that her marriage is unhappy and she wants out, do not be content with that raw datum. Explore. Say something like: "So you feel terrible about your marriage and feel trapped. What exactly is it that you feel worst about?" You are encouraging Debbie to clarify her general statement by relating concrete instances that give rise to her generalized feelings of dissatisfaction. Your probing may give Debbie the first real opportunity she has ever had to explore and vent her feelings about her marriage. Furthermore, Debbie's trouble with the law may be a consequence, direct or indirect, of her poor marital relationship. If this turns out to be the case, you will have a starting point for your later counseling sessions with her if she is placed on probation.

Probing questions should be open-ended, meaning that they cannot be answered by a simple yes or no. The type of questions should be: "Now that you know what the problem is between you and your husband, what do you plan to do about it?" rather than "Now that you know what the problem is between you and your husband, do you plan to do anything about it?" A response of yes or no to this question will force you to ask further questions, giving Debbie the impression that she is being grilled. Using open-ended questions reduces the number of questions you ask and gives the client some sense of control.

Obviously, it will sometimes be desirable to use closed questions such as "What was the last school you attended?" You will probably use closed questions most often to follow up client responses to open questions and in dealing with factual information, such as whether a client is married. Closed questions do sometimes have to be used when open-ended questions would be preferable, such as when you are working with adolescents and with mildly retarded clients who verbalize poorly. Sometimes streetwise clients will make it a practice to not volunteer any information that is not specifically requested: in order to get the information you want, you will have to rephrase your open question as a closed one. You should never stop trying, however, to get the client to speak freely by the use of open questions.

Regardless of the type of question used, you should not rush your clients by throwing questions at them in staccato fashion. Your tone of voice and rate of speech indicate clearly how you feel and whether you have really been listening to previous replies. Think of the many ways that you can say, "I'm really interested in you." Give clients ample time to think through their answers to your questions. Do not be embarrassed by silence or tempted to fill in with small talk. When the client is groping for ideas during such breaks in the conversation, small talk will interrupt the flow of thought. If the silence becomes overly long, ask the client to tell you some more about the last point you covered. Do not attempt to break the silence by putting words into the client's mouth. Clients may grasp at your idea and agree with it in an effort to please you or to avoid saying what was really on their minds. Either way, you will be recording and evaluating a response as the client's when it may actually be your own.

Listening

Evaluating responses to questions requires active listening. Active listening must be practiced. Some people are easy to listen to, others difficult. Prejudices on the part of the officer will interfere with active listening to the client as much as poor communications skills on the part of the client. When either of these is present, it is especially important to make an extra effort to really listen to what the client is saying.

Active listening requires a great deal of alertness and flexibility. Be especially alert to any recurring ideas the client presents and mentally flag them so that you can raise them later for deeper discussion. Be flexible enough to deal with issues as the client presents them. If you insist on dealing only with topics when *you* are ready for them, you may miss vital information because the client may no longer feel as disposed to discuss it as when it was first broached. Active listening, in short, implies what psychologist Theodor Reik (1956) calls "listening with the third ear." This requires not so much the mere auditory recording of actual words as listening to what the client is trying to tell you.

Clients may be telling you things they have no conscious intention of revealing. Does the client reveal self-centeredness by the overuse of personal pronouns? Does the client reveal overdependence or lack of a sense of responsibility by constantly blaming others for every little misfortune? Does the client bemoan his or her sins as vigorously as they are committed, thus perhaps revealing false remorse? What adjectives does the client use to describe significant others, and what do they reveal about his or her interpersonal relationships? What kind of defense mechanisms (to be discussed later), such as rationalization, projection, and displacement, does the client use to distort reality? This third-ear listening will tell you a lot more about your client than the face-value response of "what he did to me and what I said to her."

Restrain the urge to play Dr. Freud by reading too much into nonspecific responses at this stage, however. You do not yet have sufficient knowledge to make unsupported speculations in a report that has so much importance to the client's future. Third-ear insights should be noted for future use but should not be relayed to the sentencing judge as facts. When you begin to develop an empathetic understanding of your client and when a positive relationship has formed between you, then you may broach such issues. Of course, if you perceive something about a client's responses that applies directly to the present offense (such as rationalizing or intellectualizing about the crime) and that has implications for sentencing and supervision, it should be explored with the client then and there.

The Temptation to Interrupt Have you ever noticed that instead of really attending to what another person is saying to you, you were thinking of the next thing you wanted to say or that you interrupted that person in midsentence? And have you ever noticed how annoying this can be when others do it to you and how it causes you to lose your train of thought? When you are interviewing a client, your objective is not to score points in a debate. It is all too easy to interrupt clients when you perceive their verbal responses to your inquiries to be off the track. Do not let yourself become irritated and impatient with client digressions. Clients may be approaching the topic you bring up in the most direct way they know how. There are limits, of course, to the amount of digression that you may tolerate, but too early an interruption may prevent the emergence of significant information. Some people simply need more time to arrive at their destination. Although side excursions can be time-consuming, allowing a little extra time during the initial interview can actually conserve time when you are attempting to establish a working relationship with a client.

Keeping the Client in the Foreground Give the client the lion's share of the "air time" during the interview. Goyer, Redding, and Rickey (1968:14) have suggested that if you find yourself talking uninterruptedly for even as little as two minutes, you are failing to get through to your client; it is a good idea to reduce your talk time as much as possible. The time is the client's. You must resist the temptation to thrust your opinions onto clients. Many clients will be only too happy to allow an interviewer to babble on so that they may avoid exploring their own problems. Talk only when necessary to elicit information or to channel the interview in fruitful directions.

Further Impediments to Active Listening Other impediments to active listening against which you should guard are **daydreaming, detouring, arguing** and **rehearsing.** We are all guilty of these errors at one time or another. It is important in your chosen field to be aware of them and to reorient yourself to the content of your clients' communication as soon as you perceive yourself to be drifting away from it.

Daydreaming occurs when you are bored with what you are hearing or when you have pressing needs unrelated to the client's concerns. You veer off on your own track and leave the client behind, forgetting that the interview time belongs to the client. You must never daydream during client interviews; the client soon realizes that you have lost interest in his or her problems, and your efforts to establish a firm relationship will fail. Frequent daydreamers are out of touch with present reality. They fail in many tasks because they focus more on a future "could be" than on what is actually going on now.

Detouring occurs when a piece of communicated information reminds you of something not immediately relevant. You may then let your thoughts wander off on tangents, coming back now and again to touch the actual line of communication. When your thoughts again make contact with the client's, you can never be sure that the track you are on accurately corresponds to the client's track. Often it will not. On the highway or in an interview, detours can get you lost. Frequent detourers are inclined to be scatterbrained; they have difficulty focusing on the problem at hand.

Arguing occurs when a client makes a statement that rankles you and you cut off the client's line of communication to present your opinions. It is the client's opinion, not yours, that is the present concern. Allow clients to express and explore their feelings fully without debating them. It is important not to argue with clients, whether by actually voicing your opinions or by debating the client in your mind. Arguers tend to be either self-righteous or contentious individuals who are overly concerned with their own viewpoints.

Rehearsing occurs when, instead of attending to the client, you are considering how you will respond to an earlier statement. Rehearsers tend to be either unsure of themselves or perfectionists. They feel that no response is ever adequate if it is not carefully formulated before delivery. They seek just the right word or example to make a point. The trouble is that while you are thinking of that "perfect" response, you will have missed what the client is saying, which may be something that makes your response irrelevant.

In summarizing this section on listening and questioning, it accurate to say that no matter what your counseling orientation or the purposes of an interview, the most crucial skill you need is listening. It is the prerequisite to all other skills. If you have not really listened to what your client has been saying, you cannot formulate meaningful follow-up questions, you cannot develop rapport, you cannot begin to understand the client, and your assessment will be sloppy at best. Poor listening will frustrate and alienate clients; you may become part of their problem rather than part of the solution.

Responding: Guiding the Client's Disclosure

No matter how hard you listen, you will often have to verify a client's message to avoid jumping to wrong conclusions. When a response seems ambiguous, ask for **clarification.** Clarification involves a question like "Are you saying that ...?" or "Do you mean that ...?" Your request for clarification gives the client the opportunity to confirm or disconfirm your understanding. **Paraphrasing**, a simple restatement of the client's message in the interviewer's words, is similar to clarification. Paraphrasing is used to restate a message with *factual* content, such as a description of a person, place, event, or situation, to clarify the message, to let clients know that you have been paying attention and to encourage them to focus on the content more deeply.

In contrast, **reflection** is a rephrasing of the *emotional* content of the client's message. Reflection is useful when you want to identify how the client feels about the factual message presented to you. Feelings are not always expressed verbally but may be identified by nonverbal cues such as rigid body posture, reddening of the face, pursed lips, or tone of voice. The purpose of reflection is to help clients to become fully aware of their feelings and to encourage them to explore them.

A hypothetical dialogue illustrates these techniques. A thirty-year-old single mother of three children, Betty, has been found guilty of child endangering. Her oldest son, Jason, age nine, was hospitalized with a broken arm. A physical examination revealed that he had often been physically abused. You ask her to explain why she abuses Jason. Some possible interviewer responses follow her reply. Try to think of some replies of your own by imagining what it would be like in Betty's shoes.

> **CLIENT:** I don't really know why I do these things to Jason; I do love him. I'd do anything to change things. I'm not proud of what I did. He's a beautiful boy. I guess I just get so frustrated having to bring three children up on what the welfare pays you. You know, it's not easy trying to raise three kids. I can't get work because the kids are all so young. I just sit at home thinking about the future. I drink more as time goes on. All that sitting and drinking hasn't done much for my figure. I weigh about 210 right now. Who would want to hire a slob like me? If only I could get a job I know things would be better for us all.
>
> **INTERVIEWER** [Clarification]: Are you saying that one of the hardest things facing you right now is your inability to get work, which would enable you to make a better life for yourself and your children? Do you mean that your situation leads you to do these things to Jason?
>
> **INTERVIEWER** [Paraphrase]: You love Jason, but your responsibility for raising your family by yourself is very difficult for you. You are having a tough time of it.
>
> **INTERVIEWER** [Reflection]: You feel frustrated and angry about your inability to take care of your children as you would like. You feel terribly guilty about doing what you did to Jason. You feel embarrassed about your weight.

Interviewing the Client

Preparation

The Physical Setting The results of your interview will probably have a significant impact on your client's future; it is therefore vital that you give the client your undivided attention. Although the physical facilities in many criminal justice agencies are not ideal, it is important that the interview setting be as private and free of distractions as possible. The receptionist should be instructed to hold all nonemergency telephone calls, and a "Do not disturb" sign should be displayed on your office door. Some interruptions may be inevitable, but they must never be personal or frivolous. You must convey to your clients that the time belongs to them and that they are the only topic of importance to you during this period.

Familiarity with the Case Before interviewing the client, you must thoroughly familiarize yourself with the case materials obtained from police and prosecutor's files and use them to formulate the questions that you plan to ask. Appendix A contains a comprehensive semistructured interview schedule that is used in probation and parole agencies nationwide. It is an excellent tool for the beginning interviewer because it covers everything of importance for interviewing the typical client. The only point to remember about the schedule here is that while it begins by asking questions about clients' attitudes toward the offense and offense patterns, questions pertaining to the crime and to the client's criminal history are best left until last because these are the questions most likely to threaten the client and may require the use of interrogation rather than interviewing techniques. Clients will answer questions about the offense and about prior offenses more easily after friendly rapport has been established and they feel less threatened by the situation.

Most probation departments use an intake form, which the client fills out before meeting the probation officer. This form should request basic demographic data such as name, place and date of birth, current address and telephone number, names and addresses of family members and places of work, schools attended, and financial situation. It should also ask clients for pertinent medical information, prior involvements with the law, and their version of the current offense. A typical social history questionnaire is included in Appendix A.

Such a form serves a number of functions: (1) it gives structure to the interview, (2) it sensitizes the client to the kind of questions you will be asking, (3) it gives the client an opportunity to decide whether to be honest with you, (4) it gives you the opportunity to decide if the client has indeed been honest with you because you can check the written statement with the record, (5) it gives you insight into the client's communication skills, and (6) it minimizes the need for you to record factual information during the interview, which would stop its flow.

Initiating the Interview

A criminal justice client first meets a community corrections agency usually on referral to a probation department for a presentence investigation report (PSI) after being found guilty of a crime. Because the presentence investigation interview is perhaps the most important interview the client will experience, it will be the basis for the following discussion. Given the circumstances, the client will probably view the presentence interview as a punishment rather than as an opportunity to receive help. Because the client is not there voluntarily and may well have an ingrained mistrust and disregard for authority, it is particularly important that the interview get off to a good start.

Meeting the Client: Respect and Rapport Your first meeting with the client, who may be anxious and nervous, should convey your respect and concern. The importance of this first contact cannot be overemphasized. First impressions will certainly color much of what will follow between you and your client. It is essential, then, to establish rapport at this time. Greet your client by looking him or her straight in the eyes and offering a smile and a firm handshake. First names should not be used at the first meeting, especially with older clients. Traditionally, the superordinate individual addressed the subordinate individual by first name, whereas the person in the inferior position was expected to use the presumed superior's full title and last name. This convention was designed to emphasize social distance—something you definitely wish to avoid. (A more informal first-name relationship should be established as soon as you perceive that the client is amenable to it.) Your initial statement should be something like, "Good morning, Mr. Smith. My name is Joyce Williams. I will be your probation officer."

You have now introduced yourself and your role. Although your client is a troubled individual you are seeing because he or she has committed a crime of which he or she may be deeply ashamed, there must be no hint of a patronizing, condescending, or judgmental attitude in either your voice or your nonverbal behavior. You may have extremely negative feelings about the kind of behavior that has brought the client to you. Any attempts to deny those feelings to yourself will result in an artificial, stilted, and unproductive interview. Acknowledge to yourself that these feelings exist and that they are normal and to be expected, but also recognize that expressing them in a professional goal-oriented setting is inappropriate. If you reveal your anger or embarrassment, even subtly or unconsciously, the client will pick up on your cues and perhaps respond equally with anger or embarrassment. Negative emotions, yours or the client's, are not conducive to an effective interview. Recognition and control of feelings rather than denial and repression of them is a professional goal you should strive for.

Early in my career I had a client whose appearance and crime had a negative effect on me. She had paid neighborhood boys to have sex with her over a period of months. Although I struggled to rid myself of the sexist attitudes acquired through my socialization, I could not free myself of the notion that women were not supposed to act that way. Consequently, I perceived her crime as somehow much more odious than if she had been a man. Her physical appearance made matters worse: She was extremely obese, with multiple chins thickly folded upon an expansive bosom, and she had a body odor too strong to ignore.

I tried hard to respond positively to her, but I realized later how completely artificial I must have seemed to her. I ran through the interview, and I approached the embarrassing (both to her and to myself) question of her offense with insensitivity. In other words, I let my attitudes and feelings about my client obscure her basic humanity. The interview was purely ritual. She was placed on probation to me, but our relationship never did manage to overcome our disastrous first encounter. First impressions are indeed vital! I did learn a lot about myself and my attitudes through that encounter, and I do not think I ever made the same mistake again.

My experience with this woman underscores the desirability of examining your attitudes and prejudices about various kinds of people and their behavior before you ever have to deal with them in a field situation. Treat each person as a unique individual, not as a member of a larger group from whom you expect certain ways of behaving. A colleague of mine used to have a saying on her office wall, which she said she read at the beginning of every day "to keep me honest." It said: "There is so much good in the worst of us, and so much bad in the best of us, that it ill behooves any one of us to find any fault with the rest of us."

Explaining the Purpose of the Interview Begin the actual interview by asking your clients if they know the purpose of the interview. If not—and many clients do not—then explain the purpose fully. Tell the client the kind of information you wish to obtain, what it will be used for, and who will have access to it. Although an explanation of how a presentence investigation report will be used (to aid in sentencing decisions, and, if the client is incarcerated, in prison classification and parole hearings) can raise the client's anxiety level, the honesty will be appreciated.

It is a good idea to then ask clients if they understand what they have been told so far and if they have any questions. It is very important, however, not to respond to such questions as "What do you think I'll get?" or "What are my chances?" You do not make the final sentencing decision, and you do not wish either to raise false hopes or to generate needless anxiety. If you tell a client that you are "sure" that he or she will get probation and the client is incarcerated, that person will surely feel bitter and betrayed. One such incident may have a lasting negative affect on any dealings that client may later have with you or with any other correctional worker. Conversely, if you tell a client that he or she is as good as on the bus to prison but the client is actually placed on probation, his or her attitude toward you could be one of smug contempt: "The judge didn't buy your recommendation. Just goes to show how valuable your opinion is, doesn't it?"

Some authorities would disagree on this point, feeling that if incarceration seems probable, it is humanitarian to prepare the client. This is like the physician's dilemma when asked, "How long have I got?" An honest appraisal in either case, so the argument goes, gives the individual the opportunity to prepare by saying goodbyes and putting personal affairs in order. However, if a client thinks prison is to be expected, the goodbyes may well be to the jurisdiction. If you do offer your client an opinion that turns out to be wrong or leads the client to abscond, you have only yourself to blame. Instead, reply politely you never second-guess judges and that it is not your place to speculate. You are now ready to begin the interview proper.

Conducting the Interview

Language and Demeanor If you are using a client intake form, the interview is to clarify and elaborate on the information the client has written down. When questioning a client, you are making contact with another human being. Questions must be geared to both the vocabulary and pace of the client. Legalistic or sociological jargon, street "jive talk," and ten-dollar words should be avoided. The use of fancy phraseology will embarrass the client whose vocabulary is limited and will not impress one who is as articulate as you are. Either way, it will distance your client from you. Similarly, the use of street jive is unprofessional and will give the client the idea that you are either being patronizing or playing buddy-buddy. Use conventional and easily understandable English. Just as important, do not adopt street mannerisms such as an artificially laid-back posture or the latest fad in handshakes. Do not say or do anything that is artificial to you; it will be blatantly obvious to those used to being treated dishonestly.

The Use of Authority A final concern is the proper use of authority. Some experts on counseling feel that the use, or even the possession, of authority is detrimental to the helping process. This is not so. Authority and helping will be incompatible, however, if you use (and abuse) your authority to emphasize the moral distance between you and your client and to puff yourself up with your own importance. The bombastic "big stick" approach will only alienate clients. They will type you as "just another cop in social worker's threads" and scoff at your insistence that you want to help them.

Yet authority comes with the job, and it cannot be denied. Failure to use your authority when appropriate will be viewed as weakness by clients who value strength and who are adept at manipulating perceived weakness. Officers' authority, like their feelings, must be recognized and accepted, but used with professional restraint. Needless to say, the trappings of force, such as guns or handcuffs, should not be on display at the first meeting with the client.

Dealing with Awkward Clients Some of your clients, being fearful or angry, will act hostile or refuse to answer certain questions. They may be trying to maintain a sense of dignity and control in the only way they know. When such an attitude becomes apparent to you, do not continue with the interview as if you hoped that ignoring it would make it go away. Say something like: "Mr. Jones, I know that this is unpleasant for you and that you must be feeling a little uptight. It's quite natural for you to feel that way, lots of people do. Why don't we agree to be civil to one another? What do you say?" This lets Mr. Jones know that you are aware of his feelings, that others have felt that way, that you accept his feelings as natural, and that you are willing to start over again on a new footing.

In those rare instances when clients continue to refuse to answer questions or respond in a sarcastic, rude, or abrupt manner, let them know in no uncertain terms that this kind of attitude is unacceptable and tell them that if they continue, the interview will be terminated and they will have to come back after they have rethought their approach. You may also indicate that a persistent attitude will be conveyed to the sentencing judge. If this tactic does not work, try a phone call to the client's attorney outlining the problem; I have found this never fails to bring about a change in the client's demeanor.

Most often, however, clients are anxious to cooperate and to make a positive impression during the initial interview. They are feeling you out just as surely as you are feeling them out. Most clients are aware that their attitudes will be reported to the judge and that they may influence your recommendation. Reluctance and lack of cooperation are much more common once clients are under actual supervision than they are before. The presentence investigator and the parole board usually see clients at their best. It is the supervising probation and parole officers who are usually confronted with uncooperative clients. For this reason, it is of the utmost importance to lay the groundwork for a trusting relationship at the initial interview, when the client's frame of mind is most conducive to it. (The problem of the reluctant client is addressed in more detail in Chapter 9.)

No matter what the degree of cooperation, the client's overall demeanor will give you valuable clues for your assessment. Someone who comes to the interview smelling of alcohol or under the influence of drugs is not taking the process seriously and will obviously be difficult to supervise on probation. A servile or arrogant manner will also provide clues for character assessment and possible supervision strategies.

Such observations will assist you as you design a preliminary treatment plan or decide if it is appropriate to refer the client to a specialized agency (such as those described in Chapter 19). When you decide that a referral is advisable, discuss the matter with the client and explain your reasoning. Do not antagonize or put the client on the defensive by flatly stating that he or she has a problem. Try to steer clients toward that conclusion themselves by asking them how the problem you perceive them as having affects their relationships with others and how they would feel if they could find support in controlling it. You may then discuss the services provided by a given agency and the benefits they may derive from talking with a counselor there. Again, it cannot be emphasized enough that the initial interview is your best opportunity to begin to get a client's cooperation and compliance.

Terminating the Interview

At the end of the interview, summarize what has gone on. Your summary provides the opportunity to determine if anything important has been overlooked and gives the client the chance to change, clarify, or add to transmitted information. Ask the client if he or she has anything to add or to ask. If not, you may conclude the interview, shake the client's hand, inform the client that you will be in touch in the near future, and walk him or her to the door. Back in your office, go over your notes immediately and write down additional impressions while they are fresh. The results of your interview should also help you decide what collateral interviews will be necessary.

Interviewing the Victim

Preparation

Your first approach to the victim should be a phone call to make an appointment. Explain why you want a personal meeting and set up a time at the victim's convenience. As a courtesy, and to relieve victims of any further inconvenience, the meeting should take place in the victim's home unless he or she prefers otherwise. Some victims welcome the opportunity to speak about the crime again in the familiar setting of their own homes, but for some it is a nuisance that they would rather avoid.

When you meet with the victim, identify yourself as an officer of the court by presenting your credentials. You may then review the purpose of the interview. Make an effort to let the victim know that your presence indicates the concern the legal system has about his or her experience and that the interview is an opportunity for the victim to have some input into the sentencing process. This assurance tends to ease the pain and anger of all except the most cynical, and it returns a sense of control to those victims who feel that they have lost much of it by their victimization.

Being the victim of a crime is an intensely negative experience. Even if the crime is a nonviolent one in which the victim never had to confront the offender, the experience can leave a person with feelings of complete helplessness and violation. These feelings naturally tend to generate anger and self-blame, the latter especially among victims of sexual assault. The typical experience of the victim as the case progresses through the courts, sometimes with interminable delays, does nothing to mitigate these feelings.

Because some of the anger and self-blame may be displaced onto the presentence investigator, be prepared to encounter this natural reaction and to be sensitive in dealing with it. Your most trying experiences may be interviewing parents who have lost a child to a drunken driver or relatives of loved ones who have been brutally raped or murdered. Extreme sensitivity and understanding are absolute musts in such instances. In no case should you imply sympathy for the offender or suggest that the victim may have contributed to his or her own victimization (even if the thoughts are in your mind). Never argue with a victim or the victim's survivors. An investigator must have a self-concept strong enough to allow victims or their survivors to vent their anger without retaliation.

When Not to Interview

Interviewing child victims of sexual abuse is entirely different. It is not merely uncomfortable for a child to recount the episode; it may add to the psychological damage the child suffers. Henry Hartman, a criminal psychiatrist of many years' experience, says: "Intense emotional reactions on the part of the parents, repeated questioning by police, unpleasant appearances and cross-examination in courtrooms may all be as traumatic as or even more traumatic than the offense itself" (1978:217). There is no point in risking further trauma for the sake of a little additional insight into the offense. I have seen children who, even after long-term sexual victimization by adults, have suffered no ill effects until the relationships were discovered and the children subjected to the results Hartman lists. Such social reactions lead children to believe that much or all of the blame for what transpired belongs to them. Certainly it does not, and the investigating officer should not call up the child's residual feelings of guilt and shame in the pursuit of a "complete" PSI. Parents of the children should, of course, be interviewed and allowed to discuss the effects of the offense on their children.

Conducting the Interview

Asking for Details of the Offense It is not advisable in all cases to ask victims for the details of the offense. They have already recounted them numerous times to other officials, and the retelling may be painful for them. You should, however, offer them the opportunity to speak about the offense if they want to. You might say something like, "I know this has been an awful experience for you and you would probably like to forget it, but is there anything at all that you would like to add that you didn't tell the police or the prosecutor?" In posing the question this way you have conveyed to the victim your recognition of his or her ordeal, and you have offered the option of elaborating. The decision must be the entirely the victim's; do not press the issue in the face of obvious reluctance.

Reassuring the Victim One of the things that crime victims need most is reassurance of their safety. Many victims fear retaliation or worry that, for example, a burglar will come back. In my experience as a police officer and as a probation officer, I have never known a criminal to retaliate against the victim after the case had been adjudicated or a burglar to hit the same house twice. If such things happen, they are extremely rare. Make a clear statement to this effect to frightened victims. When the victim and the offender are known to each other, you may even suggest that if the criminal is placed on probation, you will make it a condition of probation that he or she is to have no contact of any sort with the victim. Victims need such reassurances.

Promises to the Victim It is important that you not make any promises to the victim that you cannot keep or statements regarding the defendant's probable sentence. Some states allow victims to have input into the sentencing of those who have offended against them. If your state has a law providing that a victim may make a recommendation for sentencing, you should, of course, request one. Whether these recommendations actually affect sentencing decisions is a question that has not yet been studied well. A recent study found a statistically significant relationship between victim recommendations and the sentences imposed in sexual assault cases, but the relationship disappeared when the effects of the seriousness of the crime and the offender's prior record were controlled for (Walsh 1986). Future research may show different results. In any case, do not allow the victim to think that his or her recommendation will necessarily be heeded. Be as honest with victims as you are with offenders. Do not risk the future anger and disrespect of a victim for the sake of their momentary peace of mind. Specific questions you should ask the victim are listed in Chapter 6 on the PSI report.

Terminating the Interview

End the interview with the victim by reiterating your assurances and thanks for his or her cooperation. Give the victim your card and invite him or her to call you with further concerns at any time. This invitation may again reassure the victim that he or she will not be forgotten in the criminal justice process. Finally, if it is not the practice of the prosecutor's office in your jurisdiction to apprise victims of sentencing dates, you might tell victims that you will notify them personally. At the very least, inform the victim of the final disposition of the case.

Interrogating the Client

Reasons for Interrogation

Most jurisdictions define their probation and parole officers as law enforcement officers. As a law enforcement officer, you will be responsible for monitoring the behavior of your clients. When clients break the law or some condition of their supervision or are suspected of doing so, it is your duty to question them. As you will see, your questioning under these circumstances will require a different strategy. This type of questioning is called interrogation. To those who enter the community corrections field with the notion that their only role is that of a helper, interrogation is sometimes distasteful, probably because they associate it with the old-fashioned third degree. You must not lose sight of the fact that you are functioning as both a law enforcement officer and a counselor; the two roles do not necessarily conflict. As a law enforcement officer, you may need to learn the truth about acts committed by your clients that violate the conditions of their probation or parole. Clients do not readily admit to violations. You are not doing justice to your role or to your clients if you do not interrogate them about and deal with the details of their violations.

During a PSI interview you may also need to interrogate a client who flatly denies having committed the crime of which he or she has just been convicted. This is not all that unusual. An unpublished study found that 18 percent of a sample of 416 clients denied their crimes during the PSI interview. Since denial has implications for decisions about sentencing and treatment, the investigating officer's report must go beyond recording the simple denial. Many clients will tell you that they are innocent and that they pleaded guilty on their lawyer's advice or to plea bargain. Although some innocent clients may plead guilty because their lawyers have considered the case against them to be too strong, the fact that the case is now before you makes the possibility remote. Given the legal restraints on police questioning (restraints that you do not have in the PSI situation) and the defendant's privilege of silence in court, your interrogation may be the first opportunity to get to the truth of the matter. I estimate that one out of every four clients who initially denied their guilt finally admit it under questioning and at least two more make statements that are sufficient to dispel doubts of guilt.

Distinguishing Between Interviewing and Interrogation

Interrogation is the use of systematic and formal questioning to thoroughly investigate a specific allegation against a suspect. There are two basic differences between interviewing and interrogation. The first concerns your relationship with the client: You have temporarily discarded the helping attitude of the counselor and adopted the skeptical manner of the law enforcement officer. The second concerns purpose: Interviewing is designed to gather general information; interrogation is the drawing-out of specific information that the client may be highly motivated to keep hidden—namely, whether the client did or did not commit a given act.

The process of interrogation is also different from interviewing in that it requires the interrogator, not the client, to be in control. You must control the timing, content, and wording of your questioning with your singular purpose in mind. Clients must be given only enough initiative and control to allow them to relate their stories. They must come to understand that you mean business and that for the moment you are not interested in anything but the question at hand.

If the matter about which you are conducting the interview involves a new offense and if what you learn is to be used as evidence in court, you must inform your client of his or her rights as required by *Miranda*. In *United States v. Deaton* (1972), the presiding judge stated that a probationer or parolee is probably under more pressure to respond to a probation or parole officer than to a police officer, and therefore the *Miranda* warnings should be given.

Being Confident by Being Prepared

Preparing yourself for an interrogation is both different from and similar to preparing for an interview. The major difference is that, because the client is aware that an interrogation is often a battle of wits, the atmosphere can be quite charged. If you are to conduct an effective interrogation, one that will lead you to the truth, you must convey an impression of confidence to the client. To be confident you must be fully prepared, completely familiar with all the evidence whether it supports or subverts the client's guilt. Such evidence might include police reports, victim statements, or information from an informant. Not having all the evidence available will put you at a disadvantage once the interrogation begins.

Conducting the Interrogation

Whether the interrogation takes place in your office or in a cell at the county jail, as the client's supervising officer you will, unlike a police officer, have had an ongoing relationship with him or her and will be able to dispense with the usual police lead-ins like requests for demographic information. Greet the client in a friendly but business-like way and set out your purpose by saying something like, "Jim, I've asked you to come to see me (or, I've come to see you) to get to the bottom of this matter that has come to my attention." You may then begin your questioning.

Confidence in your professionalism and in your preparation, again, is of the utmost importance. A lack of confidence, reflected by frequently referring to reports, hemming and hawing, squirming in your chair, or acting impatient will give the client the impression that the evidence may not be all that strong. You should demonstrate to the client that the evidence has convinced you that he or she is guilty. State this conviction in a nonemotional, clinical manner. Your credibility as an interrogator depends on these two points: your thorough knowledge of the matter under discussion and the client's perceptions of you as a competent professional. Do not jeopardize a positive relationship that you have worked hard to gain by becoming frustrated and angry because you feel that you cannot break down the client's defenses.

Style Despite the differences in purpose between interviewing and interrogation, much that we have said about interviewing does apply to the interrogation. You must approach the task in a completely professional manner. Any attempts to borrow the techniques of the movie detective will prove disastrous. Do not put up a "tough guy" front. The typical criminal will see through this and match you verbal blow for verbal blow and could well win the competition, because clients must often rely on such tactics to survive every day of their lives. If this happens, you reveal yourself as a phoney, and you can say goodbye to any respect your client may have had for you.

Clifford Unwin, an experienced British police inspector, says that although the interrogator must control the psychological situation, it is not wise to try for complete psychological domination. He writes: "The problem is that if the interrogator limits himself [or herself] to displays of power he [or she] may find in certain situations that he [or she] is running the risk of doing exactly the opposite. It may cause the suspect to confirm his [or her] beliefs that the interrogator is the enemy and is someone to be defied, particularly with a hardened or seasoned criminal" (1978:1875).

As Unwin implies, you should never adopt the attitude of "NIGYSOB" ("Now I've got you, you son-of-a-bitch") described by Eric Berne (1964) in his book *Games People Play*. If you project such an obviously self-satisfied attitude to clients in interrogation, you are issuing a challenge that invites resistance. You also imply that your objective all along has been to "get" rather than to help your client.

Ask Leading Questions An interrogation will often rely on **leading** questions, those in which the wording strongly encourages a specific answer. (This kind of question should never be used in an interview.) For example: Jim's estranged wife complains to you that he was drinking last night and came over to her home and slapped her around. Jim's parole conditions require him to stay sober and stay away from his wife. You may confront Jim with: "You were in the Western Bar drinking last night, weren't you? Isn't it also true that you got drunk and went over to your wife's and beat her up?" Such questions, asked in a businesslike tone, are more difficult to deny than is a simple, "Were you drinking last night?"

Reveal a Little Information Reinforce both your confidence and the client's anxiety by revealing some of the evidence you have, taking careful note of how the client deals with this information. But do not reveal all the evidence in one giant salvo. If the client successfully weathers the initial full attack, you have nothing left in reserve to spring as a surprise. Always keep clients on the defensive by letting them guess how much evidence you have. Point out inconsistencies in their story and ask them to account for them. (You can do this only if you have thoroughly assimilated the official version and paid complete attention to the client's version.)

Some clients will respond well if you state straightforwardly that alibis or protestations of innocence are "bullshit." More than once after such a remark I have been confronted with a knowing smile, followed by the real story. This usually works with a client who has been through the system before and who tends to look on what is going on between you as a game. (This, of course, depends on how serious the consequences of such an admission will be.) Other clients will react defensively to such a direct statement; with them it is preferable to state: "You haven't told me the whole truth" than to say, "You've been lying to me." The difference is subtle but real. Only experience will tell you when which approach will work best. Usually the former method is preferable with more respectable, less streetwise clients.

Let Clients Damn Themselves It is often a good ploy to let the client make statements that you know are lies, giving the impression that you accept them at face value. The awkward thing about a lie is that it requires additional lies for support. Eventually, this compounding of falsehoods should paint the client into an uncomfortable corner where the only way out is the truth. If you let clients get themselves into such a psychologically uncomfortable position and then point out the inconsistencies, they have a strong motive (the removal of psychological discomfort) to "come clean."

Taking Advantage of Client Discomfort If this does not secure the desired admission, such signs of guilt as confusion, stammering, nervous sweating, an active Adam's apple, refusal to maintain eye contact, and other emotional reactions should be pointed out to the client. Then take advantage of such signs of physiological discomfort by looking the client squarely in the eye and repeat some of your most threatening questions. You may also ask the client to repeat a story three or four times at different points of the interrogation. It is easy to be consistent if the story is true, but very hard to remember little details used to support a falsehood. That is, you can tell the truth in four different ways, but not a lie. Knowing that you are aware of their discomfort often prompts clients to unburden themselves by making a confession.

Bluffing is a weak form of interrogation. Bluffing is meant to convey to clients the impression that you have access to information that is damaging to them when, in fact, you do not. For instance, while interrogating Jack on the basis of police information that he has been trafficking in drugs, you may suggest that you have "accurate" information from "confidential informants" that he has been selling drugs. A bluff like this may pay large dividends, but it is more likely to be called. If Jack calls your bluff, all you can do is withdraw as gracefully as possible. What if he really is innocent? Your crude poker tactics will sorely offend him and perhaps do irreparable damage to the supportive relationship you have been seeking to develop with him. The cost/benefit ratio of such tactics does not recommend their use.

The Back Door Approach Some authorities on police interrogation advocate a "back door" approach (Unwin 1978), prompting a confession by downplaying the seriousness of the offense the individual is suspected of committing, conveying sympathy and understanding of why such a crime would be committed under the circumstances, blaming victims or accomplices, or intimating that the act might have been accidental. Although I have used this approach as a police officer, I do not advocate it for the corrections worker. This psychological ploy elicits confessions by relieving suspects' guilt, because the message they get is that their actions were not really that bad, others would do the same thing in their shoes, and the blame is not all theirs. While this suits police purposes by "clearing" crimes, it is counterproductive to the correctional goal. Offenders who have been given easy rationales for their actions are not amenable to rehabilitation. The correctional worker aware of his or her dual roles should not compromise one of them to satisfy the immediate requirements of the other.

Terminating the Interrogation

How you terminate the interrogation will depend on the circumstances. If the interrogation was to follow up a technical violation of supervision conditions, such as associating with known criminals, continued substance abuse, failing to report to you, or any other violation of this kind, the action you take is discretionary. You may feel it necessary to initiate formal proceedings for the revocation of probation or parole, or you may decide to resume your helping relationship. If the interrogation resulted from an arrest for a new crime, any further action on your part has to await formal adjudication.

In any case, the client should be informed of your next step as soon as you have decided what it is to be. You may be able to tell the client then and there, or you may want to investigate further and think the matter over before declaring your intentions. Either way, you should explain your decision to the client and your reasons for making it, making every effort to reestablish your working relationship with the client. Even if you decided to initiate parole revocation proceedings, most clients realize that you are only doing your job and will not permanently alienate themselves from you if you have been fair, honest, and professional with them.

Summary

This chapter has introduced you to the techniques of interviewing and interrogation. Prepare for both tasks by familiarizing yourself with all the pertinent information available. Any interview, to be effective, must begin with an effort to establish rapport. This is particularly important in criminal justice where clients are reluctant to even be in your office. Your clients, though convicted criminals, are also human beings who deserve consideration and respect. Make them as comfortable as possible and show that you are concerned and willing to listen to them.

Listening—really listening—is the most important aspect of an effective interview. Give the client the "air time" and resist interruptions and debates; the interview time belongs to the client. Encourage clients to explore themselves and their behavior, as they must, through frequent use of probes and open-ended questions. Make sure you understand what your clients are trying to tell you by using paraphrasing, clarification, and reflective techniques. Even the most awkward of clients will settle down and give you a great deal of valuable assessment information if you treat them with patience, respect, and firmness when it is required.

Interviewing victims requires special sensitivity and absolute respect for any reluctance they have to being interviewed or to approaching certain subjects. Do not dig for details of sexual offenses. (They are in the official record anyway.) It is also considered extremely inadvisable to interview child victims of sexual assault. Never argue with victims about anything, and be prepared to be used as a convenient target for their verbal anger. Finally, reassure victims as much as possible, but, as with clients, make no promises that are not within your power to keep.

Sometimes interrogation techniques are required. Any interrogation should be approached in a calm, clinical, and professional manner. Unlike the interview, the purpose of which is to gather large amounts of general information, the interrogation is geared to answering one specific question: "Did you do it?" Also contrary to the interview process, you rather than the client will control the content and pace of the interrogation. Know the evidence that supports your client's guilt, but do not jeopardize your relationship with your client by coming on like a movie detective. Some useful interrogation techniques are letting clients damn themselves and taking advantage of client discomfort. Use these recommended techniques when necessary, but always be honest and fair with the client, and be yourself.

Exercise in Listening and Interviewing

This is an exercise in listening using the CMC (Client Management Classification) semistructured interview schedule reproduced in Appendix A. Although this exercise will familiarize you with the type of questions asked in a typical PSI interview, the main purpose for the present is to give you experience in listening.

Students should be divided into pairs, one student being the interviewer and the other the interviewee. Rather than role playing, the interviewee should relate to the interviewer actual aspects of his or her life. For instance, when asked, "How do (did) you get along with your father?" the interviewee should respond accurately with his or own actual experiences. The main purpose of this interview exercise, again, is to develop your ability to listen actively. Did you ever buy a lottery ticket or bet on a ball game and then listen for the results on the radio? Think back to how you listened then. You probably sat close to the radio and faced it with intense interest. You leaned toward it, impervious to all other stimuli. That is how you should proceed with this exercise—with intense interest. Ask the questions provided in the schedule, but when appropriate use probes, open-ended questions, requests for clarification, paraphrased responses, and reflected feelings.

After the interview, write a brief social history of your partner (a PSI without offense, criminal history, and evaluation and recommendation material) based on the information obtained, then give it to the interviewee for evaluation. The interviewee should evaluate the history and your interviewing performance according to the following criteria:

1. Eye contact was maintained without gazing or staring. Yes__No__
2. Body posture was appropriate (relaxed, slight forward lean). Yes__No__
3. He/she made me feel comfortable and relaxed.Yes__No__
4. He/she made me really think about things I haven't thought about for some time by the use of probes. Yes__No__
5. He/she seemed genuinely interested in me. Yes__No__
6. He/she delivered questions without hesitation. Yes__No__
7. He/she often asked for clarification and paraphrased often.Yes__No__
8. I felt that I could tell him/her just about anything he/she wanted to know about my personal life.Yes__No__
9. He/she accurately reflected my feelings. Yes__No__
10. On a scale of 1 to 10, I would rate his/her reported accuracy of my social history as 1 2 3 4 5 6 7 8 9 10 (circle one).

After each student has taken a turn as both interviewer and interviewee, these ratings should be shared with one another. Ratings should be honest evaluations and not designed to ignore poor technique in the name of "smooth sailing." Feedback should be viewed by the interviewer as constructive. Think of it as another exercise in self-disclosure in which your partner has revealed something of your "blind self," in this case, your ability to conduct an effective interview. The benefits of these exercises will be greatly enhanced if they can be videotaped so that you will have visual and audio feedback of your interview behavior. Lastly, do not forget that this is only a first attempt. Learn from it.

References and Suggested Readings

Aubry, A., and R. Caputo. 1965. *Criminal interrogation.* Springfield, Ill.: Charles C Thomas.

Benjamin, A. 1981. *The helping interview.* Boston: Houghton Mifflin.

Berne, E. 1964. *Games people play.* New York: Grove Press.

Egan, G. 1986. *The skilled helper*. Monterey, Cal.: Brooks/Cole.

Garrett, A. 1982. *Interviewing: Its principles and methods*. New York: Family Services Association of America.

Goyer, R., C. Redding, and J. Rickey. 1968. *Interviewing principles and techniques*. Dubuque, Iowa: William C. Brown.

Hartman, H. 1963. Interviewing techniques in probation and parole. *Federal Probation* (series of four articles in March, June, September, and December).

Hartman, H. 1978. *Basic psychiatry for corrections workers*. Springfield, Ill.: Charles C Thomas.

Ivey, A. 1983. *Intentional interviewing and counseling*. Monterey, Cal.: Brooks/Cole.

Kleinke, C. 1975. *First impressions: The psychology of encountering others*. Englewood Cliffs, N.J.: Prentice-Hall.

Reik, T. 1956. *Listening with the third ear*. New York: Grove Press.

Unwin, C. 1978. Interrogation techniques. *Police Review* 85:1874-1877.

Walsh, A. 1986. Placebo justice: Victim recommendations and offender sentences in sexual assault cases. *Journal of Criminal Law and Criminology* 77:1126-1141.

Wicks, R. 1974. *Applied psychology for law enforcement officers and correctional officers*. New York: McGraw-Hill.

Chapter 6
The Presentence Investigation Report

The presentence investigation is the first step in the attempt to correct the offender's behavior. . . . It requires great skill in the study, evaluation, and supervision of offenders; familiarity with community resources; and an understanding of their subculture.

Harvey Treger

The presentence investigation report is the end product of the interviews you have completed with the offender, the victim, arresting police officers, and other interested parties. The quality and usefulness of the report depend on how well you have conducted your interviews and how well you can summarize a voluminous amount of material, making a reasoned selection of pertinent information.

You must learn to discriminate between information that is necessary and information that is merely nice to know. Too much unnecessary material will clutter the report and confuse the reader. Many reports are liberally padded with trivia that add nothing to the understanding of the client and cloud sentencing decisions. Studies exploring the decision-making process have shown an inverse relationship between sheer quantity of data and appropriate or useful decisions (Nettler 1970). If you were the sentencing judge, would you want to read fifteen pages of irrelevancies when you had perhaps ten other reports to read?

Good report writing is an art that flows from practice and feedback from classroom instructors, coworkers, supervisors, and judges. There is no substitute for practice and feedback, but a discussion of specific content areas of the PSI report should lay the groundwork for the writing of thorough, factual, concise, readable, and useful PSI reports.

Uses of the PSI Report

A brief review of the uses of PSI reports will underline the importance of making sure that your reports are well-written. Generally, PSI reports are used as decision-making aids or as treatment aids.

Judicial Sentencing Decisions

Presentence investigations to help the judge choose an appropriate case disposition serve the positivist philosophy of individualized justice. Probation officers are charged with putting this philosophy into practice by giving the courts their assessments of individual offenders and making sentencing recommendations consistent with those assessments. Numerous studies have shown that probation officers have been spectacularly successful in gaining judicial compliance with their recommendations (Hagan 1975; Myers 1979; Walsh 1984, 1985a). Given that these recommendations, which should flow naturally from the information in the PSI report, can have a profound effect on an individual's life, it is imperative that they accurately reflect the facts.

Departmental and Institutional Classification

Diagnostic information in the PSI report is used by probation departments to determine how much supervision to give clients placed on probation. Information about prior supervisions, arrest record, attitude, needs and risk assessments, and the nature of the crime can be quantified on a scale (such as the risk and needs scales to be examined later) to determine the type and frequency of supervision. For the incarcerated client, the institution uses medical, psychological, and criminal history and vocational and educational information to help determine security level, work assignments, and vocational, educational, and counseling needs.

Parole Decisions

The PSI report accompanies the client to the institution and is used as a basis for parole release decisions. The parole officer to whom the client is released also uses information in the PSI report in formulating initial treatment and supervision plans. In decisions about parole revocation, PSI information is used as a baseline to gauge the offender's progress (or lack of it) since the PSI assessment.

Counseling Plans and Community Agency Referrals

The treatment plans outlined in the PSI report guide the probation officer who is supervising the client (who may or may not be the officer who wrote the report). They also help the officer make appropriate referrals to agencies that deal with problems of the client that are beyond the officer's expertise. The PSI report is then used by the receiving agency as a planning guide, relieving the agency of the need to gather duplicate information. (Such information should not be provided to the agency, however, without the written consent of the client.)

Sample PSI Report

An actual PSI report is presented here to illustrate what such a report should contain. (Names, locations, and circumstances have been altered sufficiently to protect anonymity.) Bear its uses in mind as you examine it. This report was selected because of its quality and because it illustrates interesting applications of theories we have examined or will examine. This report is to be used not to validate particular theories, but to illustrate them.

We will explain, section by section, the kind of information required in each section of the PSI report. Then we will comment on each content area using examples from the Bloggs PSI.

THE ADRIAN COUNTY ADULT PROBATION DEPARTMENT
LOWMAN, IDAHO
PRESENTENCE REPORT

NAME: William (Bill) Bloggs
JUDGE: Joseph B. Lynch
ADDRESS: Currently in Adrian County Jail
Formerly: 780 N. 30th, Lowman, ID.
INDICTMENT # 84-3457
AGE: 26 DOB 7-25-58
SEX: Male RACE: White
ATTORNEY: S. Bonnetti
PROBATION OFFICER: Paul Corrick
PENDING CASES/DETAINERS: None
MARITAL STATUS: Married
DEPENDENTS: None
OFFENSE: Aggravated Robbery, IRC # 2911.01
Attempted Murder, IRC # 2923.02
DATE: October 19, 1984

CIRCUMSTANCES OF OFFENSE

On 6-13-84, at approximately 1:30 a.m., the defendant entered the Big Man Restaurant, located at 1324 Main St., through an open rear door and announced his intention of robbing the establishment. Armed with a .38 caliber pistol, the defendant ordered the manager to fill a bag embossed with the Lowman College seal, which he had brought with him, with the day's takings. The manager, Barry Harboume, complied with the demand and filled the bag with cash totaling $1,203.32. The defendant then picked up the bag and exited through the back door.

As soon as he left the restaurant, Mr. Harbourne called the police to the scene. Upon leaving the scene, the defendant stopped to remove his sweater, gloves, and the face mask he was wearing. The police arrived as he was doing this and spotted him. At this point, the defendant saw them and started to run. The police ordered him to stop. He did not heed this warning and kept on running. The police were firing at him as he ran. The defendant returned the fire with two rounds, one shot hitting Patrolman Williams in the leg. The defendant was able to elude the pursuing officers at this time. However, the police found a 1976 Buick Special registered to the defendant parked three buildings east of the Big Man. In making good his escape, the defendant dropped the bag containing the money and a number of personal artifacts. The bag was the aforementioned Lowman College bag containing a man's wallet with the defendant's driver's license and other identification inside. The gun was found in the grass in a storm ditch across from Ray's Auto Supply Store, located at 1200 Main.

The defendant, accompanied by his attorney, turned himself in to the Lowman police the next morning and made a full confession. He confessed to the present offense, as well as to two previous robberies of the same establishment, and one at the Big Man Restaurant at State and Glover on 4-12-84.

STATEMENT OF THE DEFENDANT

The defendant wrote out his statement for this officer. It was decided that it should be reproduced verbatim in order to preserve its flavor.

"On the morning of June 13, 1984, I robbed the Big Man Restaurant. In order to understand why I needed the money, first we should examine my childhood in order to find some underlying reason(s) for my behavior. Our family had a farm and a dog food processing business. The family hobby was hunting and trapping, totally our father's idea. The family businesses left very little time for our parents to be parents, they were most always in the position of boss.

"During the years previous to meeting the woman who became my wife (she was not my first girlfriend), I did not see myself in any real one-to-one loving relationships. Even the pets I had would be taken from me, eventually I learned not to become attached to anything for fear it would be taken away. Death of something which I had compassion for never received mourning—the dog food processing experience also made me cold in the need for caring relationships with anything. The horses I saw were many times slaughtered, shot before my very eyes, then we as a family would skin, bone, grind up, and package the meat. We even killed and trapped animals for 'sport.' The business would have been great if adults did all the work.

"I never became close friends with any girls until after I graduated from high school. Never really finding anyone who cared as much for me as I cared for them until I met Susan, it became an obsession for me to please her, at times I probably ran her life. I hated her to work so she quit a good job as a secretary. I don't think she ever asked for anything that she didn't get. Now we both admit that our direction was wrong, and we have done something about it. We have sold many of our possessions and she has a job. She still does not want to work and I don't like the idea but it's part of reality—Bill cannot make enough money! Never again will I work third shift and regular weekends, I was so busy working I did not know what was happening to my brain. The more money I made the more I spent and the more I felt the need for money, which was not real but imagined.

"Since my imprisonment, we have sadly learned the need for Susan to lose Bill, if not through imprisonment then through death. Shortly after I was arrested, Susan had a life reading, and one of the results has been this realization that she would lose Bill. In a past life she lost me through death very early, and has past Karma to overcome. I am sure of the need for Bill's punishment to correct the Karma he has for his crimes. I also know that Bill had the choice to do what he did or not to do it. What Bill does not know is this, how would Susan correct her Karma if I were not imprisoned. Would I die? This is a good question. What I have done is not easily forgivable, but I know that when I'm free, Bill will grow and hopefully will still have Susan to grow with him. I have been saved from a terrible future, no one was killed but many were hurt and hurt seriously and it will take a lot of hard work to correct the mistakes, I hope I have the chance to correct them—in this life."

It will be gleaned from the above statement that the defendant is interested in mysticism and paranormal phenomena. The "life reading" to which he refers is retrogressive hypnosis. This technique supposedly takes the client back into his or her past to elicit memories buried in the subconscious. The true initiate apparently believes that this even extends to prior existences in other times and places. The defendant believes that he lived before in what he called the "horse and buggy" days. In that life, he and his wife reversed sex roles; i.e., the defendant was the female and his wife was the male. The defendant stated that he died of a brain tumor at the age of 35 on his last sojourn on earth. He/"she" was also a robber in that life. The combination of his early death and his antisocial career drove his wife/"husband" to alcoholism (I wonder if he is not projecting his perceptions of his wife's possible reactions to his current predicament into this story). He feels that the "bad Karma" built up by their actions in the former life has to be worked out in this one.

Karma is an ethereal "something" that automatically adheres to the perpetrator of an evil act (something akin to sin). It must be canceled or "worked off" by a positive act that has a measure of good proportionate to the evil of the negative act. If this is not accomplished, the self is caught up in an endless cycle of birth and death. This belief, so the defendant states, enables him to tie everything he has done in this life to past lives of himself and his wife. He says that prison is necessary for him to equilibrate his "bad Karma." He wants to do volunteer work in the prison and upon his release to build up his reserve of "good Karma."

Although the defendant has a teleological view of life, he does not claim that he was "fated" to commit his crimes. He stated that "Bill has the free will that he was blessed with." (It is interesting to note that he often referred to himself in the third person. It is as though he disassociates himself and views himself as an object apart from himself.) He did occasionally lapse into fatalistic explanations. For instance, when asked how he was able to elude capture and avoid getting hit by police fire, his eyes turned heavenward, and he replied with a cryptic "them." Who "them" are was not made clear.

Notwithstanding the interesting story he tells, at bottom the reason he committed the robberies was simply that he "needed" more money than he was making in order to indulge his wife's expensive tastes.

STATEMENT OF VICTIM (Patrolman Frederick Williams)

Patrolman Williams stated that he and his partner responded to a robbery call at the Big Man Restaurant at about 1:30 a.m. on the morning of 6-13-84. As they came upon the scene, he noticed the defendant in a field taking off his sweater. The defendant fled as he and his partner approached, and he refused to stop when ordered to do so. Williams was chasing the defendant on foot when the defendant turned and fired two shots, one of which struck Williams in the leg. Patrolman Williams stated that his wound required six weeks off work and two weeks light duty. When asked his opinion of the defendant, and what he thought should happen to him, Williams replied: "The guy's sick; he needs help. As far as I'm concerned, you can put him away for 80 years."

PRIOR RECORD BIR # 234569 FBI # 356 953 V1

Juvenile: Adrian County juvenile authorities report no juvenile record.
Adult: 6-14-84 LPD a) Attempted Murder b) Aggravated Robbery—present offenses.
Two other counts of Aggravated Robbery nolled in CR84-4357.
One count of Aggravated Robbery nolled in CR84-4358.
LCPD, BCI, FBI, and Juvenile record checks made and received.

FAMILY AND MARITAL HISTORY

The defendant is the youngest of four children born to James and Mary Bloggs. The defendant, up until his marriage, lived his entire life on the family farm located at Box 3123, Rural Route 10, Elko, ID. Information received from the defendant's wife and certain of his siblings revealed that his childhood was characterized by excessive work demands, physical abuse, and forced incestuous relationships with his sisters. Details of the above are contained elsewhere in this report. It is quite clear that the entire Bloggs family was under the strict and uncompromising figure of Mr. Bloggs. The defendant had very little time to pursue any personal interests that he may have had, always having to acquiesce to the wishes of his father. His whole life evidently revolved around the family business, which he despised.

The defendant's older sister related that her father was "absolutely livid" when he found out that her mother was pregnant with the defendant. He did not even visit his wife in the hospital during her confinement. She further stated that the defendant would often get blamed for things he did not do, and was made to feel unwanted. She went on to relate how both the defendant and his older brother were bed wetters up to a relatively late age, and that her father would "hog-tie" them and keep them lying in bed in their urine all day. Interestingly, the defendant denied a history of enuresis to court psychologists as if to block out all memory of these extremely unpleasant occurrences.

The defendant left home at the age of 22 to take up residence with his girlfriend, now his wife, Susan Overton. This marriage took place on 9-15-84 in the Adrian County Jail. In an interview with Susan at this office, she described herself as an "old-fashioned" type who did not wish to go out to work. She described the defendant as being "jealous and possessive," adding that he is prone to "snap in and out of an explosive temper." She stated that he felt like he owned her, and that he once hung and killed a kitten of hers when he suspected that she was seeing another man. When I inquired, in light of the above negative statements and in light of the prison sentence that the defendant is facing, why she would marry him, she replied that they are "fated" to be together. She said that she could not cope with his death in their previous existence, and that she must now learn to cope with his absence in this one.

When asked why she thought that the defendant committed his crimes, she indicated the aberrant family situation previously mentioned. She stated that Mr. Bloggs slept with both of his daughters and had on numerous occasions forced them to instruct the defendant and his brother in sexual matters while he watched. On a second interview with the defendant I questioned him about this. He felt that this was "no big deal," and stated that he was about 10 when these incestuous encounters began.

While Susan believes that this sexual deviance may have been a distinct influence, she felt that the more proximate cause for the defendant's criminal behavior was his desire to satisfy her request for a big wedding, which he could not afford. It is ironic that their desire for a conspicuous and grandiose wedding may have led them to nuptials in a barren jail cell with a corrections officer as a witness. Her final statement to me was, "Don't send him to prison, he won't come back."

The defendant's father and mother were interviewed at their family farm. Mr. Bloggs is 54 years old, has two years of college, and is a self-employed farmer. He is an impressive professorial-looking person who is obviously accustomed to being in control of any situation. He spoke slowly and deliberately, and appeared to take great pains to use just the right word. He stated that he is at a loss to explain his son's behavior, that he loved him, and will continue to support him. He denied any mistreatment of the defendant beyond what he called "normal chastisement." I did not feel it appropriate to raise the issue of the alleged incest with him in front of his wife.

The defendant's mother is 53 years old, has one year of college, and describes her occupation as "housewife." She is a timid-looking soul who complements her husband's personality with a passivity which approaches sycophantic proportions. She was never able to complete two successive sentences without her husband finishing them for her. She profusely praised her husband as a father and a provider, and also denied that he was excessively punitive. One wonders if she has any knowledge of her husband's sexual abuse of their children. A computer record check revealed no criminal history for either parent.

The defendant's oldest sister, Patricia Knowles, is a high school graduate who currently drives a cab for Black and White. Pat has been married and divorced twice, and has a 10-year-old daughter and a 9-year-old son. Pat has a criminal history of child endangering and drug abuse. Pat does not presently associate with her father, stating that "He f---ed all of us kids up. He's the one that should be in jail."

Ann, the defendant's second sister, has similar feelings about her father. She is a high school graduate. She stated that she ran away from home right after graduation, and openly admits that she went to Los Angeles to become a call girl. She eventually quit that occupation after becoming pregnant (she kept her child). She is currently on welfare in Los Angeles. A check with LAPD revealed numerous soliciting arrests for Ann.

Frederick Bloggs, the defendant's older brother, could not be reached. However, Pat indicated that Fred dropped out of high school at the age of 16, has been married and divorced, and is now an "alcoholic bum" in Omaha, Nebraska. It would appear that the defendant is not the only victim of Mr. Bloggs's distasteful personality.

EMPLOYMENT HISTORY (Social Security # 302-42-9988)

At the time of his arrest, the defendant was working for Lowman Cascade as a press operator. He has been employed there since 4-14-82. He works all the overtime that he can get, and frequently brings home in excess of $400 per week. The defendant's immediate supervisor characterized him as "a good and dependable worker who gave us no trouble."

The defendant had taken the entrance examination to become a Lowman City police officer. Lt. Murdock of LCPD indicated that the defendant was to be called to the next class at the academy.

The defendant relates no other employment except at his family business.

PHYSICAL HEALTH

The defendant is a white male, 26 years of age, 6' tall, and weighs 155 lbs. He has dark blonde hair, blue eyes, and a fair complexion. He describes his current physical health as "excellent." He has suffered no hospitalizations or serious diseases, and relates no defects of hearing, speech, or vision. There is a family history of hypertension, and he feels that he is disposed to it himself. He is an infrequent consumer of alcohol, stating that the last time that he was drunk was over two years ago. He smoked marijuana rather heavily while in college, and stated that he frequently used amphetamines while working the night shift at Lowman Cascade in order to stay awake. He did not feel that he was addicted to them, however.

MENTAL HEALTH

The defendant graduated from Capital High School in 1978. He graduated 31st out of a class of 63, with a GPA of 2.27 on a 4.0 scale. School IQ testing saw the defendant obtain a full-scale IQ of 113, placing him in the 85th percentile of U.S. population IQ scores. Were his educational attainments commensurate with his IQ percentile ranking, the defendant would have placed 9th in his class. The defendant stated that he was too busy working on the farm to do justice to his studies.

Upon graduation from high school, the defendant entered Boise State University. He majored in, of all things, criminal justice. He was still attending BSU at the time of his arrest. He has obtained a cumulative GPA at BSU of 2.49. His criminal justice advisor stated that he was a "quiet student who participated very little in class, but his written work showed evidence of real independent thinking."

The Court Diagnostic and Treatment Center report indicates that their testing saw the defendant obtain a full-scale IQ score of 114, indicating a certain consistency in mental ability. It is noted that he scored significantly above average in tasks requiring nonverbal and short-term memory skills.

It is too easy to ascribe some form of mental abnormality to one who subscribes to the world view described by the defendant. It should be remembered, however, that his views are a valid discourse for millions of people in the world. I am more inclined to view his neurotic materialism as indicative of mental instability than his new-found religious eclecticism. He himself views his seemingly insatiable acquisitiveness as being responsible for his criminal actions. He was socialized in a family seemingly obsessed with making money. Neither can we discount the incestuous behavior he was forced into as a generating factor. It is clear that love was not a prevalent quality in this man's life. This deficiency may explain his clinging, jealous, and paranoid attraction to the one person (Susan) who showed a loving interest in him.

Although the CD&TC report states that he is experiencing high levels of anxiety and depression, he now states to me that he is "more at peace" with himself. He spends much of his time in his cell these days reading the Bible and esoteric literature. He describes himself as "driven to achieve," and feels that he is very aggressive in a nonviolent way. Given his crime, the hanging of the kitten, and Susan's statement about his "explosive temper," one might well dispute this description. The CD&TC report also describes him as being "in the early stages of a schizophrenic reaction, specifically of a paranoid type." His frequent reference to himself in the third person perhaps augments the impression on disassociation. Overall, this officer gained the impression that the defendant is a very bright, knowledgeable, and articulate person. He has been completely cooperative, and was a pleasure to talk with.

EVALUATIVE SUMMARY

Before the Court is a 26-year-old married male facing his first criminal conviction. He is an extremely bright, articulate, and personable young man. He evidently had a childhood in which he wanted for nothing materially, but which was characterized by excessive labor, harsh punitive treatment, and forced incestuous episodes. It is evident from the defendant's own statements, and from information uncovered in the course of this investigation, that he was severely deprived of close and loving interpersonal relationships. His father was viewed by family members as the great patriarch, or as the defendant put it: "as a boss, not a father." His father bestowed praise and approval only when the defendant met his excessive demands. Love, if there indeed was any, was withdrawn on the slightest pretext. His mother was viewed as a good person, but also as a pusillanimous alter-ego to the father.

The defendant's lack of experience of loving relationships rendered him ill-equipped to function well within one when Susan came into his life. He was obviously obsessed with making good this deficit. His relationship with Susan, now his wife, appears to have been a clinging obsession with him. He was paranoid about the possibility of losing her, and hypersensitive to her "needs," which everyone concerned agree were considerable. He wanted only the best for her, and often worked seven days a week, even while attending college, to get it for her. Even his considerable income was not sufficient to purchase all of the things he felt were necessary to ingratiate himself.

Nonetheless, we cannot overlook a string of armed robberies and the shooting of a police officer. It is evident that the robberies were well-planned and executed. In any objective sense, he was not in any desperate need of money, as he was earning a wage well in excess of average. He needed love, and his materialistic background told him that love was just another expensive commodity to be purchased with cash.

His intelligence, desire to learn, and intensity of purpose will stand him in good stead upon his release from the institution. His new-found spirituality, coupled with psychological counseling, will, I believe, function to prevent any further criminality in the future. He is well aware of the terrible crimes he has committed, and stands ready to accept the consequences. The extreme seriousness of his crimes point to the necessity of imposing consecutive sentences.

STATUTORY PENALTY

IRC #2911.01 Aggravated Robbery	"...shall be imprisoned for a period of 4, 5, 6, or 7 to 25 years and/or fined up to $10,000."
IRC #2911.01 Attempted Aggravated Murder	"...shall be imprisoned for a period of 4, 5, 6, or 7 to 25 years and/or fined up to $10,000."

RECOMMENDATION

Regarding 80-1234, Aggravated Robbery, it is respectfully recommended that the defendant be sentenced to 4 to 25 years at the Idaho State Penitentiary and ordered to pay the costs of prosecution.

Regarding 80-3456, Attempted Aggravated Murder, it is respectfully recommended that the defendant be sentenced to 5 to 25 years at the Idaho State Penitentiary, and that he be first conveyed to the Idaho Medical and Reception Center for evaluation and classification. It is further recommended that said sentences be served consecutively, and that the defendant be ordered to pay the costs of prosecution.

Respectfully submitted,

Paul E. Corrick, Probation & Parole Officer

Circumstances of Offense

It has been estimated that approximately 90 percent of all felony cases are disposed of through plea negotiations rather than by trial. Consequently, the sentencing judge is often unaware of the circumstances that brought the offender before the bench for sentencing until he or she has read the PSI. This section, then, should lay out the official (police) version of all pertinent details of the offense. It should contain basic information such as the place and time of the offense, the names of any codefendants, whether or not any weapons were involved, the name and address of the victim, and the injuries or financial loss suffered by the victim. It should also detail the circumstances surrounding the defendant's arrest: How was the defendant discovered? What was the defendant's condition at the time of arrest (drunk, high)? Did he or she resist arrest or voluntarily surrender to the police? Be concise but thorough.

Statement of the Defendant

The client's version of the offense helps you fill in gaps in the official version; the PSI interview is likely to be the client's first opportunity to tell his or her side of the story. The police are usually concerned only with the question of commission, not with the whys and wherefores of the case, and clients often seem to think that the only interest their defense attorneys have is to "sell" them the plea agreement.

Nevertheless, you must never allow a client's sob story to distract you from the facts contained in the official version. Your job is not to retry the case in your PSI. Judges do not take kindly to such efforts. Some interrogation techniques may be necessary if you are to reconcile major discrepancies between the client's story and the official version, but first listen objectively to the whole of the client's story. You must then go over discrepancies one at a time with the client until you are satisfied that they are resolved.

Do not let your humanitarian impulses get in the way if you believe that the client is trying to snow you. Note how the story is told. Is it slick and obviously memorized? Are there claims of memory loss (a favorite ploy with child molesters)? Are there major inconsistencies within the client's own version of the offense? If you think that the story is untrue, say so. This may be all you need to do to get the real story. You can be burned badly if you succumb to the natural impulse to put your unconditional faith in the poor troubled human being sitting beside you. You will be jeopardizing your credibility not only with the judge and your colleagues but also with the client. Worse, you could be opening yourself up for a lawsuit if, as a result of your report, a dangerous client who has been released on probation harms someone else. Dig hard and dig deep. If you cannot reconcile the different versions, simply note them in your report. If you believe that unresolved discrepancies are the result of deliberate deception, report this in the PSI and support the reasoning behind your belief.

An important variable to assess is your client's attitude about the offense. Is there remorse? Does the remorse appear to be genuine or is it just sorrow for getting caught? Experience will sensitize you to signs of genuine remorse. Shame, as an indication of remorse, is signaled by blushing and sighing when the crime is discussed, attempts to avoid discussing embarrassing details, stuttering, stammering, apparent confusion, and the avoidance of eye contact.

Similarly, guilty feelings are good indicators of genuine remorse. Behaviors consistent with a sense of guilt include voluntary confessions and the acceptance of complete blame, surrender to the police, a tendency to dwell on details of the offense, and the expression of a willingness to make amends. Clients who display some or all of these indicators of shame and guilt are usually those who normally conduct themselves according to conventional moral standards. Be sensitive to the inclination toward depressive states, and even suicidal ideation, among clients of this type.

Such clients are rare, however. Most will try to claim some sort of mitigation such as bad company, victim precipitation, or alcohol. In an unpublished study of 416 probation clients, 52.7 percent of them tried to shift the blame away from themselves. "Victim precipitation" is a favorite excuse in assaultive crimes, alcohol or drug abuse in property crimes. When a case has multiple defendants, fully 92 percent placed the blame on bad company, not realizing that each was the whipping boy of the other. This is not to assert that all claims of mitigation lack substance. It is your good judgment that will decide what how much credence you will give to such claims.

You should also discuss victims' losses with your clients and ask them how they feel about making restitution and whether they can do so. Restitution may include victims' medical bills, time lost from work, or replacement costs for property lost or damaged. The court may order payment of restitution either directly to the victim or to an insurance company. The client's willingness and realistic ability to pay restitution will probably be an important factor in both your recommended disposition of the case and in its actual disposition. Remember, however, that restitution may not legally be ordered if the client's plea was "no contest" rather than "guilty." This limitation displays a total disregard for victim's rights and is one of the major injustices of the criminal justice system.

Bill's version of the offense exactly mirrors the official one, and he makes no attempt to deny any aspects of it. The phrase "in order to understand why I needed the money," however, is most instructive. His story is a psychiatric delight, illustrating for us many of the ego-defense mechanisms that we will be discussing later. Constant themes throughout his statement are severe deprivation of love and the pressures of life with an authoritarian father. His love for Susan is a clinging, cloying, jealous one. He was willing to go to any lengths to buy from her the love he so desperately needed. He was painfully aware that he had grown up in a loveless environment, so much so that he "learned not to become attached to anything for fear it would be taken away." Susan was inadequately filling his deeply felt deficiency, the desperate need for love. His jealousy, and indeed his crimes, can be viewed as stemming from his unrealistic attempts to cling to someone toward whom he had finally formed an attachment.

He had convinced himself (apparently genuinely) that this attachment extended back to a prior existence. Note that the probation officer did not disparage Bill's bizarre story but tried instead to understand it and fit it into the client's frame of reference for the readers of the report. Correctly, however, he did not let this sway him from recognizing how serious Bill's crimes were: To understand is not to excuse. The probation officer also perceptively picked up on Bill's use of the third person when discussing himself and tied it in nicely with evidence from the examining psychiatrist, who indicated that Bill may have been in the "early stages of a schizophrenic reaction."

Was Bill remorseful, and if so, was his remorse genuine? He did turn himself in to the police, and he did make a full confession. Given that he left behind so much identifying evidence at the scene of the crime, however, we can hardly assume that his cooperation indicated remorse. Further damaging to an interpretation of genuine remorse is the fact that the present offense was his fourth robbery within a short time. But he did accept full responsibility for his crimes ("Bill has the free will that he was blessed with"), and he did accept the legitimacy of his punishment. The overall impression is that Bill would have continued his crime spree had he not been caught. His apparently genuine remorse was late in coming, was related to the situation he was in at the time of the interview, and could not be viewed as a mitigating factor when considering sentencing.

Statement of the Victim

Though many jurisdictions require that a victim impact statement be included in the PSI report, it is worth including even where there is no legal requirement. The statement should include the victim's version of the offense and the physical, psychological, and financial impact of the crime on him or her. You should also obtain an itemized statement of any financial losses from the victim or the insurance company. It is not unusual, although it is understandable, for victims to inflate their losses. Make it a point to solicit a statement of the victim's feelings and a recommendation regarding the disposition of the case.

Given the seriousness of this client's crimes, it was obvious from the onset that incarceration had to be the recommended disposition. Therefore, no attempt was made to ascertain financial losses to Officer Williams or the police department (whether or not the defendant can pay restitution, the courts cannot monitor payments if the defendant is under the jurisdiction of the Department of Corrections). Since Officer Williams's version of the offense was an integral part of the official version, his statement throws no more light on it. His understandably negative opinion of the defendant and what he thought should happen to him was of no value in the formulation of a sentencing recommendation.

Prior Record

Before you interview your client, you should have in hand a complete criminal history, including juvenile, local police, state Bureau of Criminal Investigation (BCI), and Federal Bureau of Investigation (FBI) arrest sheets ("rap sheets"). Most of these should be in the prosecutor's case file. Immediately on receiving the case, however, you should run your own computer check for an updated history. A computer check will also reveal any outstanding warrants for the client. If you discover that the client is wanted, find out from the issuing clerk the particulars of the warrant. It is your duty to arrest the client if the warrant is for a serious crime. For obvious reasons, your knowledge of the warrant should not be revealed until the interview is finished. Telling a client that he or she is to be arrested will not make for a productive interview. If the warrant was issued for something innocuous, such as nonpayment of traffic fines, rather than making an arrest it is probably better to tell the client to take care of the problem before your next meeting. At this point it is wise to avoid confrontation about relatively unimportant matters.

Once you have arrest records and any previous PSI reports, review this history of criminal activity with the client. Ask the client to explain any serious prior arrest and conviction, and try to see if there is a pattern in the arrests. For instance, are the crimes all of a similar type (property, sex, violent), or does the record suggest a polymorphous deviant? Is there a pattern of increasing seriousness? At what point in life did the client start acquiring a criminal record? Are any or most of the crimes related to alcohol or drug abuse? Is there a pattern of planned criminality, or do the crimes seem mostly opportunistic? Finally, are all crimes readily admitted, or does the client attempt to rationalize most of them away?

The lessons to be learned from your client's criminal history are many and valuable. In Bill's case, it is instructive that he had no previous arrests, either as a juvenile or as an adult. Yet his offenses were extremely serious. In the normal progression, a criminal graduates over a period of years from far less serious crimes to the kind of crimes Bill committed. It is so extremely rare to find a client who, at the age of 26, begins a criminal career with armed robbery that you should be immediately alerted to look for very special circumstances.

Family and Marital History

A family history should contain the names and addresses of parents, siblings, children, spouse, and any former spouses and indicate the current status of each family member (deceased, divorced, retired, imprisoned, whereabouts unknown). This data will yield important information about the client's family dynamics. Look into the client's relationship with his or her parents during the formative years: Were the parents divorced early? With whom did the client live? Did either or both of the parents remarry, and what was the relationship with stepparents? What are the client's current relationships with his or her parents and significant others—supportive or rejecting? Exploring parental reactions to the present predicament will give you access to the moral environment in which the client was raised. Collateral interviews with parents, if time allows and the case is serious enough, can be used to validate and expand on the client's perceptions.

It may be instructive to inquire into clients' friendship networks: Do they associate with known criminals? If so, why? How is leisure time spent with friends—in productive or nonproductive ways?

You should then obtain the client's marital history, if any: How many times has the client been married? Frequent marriages, common-law or otherwise, indicate an inability to form lasting relationships and a lack of responsibility. If the client has been married more than once, what was the reason for divorce? Placing the blame on the spouse may reflect an overall pattern of blaming others for negative outcomes. Find out if the client has any children from former relationships and is living up to any support obligations.

The quality of the relationship with the current spouse should be examined next. Explore the nature and extent of any major difficulties. Is the client responsibly supporting dependents, or neglecting them? A collateral interview with the spouse may prove useful. (You may conduct a collateral interview by telephone, although you lose much of the flavor if you do.) You will certainly want to find out the spouse's attitudes about the client's criminal activity and how he or she would cope if the client were to be imprisoned.

Officer Corrick's collateral interviews with Bill's wife, his parents, and selected siblings certainly paid off in terms of insight into the origins of Bill's criminal behavior. Although Bill's family was comfortably middle-class and demonstrated commitment to, involvement in, and belief in typical American success values, beneath the veneer of respectability lay an abominable family situation. Attachment, genuine reciprocal love, was clearly absent. Bill appeared to have tried very hard to gain his father's love and approval. His father, however, seems to have been a patriarchal, sadistic, sexually perverted, and overdemanding person. His absolute control over the family is in evidence throughout the report. Bill's mother "complements her husband's personality with a passivity which approaches sycophantic proportions." Note that she never mentioned anything to Corrick about the incestuous behavior that went on for so many years. It is not at all unusual for wives to deny, even to themselves, that incest is taking place. This behavior first came to light during the collateral interview with Susan. It was then necessary for Officer Corrick to verify the information, which he did with Bill himself and with two of his siblings. Potentially damaging information should never be included in a report on the basis of a single statement.

The effects of growing up under the conditions in the Bloggs family have resulted in many negative outcomes for Bill's siblings as well. Pat has had two broken marriages in four years and has a record of child abuse and drug abuse. Ann has one illegitimate child and was for a time a prostitute with numerous soliciting arrests. Fred is a high school dropout, was divorced after one year of marriage, and is an admitted alcoholic. All this, in spite of them all having access to all the objective advantages of a white, middle-class status, supports Officer Corrick's analysis of the origin of Bill's behavior as presented in the evaluation section of the PSI report.

Susan's statements indicate that she shares Bill's unusual interpretation of their relationship ("they are 'fated' to be together"). She quit her job when she and Bill started living together, and she was evidently quite happy to allow Bill to work inordinately long hours to satisfy her considerable material wants. Her comments about Bill's "explosive temper" and his hanging of her kitten provide all those who will use the PSI report with valuable insight not gleaned from either Corrick's or the diagnostic center's interviews with Bill.

Very few collateral interviews will ever be as valuable to you as the ones presented here. In less serious cases, time constraints will usually prevent you from going to the extraordinary lengths to which Corrick went here. Nor would it be especially productive if the offender fit the profile of the typical armed robber (lower-class, poorly educated, broken home, unemployed, and so on). It was the atypicality of Bill's criminal profile that led Corrick to dig as deeply into Bill's past as he did.

Employment History

The section covering employment history explores not only the client's employment but also other sources of income such as welfare, social security, or disability income. A complete, verified employment history is a vital part of any client assessment. As the theories we have examined have informed us, a steady work history, evidence of prosocial commitment, involvement, and access to a legitimate avenue to success are incompatible with serious criminal involvement. Of the 416 offenders in my unpublished 1983 study, only 55.8 percent were working at the time of the PSI interview. Of those, fully 86.6 percent were in dead-end unskilled occupations. Of the 2.8 percent who were in managerial, technical, or professional occupations, all were first-time offenders.

The name, address, and telephone number of the client's current place of employment is the first item on the agenda. To avoid jeopardizing your clients' jobs, you can verify employment by having them bring in their most recent paycheck stubs. Length of employment can be verified through tax records. Ask clients what type of work they do and if they enjoy it. Are there opportunities to move up in the company? Do they feel that their present income is sufficient to meet their basic needs? Do they criticize the company severely? Why?

Former employment must be verified directly. A standard form should be sent to former employers asking them to indicate type of work, length of service, and reason for leaving, and to evaluate a client's work performance and general character. What is the client's pattern of movement in the work force? Does the client work steadily and change jobs only to obtain a better position? Or does the client quit on any pretext after minimal periods? This information will give you a general picture of your client's level of responsibility, ability to get along with others, and general persistence. You should fully explore all gaps in employment history and ask the military for a copy of the client's service record, if any, although you may not receive it until long after sentencing.

Bill's employment history is atypically good. At the time of his arrest he had been working for more than two years for the same company. He worked hard and earned a good income. Management was very positive toward him, even planning to promote him to supervisor. He also worked part-time on the family farm and had passed the examination to become a police officer. Bill's exemplary work history obviously impressed Officer Corrick and further alerted him to dig beyond surface demographics to explain Bill's behavior.

Physical Health

Clients' physical health (self-reported, or, if necessary, verified by a physician) and its possible effects on their social and vocational functioning should be assessed for the report. Recent hospitalizations and diseases, use of medications or prosthetic devices, and drinking habits and drug abuse should be noted. Substance abuse should be a central concern because of its association with many criminal acts. For many clients drugs and alcohol are chemical substitutes for love and meaning—ways to temporarily shut out the cruelties and responsibilities of life. Look into the extent and frequency of clients' drinking, noting if they have committed any alcohol-related offenses, such as drunk driving. A useful assessment scale for alcohol use is included in Appendix C.

The extent, frequency, and type of drug abuse should be addressed next. Not all clients will be willing to admit abuse, but with time you will know when to probe. Physical indicators of drug abuse are examined in Chapter 12. A word of warning here: Some clients will exaggerate the extent of their substance abuse in the hope that blame will be shifted from them to the substance and that they will touch a sympathetic chord in the officer. My 1983 study found that 13.5 percent blamed substance abuse for their crimes. If clients claim drug dependency or if you suspect it, they should be immediately referred to a drug dependency clinic for a complete workup and evaluation.

Nothing was uncovered in Bill's physical health history that is pertinent to decisions of sentencing, classification, or treatment. He did report heavy use of marijuana while in college and current use of amphetamines. However, given the ubiquity of marijuana use among the young and his stated reason for taking amphetamines, there is no cause for undue alarm. We do note that the use of amphetamines is favored by those seeking intensified stimulation.

Mental Health

The first item for consideration under the heading of mental health is the client's education. Names and locations of all schools attended, including dates of attendance, should be listed and records requested from the client's last high school or college. From school records you should note grade point average, class standing, IQ and vocational testing, and attendance and behavioral history. If the client dropped out of high school, find out why. If you feel that your sentencing recommendation will be probation, explore the possibility of the client attending GED classes. Clients' responses to this and similar ideas will give you some idea of their motivation to better themselves. IQ and vocational testing results will give you a range of possibilities for the client, but do not be misled by low scores to dismiss a client as hopeless; a recent study found that probationers attending GED classes had significantly fewer arrests and committed significantly less serious crimes than a matched group of probationers not attending classes (Walsh 1985b).

Any psychiatric or psychological workups done on clients should be discussed with them and integrated into your own assessment. Discuss any discrepancies between the stories they have told you and those they have related to mental health professionals. Lies have an awkward tendency to be soon forgotten. Do not be afraid to disagree with or add your own opinions to those of the mental health professionals—you are a professional in your own right. Studies have shown that when the recommendations of probation officers conflict with those of mental health professionals, judges are somewhat more apt to agree with the officers (Morash 1981). The training and role expectations of mental health workers lead them to see mental pathology in nearly all cases they review. Although real mental illness does exist, a deficiency rather than a pathological view of criminal behavior is both more productive and less stigmatizing. You should never argue with mental health professionals, however, if they advise psychiatric hospitalization. Such recommendations are not rendered lightly, and you must respect boundaries of expertise.

When discussing aspects of their mental functioning with your clients, concentrate on how they feel about themselves, their aspirations, their goals, and their usual ways of coping with stress and adversity. If you feel that a particular client has some special problems that require the assistance of a mental health professional, refer the client for a workup, indicating the areas you wish the diagnostic center to explore.

We have already addressed many of the possible underlying reasons for Bill's criminal behavior. It is interesting to see how Officer Corrick integrated his own findings into those of the Court Diagnostic and Treatment Center without ever stepping beyond the boundaries of his professional expertise to contest the findings and opinions of the center's personnel. He merely added to their insights. His collateral interviews with family members gave him information unavailable to court diagnostic personnel. We know that enuresis and cruelty to animals in childhood and adolescence are predictive of violent behavior and that Bill exhibited two of them. We do not know if Bill also set fires, so perhaps we should not make too much of this; only when the three behaviors are taken together are they considered predictive. Nevertheless, Corrick was aware of Bill's late enuresis (which Bill denied to the examining psychiatrist) and his hanging of Susan's pet kitten; court diagnostic personnel were not. Would they have labeled Bill passive aggressive (shooting a policeman and hanging a kitten is certainly aggressive, but hardly passive) had they known? Nor were they aware of the sexual perversities into which Bill's father forced him and his siblings. This is an excellent example of the appropriate use of collateral interviewing. The court diagnostic center's other diagnosis of Bill as being "in the early stages of a schizophrenic reaction" was supported by Officer Corrick's observation that Bill often spoke about himself in the third person.

Other revealing pieces of information in this section help us gain a clearer picture of Bill. Whereas his high school GPA of 2.27 is respectable, it is considerably below what one would expect from someone with an IQ in the bright-normal range, as is his class standing. Is this indicative of an underachiever or, as Bill claimed, of someone kept too busy working for his father to do justice to his studies? The consistency of IQ test scores taken seven years apart reveals that regardless of any other mental problems Bill may have had, he suffered no deterioration of intellectual functioning.

Alert students will have noted an important piece of information that Officer Corrick reported but did not comment on: Bill "scored significantly above average in tasks requiring nonverbal and short-term memory skills." We noted in the section on psychopathy that a performance IQ that is clearly in excess of a verbal IQ has been considered by many authorities as a clear marker of psychopathy. Unfortunately, Corrick did not report the performance and verbal IQ subscales but only the full-scale score. We do not know, therefore, if Bill's performance IQ was "clearly in excess" of his verbal IQ. However, this piece of information in conjunction with Bill's enuresis, cruelty to animals, apparent inability to form close loving relationships, and history of deprivation of love renders plausible the application of the psychopathic label. Had Corrick picked up on this (assuming that he was aware of the theory behind it), he might have been led to investigate further along those lines. This observation again underscores the necessity for criminal justice workers to be conversant with criminological theory.

Finally, though it is clear that Officer Corrick was very much impressed with Bill, he did not let that cloud his judgment when he made his sentencing recommendation.

Evaluative Summary

The evaluative summary is the most challenging section of the PSI report to write. You are drawing reasoned conclusions from the facts in your report. This section represents the distilled wisdom of the investigator and separates the true professional from the data-gatherer. It is the product of a disciplined effort to organize, synthesize, and analyze your collected data. No new data should be included in this section; your sole task here is to draw meaning from what you have already reported.

Since this section requires you to make value judgments, you must make every effort to minimize any emotional reactions you may have for or against clients. You must fully appraise your subjective feelings by asking yourself: "Why do I feel this way?" The impressions of the offender conveyed by the tone of your report may have a major impact on the offender's future. Emotion-laden terms, such as "morally bankrupt" or "a picture of womanly virtue," reveal more about the investigator's attitudes than the client's and should not be part of a professional report. If you find that your client evokes this kind of heavy emotional response, it is a good idea to consult with your supervisor or your colleagues before writing this section, in order to clarify and objectify your thoughts.

This does not mean that you should not take a firm and positive stand. Indeed, as a professional this is your duty. Ambiguous, "wishy-washy," hedging statements reveal an investigator who is uncomfortable in the role and uncertain of his or her expertise. Beating around the bush undermines the authority of the entire report and causes the reader to have doubts about the advised plan of action.

All strong statements should, of course, be firmly grounded in the information set down in other sections of the report. Of the utmost importance is your evaluation of your clients' strengths and weaknesses, their patterns of criminal behavior, their potential for reform, and their amenability to treatment and training. This evaluation requires a thorough knowledge of community resources as well as of the offender. It serves as the basis for a treatment plan, which is the logical conclusion of the evaluative summary.

The treatment plan should be realistic. A recommended treatment plan that cannot be implemented is frustrating to the person who must act on your recommendations. One client who had committed a string of armed robberies had been released on parole after serving ten years and was again in jail for a parole violation for yet another robbery. His officer recommended that he be allowed to go to another state under the care of a Christian youth camp. The officer had been convinced by the client and by the client's spiritual counselor that he was a "born-again Christian." The officer skillfully sold his recommendation to the sentencing judge, who allowed the client to go. When this 53-year-old man found himself surrounded by youths and expected to work for his daily bread, he left the camp and committed further crimes before he was apprehended. Needless to say, the officer found his credibility seriously compromised.

In formulating a treatment plan, give the threat your client poses to the community equal consideration with the client's rehabilitative needs. Clues to this threat are provided by the nature of the present offense and by the length and seriousness of the client's criminal record. You should weigh alternative plans in terms of their advantages and disadvantages for the client and the community. Give the reasons why you have rejected some plans and completely justify the chosen plan in

Perspectives from the Field

Interviewing in Presentence Investigations

Marilyn West

Marilyn West is a presentence investigator with the Fourth District (felony) Court, Ada County, Idaho. She is a graduate of Northwest Nazarene College. She is active in many community organizations working for criminal rehabilitation. She is a member of the Fourth Judicial District Sexual Abuse Task Force.

In most jurisdictions presentence investigations are prepared by probation officers. In some jurisdictions there are people whose work consists solely of doing presentence investigations reports (PSIs). I am one of those people.

A PSI is a necessary and vital function of the criminal justice system, but because it is confidential, few people outside of the criminal justice system know that these reports exist. This makes being a presentence investigator a real conversation-starter. People are intrigued to hear that someone is in charge of gathering all sorts of background information on felony criminals and presenting it to the court. People who have served on juries often express concern that the criminal histories of defendants are not made known to juries. Former jurors are relieved to learn that there is a point in the process where these histories are taken into consideration.

Because our PSI reports make sentencing recommendations, we have to make sure that our information is factual and our conclusions well-grounded. This involves interviewing large numbers of people who know the defendant, including friends, relatives, and professional contacts. PSI reports are also a conduit for defendants and victims to express their feelings to the court.

Normally, the investigator has contact with the defendant for about three weeks following a guilty verdict or guilty plea. The goal of the presentence process is not to conduct actual rehabilitation, it is to do a diagnostic workup. Of course, a good workup can go a long way toward a beginning in the ultimate goal of rehabilitation. Good interviewing skills are an absolute necessity if you are to perform a good diagnostic workup. You can't simply "ask questions" and expect to get meaningful answers in criminal justice settings. You'll always get answers to your questions regardless of how they are asked, but the answers won't necessarily be helpful or truthful. You must establish a relationship in which the defendant can feel comfortable in revealing intimate information to you. That's quite a challenge.

We are obliged to be objective in our reports. This requires a special effort because a lot of emotions can surface during the investigation. The victim's side of the story often arouses our feelings, and often we discover traumatic or tragic circumstances in the defendant's past that stir our sympathies as well. This type of emotional information rarely comes to light in police or prosecutor's investigations and is of little concern to them. But we have to decide how much of this information is necessary to us in the formulation of our recommendations to the court. Overall, our goal in constructing the recommendation is the same as that of the sentencing judge: to protect society. Perhaps one of the most valuable functions the presentence investigator performs is that of making specific recommendations. It is not enough to simply recommend that a person be treated for some problem. We have to recommend the specific resource, keeping in mind such practical matters as the appropriateness, cost, and availability of treatment. In order to make these recommendations we must keep ourselves current on what is available in the

Perspectives From the Field (continued)

treatment community. This means that we have to become quasi-experts in many treatment fields. Several people in our office are active in community treatment organizations for such problems as alcohol and drug abuse or sexual abuse. We are also charged with offering our opinion to the court as to whether an individual is capable of being rehabilitated. As you can imagine, this is sometimes a tough question. We have to supply ample information to show what our opinions are based on. Again, this underscores the absolute necessity of good interviewing techniques.

It is a challenge to obtain a valid profile of an individual's life in the space of a few weeks. It makes me feel good when my recommendations are confirmed by judges or when probation officers come up to me and say something like, "Your report on so-and-so was right on the money. Now maybe we can draw his attention to some of the things he's doing to get himself in trouble, and maybe we can show him some of the ways to stay out of trouble." That's what this business is all about.

---

terms of both client and community concerns. Treatment plans that involve other agencies should be formulated in concert with them. Their special expertise may uncover deficiencies in a client's character or motivation that renders him or her unsuitable for the plan you have in mind. If this be the case, respect their professional evaluation and concentrate on an alternative plan.

Officer Corrick begins his evaluative summary by reiterating the fact that the present offense is Bill's first conviction and by describing his positive feelings about the client based on objective criteria and on his dealings with him. He than launches into a thoughtful examination of the possible origins of Bill's behavior. He emphasizes the lack of love, the punitive and incestuous milieu in which Bill grew up, and the excessive acquisitiveness of both Bill and Susan. After reading this evaluation, you feel you know Bill fairly well without ever having seen him. This is the ideal for which you should strive.

Officer Corrick did not outline a treatment plan for Bill because he felt that Bill's crimes were serious enough to warrant incarceration in spite of Bill's "first offender" status. Corrick seemed to feel that the experience of being caught, incarcerated, and having the opportunity to examine his behavior would deter Bill from future criminality.

Recommendation

Like the denouement of a mystery novel, the recommendation should flow logically from all the preceding information. It also should be consistent with what the law of the state requires. Certain crimes, such as murder, rape, and aggravated robbery, are not probationable; certain other crimes may contain elements that render them nonprobationable. As an officer, you must be aware of the penal codes of your jurisdiction.

The recommendation should concisely state the number of years the client is to spend in prison or on probation. If you recommend probation, state any recommended special conditions, such as amount of restitution and the name and address of payee, attendance at alcohol or drug centers, fines to be paid, or the amount of time that you feel the defendant should serve locally in jail or a work release program.

Corrick's estimation of community feelings, the possible threat Bill posed to the community, and the extreme seriousness of the offense led him to recommend that Bill serve two consecutive prison sentences of four to twenty-five years and five to twenty-five years. The judge imposed those sentences. What would you have recommended?

PSI Checklist

The most useful summary of this chapter takes the form of a checklist of factors to be considered in any presentence investigation. Styles and formats of PSI reports vary; some areas we have discussed, such as the victim's statement and the officer's recommendation, may be optional in your department. No matter what must be included, remember one thing above all: the PSI will have a significant impact on your client's future. Accuracy is of the utmost importance.

1. *Circumstances of present offense(s)*: A concise summary of relevant details of the offense(s) for which the client is to be sentenced.
2. *Client's version:* How does the client's version differ from the official version? What are the client's overall attitude and attitude about the offense? The officer should make judgments about these questions.
3. *Prior record*: A complete and verified criminal history of the client, noting any patterns of criminality.
4. *Family history*: Family demographics, characteristics, conflicts, migrations, child-rearing practices, marital history, and so on.
5. *Employment history*: A complete and verified history of the client's employment and financial situation.
6. *Physical and mental health*: Recent hospitalizations and diseases, drug and alcohol abuse, level of intellectual functioning (school grade completed, GPA, IQ), vocational training, and psychological information.
7. *Evaluative summary*: A capsule version of the entire report, evaluating its overall meaning; the officer's professional assessment of what is to be done to amend the client's behavior.

References and Suggested Readings

Clear, T., V. Clear, and W. Burrell. 1989. *Offender assessment and evaluation: The presentence investigation report.* Cincinnati: Anderson.

Division of Probation, Administrative Office of the United States Courts. 1978. *Presentence investigation report.* Washington, D.C.: GPO.

Hagan, J. 1975. The social and legal construction of criminal justice: A study of the presentence process. *Social Problems* 22:620-637.

Mangrum, C. 1975. *The professional practitioner in probation.* Springfield, Ill.: Charles C Thomas. (This book, by a practicing probation officer, offers an excellent examination of all the many roles played by the probation officer).

Morash, M. 1982. A case study of mental health professional's input into juvenile court decision making. *Criminal Justice Review* 7:48-56.

Myers, M. 1979. Offended parties and official reactions: Victims and the sentencing of criminal defendants. *Sociological Quarterly* 20:529-540.

Nettler, G. 1970. *Explanations.* New York: Harper & Row.

Walsh, A. 1984. Gender-based differences: A study of probation officers' attitudes about, and recommendations for, felony sexual assault cases. *Criminology* 22:371-387.

Walsh, A. 1985a. The role of the probation officer in the sentencing process: Independent professional or judicial hack? *Criminal Justice and Behavior* 12:289-303.

Walsh, A. 1985b. An evaluation of the effects of adult basic education on rearrest rates among probationers. *Journal of Offender Counseling, Services & Rehabilitation* 9:69-76.

Chapter 7

Assessment Tools and Guidelines

Justice consists of treating equals equally and unequals unequally according to relevant differences.

Aristotle

Aristotle's comment signifies the philosophy of individualized justice underlying the effort to operationalize justice by assigning numeric scores on assessment scales. These tools attempt to determine Aristotle's "relevant differences" so that justice can be done as equitably as possible.

Everyone benefits from the more structured and reasoned approach to decision making made possible by research-grounded tools such as those presented in this chapter. Offenders benefit by being treated more justly and consistently than was previously the case, and the community is better served by more accurate assessment of the risks offenders pose. The assessment and guideline approach is used in many jurisdictions to set bail; in prosecutor's offices it is used to screen cases for dismissal or prosecution and to guide plea-bargain arrangements. It has been argued that hundreds of millions of taxpayer dollars could be saved with little additional risk to the community if adequate numerical guidelines were developed to reduce jail and prison overcrowding (Marsh & Marsh 1990).

This chapter explains the assessment tools used in many probation and parole agencies. They are filled out by the processing officer on the basis of his or her evaluation of the offender. When your instructor assigns PSI interviews, you will have actual cases for practice interviews and assessments. If you are role-playing the offender, you will have access to information supplied by the offender. It is the officer's task to elicit this information from the offender using the interviewing techniques described in Chapter 5. If you are role-playing the interviewing officer you will have only the case materials normally available from sources other than the offender, such as circumstances of the offense, criminal record, victim statements, and school records. Drawing on the information from these sources and the information you elicit from your client, you must evaluate the client, make a realistic recommendation, and formulate a treatment plan.

There are no "correct" answers. There are only good or poor evaluations, realistic or unrealistic recommendations, and workable or unworkable treatment plans. As you reach each section in the practice PSI reports, reread that section in Chapter 6 to determine if you have considered everything pertinent before deciding on an evaluation and recommendation. Do not hesitate to recommend imprisonment if you feel that is the appropriate disposition. However, for the purposes of formulating a treatment program, assume probation placement even if you recommended imprisonment. All the assessment tools covered in the following discussion appear in Appendix A.

The forms and scales in this chapter are presented in the sequence that they are encountered in the field: Clients fill out the social history questionnaire before meeting the officer assigned to the case, the officer may then use the structured interview schedule and will next complete the sentencing guideline. The risk and needs scales are completed after the client is sentenced to probation or granted parole, as are the treatment plans. Thus, we begin with the social history questionnaire.

Social History Questionnaire

The first tool you should become familiar with is the social history questionnaire (SHQ). An intake officer or the agency receptionist gives this questionnaire to the client referred for a presentence investigation; it is to be filled out completely before the client meets with the presentence investigator. Students role-playing offenders in practice exercises should use the data provided by their "offender" PSI reports to complete the form. Each item is self-explanatory.

Client Management Classification Assessment Instrument

The second tool is the Client Management Classification Assessment Instrument (CMC), a semistructured interview schedule. The CMC was developed for the Wisconsin Bureau of Community Corrections after much study and research. Whereas the SHQ deals primarily with factual demographic data, the CMC guides the investigator in exploring client attitudes and feelings and in supervision and treatment planning. When using this schedule, it is not necessary to repeat the questions exactly as they are printed. There is enough leeway for you to incorporate your own style into the questions and to allow for unusual situations. However, the meaning of each question should be preserved in the translation into your own words. Questions about the crime and criminal history should be left to the end of the schedule, after you have generated sufficient rapport to make these questions less threatening.

The CMC is scored so that probation and parole officers can assign clients to one of four treatment modalities (selective intervention, environmental structure, casework control, and limit setting). Scoring, a rather complicated procedure for the uninitiated, is accomplished by using eight templates (cardboard sheets with holes punched in them that fit over a scoring guide). Probation and parole officers attend three-day workshops and extensive follow-up training before they are considered able to use this system to its fullest; to attempt to explain it thoroughly is well beyond the scope of this book. In fact, the training material for the CMC constitutes a book in itself. The interview schedule included here is simply a guide to the kind of questions you should be asking your clients and an introduction to the CMC system of client classification. The classifications obtained from scoring the CMC are highly correlated with the classifications obtained from the far more succinct risk and needs scales that will be explained later in this chapter.

Nevertheless, it is useful for you to have some idea of the types of clients who fall into each of the four classifications. The following descriptions are paraphrased from those in the CMC training manuals.

Selective Intervention

Clients in the selective-intervention category require the least time and present the fewest supervision problems. As the term implies, the supervising officer will intervene in the client's life only as needed. Clients in this category almost always fall into the low-risk category as determined by the risk and needs scales. They generally have relatively stable and prosocial lifestyles, and their current offense is often their first. Their offenses can be viewed as a temporary lapse or suspension of an otherwise normal value system. They tend to show strong indications of guilt and embarrassment. Without allowing them to intellectualize or minimize their criminal acts, you should avoid increasing guilt and criminal identification in these clients.

These clients respond best to a warm, supportive relationship with their officers and to rational problem-solving approaches to counseling. Avoid giving them the impression that you are trying to run their lives for them or that you do not trust them. If your agency uses a minimal contact system, allowing low-risk clients to report by mail or telephone, make sure that clients know that you are available to help them through temporary crises or with emotional problems that might otherwise prompt further criminal activity. These clients should not be put on minimal supervision or write-in status until any needs for treatment are satisfactorily met.

Environmental Structure

Clients who need environmental structure generally fall into the low end of the medium-risk category and require regular supervision. Intellectual, vocational, and social deficits contribute considerably to their criminal activities. They tend to lack foresight, to have difficulty learning from past mistakes, and to be overly dependent on others like themselves for acceptance and approval. They are not usually committed to a criminal career, and malice as a motivation for criminal activity is rare.

These clients need help to develop or improve intellectual, social, and work skills, find alternatives to associations with criminal peers, and increase control of impulses. You should be more directive and concrete with these individuals than with selective-intervention clients. Move slowly to build a success identity for your clients by balancing your expectations of them with their present coping resources (this theme is taken up in the next chapter). You may often have to do things with and for them initially (such as taking them job hunting), but be careful not to foster dependence. Many clients in this category can, with a warm and accepting officer who knows the community resources available, become productive citizens.

Casework/Control

Casework/control is for clients who need more intensive casework and tighter control of their activities. Clients in this category are at the high end of the medium risk and needs scale. Their lives evidence a generalized instability. They lack goals and have difficulty with interpersonal relationships and in finding and keeping employment. They tend to have had chaotic and abusive childhoods, which they repeat with their own families. Alcohol and drug abuse is common among these offenders; many of their criminal convictions reflect this abuse.

These clients need the same kinds of help as environmental structure clients but they are harder to help because of their substance abuse and greater emotional problems. These clients require a great deal of your time, as well as considerable coordination of auxiliary programs. Attendance and involvement with outside programs must be strictly monitored, and the clients should be allowed to suffer the consequences of noncompliance, such as short periods in jail. In short, use all the leverage at your disposal to promote client compliance. These clients will severely try your patience and professional competence, but they can be turned around by a knowledgeable, caring, no-nonsense officer.

Limit Setting

Clients who need their officers to set strict limits for them are high-risk on the risk and needs scale. They are comfortable in their criminal lifestyles and demonstrate a long-term pattern of criminal activity. They delight in their ability to beat the system and tend to minimize or deny any personal problems. They see themselves as being individuals who have simply chosen a criminal lifestyle. Indeed, in comparison to structured-environment and casework/control clients, they often show superior ability to function normally (if not morally) in society.

Clients in the limit-setting category are typically assigned to a special intensive-supervision officer. Intensive-supervision officers usually have small caseloads that allow them the time necessary to supervise high-risk clients. Protection of the community through surveillance and strict client control (often with the cooperation of the police) is of primary concern. High-risk clients, who are extremely manipulative, will often test your resolve. Any failure on your part to act assertively will be interpreted as weakness. Thus you must always be prepared to confront them about even minor infractions of the rules. If you do not, you will not be respected, and you can be sure that they will escalate their violations.

These clients respond best to the techniques of reality therapy (see Chapter 9) and to rational discussion, because their criminal behavior is often more a function of choice than of emotional or intellectual deficiencies. Figuring the cost/benefit ratio of crime as explained in Chapter 11 may be beneficial to these clients. Since they also tend to be energetic and to have adequate intelligence, they have capabilities that can be channeled into profitable and legal endeavors. Try to give them challenging and innovative opportunities to find satisfying alternatives to a criminal lifestyle.

When clients have defeated all your best efforts, have repeatedly sabotaged treatment plans and exhausted existing programs, and plainly lack any motivation to change, it may be appropriate to discontinue major efforts to restructure their lives. Expect nothing more than legal conformity from them, but make it crystal clear that any violation, no matter how minor, will result in official action.

Felony Sentencing Worksheet

The Felony Sentencing Worksheet (FSW) is one of several widely used sentencing guidelines. Sentencing guidelines were developed as a compromise between factions in criminal justice, one believing that punishment should fit the crime and the other that punishment should fit the offender and lead to rehabilitation. Both of these positions are addressed in the FSW, with seriousness of offense more heavily weighted than the character of the offender.

Guidelines also attempt to minimize disparities in sentencing for similar crimes and similar criminals. They are aimed at containing judicial discretion and promoting consistency by setting sentencing norms based on the past practices of judges confronted with similar cases. Implicit in the idea of guidelines is the notion that disparity flowing from variation among crimes and offenders is acceptable, but disparity shorn of just or coherent reason is not. Sentencing guidelines may be viewed as an application of Aristotle's definition of justice as relying on relevant differences.

The probation officer scores the FSW by assigning the numerical scores on the basis of the legal and social factors addressed in each subsection. Some sections seek only factual data, such as the degree of offense, multiple offenses, prior convictions, and repeat offenses. Other sections, covering culpability, mitigation, and credits, require a great deal of interpretation. Do not be surprised if you and your classmates arrive at different FSW scores for the same data. Since judgments are called for, the FSW allows for the intrusion of philosophy into its scoring. A recent study showed that the FSW is differentially scored by practicing probation officers according to ideology, with conservative officers assigning significantly higher scores (Walsh 1985). Sentencing by arithmetic is not impervious to ideological intrusion, but it does constitute an improvement on unstructured sentencing.

An early study of the effects of the FSW on sentencing found it to have a predictive accuracy of 85 percent;

that is, judges imposed the suggested sentence in 85 percent of the cases, with 8 percent sentencing more harshly and 7 percent more leniently (Swisher 1978). This study was carried out a year after the FSW was first implemented. Judges may have been more willing to abide by the guidelines initially because of the novelty effect. It is of utmost importance to develop value-free guidelines and then to make the sentences suggested mandatory unless special circumstances prompting different sentences can be fully justified in writing.

After scores have been added for both the offense and the offender categories, they are applied to a grid on the reverse side of the FSW. At the point at which they intersect, the grid indicates a suitable sentence. These are suggested sentences only. Do not hesitate to recommend sentences that are not consistent with the grid if you feel you can justify an alternative. In fact, it is probably a good idea for practice purposes to ignore the scoring of the FSW until after you have decided on a recommendation. Then score the FSW and see how close your decision comes to the suggested sentence.

As a quick exercise, let us score Bill Bloggs on the FSW. He was a first offender and thus is scored zero on the "offender rating" section of the sheet. In the "degree of offense" subsection Bill would receive the maximum number of points, four, because both of his crimes were first-degree felonies. In the "multiple offenses" category he would receive two points because he was convicted of both aggravated robbery and attempted aggravated murder. In the "actual or potential harm" category he would receive two points for wounding the police officer. With eight points he is already beyond the FSW's range for probation. One could also assess two points against Bill in the "culpability" section for "shocking and deliberate cruelty," and deducting any points in the "mitigation" category could not really be justified. Bill therefore would get ten offense-rating points, a score that places him in the upper-left square of the grid.

Risk and Needs Assessment Scales

Risk and needs assessment scales are part of the Client Management Classification System and are designed to be used with the CMC interview schedule. The system has two separate scales that assess the client's "risk" and "needs." (The scales and a complete scoring guide are reproduced in Appendix A.) Client risk refers to the probability that the client will commit another crime and to the threat the client poses to the community. It is assessed by assigning numerical scores on variables known to correlate with recidivism. The earlier a criminal career begins, the more involved the offender is in it, the more addicted to chemical substances, the less legitimately employed, and the more negative the attitude, the more likely the client is to commit another crime. The more likely clients are to reoffend, the greater the risk they represent to the community and the more closely they must be supervised. It is the practice in many jurisdictions to move clients up one level of supervision higher than the score indicates where there is a history of assaultive offenses.

Client need refers to deficiencies in personal repertoires and lifestyles that may be deterring them from a conventional moral pattern of behavior. The needs section is where the probation and parole officer's counseling skills and knowledge of community resources are of great value. Scores on both sections of the scale tend to be highly correlated: A client who is high-risk tends to have high needs, and clients with few needs are not high-risk.

Complete a risk and needs scale for each client for whom you write a practice PSI. As you do this, be mindful of the need for complete accuracy: The safety of the people of the community and the rehabilitation of your client both depend on the accuracy of your assessment. Read the instructions carefully before you assign any points. Place your client at the appropriate level of supervision.

How would Bill Bloggs do on the risk and needs scales? On the risk scale, Bill would be assessed only three points (he was between the ages of eighteen and twenty-nine at the time of his offense), but the "assault factor" would automatically move him up one level of supervision in most departments.

In the "emotional stability" section of the needs scale, I would assign Bill two points. On the one hand, given some of his weird behavior and statements, a two might not be enough. On the other hand, his symptoms do not prevent him from functioning adequately. I would also assess three points against him in the "living arrangements" category. The only other assessment that might be justified is one point for "situational or minor difficulties" under "financial status," but I would assess another five points under "officer's impressions," for a total of eleven points.

Supervision Level Matrix

On the basis of scores obtained in both sections of the assessment scale, clients are placed under minimum, medium, or maximum supervision. These levels closely correlate with the case management classification system derived from the CMC. Correct assessment of clients at this point contributes greatly to the efficient use of officers' time. The time not wasted in overservicing low-risk and low-needs clients can be fruitfully spent with those who require more attention.

Five cells of the supervision level matrix represent maximum supervision, three represent medium, and a single cell represents minimum supervision. Only clients with ten or fewer risk points and thirteen or fewer needs points fall into this minimum category. Do not be alarmed by the number of cells calling for maximum supervision. It has been empirically determined that only about 15 percent of probation and parole clients fall into these five cells. About 50 percent of the clients will fall into the medium level of supervision, and the remaining 35 percent will require only minimal supervision (Idaho Dept. of Corrections n.d.:19). These figures will vary according to the probation/parole granting practices of a given jurisdiction. If a jurisdiction relies heavily on community-based corrections, the number of clients requiring maximum and medium supervision will be much higher than in jurisdictions that are reluctant to grant probation and parole,

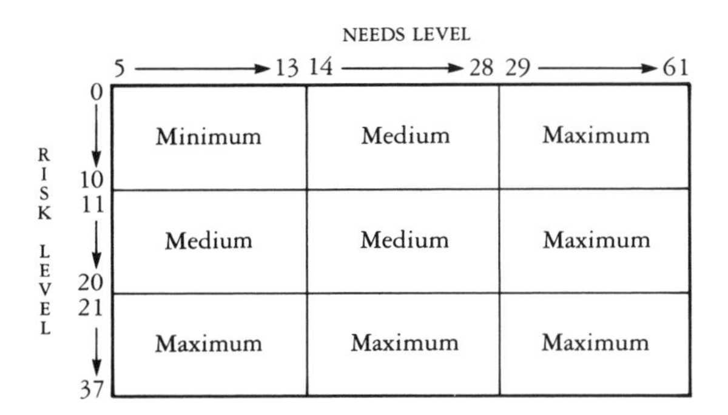

Figure 7-1 Risk and needs supervision level matrix

where the number of clients requiring minimum supervision might be 60 to 70 percent.

If we apply the supervision level matrix (Figure 7-1) to Bill Bloggs, we discover that Bill's level of supervision without the assault override would have been minimum. That level is clearly untenable for someone who has committed the kind of crimes Bill did (though this level might be fine if he were being classified for parole rather than probation and if information from prison authorities justified it). This classification problem underscores two points: (1) Bill was clearly an atypical case, and (2) the suggestions of these scales, based as they are on the "typical" criminal, are not cast in stone. In the extremely unlikely event that Bill had been placed on probation, you would have been seriously remiss if you had followed these guidelines unquestioningly.

Supervision Planning

Having found the appropriate supervision level, you must now formulate a plan for the offender's rehabilitation. Treatment plans must represent a balance between the client's treatment needs and the client's present coping resources (see Chapter 9). You have identified the client's needs, so the next task is to prioritize them according to their influence on his or her legal difficulties. The supervision planning form will be useful here. It asks the officer to list the client's strengths/resources and problems/weaknesses. In rank-ordering problem areas, give extra weight to the problems most amenable to speedy change so that the client can begin to develop a success orientation.

Be particularly alert to what may be a primary or "master" problem, a particularly debilitating one that may be the source of most of the client's other problems. For instance, lack of education and employment, poor financial status, and poor spousal relationships are highly interdependent areas that might be mitigated by meaningful vocational training and employment. All these areas, as well as others such as the influence of criminal companions, may themselves be dependent on substance abuse. If evaluation of the client's problems leads you to believe that most of them are secondary to substance abuse, the obvious plan is to give substance abuse top priority for change.

With the client's rehabilitative needs identified and prioritized, you are ready to draw up a tentative supervision plan according to the form reproduced in Appendix A. The tentative supervision plan includes a problem statement, long-range goal, short-range objectives, probationer/parolee action plan, and officer/referral plan.

For instance, an officer may identify alcoholism/problem drinking and vocational training as priorities for immediate attention. Alcoholism can be identified by the client's score on the MAST scale (see Appendix C) and by alcohol-related legal problems on the record. A second problem that may be identified is a client's lack of marketable skills for worthwhile full-time employment.

The long-range goals, therefore, would be to maintain sobriety and complete vocational training. As we will see in Chapter 9, a good plan should be simple, specific, and something the client must do as soon as possible rather than stop doing. The officer might state the short-range goal to be two days of sobriety and attendance at the next AA meeting. The officer will then formulate a probationer action plan and ask the client to commit to it by signing it. The officer's commitment to the plan may be expressed in the plan by a promise to attend the first AA meeting with the client and to refer the client to an alcohol treatment facility for evaluation and treatment recommendations. The procedure for the second problem should be similarly simple and focused.

The reassessment plan will be implemented after the outcomes of the tentative plans have been determined. For instance, the alcohol treatment facility may advise more intensive treatment or conclude that the officer has overemphasized the client's drinking problem. The officer will plan the next supervision phase accordingly. If the client has successfully completed vocational training after referral, the long-range plan may now be for the client to secure and maintain full-time employment, with the short-range plan being to file a designated number of applications for employment every day until the client has a job. Supervision plans must be frequently changed as circumstances dictate.

Every six months there should be a reassessment of the client's risk and needs; the client may be placed in a higher or lower supervision category depending on the progress or lack of progress in the preceding six months.

A Final Word About the CMC System

It is important that neither the seasoned officer nor the student view the CMC system as just bureaucratic paper-pushing. The officer used to supervising clients on the basis of intuition or experience will indeed see it as extra work. I was one who complained about filling out forms when the system first came out, but once I got used to it, I became a committed convert. The CMC system is actually an efficiency-enhancing device that will ultimately save time.

A recent study (Lerner, Arling & Baird 1986) found that high-risk clients on CMC supervision experienced 8 percent fewer parole revocations than regularly supervised ("seat of the pants") high-risk clients. CMC medium-risk clients experienced 6 percent fewer revocations than non-CMC medium-risk clients. Both these differences are statistically significant. They also represent ninety-five fewer parole violation reports, and that saves a lot of time. More importantly, ninety-five clients were saved from the futility of the revolving prison door because their needs had been identified and efficiently met. CMC supervision of low-risk clients resulted in only 1 percent fewer (6 percent versus 7 percent) revocations than the regularly supervised low-risk clients. This seemingly insignificant difference is more a function of the generally good performance of low-risk clients than of poor application of the CMC system to them.

What do field practitioners think of the system? Michael Schumacher, Ph.D., the chief probation officer of Orange County, California, is an enthusiastic supporter:

> Probation programs... can no longer rely upon the assertions of "doing good" for people based upon a subjective model of human behavior. The risk/needs approach provides an objective look at offenders based on characteristics that have been shown to have some predictive value for the success or failure of other probationers. It supports a healthy balance between the peace officer role [and the] social work role. It is a tool that has been a long time coming and shows promise for probation supervision as a major factor in the resocialization of offenders. Longitudinal research conducted in jurisdictions where this system has been fully implemented has shown encouraging results in the reduction of criminal behavior by probationers. If this system is properly implemented, I am convinced reductions in recidivism rates will result (1985:454-455).

References and Suggested Readings

Lerner, K., G. Arling, and C. Baird. 1986. Client management classification: Strategies for case supervision. *Crime and Delinquency* 32:254-271.

Marsh, R., and D. Marsh. 1990. Jail overcrowding: Who makes policy? *Journal of Contemporary Criminal Justice* 6:167-175.

Schumacher, M. 1985. Implementation of a client classification and case management system: A practitioner's view. *Crime and Delinquency* 31:445-455.

Swisher, T. 1978. *Sentencing in Ohio*. Columbus: Ohio State Bar Research Foundation.

Walsh, A. 1985. Ideology and arithmetic: The hidden agenda of sentencing guidelines. *Journal of Crime and Justice* 8:41-63.

Chapter 8

Nondirective Counseling: Theory and Practice

Love is the increase of self by means of other.
Spinoza

Robert Martinson's article "What Works? Questions and Answers about Prison Reform" (1974) provided much grist for the mills of those who subscribe to a "lock 'em up and lose the key" philosophy. They were so excited about Martinson's alleged findings that the rhetorical "what works?" was translated into the nihilistic "nothing works." The Martinson report was interpreted as a justification for terminating all efforts to rehabilitate criminals in favor of punishing them, preferably by long periods of incarceration.

Disregarding the prohibitive cost of incarcerating all convicted criminals (see Walker's excellent 1985 analysis of the financial waterfall needed to implement this philosophy), to consign all convicted criminals to prison is both morally inhumane and socially insane. Nearly all incarcerated felons will leave prison some day, and they will emerge harder, crueler, more savage, and more bitter than they were before they went in. The United States already incarcerates more people than does any other country with humanitarian pretensions. Yet the call for more and more punishment continues to find receptive ears.

It is true that many correctional programs did not work, for a variety of reasons. Gendreau and Ross, two researchers in the forefront of efforts to revive the rehabilitation ideal, explain:

> The programs recorded in the literature which have failed (and earned treatment a bad name) did so because they were derived from conceptual models (e.g., psychiatric, nondirective counseling methods, clinical sociology) that made little sense in terms of offender populations or were applied to inappropriate target populations or sought to affect behaviors which were unrelated to crime. They failed because they were badly managed, because they were not sufficiently intensive, and because they employed staff who were inadequately skilled, who exerted insufficient effort or who were not aware or supportive of the program's techniques and goals (1981:47).

What Gendreau and Ross are saying is that rehabilitative efforts must be based on theories and methods that are specific to the clientele being dealt with (which does not mean that the methods they mention as ineffective have nothing to offer) and must be conducted by caring individuals who fully believe in what they are doing and are trained to do it properly.

Before we can determine that something does or does not work, we first have to define thresholds. A rehabilitation program is not a machine that either works or doesn't. Nothing works for all human beings, and nothing will ever work all the time. If it did, we would be not human beings but programmed robots. So when we talk about programs working or not working, we recognize that none will work for everybody all of the time.

What rate of success is acceptable before we say a program works: 90 percent, 80 percent, 50 percent, 10 percent? Of the 231 studies that Martinson reviewed, 48 percent reported some success. If your criterion for success is a demanding 100 percent, then indeed nothing works. A 48 percent success rate (however "success" was defined in the original studies) is cause for optimistic celebration. Walker (1985:170) reports that other reviews of similar studies found success rates of between 67 percent and 77 percent. In a later review of rehabilitative programs, Gendreau and Ross (1987) found evidence for a great deal of success. They conclude that "it is downright ridiculous to say that 'nothing works.'" This review attests that much is going on to indicate that offender rehabilitation has been, can be, and will be achieved" (1987:395). Let us then dismiss the pessimism of the "nothing works" crowd and explore counseling theories designed to help those caught up in the criminal justice system resolve their problems.

Counseling

What Correctional Counseling Is Not

"Beware of helpers. Helpers are con men who promise you something for nothing. They spoil you and keep you dependent." John Stratton, an experienced supervising probation officer, opens his insightful essay on "counseling con men" (1975:125) with this statement by Fritz Perls, a statement that all who aspire to a helping profession should think about. We enter the so-called helping professions with noble motives; it makes us feel good to "help" the troubled and the less fortunate. But the point of helping is not to make us feel good, it is to help our clients help themselves to feel better and become more productive members of society. We should never do for our clients what they can do for themselves. If we do, we foster client dependence, the inability to be responsible and to stand on their own two feet, and, to use a current buzzword, we "enable" them to persist in self-destructive and immature behavior. This is not true helping or counseling. Certainly, our clients may lean on us—but only if they lean on us in order to lift themselves.

Too many corrections counselors see their roles differently. They think they must "straighten out" their clients' behavior and "adjust" their attitudes. They try to do this via directives and well-meaning advice. There is indeed much about correctional casework that is coercive. But in exercising the required restraint and constraint, we will be far more successful if we treat our clients with respect and enlist their cooperation, just as we would if we were counseling in a noncoercive setting, say, marriage counseling, where there is no authoritative relationship between counselor and client.

It is best for a counselor to avoid giving advice unless it is specifically requested. As Meier states: "Friends and family give advice; counselors generally don't, particularly in the initial stages of relationship building" (1989:19). Even advice from family and friends is usually not well-received or attended to unless it is requested—uninvited advice often irritates. As authority figures, we can force our advice on clients and even force them to follow through with it, but meaningful and lasting results can only be achieved if clients are personally convinced of its usefulness. Learning and discovery can ultimately only come from within; helping the client to become open to learning is the real challenge for the counselor.

What Is Counseling?

Our first task is to differentiate between the terms "counseling" and "psychotherapy." Some claim that there is no essential difference since the definitions and roles of the two terms are interchangeable. Further, the same theories are presented in both counseling and psychotherapy texts. However, in keeping with earlier advice to respect boundaries of expertise, we must stress the differences between the two.

Psychotherapy is practiced by psychiatrists or psychologists with many years of highly specialized training. True, they employ many of the same techniques used by those engaged in counseling, but they have a deeper theoretical understanding of the causality of the conditions they are treating.

The term "treating" delineates another important distinction between psychotherapy and counseling. Psychotherapists think of their patients' problems in terms of pathology; counselors must interpret their clients' problems as deficiencies. Psychotherapy differs from counseling in the depth and seriousness of the problems it deals with and in the intensity of the treatment. If we laid all the psychiatrists and psychologists in the world out couch to couch, we would not have nearly enough to help all our criminals, the vast majority of whom do not require "treatment." That's why we need counselors.

Counselors attempt to help their clients with specific life-adjustment problems and to develop the personality that already exists. Psychotherapists attempt to help their patients restructure their basic personalities over a long period of time. To put it another way, psychotherapists deal primarily with *intra*personal conflicts, counselors with *inter*personal conflicts. When a client is obviously in need of treatment that exceeds your capability as a counselor, do not hesitate to relinquish the case to someone more qualified to deal with it.

Similarity between Interviewing and Counseling
Counseling is a series of concerned responses offered to clients who have problems that adversely affect their functioning. Counseling is an extension of the interviewing process that uses the same communications skills and techniques. However, "techniques" are secondary to the warmth, acceptance, and understanding the counselor brings to the task. Good (that is, open, warm, accepting, and empathetic) counselors operating with different theoretical perspectives are more similar to one another than are good and poor counselors with the same theoretical perspective (Lytle 1964). In other words, all the counseling methods and theories we will examine are only as good as the person putting them into practice. If you work on improving the quality of the self you bring to the counseling process, the techniques will come easily to you.

Differences between Interviewing and Counseling
Although counseling is an extension of the interviewing process, there are certain differences between interviewing and counseling in a criminal justice setting. First, you are more likely to encounter client resistance during the counseling process than during the interviewing process. During the PSI interview or parole hearing, the client is fairly anxious to seem contrite and cooperative because he or she knows that you make recommendations afterwards. Once there has been a disposition, clients tend to lose some of their motivation to cooperate along with the anxiety about the disposition of the case. This tendency is a good reason to make the best possible effort to establish a working rapport during the initial interview, when the client is fairly amenable; you will find it much harder to develop later on. Do not be disheartened if you do perceive a change in some clients after case disposition; accept it as a professional challenge.

Second, once you have a good working relationship with your clients, you can be ready to communicate with them at a deeper level in successive counseling sessions by carefully developing an empathetic understanding of them. You no longer have to gather large amounts of data, so you are free to concentrate on specific problem areas. Therefore, counseling differs from interviewing in its depth.

So, what is correctional counseling? William Lewis, a psychologist with many years of experience counseling offenders, defines it as "ongoing, positive, interpersonal relationships as the vehicle through which a variety of systematic verbal techniques can be applied to increase the counselee's *feelings* of self-satisfaction, *and* improve his [or her] *actual* social adjustments" (1989:71, emphasis in the original). The correctional worker who can do this has a positive and integrated sense of self and can serve as a model of growth-inducing interpersonal relationships.

Counseling Theories

With this brief introduction to counseling, we turn to five of the most popular theories of counseling, two in this chapter and three in the next. Important aspects of counseling will be illustrated in the context of the theories that most strongly emphasize those aspects. We will pay special attention to processes for generating rapport and empathy and to techniques for dealing with reluctant, resisting clients.

You may view the large number of theoretical orientations to counseling (and there are certainly far more than the five presented here) in two ways. You may consider them to be so much clutter, demonstrating a lack of scientific rigor in the field. Or you may regard them as a rich mine of possibilities in which you can dig for counseling gems. No single theory will apply to all the problems and concerns with which you will deal, and no one theory will exhaust the uniqueness of each client. There is a profound statement whose author is lost in time: "Each person is like all other persons, like some other persons, and like no other person." It follows that certain insights from one counseling theory may apply universally, only some of the time, or not apply at all on some occasions.

The more theoretical insights you have in your repertoire, the better you will be able to respond successfully to the diversity of clients and problems you will encounter. Loyalty to a single theory may severely limit your effectiveness by leading you to stretch everything to fit the theory and to ignore whatever will not. Good counselors develop a unique, flexible, and workable style of their own. If you use an eclectic approach, picking and choosing those elements that fit your style and serve your needs with a given client, you will begin to discern some of the common threads woven into all theories. The agreement of greatest importance among all theories is the vital necessity of all human beings to love and be loved.

This chapter focuses on psychoanalysis and client-centered therapy, the next on transactional analysis, rational emotive therapy, and reality therapy. Psychoanalysis and client-centered therapy are nondirective forms of counseling. They put great faith in the ability of clients to discover their own capabilities and find their own directions. The counselor plays a relatively passive role and is reluctant to impose his or her values on clients and direct them. Psychoanalysis and client-centered therapy are rarely used in a correctional setting, primarily because they are not directive enough, the terminology and concepts are too abstruse, and the methods are difficult for the non-specialist to apply. But they have been included because they offer certain unique insights, which we will outline as we go along.

Psychoanalysis

Although psychoanalysis is beyond the boundaries of expertise for the nonpsychiatrist or nonpsychologist, it contains useful insights into the nature of human beings. Whereas the other four theories focus primarily on the present, psychoanalysis emphasizes the role of the past in shaping current behavior. Since so many emotional and behavioral difficulties stem from past experiences, it is important to explore a client's past as a vehicle for understanding his or her present.

According to Fine, "the technical task of psychoanalysis has been to elucidate the nature of love" (1973:16). Freud himself has stated that happiness exists in "the way of life which makes love the center of everything, which looks for all satisfaction in loving and being loved" (1961:29). The psychoanalyst explores the patient's childhood to uncover reasons for an inability to love. We will relate what follows to the life history of Bill Bloggs as recounted in his PSI report. (Again, reference to the Bloggs case illustrates but does not validate the theory.)

The psychoanalytic theory that the personality has three parts—id, ego, and superego—is too well-known to warrant extensive treatment here, so the id will be defined simply as the biological source of the organism's energy, the driving force of the personality. Its only goal is to gratify its urges—to seek pleasure and to avoid pain. The superego is the counterforce to the id, exercising socially derived moral prescriptions and proscriptions. We call individuals who give free reign to the id nasty names like "psychopaths" or "criminals," and we call individuals with an overly powerful superego slightly less offensive names like "neurotic" or "conformist." The ego synthesizes the biological and social demands on the organism. Well-balanced people with egos are able to gratify their id drives within the bounds of moral restriction placed on them by their superegos (their conscience).

The value of Freud's theory of personality lies in the recognition of both the "beast and angel in man" (Wrong 1968). The bestial side of humanity is the side that most concerns the criminal justice worker. As a criminal justice worker, you must help clients to understand themselves and to enlist that understanding in the task of strengthening the rational ego "so that it can appropriate fresh portions of the id. Where id was, there shall ego be" (Freud 1965:80).

Psychosexual Stages

Psychoanalysis stresses the great importance of the three psychosexual stages of early character development: the oral, the anal, and the phallic (other stages have been identified, but the first three are generally considered the most important in terms of their effects on personality development). Each stage represents the child's first encounters with external restraints on natural urges coming from the id. These encounters generate negative feelings in the child, such as hostility, hatred, anger, and destructiveness. Since the display of these feelings invites negative reactions from other people, the child learns to repress them, causing a later inability to accept and express real feelings. This barrier to self-knowledge must be breached in any counseling session.

Oral Stage: From Birth to Age 1 The oral stage encompasses the first year of life, which, according to modern neurophysiology, is the critical period when the neuronal pathways are laid down. This is the time when the child learns love and security and when the template for the child's basic personality is formed. At the mother's breast, the infant satisfies its hunger and needs for tactile stimulation. These are unconditioned needs (they do not have to be learned), the satisfaction of which the infant "loves" because they are intrinsically rewarding. When the infant identifies the source of its pleasure, it develops a love for that source that is stronger than the love of the pleasures the source affords. In this sense, then, love for mother is a response conditioned by the continual associations made between her and the pleasures she provides.

Negative behaviors, such as acquisitiveness and aggression, may develop when these needs are not adequately met. According to this theory, these behaviors are substitutes for what the individual really needs—love. The child feels unworthy, unwanted, and unaccepted and grows up to be mistrusting and rejecting of others. These individuals cannot accept either themselves or others because they have not experienced acceptance. Early love experiences are a safeguard against this kind of negativism.

This does not mean, of course, that all people who exhibit these negative characteristics have experienced an unloving childhood or that individuals who did experience an unloving childhood will necessarily exhibit them. The theory merely asserts that individuals who have experienced a childhood marked by a lack of love are more likely to behave negatively as adults than those individuals who were surrounded by love as children.

Consider the early life experiences of Bill Bloggs. It was plain that he was an unwanted child from the start. Was he not, by his own admission, socially isolated? Did he not seek to win Susan's love by purchase? Can we not see his extreme materialism and bursts of aggressive behavior as stemming from his lack of love during the oral stage of his life?

Anal Stage: Ages 1 Through 3 In the anal stage the child first encounters discipline. Before this state, the child has received a series of admonitions such as "Don't touch that oven!" or "Stop hitting the cat!" but in the anal stage the child encounters "real" discipline aimed at self-mastery by learning to control bodily functions through toilet training. Toilet training is important in psychoanalytic theory because it is the first time the child must suppress natural urgings until they can be satisfied in an appropriate way in an appropriate place. While the child tends to rebel against the unnaturalness of toilet training, once the training is completed, he or she takes pride in the accomplishment. Parents should encourage this sense of mastery by allowing the child to explore and to make mistakes, making it clear that it is permissible to make mistakes if one learns by them. If parents are constantly critical of the mistakes the child makes, the child will be reluctant to explore and expand. If parents show exaggerated concern and do everything for the child, the child will not develop a sense of independence and autonomy. The children of such parents may be stuck forever in a "no-can-do" mode, lacking the self-confidence to expand their horizons and thinking poorly of themselves.

It is easy to view Bill's parents, especially his father, as being hypercritical of him during his formative years. Bill's whole life seemed to revolve around doing things to please his father. The fact that he did not leave home until he met Susan suggests a strong sense of dependency. His hanging of the kitten, his bursts of extreme temper, and, not the least, his shooting of a policeman point vividly to his inability to express his feelings appropriately.

Phallic Stage: Ages 3 Through 5 The phallic stage is a period of early development of conscience and sex-role identification; during this stage, children become aware of their genitals. Masturbation usually beings at this stage, and parental response to the discovery of this activity can have serious consequences. If parents are overly moralistic, defining masturbation as something that "nice boys and girls don't do," they set the stage for the overcontrol of the superego. Such rigid conformity to puritanical morality may preclude the enjoyment of intimacy with others later in life because of inadequate sex-role identification.

We have no information about Bill's experiences during the phallic stage, but it takes no great flight of imagination to see Bill's father as a real authoritarian moralist. Bill did have great difficulty forming intimate attachments with others, and perhaps his belief that he was a woman in his "previous existence" indicates sex-role ambiguity. Bill's forced incestuous experiences would have seriously conflicted with any early development of a moralistic conscience. The relaying of highly incongruous prescriptive and proscriptive messages to children is the basis of the so-called double-bind theory of schizophrenia because it undermines the child's foundations of reality (Bateson, Jackson, Haley & Weakland 1956). Bill did have an unusual view of reality, and he was deemed to be in the early stages of schizophrenic reaction.

Defense Mechanisms

The identification of a patient's defense mechanisms is an important part of the psychotherapeutic process. Defense mechanisms, which operate at an unconscious level (the individual is unaware of them), function to protect the ego from a threatening reality by distorting it. Defense mechanisms are not necessarily pathological; we all use them to some extent, and they can even be psychologically adaptive. Only when they contribute to a pattern of avoiding reality do they become matters of great concern. There are numerous defense mechanisms listed in the psychoanalytic literature. We will discuss only those seen most often in a criminal justice setting.

Denial is the blocking-out of a portion of reality that is threatening to the ego. Sexual feelings and activities are often subject to this defense mechanism. Child molesters, who may be otherwise quite respectable, will often deny to themselves what they have done. This is not simply "forgetting" (repression), but refusal to recognize that it happened. Bill's denial of his enuresis may have been an attempt to deal with the residual anxiety he felt about being "hog tied" and whipped when he wet his bed, and his statement that his incestuous experiences were "no big deal" seems to be an attempt to divorce himself from the possibility that he could have welcomed them.

Rationalization is the process of finding acceptable reasons for behavior or experiences in order to soothe a damaged ego. This is a definite favorite of criminal justice clients. Bill recited a litany of experiences to make Corrick understand "some underlying reason(s) for my behavior," thus creating the impression that he was more wronged than wrong. Rationalization helps us to maintain an acceptable self-image by downplaying our own badness or inadequacies; we parcel out blame or disvalue what we want but cannot get ("I didn't get the job because this is a racist society and I'm black. Who wants that stupid job anyway?").

Fixation is being immobilized at an earlier stage of personality development because the more mature stage is fraught with anxiety. Many criminal justice clients have a childlike attachment to the present because stepping into the future is stepping into the great unknown. Many have developed a pattern of helplessness through their dependence on the welfare system, which is the only financial "parent" many have ever known. To expand one's capacities and explore one's potential is not a lesson imparted by the culture of poverty. As a criminal justice helper, you are charged with helping your clients to develop a realistic orientation to the future by attempting to enlarge their sense of self-worth and of the possible.

Displacement is the transference of feelings about someone or something onto another person or object because the original person or object is either inaccessible or too powerful. Anger or aggression is often displaced onto the innocent. Wife and child battering is often a displacement of aggression generated by others too powerful to attack directly. All too often criminal justice clients have much pent-up anger, the source of which they find difficult to identify. Further, they have not learned to express their feelings in appropriate ways, so they vent them on "safe" targets. Bill's explosive temper and the hanging of the kitten would be interpreted by the psychoanalyst as a displacement of the anger he felt toward his father onto nonthreatening targets.

Intellectualization is common among better-educated criminal justice clients. They will often try to assail legal reality by intellectualizing their crimes away. The marijuana dealer who launches into a monologue accusing society of hypocrisy, the petty forger who cites chapter and verse on white-collar crime, and the thief who discourses plausibly on corporate irresponsibility are all trying to avoid the reality of their own malfeasance. You may certainly accept the legitimacy of their position, but you must also impress on them that the issue is not the behavior of others but their own and that they cannot avoid confronting their behavior by trying to refocus the discussion elsewhere.

Projection is the mechanism by which people attribute to others the feelings they refuse to see in themselves. We are often most troubled by the behavior of others when it mimics our own repressed urges. The rough treatment of child molesters in prisons may be viewed as an attempt by other inmates to convince themselves that they could not possibly harbor such evil urges themselves. Clients who feel that no one understands or likes them, who harbor hostility toward others, are projecting their negative feelings about themselves onto others, protecting the ego by confusing self with other. Often expressions of hostility and hatred of the world by criminal justice clients are really expressions of self-hatred. If you can help clients to develop more positive feelings about themselves, they will develop better attitudes toward the world.

Lessons and Concerns

The primary usefulness of psychoanalytic theory for the criminal justice worker is that it offers insights that make it easier to understand clients' struggles with themselves and with the outside world. The defense mechanisms are particularly useful in understanding client resistance to the helping process.

A little knowledge, Alexander Pope said, is a dangerous thing. The criminal justice helper lacks the training necessary to put the techniques of psychoanalysis into practice. To attempt to do so could have negative consequences. Psychoanalysis is also too time-consuming and complex for the criminal justice context. It is an approach better suited to those free to seek absolution for their sins, those who enjoy richer vocabularies and fatter wallets than the typical correctional client. Many psychiatrists and psychologists themselves have turned to more simplified methods to deal with the problems the typical client presents—methods that have generally been found to be more productive of change because few clients require total personality restructuring. Using psychoanalysis for minor life-adjustment problems can be like swatting flies with a baseball bat. But this is not to belittle the often profound theoretical insights into human nature this theory provides.

Client-centered Approach

Carl Rogers developed his client-centered (or person-centered) approach to counseling in response to the deficiencies he perceived in psychoanalysis. As an existentialist/humanist thinker, he rejected the determinism of Freud's psychoanalytic theory in favor of self-determination and faith in the natural goodness in humankind. Rather than viewing individuals as being driven by irrational biological impulses (which Rogers saw as implying that humans were basically antisocial), this approach sees human beings as basically good, self-driven, and possessing an innate capacity for self-actualization (the tendency to become all that we are able to become). Self-destructive behavior and attitudes arise from faulty self-concepts and an inability to grasp the fundamental truth that we are free agents in charge of our own destinies. Although this kind of thinking may be somewhat Pollyannaish in that it refuses to see the beast in man, it is ennobling in its enunciation.

As is the case with all counseling theories, the basic process of client-centered therapy is designed to improve the self-concept. Rogers defines counseling as follows: "The process by which the structure of the self is relaxed in the safety of the relationship with the therapist, and the previously denied experiences are perceived and then integrated into an altered self" (1952:70). Client-centered therapy eschews searching for causes and the teaching of counseling techniques in favor of asserting the absolute primacy of the client/counselor relationship. What the counselor brings to the relationship in terms of the quality of the self is far more critical than the technique adopted.

The absence of loving human relationships is the basic reason that isolated, alienated, lonely, and self-destructive clients turn to a counselor for help. It follows that the client must form a positive relationship with at least one other person if anything meaningful is to be accomplished. That one other person is the counselor. Although the burden of discovering the true goodness of the self is placed squarely on the shoulders of the client, the burden of establishing a relationship in which it may be accomplished is on the counselor: "If I can provide a certain type of relationship, the other person will discover within himself the capacity to use that relationship for growth and change, and personal development will occur" (Rogers 1961:33). The counselor functions as a kind of midwife, wresting out of the client the goodness that is already present awaiting birth.

Can the correctional worker provide the "love" that Rogers considers so important? Unfortunately, the English language is such that the term love is either confined to romantic love or used indiscriminately as an intense form of liking ("I love golf," or "I just loved that movie"). William Lewis tells us how we can meet a client's need for love:

> A correctional worker can meet the need for love, for example, at the young adult level through such means as courtesy; showing genuine interest and concern; giving instructions in a friendly, respectful way (as opposed to grumpy or profane barking); giving honest praise for work well-done; and asking for opinions and respecting them as worthwhile (1989:28).

Evans et al. (1989:3) have characterized Rogers as the "listening counselor." The techniques of client-centered therapy are those we talked about in Chapter 5: active listening, clarification, reflection of feelings. If you were to watch a client-centered counselor at work you could get the impression that nothing is going on. The counselor simply listens intensely to the client while making occasional verbalizations such as "Yes, please go on," "Uhuh, uhuh," "Mm," and "Once again, please," and with other signs of approval such as smiles and nods. These verbal and visual signs of approval are designed to reinforce the client, and such reinforcement is considered vital in the counseling process. Clients tend to talk about topics that are reinforced, and not about topics that are not. People's verbal and nonverbal behavior can be systematically shaped in desired directions by such simple acts of reinforcement (Evan et al. 1989:5-6).

However, Rogers is much more concerned with the client/counselor relationship and the personal attributes of the counselor than with techniques. The three main attributes that the counselor must bring to the relationship are unconditional positive regard, genuineness, and empathy.

Unconditional Positive Regard

According to Rogers, many negative self-feelings and psychological problems develop because others place conditions on their acceptance of us. They like us or love us "if" we are or "if" we do what they would like us to be or do. Since we all want to be liked, loved, and accepted, we tend to conform to these conditions. Our conformity to the expectations of others leads us to an inauthentic self-image. In order to function as psychologically healthy people, we must set our own standards of behavior and self-acceptance. We have the ability to be fully authentic human beings, but we must first experience unconditional positive regard from at least one person. For Rogers, the counselor fills that role.

Unconditional positive regard occurs when the counselor communicates a full and genuine acceptance of the client's personhood, warts and all. Acceptance must not be contaminated by judgments that the client's attitudes, feelings, or behavior are wrong or bad. This does not mean that the counselor accepts illegal or immoral behavior; it means that the counselor accepts and values the client's essential humanity in spite of his or her attitudes and behavior. This acceptance sets clients free to examine their own behavior in a non-threatening atmosphere, so that they may themselves realize that their attitudes and behavior are self-defeating. (Officer Corrick appears to have had a positive feeling about Bill Bloggs, while at the same time soundly condemning his behavior in the PSI report.)

"Unconditional positive regard" is an ideal to be striven for, not an all-or-nothing requirement. It is most unrealistic to think that you can develop this kind of relationship with all of your clients, or even most of them. Any relationship between two people is a chemical mix that may blend or explode. Clients who are determined to make your life as difficult as possible will read only weakness or patronization into your efforts to establish a positive working relationship. Most, however, will respond to your warmth with warmth of their own. The degree to which you can achieve the kind of positive regard that Rogers talks about is largely the degree to which you will succeed in your efforts to turn your client's life around. At the very least, respect the basic humanity of the client. Be cautious, however, that the client does not become dependent on you and that you do not use the relationship possessively to fulfill your own needs for positive regard.

Genuineness

The counselor must be genuine with the client, accepting and dealing with all the feelings, positive or negative, generated by his or her interaction with the client. Since it is the task of the counselor to help the client become more aware of internal incongruities, it is highly desirable that the counselor present an authentic integrated self to the client. Pretensions, game playing, and facades must be avoided at all costs. The counselor who displays a false front feels a lack of congruence between the real and the ideal self—which is precisely the vulnerable state the client is assumed to be in. The aim of self-disclosure exercises for the neophyte counselor is to develop an authentic and congruent sense of self, so that the counselor's transparent and authentic self permeates freely into the client.

It is not true that only a "fully authentic" counselor can effectively counsel clients. Human genuineness or authenticity is on a continuum and must be developed. It is interesting to see how the giants of the human sciences agree on this subject of human authenticity. Freud, Marx, and Maslow, despite radically different ideological orientations, all agree that the ability to love and be loved is the key to human authenticity (Walsh 1986).

Empathy

Empathy is the counselor's capacity for participating in the feelings of the client. It implies more than an intellectual understanding of the client's feelings. It goes beyond cognitive knowledge about the client to fusion with the client, causing the counselor to experience the client's feelings as if they were the counselor's own.

This implies a subjective understanding that is granted only to those who have walked in similar shoes. Mayeroff describes the empathetic ability thus:

> To care for another person, I must be able to understand him and his world as if I were inside it. I must be able to see, as it were, with his eyes what his world is like to him and how he sees himself. Instead of merely looking at him in a detached way from the outside, as if he were a specimen, I must be able to be with him in his world, "going" into his world in order to sense from the "inside" what life is for him, what he is striving to be and what he requires to grow (1971:41-42).

This definition of empathy is like the definition of unconditional positive regard—beautiful in its conceptualization but probably impossible to attain. Yet many books on counseling contain such statements as "Respond to the client with empathy." This gives the beginning counselor the mistaken impression that "getting into" a client's frame of reference is not much more difficult than attaching tab A to block B when assembling a toy. This could be falsely reassuring and dangerously misleading.

Developing Accurate Empathy Is empathy possible between persons of different races, social strata, and educational backgrounds? For example, can a white, middle-class, college-educated corrections worker really "participate" in the mind-set of a black semiliterate street person? Yes, but only in a limited sense. The ability does not come naturally or easily. It takes hard work, both in examining your own values, prejudices, and stereotypes and in assimilating as much knowledge as you possibly can about the causes and reasons why offenders live and behave the way they do. Your ability to empathize with your clients will increase in direct proportion to the time you spend trying to understand them, and yourself. Even then, it may be counterproductive to convey to clients that you "understand" their problems until you have actively listened a number of times to what they have to say. That is why empathy was not stressed in the chapter on interviewing, but listening was: active listening is a prerequisite to empathy.

Egan (1982) distinguishes between what he calls primary and advanced empathy, both of which he subsumes under the general term "accurate empathy." Primary empathy "means communicating initial basic understanding of what the client is feeling and of the experiences and behaviors underlying these feelings." For instance, anger, depression, and anxiety are common to all people, regardless of their unique experiences.

Advanced empathy "gets at not only what clients clearly state but also what they imply or leave only half-stated or half-expressed" (Egan 1982:89). This is exactly what Reich (1956) means by "listening with the third ear." However, it is used differently in an initial interview and in a counseling setting. In the interview the primary task is to assess the client, and the secondary task is to prepare the groundwork for future counseling sessions. You are listening to what clients are implying or leaving half-expressed to gain the best initial understanding you can of where they are. The initial interview is simply too soon to challenge clients about what you think they are implying or half expressing. Trust is not yet established, you have very limited knowledge of clients, and it would be easy to make a major mistake in your judgments and interpretations. Even if you are right, clients may not be ready to verify your insight and may deny it. Once a client has denied some facet of the deeply private self, it becomes more difficult for him or her to admit it later. It is frightening to be forced to confront a negative feature of the self that has formerly been repressed. Do not risk erroneous assumptions or provoking the client's denial by premature attempts at advanced empathy.

Empathy, then, is a series of responses rendered by the counselor with a developed sensitivity to the client's unique set of feelings about the world and his or her place in it. You are, in effect, thinking *with* your clients rather than *about* them.

Examples of Empathetic Responses A counselor's responses are never neutral; they are either constructive or destructive. This is particularly important for criminal justice clients because they are stuck with you, for better or worse, during their correctional supervision. Constructive responses involve clients in self-exploration so that they may find solutions to their troubles themselves. Fully involving clients means accepting the reality of their problems and reflecting them back. For example, suppose that Tony tells you that he finds his job as an assembler in a factory boring, unsatisfying, and unsuitable for his talents and ambitions. He wants to quit. You want him to keep his job, knowing that jobs are hard to find, that he has financial obligations, and that "the devil finds work for idle hands." You say: "Tony, you feel that your job makes you feel depressed and less than worthy and productive. I can understand that because I've had jobs that made me feel that way too. What is it in particular about your job that makes you feel depressed, Tony?"

What have you accomplished in these three sentences? First, you have recognized the reality of Tony's problem and the fact that it is a genuine concern for him. Second, you have reflected his feelings about the problem, thereby making him aware that you have understood him correctly. Third, you have shown empathy by self-disclosure of your similar experiences. This reinforces Tony's perception that you recognize that his problem is real and gives him a feeling of commonality with you. It will also make him more receptive to any plan of action you decide on together, since you have modeled the plan in your own life experience. Fourth, you have probed further by using an open-ended question to get Tony to identify specific conditions, circumstances, or situations that arouse his negative feelings. Your response has generated a positive atmosphere that will facilitate further exploration, leading, you hope, to an acceptable plan for dealing with the problem. In short, you have made excellent use of accurate primary empathy.

Contrast the positive response to Tony's concern with this: "Tony, you're always complaining about something. This business about your job is all in your head, it does you no good to dwell on it. How can you expect a better job with your education? Besides, you can't quit without my permission, so relax and forget it, buddy."

What have you accomplished here? First, by responding from your frame of reference rather than Tony's, you have denied the reality of the problem and of his feelings about it. Second, you have denigrated him by calling him a complainer and belittling his education. Third, you have distanced yourself from him by (1) showing a lack of concern and understanding, (2) emphasizing differences in educational levels, and (3) emphasizing your authority over him. Furthermore, by telling him to "relax and forget it" you have guaranteed that he won't. Instead, you will have exacerbated his negative feelings and left him to deal with them in a possibly destructive way. You can bet he will not come to you again with his concerns. In short, Tony will be influenced by the second response just as he would by the first. The second response, however, generates feelings in Tony that will destroy his relationship with you. Your lack of professional concern will make your job more difficult and may well lead Tony to quit his job despite your warning that he cannot. This, in turn, may lead to a technical violation or further criminality.

Suppose Tony responds to your primary empathy this way: Sitting with his folded hands resting on his thighs and looking at you (a nondefensive, open, and trusting demeanor), he says: "Well, Joyce, I didn't mind the job so much when I was on days. It's this night shift stuff."

He straightens up, looks away, and raises his voice slightly (some defensiveness, embarrassment, and anger creeping in) "My wife complains that I don't spend enough time with her. We used to go out dancing once or twice a week, but now I can't because I'm working, or I'm too damn tired on the weekend."

He sits up straight and grasps the arms of his chair. His face reddens a little, and his speech becomes faster and louder (a strengthening of his defensiveness, embarrassment, and anger): "She goes by herself, though. I don't like that, and I tell her so. We've had quite a few arguments about that crap."

You now realize that Tony's job is not the real cause of his depression. His more substantial concern is his wife's dissatisfaction, and his statement contains some significant intimations that he is concerned about the possibility that she may be doing more than just dancing with other men. You might try the following dialogue with Tony:

> **COUNSELOR:** Are you saying that it's not the job itself that you want to quit, but you'd like to get off the night shift? (clarification)

TONY: Yes, I think things might be better if I went back on days.

COUNSELOR: The night shift leaves you without much time or energy to devote to your wife, and this is causing some friction between you. (paraphrase) You are angry and upset because she goes to the dance by herself. (reflection)

TONY: You bet I am! I've told her that it's not right for a married woman to go dancing by herself.

COUNSELOR: Tony, I can understand your annoyance with your wife, and I know that the two of you have talked about it. Why do you think she continues to go when you have told her that you dislike it? (probe)

TONY: I don't know. We get so mad at each other when we talk about it that I think she does it out of spite. [Angry arguments do have a way of leading one of the participants to act in uncharacteristic ways in order to "get back."]

COUNSELOR: What do you think she would do if you let her know your feelings without getting upset? (open-ended question designed to get Tony to think about his wife's possible reaction to a rational discussion of the problem rather than an emotional confrontation)

TONY: I don't really know. We don't argue that much about other things. I don't mind her having some fun, but dancing? My wife's an attractive woman—I see the way men look at her. (Tony's reply indicates that, except for this one issue, quarreling is not a major feature of his marriage. He quickly disposes of your question and gets down to his real concern.)

COUNSELOR: You like your wife to enjoy herself, but you find it unsettling for her to do it in this way because she's in the company of other men. (paraphrasing and reflecting) Am I hearing you say that you're concerned that one of her dance partners might make a play for her? I wonder if she realizes that she's hurting you this way. (clarifying your perception of Tony's underlying feeling and using advanced empathy)

TONY: I guess I am kind of jealous. I really love Carla, and it eats me up inside to think she might be playing around behind my back. I haven't admitted this to myself before today. I suppose I didn't want to think about it. What do you think I should do, Joyce? You've made me realize that I don't really want to quit my job—it pays good money and I have my restitution and fine to finish paying—but I don't want to lose Carla. (Tony is now asking for your advice, which up until now you have resisted giving. He will be more receptive now that he has explored the problem himself and has explicitly requested advice. You have also led him to identify for himself what he was feeling—jealousy. This is much better than simply coming out and asking him, "Do you feel jealous?" He might well have denied the embarrassing feeling if you rather than he had approached the issue directly.)

COUNSELOR: I don't think it's a question of either quitting your job or losing Carla. I might suggest two courses of action for you to think about. First, you could speak with your boss to see if there is any possibility at all of getting back on days, even if it means a different job. Regardless of whether or not this is possible, you could discuss your feelings openly with Carla as you have done with me. Do this without any hint of accusation or anger, and she'll be more likely to respond the same way. Since you seem to enjoy dancing yourself, try to arrange it that the two of you can go together at least once a week. What do you think about these suggestions, Tony?

This exchange illustrates both primary and advanced empathy. You went beyond the initial problem that Tony presented to you and probed for a deeper concern. You skillfully led him to explore feelings that he was reluctant to admit to himself, and you offered him, at his request, some helpful suggestions for dealing

ing with them. It took a great deal more time than it would have taken to tell him to stop complaining, but you may have gone a long way in helping Tony to save his job and his marriage. And you have probably actually saved yourself time and trouble in the long run.

What Accurate Empathy Is Not Now that you have a good idea what accurate empathy is, you must understand what it is not. Empathy does not mean that you condone wrong behavior. If Tony were to tell you, for example, that he goes out and gets drunk because he cannot stand Carla's imagined infidelities, nagging, and denigration of him and asks you what you would do in a similar situation, he has put you in a spot. He is asking for your sympathy, understanding, and self-disclosure. It is a poor kind of empathy to say, "I guess I'd do the same thing," even if you might. That reply would imply that you are condoning his behavior.

But if you reply that you certainly would not do so, Tony will perceive you as critical and judgmental. It would be better for you to say, "I'm sure that your wife's behavior makes you feel terrible. I'm not sure what I would do myself. I think I might seek marital counseling. Do you think that's a possibility for you?" This reply relieves you of the appearance of condoning the client's behavior while at the same time recognizing his feelings and offering a constructive alternative.

Lessons and Concerns

The primary reason for including the client-centered approach in this discussion is its emphasis on the client/counselor relationship. We all attend more to the concerns of those whose good graces we value than of those whose judgments do not concern us. Objective understanding and special techniques are not necessary to bring about change in the kind of relationship Rogers emphasizes.

Although client-centered counseling can be fruitful in some counseling settings, is it fully practical in the criminal justice setting? Unconditional positive regard, genuineness, and empathy as described here are the qualities we manifest only in a truly intimate love relationship with people who are truly special to us. If we are not "in love" with our clients, is there not a major conflict between being genuine and expressing to clients that we accept them unconditionally? Isn't there also a real danger that we will avoid necessary confrontation with a client in order not to upset the close relationship deemed to be so important? Do we not need to set conditions on our acceptance?

As a criminal justice counselor, you must allow positive regard for your clients to be conditional. This does not mean that you refuse to accept their basic humanity or that you pass unnecessary judgment on their past behavior. What it does mean is that you place unambiguous conditions on their future behavior, confront them without fear, and let them suffer the consequences when they fail to meet the conditions. Empathy, too, must be guided in responsible directions.

Nevertheless, establishing a positive working relationship with clients is important. Unconditional positive regard, genuineness, and empathy are, please recall, continuous variables that you present to your clients in varying degrees. The degree to which you do present them depends on the quality of your self-concept in interaction with the self-concepts of your clients. It is true that you cannot always be your "genuine self," but you should not suffer a sense of personal failure if you feel a lack of acceptance of the client or an inability to empathize fully with his or her view of the world.

A final point about the powerful influence of establishing positive relationships with clients comes not from criminal justice or counseling research but from medical research. Dr. William Knaus and his colleagues at the George Washington University School of Medicine set out to discover what variable is most important to survival of patients in intensive care units (ICUs). Using advanced statistical techniques, they looked at such variables as technological sophistication, professional expertise of physicians and nurses, prestige of hospital, research funding, and patient/caregiver ratio. Their examination of 5,030 ICU patients in hospitals across the United States over a period of five years found that none of these variables was the crucial one. The crucial variable was the quality of the relationships between doctors and nurses and between nurses and patients. The hospitals that allowed nurses to function semiautonomously and to interact with patients at an emotional level (what nurses call primary-level nursing) were the hospitals with the best ICU survival rates

Perspectives from the Field

Getting Back in the Race

Lindsey Whitehead

Lindsey Whitehead is the chief probation officer of the Lucas County Adult Probation Department, Toledo, Ohio. He was a probation officer and unit supervisor for seven years before becoming chief. He holds master's degrees in guidance and counseling and public administration. He is also a Certified Alcoholism Counselor (CAC).

A few days ago as I was returning from lunch, I saw a young man who looked vaguely familiar to me leaving the probation department. As he approached me, he smiled and asked, "How are you, Mr. Whitehead? You don't remember me, do you?" I wasn't very sure of what the relationship between us had been, but after talking with him for a few moments the memory was clear.

The last time I had seen him was in 1978 when I was his probation officer. He was eighteen or nineteen years old at the time and was on probation for his first felony conviction as an adult. He had been convicted of robbing a carry-out store. This young man's social history was very typical of those who find themselves in trouble with the criminal justice system: He was from a broken home, lived in poverty, was inadequately educated, was unemployed, and his spirit had been demoralized.

During the time that he was on probation he obtained his GED and enrolled in a vocational school to learn welding. Upon completion of training he was immediately hired as a welder by a local company.

"But why is he here at the probation department?" I wondered. "Is he in trouble again?" He explained apologetically that he had been caught with some cocaine and was now serving another term of probation. He further explained that this was the first time that he had been in trouble with the law for nine years and that he was still working as a welder with the same company and trying to be productive.

A few years ago, a young mother of beautiful twin girls was placed on probation for forgery. She had little motivation to do anything to try to improve her pathetic situation. But through the persuasion and leverage of the probation department and the court, she enrolled in the department's GED program. At first she didn't like it, but in time she became enthusiastic and was a willing participant. At the graduation ceremony, as her daughters looked on, she was extremely proud as she walked across the stage to be recognized for having completed her GED. She had come to realize that her efforts could result in positive changes in her life and that, at the very least, her probation officer considered her worthwhile and cared for her.

There is nothing unique or unusual about these two cases. Similar experiences are repeated daily in probation and parole departments throughout the country. Pencil and paper can no doubt demonstrate a lack of success in the community corrections function, and perhaps this is so. But those of us who are in the trenches often have the opportunity to see the human spirit triumphant over what could have been lost lives. A probation or parole officer cannot run the race for those who have dropped out or for those who never got into the race in the first place. But it is encouraging, if only occasionally, to see people pick themselves up and get into the race of life through the help of caring and professional probation and parole services.

(Holzman 1986:56). The researchers expressed their surprise at this finding; Carl Rogers would have responded with a knowing smile.

Summary

Psychotherapy differs from counseling primarily in the depth and intensity of treatment. Psychotherapists attempt to restructure the basic personalities of patients who have intrapersonal conflicts; counselors deal with interpersonal conflicts and problems of everyday living. Be alert to those clients whose problems go beyond your professional ability.

In essence, counseling is an extension of the interviewing process, but there are differences as well as similarities between interviewing and counseling. Many of the techniques they use are the same. The quality of the counselor's self—your warmth, acceptance, and understanding—is the most important ingredient in both situations. Counseling requires communication with clients at a deeper level about more specific issues. You will accomplish this more easily if you have developed a positive relationship with them during the initial interviews.

Freudian psychoanalysis offers profound insights into human nature. It emphasizes the importance of the psychosexual stages of development, especially the importance of love at the earliest stages. The identification of defense mechanisms is useful in criminal justice, particularly denial, rationalization, fixation, displacement, intellectualization, and projection. You will never use the techniques of psychoanalysis in your dealings with clients in the same way that you will use the techniques derived from other theories. Its usefulness to you as a criminal justice worker lies in its illumination of human nature.

Client-centered therapy shares with psychoanalysis its passive and nondirective approach. This theory asserts the absolute primacy of the client/counselor relationship. Client-centered counseling rests on three attributes that the counselor must offer to clients: unconditional positive regard, genuineness, and empathy. Since many psychological problems are the result of conditions that others attach to their acceptance of a person's self-worth, it is vital that the counselor accept clients unconditionally as individuals of worth.

The counselor must also be genuine; pretensions, dishonesty, and game playing must be avoided at all costs. Because the counselor's authenticity will provide a model for the client, the counselor should always strive to improve his or her own authenticity.

The final necessary attribute is empathy. It is difficult to achieve because it implies the ability to participate actively in the mind-set of another; to actually walk in that person's shoes. Primary empathy is the communication to the client of an initial basic understanding of what he or she is saying. Advanced empathy implies a deeper understanding, a reading between the lines. Empathy is something that is developed only by experience, by learning all you can about human behavior, and by really caring about what the client is trying to communicate.

References and Suggested Readings

Bateson, G., D. Jackson, J. Haley, and J. Weakland. 1956. Toward a theory of schizophrenia. *Behavioral Science* 1:251-264.

Egan, G. 1982. *The skilled helper*. Monterey, Cal.: Brooks/Cole.

Evans, D., M. Hearn, M. Uhlemann, and A. Ivey. 1989. *Essential interviewing: A programmed approach to effective communication*. Pacific Grove, Cal.: Brooks/Cole.

Fine, R. 1973. Psychoanalysis. In *Current psychotherapies*, edited by R. Corsini. Itasca, Ill.: Peacock.

Freud, S. 1961. *Civilization and its discontents*. New York: Norton.

Freud, S. 1965. *The new introductory lectures on psychoanalysis*. New York: Norton.

Gendreau, P., and R. Ross. 1981. Offender rehabilitation: The appeal of success. *Federal Probation* 45:45-48.

Gendreau, P., and R. Ross. 1987. Revivification of rehabilitation: Evidence from the 1980s. *Justice Quarterly* 4:349-407.

Holzman, D. 1986. Intensive care nurses: A vital sign. *Insight* 56 (December).

Perspectives from the Field

Love Is Not a One-Way Street

A Probation and Parole Counselor

This job involves working with people with low IQs, low educational backgrounds, poor work records, and low incomes. The people I work with are very manipulative. I have to be direct, quick to assess what I think they should do, and not hesitate to tell them to do it. If you are planning to do correctional work, you should be aware that this job involves many failures and that you can't help everyone. Sometimes when you can't help them adjust to the community, then the best help you can give them is to keep them out of the community—by holding them in jail.

Most of the people that I work with have no great desire to see me. They feel that probation is not an opportunity. It is just an obligation they must complete for the court or the parole board. Many of them do not trust me and never will. And I must say that many of them I cannot trust either. A lot of my job involves verifying, through other sources, what my probationers and parolees have told me. I have found that the best way to develop rapport in dealing with these people is to be stern, not let them manipulate you, and above all be fair.

Did my counselor education program prepare me for working in the field of corrections? Sure, it did. It helped me to communicate with the people I deal with by being concrete and truthful in what I say to them and by making me a more active listener. It helped me to know how to show my feelings and concerns in dealing with people. It also helped me to know how to write concise, meaningful reports and understand the results of tests I must verify. It did not prepare me for the people I work with. Being warm, accepting, and trusting won't work with people who haven't learned self-acceptance and a sense of social responsibility. You've got to start them at another level and try to work them up to the other ones. Love is a two-way street, and if you don't believe it, you'll break your neck and maybe your heart too.

I don't get much sleep, but I sleep sound. Counselors, no matter where they work, are responsible to lots of people, not just their counselees. We're responsible to our profession, to ourselves, and to our society. So I'd stack my kind of counseling against all the rest when it comes to measuring up to responsibility. Sure, my kind of counseling may lose a few counselees along the way, but just count up how many others we saved.

Reprinted with permission from C. Gressard and K. Hume, "Special Populations," in Being a Counselor, *edited by J. Brown and R. Pate, Jr. (Monterey, Cal.: Brooks/Cole, 1983).*

Lewis, W. 1989. *Helping the youthful offender: Individual and group therapies that work.* New York: Haworth.

Lytle, M. 1964. The unpromising client. *Crime and Delinquency* 10:130-134.

Martinson, R. 1974. What works? Questions and answers about prison reform. *The Public Interest* 35:22-54.

Mayeroff, M. 1971. *On caring.* New York: Harper & Row.

Meier, S. 1989. *The elements of counseling.* Pacific Grove, Cal.: Brooks/Cole.

Reich, T. 1956. *Listening with the third ear.* New York: Grove.

Rogers, C. 1952. Client-centered psychotherapy. *Scientific American* 187:66-74.

Rogers, C. 1961. *On becoming a person.* Boston: Houghton Mifflin.

Stratton, J. 1975. Correctional workers: Counseling con men. In *Correctional casework and counseling,* edited by E. Peoples. Pacific Palisades, Cal.: Goodyear.

Walker, S. 1985. *Sense and nonsense about crime: A policy guide.* Monterey, Cal.: Brooks/Cole.

Walsh, A. 1986. Love and human authenticity in the works of Freud, Marx, and Maslow. *Free Inquiry in Creative Sociology* 14:21-26.

Wrong, D. 1968. The oversocialized conception of man in modern sociology. In *The sociological perspective,* edited by S. McNall. Boston: Little, Brown.

Chapter 9

Directive Counseling: Theory and Practice

To love and to be loved is as necessary as the breathing of air. Insofar as we fail in loving we fail in living. The most important thing to realize about the nature of human nature is that the most significant ingredient in its structure is love.

Ashley Montagu

The theories we examined in the last chapter are passive and nondirective; the counselor who relies on them helps clients to give birth to their own solutions for what ails them. The theories presented in this chapter are active, directive, and didactic, with the counselor as involved as the client. These theories—transactional analysis, rational-emotive therapy, and reality therapy—were all formulated by psychotherapists who had become dissatisfied with the passive methods of traditional psychoanalysis and the extraordinary length of time it requires. All three theories were designed to identify and deal with problem areas quickly and take a cognitive rather than an emotional approach. The creators of the theories realized that most clients, especially criminal justice clients, need active assistance as they work to become rational, responsible, whole individuals.

Transactional Analysis

Transactional analysis (TA) is the brainchild of Eric Berne, a psychiatrist best known for his book *Games People Play* (1964). TA stresses the cognitive and behavioral aspects of personality rather than the emotional. If a person gains emotional insight from TA it is by gaining intellectual insight or changing behavior patterns. Any insight or change is achieved by examining the transactions the client has with others. A transaction occurs when two or more people interact together; the analysis is the process of exploring and explaining those transactions. TA shares with psychoanalysis the assumption that human behavior is profoundly influenced by the events of early childhood, particularly events that tell the child that he or she is loved or unloved.

Berne (1966:214) considered the greatest strength of TA to be its use of colloquial, simple, and direct terms easily understood by all: "Transactional Analysis, because of its clear-cut statements rooted in easily accessible material, because of its operational nature, and because of its specialized vocabulary (consisting of only five words: Parent, Adult, Child, Game, and Script), offers an easily learned framework for clarification." TA clients soon acquire a simple vocabulary to use with the counselor to identify problem transactions.

Scripts

Scripts are "memory tapes" that we all carry around with us. The most important scripts are recorded in early childhood because children tend to accept messages unquestioningly (lacking the maturity to do otherwise). The messages communicated by our parents during this critical period contribute strongly to our later evaluations of ourselves as worthy ("okay") or unworthy ("not okay"). By the time we are mature enough to question messages, verbal and nonverbal, about our Okayness, the questioning is influenced strongly by the powerful scripting we received in our most impressionable years. If the preponderance of messages told us that we were loved, respected, and appreciated, we will see ourselves as okay. If not, we will see ourselves as not okay. Because of the deeply etched early recordings, these evaluations of okayness tend to persist throughout our lives regardless of the messages we later receive.

Related to these early recordings is the intense human need for what Berne calls "strokes." People hunger to be touched both physically and emotionally. If they do not receive these strokes—remember the discussion of love deprivation in Chapter 3?—they will not become psychologically healthy human beings. Much of our time, Berne says, is structured around the pursuit of positive strokes (seeking assurances that we are loved). Positive strokes lead to positive scripting tapes, negative strokes to negative tapes. TA theorists believe that to change negative scripts to positive clients need direction from a strong "parent" figure, in the form of a counselor.

Four basic life positions issue from our scripting and act as backdrops in our interactions with others throughout our lives.

1. "I'm not okay; you're okay." This position is common in children. When they are punished they often feel "not okay." But their godlike parents, upon whom they depend, are naturally okay in their little minds. You will find this life position in many of your clients, especially substance abusers. They are often depressed and will have what Glasser calls in reality therapy a failure identity. At least a client with this life position will consider you okay, so you can concentrate on building up his or her own okayness.
2. "I'm not okay; you're not okay." This is the scripted life position of abused children who are led to question the okayness of their parents rather early in life. A person like this views the world as hostile and futile, for the person is unloved and unloving. Such a person may withdraw into the fantasy world of schizophrenia. (See the case history of Greg in Chapter 15).
3. "I'm okay; you're not okay." This, too, is the position of abused children who have questioned the okayness of their parents. However, they have somehow come to view themselves as okay from their own circumscribed perspective of okayness. Loners, they tend to project blame for all their problems onto others. The psychopath operates from this life position in its extreme.
4. "I'm okay; you're okay." This is the life position from which correctional workers must operate. To do your job adequately you must be convinced of your okayness; to do it well you must strive to generate your clients' okayness. The goal of transactional analysis is a relationship between

counselor and client with mutual convictions of "I'm okay; you're okay." That is, clients must get rid of the negative scripts left over from childhood and their own power and okayness.

Games

TA views games as exchanges of strokes that are unauthentic because they have ulterior motives. Games happen when individuals interact with one another from one of the first three life positions. The payoff from playing a game in which the player's time is structured around getting strokes (or giving them to those in positions of authority) is a storehouse of bad feelings that serve only to reinforce negative life scripts. Only from an authentic "I'm okay; you're okay" position can individuals engage in meaningful, game-free interpersonal relationships.

Games are very much a part of criminal justice supervision and counseling. You must learn to identify them quickly and expose them, for they are dishonest and destructive. You might even find yourself playing games with your clients. We have already mentioned one that law enforcement officers might play in interrogation: "Now I've got you, you son-of-a-bitch" when they are using clients for power strokes. Another common one is "I'm only trying to help you," used by gentler souls seeking acceptance strokes. Both of these games, of course, issue from an "I'm okay; you're not okay" position.

Offenders are good at playing games—they have had lots of practice. You will quickly find out that they are much better at it than you are (a compliment to you). A real value of TA is the ability it gives the correctional worker to expose them. Games you will run into often are "Poor me" (scratching for sympathy and "understanding"), "If it wasn't for ..." (ditto), and "Ain't it/I awful?" (false remorse). Corrections workers who are acceptance seekers or ineffectual will easily fall for KIUD ("Keep it up, doc"). Acceptance seekers are suckers for clients who continue to behave irresponsibly while telling them they are doing a great job. The payoff for KIUD clients is that their counselors will probably let them get away with considerable misbehavior.

Yet another game, common in prison settings, is HDIGO ("How do I get out of here?"). Clients soon learn to tell counselors just what they think the counselor wants to hear. They learn the latest social science explanation for their behavior and spew it back while shaking with "self-understanding" and "remorse." Of course, self-understanding and remorse are part of your goals for each client, but all counselors must learn to distinguish the real goods from self-serving manipulation of the counseling setting. It is easy, and very human, to accept the game as the real thing because it verifies your effectiveness as a counselor. Do not fudge the data for easy self-strokes. If you accept the game as the real thing, the client will have won the battle but will lose the war against his or her criminality.

Parent, Adult, Child

Parent (P), Adult (A), and Child (C), or PAC, are all ego states: three distinct systems of feelings and thinking related to behavior patterns. Each ego state perceives reality differently: the parent judgmentally, the adult comprehensively, and the child prerationally. We all slip in and out of these states in our various transactions, with one usually dominating the others.

The Parent is critical, controlling, and moralizing, just like Freud's superego, but the Parent has a good side. The good Parent is the Nurturing Parent, who reacts to others with care, dignity, and respect and makes demands that are not overbearing. This is the kind of parental figure that the TA counselor should be. The Critical or Examining Parent is domineering, self-righteous, and authoritarian. The person who always operates in the parental mode (the Constant Parent) excludes the reality of the adult mode and the playfulness of the child. Freud would call the Constant Parent neurotic. You will rarely find the Constant Parent among your clients. If you do, they will almost inevitably be sex offenders against children.

The Adult is logical, realistic, and objective and much better able to judge when it is appropriate to allow the less characteristic ego states expression than is either the Parent or the Child because of a comprehensive and realistic integration of past experiences. Like the Parent, though, the Constant Adult will enjoy little feeling or spontaneity. You will not, almost by definition, find the Adult among criminal justice clients. You will, I trust, find many among your colleagues.

The Child is spontaneous, fun-loving, and irresponsible. Many of your clients will be of this type. The Adapted Child, one who enjoys appropriate fun and laughter, is okay. The problem is the Constant Child, one who consistently refuses to grow up and behave responsibly. The exclusion of the restraining influences of the Parent and the Adult means the exclusion of conscience—the total absence of which is psychopathy.

One or another of these ego states predominates in each individual. Berne (1966) has denied the apparent equivalence of the ego states to the Freudian id (Child), ego (Adult) and superego (Parent); he considers them all to be aspects of the Freudian ego only. Further, Berne states that whereas the id, ego, and superego are "theoretical constructs" (inferred entities not amenable to observation), his ego states are "phenomenological realities" (amenable to direct observation). Let us see how we can make these direct observations.

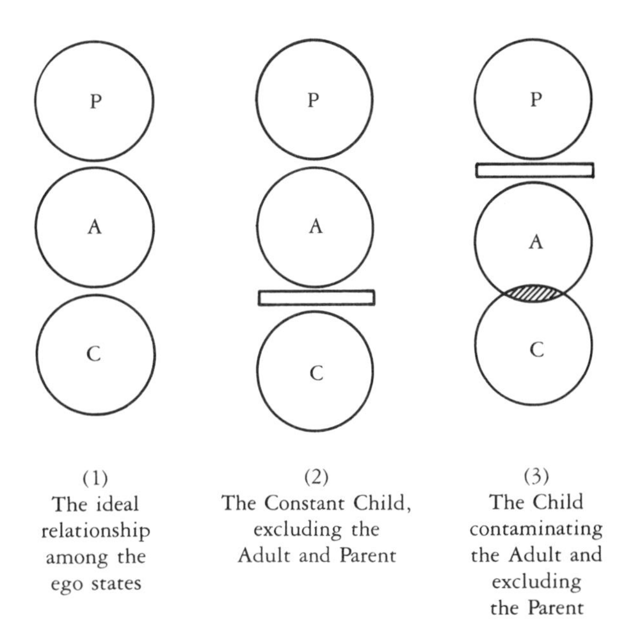

Figure 9-1 Ego states

Structural Analysis

The process of making these observations is known as structural analysis. TA seeks as a goal that every client become an expert in analyzing his or her own transactions, and structural analysis is a tool clients use to learn the content and functioning of their ego states. If clients can identify their characteristic ego states, they can better understand their options for change.

Ideally, the Parent, Adult, and Child should be distinct states with clear-cut boundaries, as they are in part 1 of Figure 9-1. Like the Freudian ego, the Adult holds the executive position but admits the Parent and Child when appropriate. Two problems arise in personality structure as viewed in structural analysis: exclusion and contamination.

Exclusion (Figure 9-1, part 2) occurs when ego-state boundaries are so rigid that free movement across them does not occur at appropriate times. The fundamentalist puritan who views all sensuous enjoyment as sin or who lives a life bound by unexamined strictures is an example of the Constant Parent who excludes the Child and the Adult. But criminal justice workers have little need to worry about puritans. We do have to worry about the Child who excludes the Adult and Parent, the complete opposite of the Constant Parent, doing everything that the Constant Parent would not and nothing that the Constant Parent does do.

Contamination (Figure 9-1, part 3) occurs when the content of one ego state gets mixed up with the content of another. We think of contamination in terms of the intrusion of either or both of the Parent or Child states into the rational boundaries defining the Adult state. Contamination of the Adult by the Parent often involves assumptions left over from our early scripting that distort objective thinking. In Chapter 5 I related how my prejudices about proper behavior for women intruded into my Adult when I interviewed the woman charged with sex crimes against children and ruined the client/counselor relationship. Bill Bloggs's Adult was certainly contaminated by his Child. He wanted success, Susan, a grandiose wedding, and lots of money, which are not wrong in themselves. But Bill wanted it all right now.

Complementary and Crossed Transactions

Transactions can be either complementary or crossed; the ideal transaction is complementary. A complementary transaction occurs when a verbal or nonverbal message (the stimulus) sent from a specific ego state is reacted to (the response) from the appropriate, or complementary, ego state of the receiver. In TA communication, complementary transactions occur when stimulus and response lines on a PAC diagram are parallel.

The lines representing a crossed transaction in a PAC diagram are not parallel. Crossed transactions occur when a stimulus sent from one ego state meets a response from an ego state other than the expected one. Though crossed transactions usually cause trouble in our interpersonal relationships, they can be beneficial if the unexpected response leads the sender to adjust to a more appropriate ego state. Figure 9-2 illustrates some complementary and crossed transactions.

In part 1 we have Parent-Parent communication. This might be two new probation officers discussing the "ignorance" and "immorality" of "welfare mothers cheating on the system." The Adult may never enter into their conversation to explore the whys of the behavior. If one officer suddenly shifts into the Adult mode (indicated by the dotted line), the conversation may not be as congenial as when they were transacting at the same level, but the shift may bring the conversation to a more appropriate Adult-Adult state, at which point the ego states are again complementary. Do not engage in complementary transactions for the sake of congeniality when you know that another ego state is more appropriate. As Rogers would say, "Be genuine, be yourself."

Part 2 represents Adult-Adult communication, perhaps between prison counselor and offender discussing a problem of the client from a mutual "I'm okay; you're okay" position. The counselor does not contaminate the Adult by talking down to the inmate from the Parent ego state or make light of the problem by joking about it from the Child ego state. These possible crossed transactions are illustrated by the dotted lines.

Part 3 illustrates a Child-Child transaction, perhaps you and your colleagues planning a Christmas party. Obviously, you should never interact with your clients at this level—unless the occasion is innocuous, like sharing a joke. A crossed transaction in this context could be something like refusing to take part in the

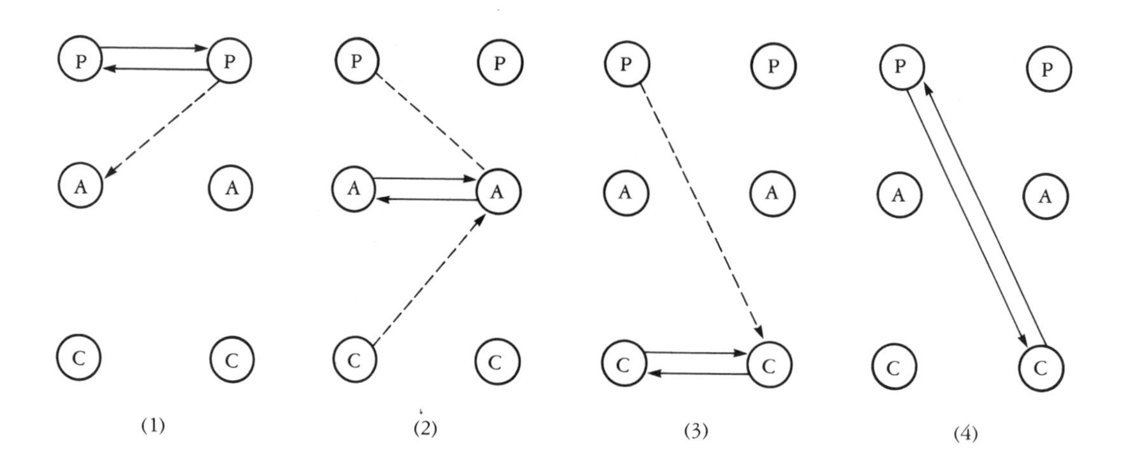

Figure 9-2 Complementary and crossed transactions

office festivities because they are "frivolous," or responding to the client's well-meaning attempt at levity with a cold stare. These responses would both reflect a Critical Parent ego state intruding into an appropriate Child-Child transaction.

Part 4 illustrates a complementary transaction even though the parties are interacting from different ego states (the lines are still parallel). An example would be a parole officer chastising a client about irresponsible behavior. The officer confronts the client from a parental ego state, and the client responds as a child might when caught with a hand in the cookie jar: "You're always picking on me." This transaction is complementary because a Parent-Child stimulus has evoked a Child-Parent response. Had the officer confronted the client from the Adult ego state, asking for an explanation of the behavior, and had the offender responded from the Child state, the transaction would have been crossed.

Remember, any crossed transaction can lead to difficulties in interpersonal relations unless the crossover is designed to shift the transaction to a more appropriate level. In general, crossed transactions usually follow when one party or the other operates from one of the first three life positions, which include various combinations of "not okay" attributions.

Lessons and Concerns

The beauty of transactional analysis is the way it simply illustrates the consequences of feelings one has about the self or about others in everyday transactions. Berne's genius was his ability to transform complex ideas into colloquial language and easy-to-follow diagrams. These ideas can be relayed with relative ease to clients so that they may analyze their own feelings and behaviors. The emphasis on manipulation and game playing is especially useful for criminal justice workers. Finally, TA describes in a neat, linear fashion how early deprivation of love leads to poor self-concept, how poor self-concept can lead to a negative image of others, and how negative feelings lead to poor interpersonal relationships.

On the other hand, TA may have all the vices of its virtues. There is a danger that an inexperienced counselor may see counseling simply as an intellectual exercise in identifying life positions and doing structural analyses. The very simplicity of the theory invites this kind of truncated counseling. It is too easy to hide beneath covers stitched from nifty diagrams and cliche phrases such as "strokes" and "games." You must involve your clients' emotions and feelings in the counseling process as well as their heads.

This is one reason for an eclectic approach to counseling. All these theories have something to offer, but although some offer more than others, none offers everything. Used in conjunction with client-centered therapy's emphasis on the nature of the client/counselor relationship, TA can be a powerful counseling tool.

Rational-emotive Therapy

Rational-emotive therapy (RET), founded by Albert Ellis, takes issue with the assumptions and practices of both psychoanalysis and client-centered therapy. Psychoanalysis is concerned with the darkness of the unconscious mind and nonrational biological drives; client-centered therapy zeroes in on the emotional rapport of the client/counselor relationship. RET fully recognizes that we share biological drives and emotional states with other species, but considers them of minor importance compared with cognition, a unique quality of humankind. Problem behaviors arise from faulty thinking and irrational beliefs; they can be corrected once clients can acknowledge that their beliefs are at odds with logic.

It follows that the RET counselor takes an active role in the counseling process and considers the quality of the client/counselor relationship secondary to what takes place within that relationship. RET counseling is highly directive, didactic, challenging, and often confrontive and painful for the client. Before we get into the meat of RET counseling it is necessary to learn something of Ellis's ideas about human personality.

The A-B-C Theory of Personality

RET counseling revolves around Ellis's A-B-C theory of personality: A is the experience of an objective fact, a so-called "Activating event," B is the subjective interpretation of or Belief about that fact, and C is the Consequence, the emotional content accompanying the meaning (B) that the experience of the fact (A) has for the individual. Most people view an activating event as causing the emotions they're experiencing ("I'm happy/sad/depressed/suicidal because she asked me for a divorce") in the following way:

Activating Event A ⟶ C Consequence
A leads directly to C

Ellis says no, there is always an interpretive process that goes between A and C that really determines the consequences:

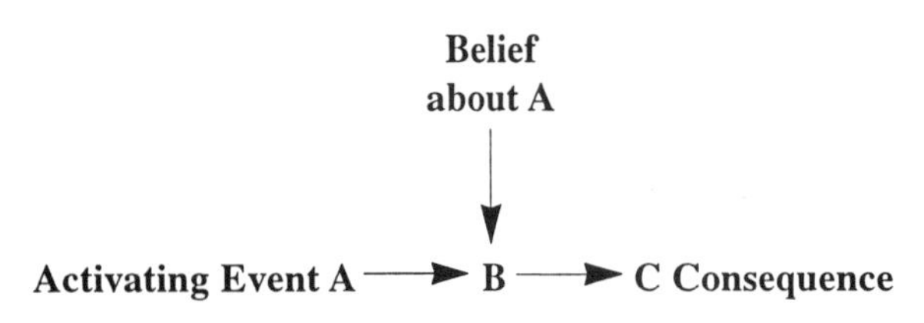

A leads to B, which leads to C

The important point for the RET counselor is that A is not the direct cause of C, but that B, the individual's belief about A, causes C. If A caused C, then everyone experiencing the same A would experience the same C, which is obviously not the case. The reason everyone experiencing the same activating event does not experience the same emotional consequence is that the intervening belief about A differs from person to person. As Shakespeare said in *Hamlet*: "Nothing is good or bad, but thinking makes it so."

According to RET theory, problems of living result from illogical and negative thinking about experiences (the interpretive processes) that the client reiterates in a self-defeating monologue. The client is reluctant to let go of irrational beliefs because they serve to protect a fragile ego. ("She's to blame for my depression because she's the one who asked for the divorce.") This process resembles the Freudian defense mechanism of rationalization—a mechanism that serves the self-consistency motive. It is the counselor's task to attack such self-damaging mechanisms directly and challenge the client to reinterpret experience in a growth-enhancing fashion. Empathizing with the client's definition of reality in the Rogerian manner only serves to reinforce faulty thinking and is counterproductive. Passive listening to a client's monologue, as in psychoanalysis and client-centered counseling, is replaced by an active dialogue between counselor and client. Counseling is not a warm relationship of relating partners; it is more like a teacher/student relationship, complete with lectures and homework assignments.

The RET counselor operates from the assumption that even when clients come to understand the origins of their behavior they often cannot make the vital link between those origins and current behavioral problems. RET counselors will rapidly cut short any client attempt to "explain" behavior by asking, "But what are you doing to correct it?" RET counselors quickly cut through the quagmire of reasons, causes, explanations, and rationalizations to nail clients down to one or two basic ideas that are the "real" reason for their disturbed behavior. Once those ideas are identified, the RET counselor challenges the client to validate them. When the client cannot, the counselor points out the lack of a reality basis for them.

This business of tearing into a client's irrational ideas should obviously not be done dogmatically or condescendingly—"God, what a damn stupid idea! How can you be so dumb?" It must be accomplished in a way that does not move the client either to dig in defensively or to completely cut you off—"Alex, do you really believe what you're saying is true?" If the RET counselor needs backup, many will suggest bibliotherapy, the practice of having clients read books that the counselor knows will challenge their views (see Chapter 14 for the use of bibliotherapy with a sex offender). Some clients will also be asked to keep journals of their daily activities and thoughts. The whole idea is that when individuals have indoctrinated themselves with false and irrational ideas about themselves that lead to self-devaluation, the RET counselor must reindoctrinate them with more positive thoughts about themselves through reality-based logical thinking.

MUSTurbations

Ellis has identified eleven irrational ideas as pervasive in our society, highly irrational, and leading to "widespread neurosis." He calls these ideas *MUSTurbations* and says: "I now see that I have given up any addiction to MUSTurbation many years ago—to thinking that I must do well; that others must treat me considerately or fairly; and that the world must provide me with the things I want easily and quickly" (1982). Most of us are addicted to some degree to certain of these MUSTurbations. Examining them will help you to identify self-defeating "musts," "shoulds," and "oughts" in both your own thinking and that of your clients. Six of these ideas described in Ellis's delightful little book *A New Guide to Rational Living* (1975) are especially applicable to criminal justice clients (and sometimes criminal justice workers as well).

1. *It is essential that one be loved or approved by virtually everybody.* We would all like our desires for universal approval to be satisfied, but we do not really need them to be. You would hardly be human if you did not derive intense satisfaction from the positive judgments of others, but preoccupation with your own demands for love and approval prevents you from seeing the lovable traits in others; by not concentrating on your demands that you be loved, you free your psychic energies so that you are able to love. Furthermore, if you believe that you are not a worthy person unless you are universally liked, you guarantee that you will be insecure and self-disvalued because you are chasing an unattainable rainbow.
2. *One must be perfectly competent, adequate, and achieving to be considered worthwhile.* This is a trap into which the beginning criminal justice counselor often falls. A fair percentage of clients will reoffend no matter what the counselor does to rehabilitate them. If you regard that as a personal failure, you denigrate yourself and your clients' responsibility for their own lives. A perfectionist will never succeed in criminal justice work. As long as you have done your best, you are a worthwhile person. We must all develop the courage to be imperfect and not to experience failure as catastrophic.
3. *Unhappiness is caused by outside circumstances over which we have no control.* We allow ourselves to be emotionally upset about outside circumstances by our mental interpretations of them. True, some outside circumstances so powerfully assault our lives that it is unreasonable not to expect a negative emotional consequence, but other circumstances are only as defeating as we let them be. The rational person avoids exaggerating unpleasant circumstances and looks for the growth potential in them. Many criminal justice clients are overwhelmed by relatively innocuous unpleasant experiences and turn to chemical comforts like the bottle or pills.
4. *It is easier to avoid personal responsibilities than to face them.* You can hide from your responsibilities only for a short while. When your head does emerge from the sand, the responsibility is still there. It may well have grown. The rational person knows that it is less painful to attend to a responsibility than to deny or avoid it. The criminal justice client does not. These clients have mastered avoidance of personal responsibilities because they all too often lack the self-confidence to attend to them. It is the counselor's task to make the client see how nonattendance to responsibility snowballs.
5. *One must have someone stronger than oneself on whom to depend.* Many criminal justice clients are in a dependency mode. They lack the self-reliance to live a responsible, self-motivated life. Overdependence on others or on chemical substances places the individual at the mercy of life's crutches. The rational person, although occasionally dependent on others, minimizes other-dependence and takes charge of his or her own life.
6. *Past experience determines present behavior, and the influence of the past cannot be eradicated.* Although it is true that our values are largely programmed by our past experiences and

that it is difficult to overcome their influence, our behavior is not bounded by them. We can transcend our experiences by accepting and analyzing the effect they have on us and by refusing to be determined by them. Typically. criminal justice clients have not recognized their capacity for self-directed change and allow themselves to be blown hither and thither by environmental conditions, past and present. It is your job to encourage your clients to examine their past experiences, realize how they have influenced their negative attitudes and behavior, recognize that those past experiences are not excuses for present behavior and that they possess the human capacity to break the chains of experience, and move toward the goal of self-responsible behavior.

Lessons and Concerns

RET emphasizes that problems arise from the faulty operation of that which is unique to humankind: the capacity to think. Illogical thought processes are easier for the counselor to deal with than are emotions per se or the vagaries of biological drives. You must ask yourself, however, if emotional problems are so easily assuaged by pointing out that they are the result of faulty thinking. One philosophical wag has opined that the sole function of the neocortex (the thinking brain) is to rationalize the emotions and behaviors generated by the mammalian and paleo cortices (the emotional and instinctual centers of the brain). Freud himself was said to believe that his "talking cures" were effective only with educated, middle-class patients who had well-developed capacities for rational thought. This is not an apt description of the typical criminal justice client.

Are cognitions really more basic and potent than emotions, as Ellis seems to think? How often have you realized how utterly stupid it was to feel a certain way, wished very much that you did not, but continued to do so anyway? As Ellis himself often points out, we think and emote almost simultaneously; but do we feel bad because we think bad, or do we think bad because we feel bad? Certainly, we can change our thoughts whether they are preceded or followed by our emotions, but we need to address emotions as well. One way to do this is to acknowledge that the past is more important to the understanding of the present than RET admits. Obviously we cannot change the past, but it invariably insinuates itself into the present via our memory tapes. Unless we understand why this happens, confront it, and move on, we will continue to think irrationally.

Some may criticize RET for insisting that rationality and irrationality always be defined from a law-abiding middle-class point of view. The insights of anomie and differential association theories tell us that under certain condition crime is rational (a fit between a goal and the means by which it is sought). Nevertheless, as Ellis says, the counselor's values and attitudes are legitimate therapeutic tools. Many clients, though by no means all, can learn valuable self-insights from an active counselor, especially if the counselor also draws lessons from client-centered therapy and establishes a warm relationship before confronting the client. Finally, RET, with its teacher/student relationship, is more realistic and genuine than client-centered therapy in a criminal justice setting—provided that "teacher" is not confused with "preacher."

Reality Therapy

Reality therapy, founded by William Glasser, has become a favorite counseling approach among those who work in community and institutional corrections. In fact, Glasser developed the basic ideas of reality therapy in a correctional setting while he was a staff psychiatrist at the Ventura School for delinquent girls in California. Thus, unlike other counseling models, it is based on the realization that corrections workers have a professional responsibility to hold offenders accountable for their irresponsible behavior. Reality therapy also shares with TA the happy quality of being relatively easy to understand:

> The principles of reality therapy are common sense interwoven with a firm belief in the dignity of man [and woman] and his [and her] ability to improve his [or her] lot. Its value is twofold: it is a means by which people can help one another, and it is a treatment technique,

> applicable regardless of symptomatology. It is simple to learn albeit somewhat difficult for the novice to practice. Experience, not extensive theoretical grooming, is the key to accomplishment (Rachin 1974:52).

The reality therapy approach integrates the outstanding features from other approaches we have examined into a single theory that can be applied without modification to the criminal justice client. Like psychoanalysis, reality therapy recognizes that before people can function well they have basic needs that must be met; basic needs for love and a sense of self-worth.

However, reality therapy does not dwell excessively on deficiencies. Rather, like RET, it moves the client away from bemoaning past privations toward concentrating on present self-defeating behavior, teaching the client how to become a more lovable and worthwhile person. It is also like RET in that it is didactic, concerned with the present, and action-oriented. Unlike RET, however, it recognizes the problems inherent in calling antisocial behavior "irrational"; it substitutes "irresponsible." This is not just a semantic difference. Rationality is seen in terms of the positive or negative consequences for an individual of his behavior. In contrast, responsibility is seen in terms of the positive or negative consequences of behavior both for the individual actor and for others. As we have seen, it is possible to be rational and engage in criminal activity; it is not possible to be responsible and do so. The reality counselor will not hesitate, however, to point out self-defeating irrational thinking, just as the RET counselor will not hesitate to point out irresponsible behavior.

The reality counselor thus shares with the RET counselor a hard-nosed, no-nonsense approach to clients: behavior is either responsible or irresponsible, period. But, like client-centered counseling, reality counseling recognizes the importance of a warm, sensitive, and open relationship with the client as a prelude to effective counseling. Positive (though not unconditional) regard, genuineness, and empathy are stressed, without the syrupy connotations attached to them by client-centered therapy.

Theoretical Backdrop

William Glasser believes that those who engage in any kind of self-defeating behavior, including criminality, suffer from the inability to fulfill basic needs adequately. If these needs are not met, the person will fail to perceive the reality of his or her world correctly and will act irresponsibly. By "reality" Glasser means that the individual perceives accurately not only the immediate consequences of a given action but also the remote consequences. To act responsibly, clients must be helped to face the reality of the world they live in; to face reality, they must be helped to fulfill their basic needs. These basic needs are the need to love and be loved and to feel worthwhile to ourselves and to others.

Glasser describes how these two needs are interrelated: "Although the two needs are separate, a person who loves and is loved will usually feel that he [or she] is a worthwhile person, and one who is worthwhile is usually someone who is loved and can give love in return" (1975:11). When these needs are met, a person can develop a "success identity"; when they are not, the person develops a "failure identity," which results in irresponsible behavior.

A failure identity is what Berne calls in TA an "I'm not okay" life position; a success identity is an "I'm okay" life position. Glasser feels that a person's basic identity (success or failure) is in place by the age of four or five. If we are loved and encouraged to learn, explore, and experience, we will have a success identity. If we are unloved, neglected, and stifled, we will have a failure identity. The whole process of reality therapy is an effort to help clients attain a success identity, to enhance their self-esteem by guiding them from success (however small) to success. It is quite true that nothing succeeds like success—and nothing fails like failure.

Glasser's theory nicely ties in at the psychological level with the sociological insights of Hirschi's control theory. The lack of a loving relationship with significant others (attachment) leads to a generalized lack of concern for the expectations and values of the larger society. This lack of concern leads to lack of commitment to a prosocial lifestyle, failure in school and in the job market, and a failure identity. Without a prosocial commitment, the individual does not know enough people with success identities to model responsible behavior patterns, but instead associates with those who have failure identities, justifying themselves and their behavior by a set of beliefs that are contrary to conventional morality. If early deprivations are severe enough, the individual may develop a psychopathic personality.

Although reality therapy refers to causes of behavior, it stresses that the causes of behavior are not excuses for that behavior. Reality therapy agrees with the client-centered and RET perspectives that the individual is ultimately responsible for his or her own "identity." Like client-centered therapy, reality therapy asserts that there is a "growth force" within us all that strives for a success identity. Reality counseling attempts to activate that force by helping clients to learn who they are, how to interact with others in a responsible way, and how they can be more fully accepted by others. It charges the counselor to be a continuing model of personal responsibility. Once again, the counselor must work to become the best person he or she is capable of being.

In an interview with Evans (1982), Glasser enumerated seven steps that the counselor must take to effect meaningful changes in a client's behavior. Paraphrased, they are:

1. Get involved with clients, develop warm rapport, show respect.
2. Understand clients' personal histories, but deemphasize the past in favor of what they are doing now.
3. Help clients evaluate their attitudes and behavior and discover how they are contributing to their failure identities.
4. Explore with them alternative behaviors that may be more useful in developing a success identity.
5. After alternatives have been chosen, get a commitment in writing to a plan of change.
6. Once the commitment has been made, make it clear that excuses for not adhering to it will not be tolerated. Emphasize that it is the client's responsibility to carry out the plan.
7. Do not be punitive with clients, but allow them to suffer the natural consequences of their behavior. Attempting to shield clients from natural consequences reinforces their irresponsibility and denies the self-directedness of their actions.

The Reluctant/Resistant Client

The attitudes and techniques of reality therapy are particularly useful in counseling reluctant or resistant clients. Most counseling theories assume a voluntary client who has actively sought help, although most clients, even self-referred ones, exhibit reluctance or resistance at times (Paradise & Wilder 1979). Some authorities even consider voluntary and welcomed interaction with the counselor as an essential prerequisite to the helping process. Reality therapy makes no such assumption. It recognizes that most criminal justice clients are inclined to demonstrate resistance. None of them is in your office by choice.

Recognizing Reluctance and Resistance Client resistance can range from sullen silence to telling you only what they think you want to know to outright hostility. Most verbal resistance does not take the form of angry name-calling and challenges. It is more often a series of responses like "I don't know," "maybe," "I suppose," and "you're the boss." In the vocabulary of TA, the client is acting from a hostile Child ego state. Nonverbal resistance can reveal itself in frequent finger and foot tapping, negative headshakes, smirky smiles, and arm folding (erecting a barrier; a gesture of defiance). This kind of verbal and nonverbal behavior can be disconcerting to the beginning counselor who "only wants to help" (TA's nurturing parent) and is desperately trying to be liked.

A counselor whose intentions are good and who is doing all the things learned in Counseling 101 to establish rapport finds it difficult to accept the client's reluctance and negativism (the transaction is crossed). All of us enjoy positive feelings; few of us are good at dealing with negative feelings, our own or those of others, because they require confrontation. Rather than acknowledging and dealing with negative feelings, the beginning counselor often tries to deny, downplay, or redirect them (trying to maintain an inappropriate complementary transaction). The negative feelings must be acknowledged and worked through with the client (temporarily crossing the transaction so that it can be reinitiated at a more appropriate Adult-Adult level). The process requires extra effort from the counselor; it is all too easy to coast, avoiding uncomfortable issues. A counselor with a strong, integrated self-concept is not afraid to confront negativism.

Reasons for Resistance Why do criminal justice clients resist well-meaning attempts to help them? For one thing, they do not come into your office asking what you can do for them; they are much more concerned about what you can do to them. You are a symbol of the authority that many clients have spent a good proportion of their lives resisting. To cooperate with you may well seem to them to be an admission of weakness, and they are not anxious to admit weakness, especially to a representative of "the system." Resistance is a defense mechanism designed to protect the ego from the disconcerting feeling of loss of autonomy.

Clients also may not want to cooperate because what you want and what they want are two totally different things: You want them to act responsibly and obey the law; they want to get out of your office and out of your life. The very fact that clients are in your office involuntarily is enough to generate resistance. The principle of psychological reactance tells us that whenever people's sense of autonomy is threatened by forcing them to do something—even if they would otherwise have done it voluntarily—the natural inclination is to resist. Finally, ask yourself why clients would want to surrender themselves to a person they do not yet trust and to a condition they see as manipulative, for purposes with which they do not, at least for the present, agree.

Dealing with Resistance The first thing you must do with resisting clients is to acknowledge their feelings by reflecting them back and giving clients the opportunity to vent them. You need not share a client's views of you or "the system" in order to acknowledge the client's right to hold them. Arguing with clients will only strengthen their resolve. You may even tell them that you do not mind if they feel the way they do as long as they behave responsibly.

Clients must be reminded that probation or parole is a privilege granted conditionally and that they may not abuse it. You can let resistant clients know that you understand their desire to get out of your office and out of your life—and that you share this desire with them. That joint objective provides a mutually agreeable starting point. You can then begin to delineate the conditions under which your mutual goal can be achieved. Emphasize that you are responsible for implementing the conditions of probation or parole, that noncompliance will not be tolerated, that both of you have a vested interest in successful probation or parole, that it should therefore be a cooperative endeavor, and that a negative or hostile attitude could seriously endanger your mutual goal: "Let's help each other out." In the vocabulary of TA, the statement of expectations is a Parent-Child transaction, and the negotiation of a treatment contract is an Adult-Adult transaction.

This approach is the one the reality counselor would take. Reality counselors do not punish the client by returning hostility for hostility, but let it be known that the client will be allowed to suffer the natural consequences of noncompliant behavior. The counselor is strong enough to deal with negative feelings in a constructive way by a judicious use of authority. He or she is straight with the client without being authoritarian. The client is allowed the dignity of expressing attitudes contrary to the counselor's but is told immediately that nonapproved—that is, irresponsible—behavior is not permitted. Criminal justice clients much prefer and respect directness rather than sweet-talking and beating around the bush. The counselor enlists the client's help to reach a goal desired by both parties. A shared purpose gives meaning to the client/counselor relationship. The ability to draw clients into their own rehabilitation is the major skill of reality therapists (Glasser 1975:25).

This area of general agreement between yourself and a resisting client is then channeled to specific areas of concern by a concrete plan of action. Initial plans should have small goals to maximize the probability of successful completion. They should also be formalized in writing and signed by the client and by yourself. (See the tentative treatment plan in Appendix A.) This says to the client, "Your signature attests to your commitment to achieve this goal and mine attests to my commitment to support you." Adherence to a plan begins the process leading to a "can-do" success identity and engenders a sense of responsibility for living up to agreements. Glasser emphasizes the importance of commitment: "Commitment is the keystone of reality therapy. It is only from the making and following through with plans that we gain a sense of self-worth and maturity" (Glasser & Zunin 1973:303). Moreover, keeping the expectations of the action plan modest often overcomes a client's reluctance to comply.

Treatment and Supervision Plans

Balance In order to minimize reluctance, resistance, and probability of failure, treatment and supervision plans should be consonant with the client's present coping resources. These resources—intelligence and educational levels, financial situation, self-concept, strength of interpersonal relationships, and so on—are known to you from previous interviews and the needs assessment scale. Similarly, watch for problem areas to be addressed in the treatment and supervision plans. Balanced plans are plans whose demands on your clients neither undertax or overtax the resources they have available to implement them. The principle of balanced plans is illustrated in Figure 9-3.

The diagram is divided into three sections, one balanced and two unbalanced. The upper-left triangle represents an unbalanced condition in which high coping resources are paired with low treatment expectation. The lower-right triangle represents the opposite. Sam is in the undertaxed section because he has high coping resources, yet low demands have been placed on him. Sam will be quite content if you allow him to slide along without having to do anything to correct the problems that led to his criminal behavior. Of course, Sam may be a first offender who needs no treatment plan and who is best left alone. But if there are clear problem areas that may lead him to reoffend, you must take advantage of whatever strengths are represented by his relatively high coping resources to encourage his growth toward responsibility.

Nick's situation is the opposite: Heavy treatment demands have been made on his limited coping resources. The dilemma here is that the very reason Nick requires more intense treatment is that he has few coping resources. But the lack of resources indicates that he probably will not be able at present to meet those demands. Nick is in a "Catch-22" situation. If you insist on maintaining his present level of treatment, you will be setting him up for resistance and failure, with all their consequences. Present treatment demands must be lowered so that they are commensurate with Nick's present capacities to cope with them. As his capacities increase you may negotiate more demanding treatment goals with him.

The treatment goals set for Al and Mary are balanced with their present coping resources. Mary's coping resources are equal to Sam's, but she is being challenged to use them for personal change and growth. Al has extremely low coping resources and thus probably needs a higher level of treatment than Mary, but his present resources are not strong enough to allow for the same level of treatment. As his resource strength increases (as he slowly builds up a success identity), so may the demands that you negotiate with him. Do not undertax or overtax your clients' coping resources; move them slowly toward the ultimate goal one simple step at a time.

Simplicity To change a failure identity to a success identity, a good plan should be

- Uncomplicated, simple, unambiguous, concrete, to the point: "Attend AA tonight at 6 o'clock."

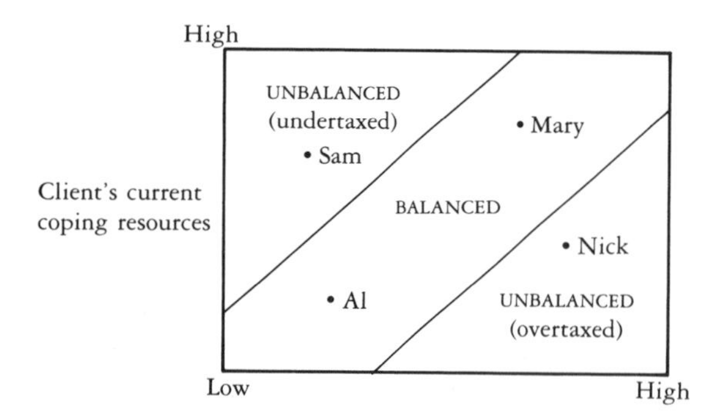

Figure 9-3 Balancing treatment goals

- Active—something to do, not stop doing: "Attend AA tonight at 6 o'clock," not "Stop drinking alcohol."
- Something that can be done as close to "right now" as possible: "Attend AA tonight at 6 o'clock."
- Entirely dependent on the client's actions for fulfillment, not contingent on the actions of others: not "Attend AA tonight at 6 o'clock if your husband lets you skip the grocery shopping."
- Something that can be done every day or as often as possible: "Attend AA tonight at 6 o'clock and every Tuesday and Thursday at the same time and place for the next month."
- Specific as to what, where, when, how, and with whom it is to be done: "Attend AA tonight at 6 o'clock at St. Anthony Church on Pine Street. The counselor will pick me up at home for the first meeting to introduce me to other members."

The first plan need not be quite so active as this example. It can be as simple as being on time for the next appointment. Whatever the plan, get it in writing and signed by both you and your client.

Orientation toward Progress To build a success identity, subsequent plans should be designed to build on the client's strengths rather than on obvious weaknesses. Too early an emphasis on major weaknesses creates too great a chance of failure, thus reinforcing the client's failure identity and generating further reluctance and resistance. For instance, if JoAnn lacks a high school diploma but could successfully complete a GED program, show her that you have confidence in her capabilities and try to secure an agreement from her to enroll. But do not forget that this goal must be balanced with her capacities. Do not insist that she commit herself if she is seriously reluctant. You might instead persuade her to take one placement test. She may well be more receptive to the entire program if the test shows that she could do well. A recent study comparing rearrest rates between probationers enrolled in a GED program and probationers not enrolled found that those enrolled were significantly less criminally involved over a three-year period. Notice the "success identity" theme in the conclusion of the paper:

> The sense of personal accomplishment, the sense of participating in a socially valued endeavor, the anticipation of legitimate employment, and the idea that the "system" finds one worthy enough to make an investment in time and resources to provide one with a second chance may be sufficient to put the scotch to an incipient criminal lifestyle (Walsh 1985:76).

The secret of counseling in criminal justice is, then, to temper your necessary authority in order to direct your clients' actions along acceptable avenues, while always showing concern for their basic humanity. Try to view client resistance as a normal response to coercion, perhaps even a psychologically healthy one. Examine your own resistance to self-growth and development and your own behavior with clients to see if you might be doing something to generate resistance. For instance, you may be a little too directive, too authoritarian, or in too much of a hurry to accomplish your goals. Especially examine the possibility that your goals for the client are not balanced with the client's present level of coping resources. As Newman has put it:

> One of the first major accomplishments of treatment comes about when the offender becomes aware, both intellectually and emotionally, that the officer represents not only authority with the power to enforce certain restraints and restrictions but that he [or she] is also able to offer material, social, and psychological aids (1961:38).

We must not forget that counseling is a difficult and sometimes draining enterprise. You cannot expect to be an expert simply by reading, but with experience and caring each counselor becomes better and better and begins to evolve a unique personal style. As Peoples puts it, treatment is often a "maze," but "the significant point to emphasize is *do something*. Shelve the paperwork, forget the coffee, get out of the office—and counsel. Risk a little involvement with the human beings on your caseload. Learn, teach, and grow with them in experiencing the most vital quicksilver of all, human behavior" (1975:372).

Perspectives from the Field

When Cultures Clash: Resistance and Persistence

Roman C. Peña

Roman Peña received B.A. and M.P.A. degrees from Idaho State University. He spent four years with the Utah Department of Corrections as a correctional counselor at a halfway house house. He is currently a probation and parole officer with an intensive supervision caseload.

I had only been in the intensive supervision program for three weeks when I was notified that I would be getting a new parolee called "Casey Jones." Reviewing Casey's inmate file and conversing with various sources, I became aware of Casey's Aryan Brotherhood affiliation. The Aryan Brotherhood is a white supremacist group that is active and powerful within prison walls. Well, here's Roman, very much a non-Aryan, going to be this racist's parole officer. Although Casey's involvement in the Brotherhood was minimal, just the fact that he chose to identify with this group and their values was enough for me. I immediately contrived ways of defending myself in the event of confrontation.

Sure enough, seated across the interviewing table the next day was Casey. His face and mannerisms displayed hate and anger. I knew that he knew about me from his own sources. As I asked him the required questions and advised him of his responsibilities, he'd respond with abrasiveness and sarcasm. It was tempting to retaliate, but I knew that it was necessary to maintain a professional demeanor.

The first two months of continual daily face-to-face visits were uneventful. Casey's attitude didn't improve, and I often hoped that he would abscond supervision. Nevertheless, he was content with doing as little as possible in most areas of concern, and he managed to stay within the "gray zones" of behavior and attitude. His welcoming remarks to me at home visits were, "Yeah, what do you want?" and "Not you again!" His acquisition of a guard dog became part of our power struggle. Casey enjoyed watching my approach to the front door, as I tended to proceed with some trepidation. His enjoyment was short-lived, as the dog befriended me.

Two more months passed until Casey experienced the setback of being laid off from his job. Casey started showing signs of worry. I couldn't help feeling that his negativism was a factor in his layoff. Christmas was only three weeks away, and the job market was stagnant. One day an employer from a local mobile home factory called me up and asked me if I knew of someone who'd like a job installing mobile home windows. I quickly notified Casey. He got the job. From that point on he began to be more friendly. He'd even greet me at the door with a friendly "Hello!" He began to share personal problems. I listened intently and offered guidance when possible. Casey completed his six-month intensive parole period and was transferred to regular parole supervision.

Casey's new parole officer was—are you ready for this—a Mr. Rodriguez. Rodriguez was firm yet fair with Casey. He told him that there would not be any sidetracking on cultural issues. Compliance with supervision standards was to be the priority. Casey agreed to cooperate with him the best that he could. One day Casey called Rodriguez on the telephone. Rodriguez's face showed concern and empathy as he consoled Casey on the death of his newborn son. This was a major turning point in Casey's life. He became increasingly receptive to assistance and cooperative in matters of supervision.

As I now submit Casey's final recommendation for discharge to the parole board, I remember our first two months in the program together. I've witnessed a miracle in human relations, not only in Casey but also in myself. Casey's parting words to me were, "You know, you're not so bad after all—for a Mexican. Thanks for everything." For some reason his Aryan values and my Mexican culture seemed so insignificant.

Lessons and Concerns

Reality therapy is a relatively simple method of counseling that stresses responsible behavior, and it can be fruitfully applied by professionals within the criminal justice setting. Its "one small step at a time" approach to developing clients' success identities is particularly useful, as is its directive and confrontive stance within a no-nonsense but warm client-involved relationship. It asserts that the origin of many clients' problems lies in early and protracted deprivation of love. Finally, a number of studies have concurred with Rachin's (1974:53) conclusion that "Correctional clients who have proven least amenable to conventional treatment methods respond well to reality therapy."

At times I have used the vocabulary of TA when explaining reality therapy to bring the concepts home more strongly. Clients will also better understand the supervision and counseling process if they are introduced to the simple vocabulary that is the great strength of TA. The integration of this vocabulary into the reality therapist's repertoire should prove very useful.

Glasser may, however, be overly facile in dismissing mental illness as merely "irresponsible behavior." We are coming more and more to the realization that much of what has been termed mental illness originates in chemical and endocrinal imbalances. To treat individuals as irresponsible when they are demonstrably ill does them a disservice, to say the least. The criminal justice counselor must recognize when clients are behaving "irresponsibly" due to no real fault of their own and refer them to a mental health specialist.

Summary

This chapter has outlined the three counseling approaches most often used in criminal justice settings. These theories have found a place in corrections because they are easy to understand and apply, they emphasize the clients' own responsibility for change, and they include equal involvement of client and counselor.

Transactional analysis is built around five simple words: Parent, Adult, Child (the ego states), Game, and Script. Much of our behavior is a playback of scripts laid down during infancy and childhood. The kind of scripts we have in our heads depends on the quantity and quality of the strokes (love) we received early in our lives. Our scripting leads to the four basic life positions from which we carry out our transactions with others: "I'm not okay; you're okay," "I'm not okay; you're not okay," "I'm okay; you're not okay," "I'm okay; you're okay." The large majority of your clients will be operating from one of the first three; counselors must strive to conduct all their transactions from the fourth, the "I'm okay; you're okay" life position.

Parent, Adult, and Child are three distinct ego states we slip into and out of during transactions. Criminal justice clients tend to operate mostly from the Child ego state. Many of them exclude the Parent altogether, and their Adult states are frequently contaminated by the intrusion of the Child. When interacting with clients, operate from the Adult ego state, and strive to get your clients more involved with their Adults.

Rational-emotive therapy emphasizes that most of the problems of living we experience are the results of irrational thinking. It is not facts, events, or situations per se that cause us emotional problems, it is what we allow ourselves to think about those happenings. If we could think more rationally, we would have far fewer emotional problems. The counselor's task is to strip away the client's negative, self-defeating thinking.

Ellis identifies eleven irrational ideas that are pervasive in our society, of which six are particularly useful to clients and workers in criminal justice. You will find it rewarding to assimilate these six ideas into your operating philosophy.

Reality therapy views self-defeating behavior as the result of not having certain basic needs adequately met. These needs are the need to love and be loved and the need to feel worthwhile. People who do not have these needs met tend to develop a failure identity. Your task is to help your clients acquire success identities by becoming actively involved with them.

Reality therapy is especially useful in dealing with resisting and reluctant clients, of which there are many in the criminal justice field. Clients resist your help because you are a symbol of the authority they have spent much of their lives resisting. They also resist because they are not in voluntary association with you.

Recognize and confront their resistance rather than ignoring or downplaying it. Allow them the dignity of their opinions, but make it clear that nonconforming behavior will not be tolerated. Indicate that you will allow them to suffer the natural consequences of non-adherence to the conditions of their supervision.

In order to minimize resistance and develop clients' success identities, treatment plans must be balanced with each client's present coping resources, neither overtaxing nor undertaxing them. Overtaxing invites resistance; undertaxing is not growth-producing. Treatment plans should be as simple and as concrete as possible and should be in writing and signed by both parties.

Exercise in Primary and Advanced Empathy

The exercise in interviewing emphasized practice in listening to what your partner had to say. In these exercises in counseling you will be more active. Not only will you be intensely listening, but you will be communicating to your partner that you understand where he or she is coming from. You will use all of the techniques outlined in the chapter on interviewing, including paraphrasing, clarification, and reflection of feelings. Do not be content with vague statements from your partner; call for specifics.

If you are the person being counseled, choose a topic that is of concern to you, one with emotional content, such as the loss of a loved one, the breakup of a romantic relationship, the inability to get along with someone of importance to you, or a perceived personal defect. These make for realistic counseling sessions. You will learn how a client feels when revealing intimate information, and the counselor will practice pulling out deep feelings that the client may be reluctant to express. However, please do not choose a topic that is too painful to discuss with an inexperienced counselor. This exercise should be both productive and relatively safe. Take ample time, therefore, to decide on a topic.

After you have been through a short counseling session, you and your partner should identify strategies for understanding and amelioration of the problem discussed. Perhaps you could do some structural analyses on the client's important relationships: Do you see a pattern of crossed transactions? What is the client's typical ego state? Does the client agree? Is the client's usual state consistent with what Berne would predict from the client's history of strokes? How about irrational ideas the client may be working with? If the counselor did not identify them in the session, maybe you can now do it together as a team. Finally, can you together define a simple plan to begin eliminating the problematic behavior or feelings of the client? The exercise should be fun if approached from a mutual "I'm okay; you're okay" position.

Counseling "Real" Clients

Working with PSIs written as interviewing and assessment exercises, you can practice criminal justice counseling by teaming up the partner you had earlier to explore more fully the problems and concerns discovered during the PSI process. These problems may be alcoholism, child molestation, drug abuse, negative self-concept, or anger and aggression. The student counselor should determine what referrals, if any, might be beneficial to the client. Explore these problems in turn from each of the three counseling perspectives discussed in this chapter, and then devise some simple "success identity" plans appropriate to your client.

If you are role-playing the client, before the counseling session think deeply about being in the offender's shoes (empathy) so that you can present a realistic challenge to your partner's counseling skills. Much of your partner's success in this exercise will depend on how well you can capture the feelings of the offender. An added bonus for you will be a greater ability to view the world from the offender's perspective.

References and Suggested Readings

Bateson, G., D. Jackson, J. Haley, and J. Weakland. 1956. Toward a theory of schizophrenia. *Behavioral Science* 1:251-264.

Berne, E. 1964. *Games people play*. New York: Grove Press.

Berne, E. 1966. *Principles of group treatment*. New York: Oxford University Press.

Brown, J., and R. Pate, Jr., eds. 1983. *Being a counselor: Directions and challenges*. Monterey, Cal.: Brooks/Cole.

Ellis, A. 1975. *A new guide to rational living*. Hollywood, Cal.: Wiltshire.

Evans, D. 1982. What are you doing? An interview with William Glasser. *Personnel and Guidance Journal* 61:460-462.

Glasser, W. 1972. *The identity society*. New York: Harper & Row.

Glasser, W. 1975. *Reality therapy: A new approach to psychiatry*. New York: Harper & Row.

Glasser, W., and L. Zunin. 1973. Reality therapy. In *Current psychotherapies*, edited by R. Corsini. Itasca, Ill.: F. E. Peacock.

Lytle, M. 1964. The unpromising client. *Crime and Delinquency* 10:130-134.

Newman, C. 1961. Concepts of treatment in probation and parole supervision. *Federal Probation* 25:34-40.

Paradise, L., and D. Wilder. 1979. The relationship between client reluctance and counselor effectiveness. *Counselor Education and Supervision* 19:35-41.

Peoples, E. 1975. Sorting from the treatment maze. In *Readings in correctional casework and counseling*. Pacific Palisades, Cal.: Goodyear Publishing.

Rachin, R. 1974. Reality therapy: Helping people help themselves. *Crime and Delinquency* 20:45-53.

Vriend, J., and W. Dyer. 1973. Counseling the reluctant client. *Journal of Counseling Psychology* 20:240-246.

Walsh, A. 1985. An evaluation of the effects of adult basic education on rearrest rates among probationers. *Journal of Offender Counseling Services & Rehabilitation* 9:69-76.

Chapter 10
Institutional Assessment and Classification

Through its diagnostic and coordinating functions, classification not only contributes to the objective of rehabilitation, but also to custody, discipline, work assignments, officer and inmate morale, and the effective use of training opportunities.

Morris v. Travisono (1970)

J. Arthur Beyer

Classification is simply a method of ordering the way we relate to or deal with objects, situations, or people. Virtually all of us classify the weather as warm and sunny or cloudy and cold, thus permitting us to make reasoned decisions about clothing and activities for the day. Within a prison setting, classification as a management tool allows prison administrators to maintain institutional order and safety through the allocation of resources for inmate services.

We classify people as well. We call them Republicans, Democrats, conservatives, liberals, alcoholics, criminals. We may subjectively classify individuals and groups on the basis of our own experiences, perceptions, and prejudices. Regardless of

---

J. Arthur Beyer, Ph.D., is a former sergeant with a city police agency in Idaho. He has also been a housing unit counselor, involved in classifying inmates, and later a security lieutenant at the Idaho State Penitentiary. He also has experience as a probation and parole officer. He has published articles on juvenile delinquency and prison classification.

how we arrive at our classifications, we tend to respond to the person classified in a manner consistent with our own beliefs.

Professional practitioners in all disciplines have elaborate systems for classifying the phenomena of their disciplines. These practitioners have gone beyond subjective methods. For instance, psychologists and psychiatrists classify various behaviors using a manual called the *Diagnostic and Statistical Manual of Mental Disorders (DSM-III)*. The DSM-III multiaxial system classifies the characteristics of individuals in terms of clinically important factors. It provides a common understanding for the family of mental health professionals and thus facilities management of caseloads and the implementation of treatment modalities.

Unfortunately, there is no tidy DSM-III for the classification of institutionalized offenders. Although the causes and treatment of criminal behavior have been important to the criminal justice agenda since it was first suggested that there might be alternatives to flogging, mutilation, and torture, there are several reasons for the lack of consistency in prison classification.

First, classification (prediction) procedures are of three types: (1) anamnestic, based solely on a individual's past behavior, (2) clinical, based on expert diagnosis and evaluation, and (3) statistical or actuarial, based on a comparison of individual behavior patterns with similar behavior patterns of others (Morris & Miller 1987).

Second, there is a problem with false-positive (Type I or Alpha Error) and false-negative predictions (Type II or Beta Error). When we predict that the behavior of an individual poses a risk to society when it does not, we have made a false positive prediction. The individual is thus unjustly deprived of rights. Conversely, if we make a false-negative prediction (i.e., predicting no risk from an offender when there is risk), we tend not to take the steps necessary to protect others. The latter situation is illustrated by the Jeffery Dahmer homicides in Milwaukee; the police made a false-negative prediction and failed to intervene.

Legal and ethical questions arise from the problem of false-positive and false-negative predictions. If offenders who pose a real and present risk to the prison population are not classified in a way that protects others (false negative), institutional security and order are threatened. On the other hand, if we deprive offenders unjustly of rights and privileges afforded under the U.S. Constitution and correctional agency policy (false positive), we become excessively punitive at great fiscal cost to society. In either circumstance, violations of the Eighth (cruel and unusual punishment) and Fourteenth (due process) Amendments to the U.S. Constitution may be alleged. Correctional agencies may then be drawn into lengthy litigation, which is costly to the public.

A closely related problem deals with predicting individual behavior. The complexity of the human organism precludes 100 percent accuracy in predicting individual behavior. We can classify an individual as belonging in a particular group whose members have the same characteristics. For example, we know that young males have a greater propensity to commit crime than other groups, and we know that the early onset of criminal behavior, the seriousness of the first offense, and the frequency of offending predict future criminality. The group as a whole may present a significant risk to society—but the individual offender may not. The best formal predictions of individual criminality are not much better than chance predictions (Farrington 1987; Steadman 1987).

Finally, unlike "free world" classifications, predictions within the criminal justice system may deprive individuals of their liberty and access to goods and services. The decision process for classifying individuals is far from perfect. Because of the possibility of diminution or loss of freedom, classification procedures must be as objective as possible; they should not be capricious and arbitrary. Standardized procedures encourage fairness for the offender, for the institution, and for the public.

Historical Overview

To understand and appreciate client classification as it is practiced today, it is important to understand the history of classification in penology. Early attempts at classification consisted simply of separating men from women and children within prisons. In the late 1700s, the Walnut Street Jail in Philadelphia inaugurated a classification process to separate serious offenders from others. Serious offenders were placed in isolation and were not allowed to work or interact with other prisoners (Lewis 1967:17). Fifteen years later in 1804, the Charleston Prison in Massachusetts established a trilevel system of classification based on prior convictions. Each group had a distinctive uniform, and the three groups were segregated from one another in quarters, prison work, and access to amenities. First-time offenders were given the best quarters, job assignments, and food. Second-time offenders were allowed only two meals a day and performed less desirable work. Third-time, or habitual, offenders did the most menial tasks and received the worst food (Lewis 1969:71).

In the early 1800s, prison administrators experimented with a variety of custodial and classification systems. The system that became the model for most prison construction for the next 150 years was the Auburn Prison, opened in New York in 1819 (Allen & Simonsen 1981:37-38) as a maximum-security prison, with harsh conditions of confinement. Little effort was invested in making inmate classification an integral part of prison administration.

In 1959, criminologists Richard Korn and Lloyd McCorkle (1959) proposed a broad classification of crime and criminals according to legal designation, personality type, life organization, and offense type (such as sex offenses and drug offenses). This set the scene for more sophisticated typologies. But it was the courts as much as anything else that gave impetus to better classification systems.

Until 1970 the courts generally avoided interfering in classification decisions, recognizing "that discipline and the general management of such open institutions are executive functions with which the judicial branch will not interfere" (*Cohen v. U.S.*, 25 F. Supp. 679, ON.D. GA., 1966e at 688). However, in 1970, the Federal District Court in Rhode Island ordered that a meaningful, nonarbitrary classification system be implemented. The court recognized that inmate classification is a management tool that enables the prison administrator to allocate scarce resources to areas where they will do the most good: Classification is essential to the operation of an orderly and safe prison. It is a prerequisite for the rational allocation of whatever program opportunities exist within the institution. It enables the institution to gauge the proper custody level of an inmate; to identify the inmate's educational, vocational, and psychological needs; and to separate nonviolent inmates from the more predatory (*Morris v. Travisono*, 310 F. Supp. 857 O1970e at 965).

The courts charged correctional administrators to minimize the risk of injury to the public, to inmates, and to the correctional staff by placing each offender in the least restrictive setting consistent with the stated goals and with the needs of the offender. Inmate classification is perhaps the most encompassing aspect of inmate supervision.

SECURITY LEVELS

SECURITY ELEMENTS	I (MINIMUM)	II (MEDIUM)	III (MAXIMUM)
Housing	Dormitories, cubicles, or rooms	Rooms and/or multiple cells	Single cells, very secure, with heavy duty hardware
Perimeter Security	None, or single fence; occasional patrol	Double fence; electric alarm system; patrol of perimeter or towers	A combination of double fence; wall; towers; constant armed perimeter surveillance; and electronic alarm system
Internal Security Measures	Inmate census taken at least 3 times daily	Inmate movement controlled by pass system; formal census at least 4 times daily, plus frequent informal census	Frequent informal census; capability to quickly separate the inmates into groups of 50 or less; directly supervised and/or escorted when outside cellhouse or living area; formal census taken at least 6 times daily

Figure 10-1 Physical security levels

Security and Custody

Security levels (see Figure 10-1) are of a physical nature. They refer to environmental factors of perimeter security like towers, patrols, and other detection devices. Custodial levels (Figure 10-2) refer to the degree of supervision the inmate receives. Programs are the activities that are provided, such as educational and vocational opportunities, counseling services, and recreational and hobby activities. Figure 10-2 makes it clear that access to jobs and programs is an inherent function of custodial classification.

Classification Data

Standards and Principles of Classification

The DSM-III classification of behavior in society in general provides an organized, systematic, and established procedure for assessing client characteristics, which in turn allows for differential treatment modalities. In institutional corrections, though not all criminals exhibit the same behavior or present the same security risk, we have tended to treat all inmates alike.

CUSTODY LEVELS

ACTIVITY	MINIMUM	MEDIUM	MAXIMUM
Observation by staff	Occasional; appropriate to situation	Frequent and direct	Always supervised when outside cell
Day movement inside facility	Unrestricted	Observed periodically by staff	Restricted; directly observed or escorted when outside cell
Movement after dark	Intermittent observation	Restricted, with direct supervision	Out of cell only for emergencies. In restraints when outside cellhouse, or as approved by watch commander
After evening lockdown	Intermittent observation	Escorted and only on order of watch commander	
Meal periods	Intermittent observation	Supervised	Directly supervised or in cell
Access to jobs	Eligible for all, both inside and outside perimeter	Inside perimeter only	Only selected day jobs inside perimeter, or directly supervised within the housing unit
Access to programs	Unrestricted, including community-based activities	Work and recreation, inside perimeter; outside perimeter only as approved by C.E.O.	Selected programs/activities inside the facility perimeter, as approved by C.E.O.
Visits	Contact; periodic supervision, indoor and/or outdoor	Contact, supervised	Noncontact or closely supervised (1-1)
Leave the institution	Unescorted/escorted	Direct staff escort; handcuffs, with chains and leg irons (optional); armed escort (optional)	Minimum of two escorts with one armed, full restraints; strip search prior to departure and upon return
Furlough	Eligible for unescorted day pass and furlough*	Eligible for staff-escorted day pass or furlough*	Not eligible

*DEFINITION: Day Pass—Permits inmate to be away from institution only during daylight hours. A furlough authorizes overnight absence from the facility.

This custody classification system is used as a guideline to determine the following:

1. Assignment is made to an institution that provides the level of security consistent with the inmate's custody requirement.
2. Assignments are made to institutional programs that are consistent with custody needs. These assignments include housing, work, and other programs such as education, visiting, and any activity that involves risk to staff, other inmates, or the community.

Figure 10-2 Custodial levels

There are three general explanations for the etiology of crime: the sociogenic, the psychogenic, and the biogenic or sociobiological (Steel & Steger 1988).

Our parent discipline, sociology, provides a home for the sociogenic school, which looks to environmental factors to explain aberrant behavior. It tends to downplay individual differences that cannot be explained in terms of environmental variation. Sociology, says Jeffery (1979:113), assumes equipotentiality, meaning that we all have the same potential for both good and evil. This school says that society causes crime. What we eventually become is the product of variation in the environment, with individual differences being constant.

Psychology, or the psychogenic school, looks at individual proclivity and motivation to engage in criminal behavior. Although not discounting environmental influences, this school looks to the individual's mental processes to explain "acting out" behavior. A third approach, the biogenic or sociobiological school, looks to physical, neurological, biological, and chromosomal abnormalities to explain crime. In this school, prenatal and postnatal trauma, chemical imbalances, endocrine abnormalities, and other biological dysfunctions are considered a major factor in criminal behavior.

Each of these perspectives on criminal behavior has had its turn in corrections. The changes of orientations and goals caused by the cyclical exchange of sociological and psychological perspectives has led to pessimism and a "lock 'em up" attitude.

Criminology as an emerging discipline is beginning to find new ways of examining corrections. Jeffery (1979) feels that by drawing on chemistry and biology, including the work being done on nutrition, and incorporating sociological and psychological insights as well, we will better understand criminal behavior and thus better understand the correctional process.

To standardize inmate classification on a national level and to respond to court mandates, the American Correctional Association (ACA) has established standards for classification on the basis of research conducted by professional practitioners. These "Principles of Classification" were developed by the National Institute of Corrections. (See Appendix B.)

Reception and Diagnostic Unit

Once sentenced, offenders are transported to the designated prison. For first offenders, this may be the most frightening experience of their lives. Consider the confusion and fear that the offender must experience in coming to grips with the consecutive ordeals of trial, conviction, sentencing, and arrival at the "big house."

On arrival, all offenders are considered close-custody inmates pending initial classification. The function of the security staff at this point is to instill the reality of prison security into the new inmate. Security personnel are armed and present, orders are given, and compliance must be immediate. Inmates are stripped naked and searched, and all their property is seized. Depending on who conducts the search, the policy of the institution, and security considerations, the search may include body cavities. The strip search is perhaps the greatest invasion of privacy possible. Inmates are then ordered to shower, with instructions to apply a delousing agent to all body hair. At no time during these initial processes is an inmate allowed out of sight of a member of the correctional staff. After the shower, inmates are issued a prison uniform and a number. All vestiges of individuality are removed. The inmate has become a nonentity, totally vulnerable and dependent on his or her keepers. Although this process is demeaning, it is unfortunately necessary as both a security and a sanitation precaution.

Inmates stay in the reception and diagnostic unit from two to three weeks, during which time they will be closely observed by security and programming staff. Observations of adjustment and behavior are forwarded to the classification committee for consideration in their evaluations.

Tests

During the reception and diagnostic period, inmates will be seen by medical staff and will be tested in accordance with the policies of the state and institution. The tests may include the Nelson Reading Skills Test, the General Aptitude Test Battery (GATB), the Wechsler Adult Intelligence Scale (see Chapter 3), the Minnesota Multiphasic Personality Inventory (MMPI), the Human Synergistics Lifestyle Inventory, and the Myers-Briggs Type Indicator (MBTI).

Nelson Reading Skills Test The simplest of these tests for the inmate is the Nelson Reading Skills Test. It is designed to evaluate the offender's reading grade and vocabulary levels. This test tends to establish offender eligibility for subsequent testing. If the offender does not read and understand written communications at least at the sixth to eighth grade level, subsequent tests will be invalid.

General Aptitude Test Battery The General Aptitude Test Battery is often used by governmental employment services to measure aptitudes considered significant in many occupations. The GATB is not normally administered to anyone who does not read at least at the sixth grade level. Although it was designed to test adults and high school seniors, tables have been devised for converting scores for those reading at less than twelfth grade level. The GATB tests the following:

1. *General learning ability* (G). The ability to understand instructions and underlying principles; the ability to reason and make judgments.
2. *Verbal aptitude* (V). The ability to understand meanings of words and the ideas associated with them and to use them effectively. The ability to comprehend language and to understand relationships among words and the meanings of whole sentences and paragraphs.
3. *Numerical ability* (N). The ability to perform arithmetic operations quickly and accurately.
4. *Spatial ability* (S). The ability to comprehend forms in space. Often described as the ability to visualize objects of two and three dimensions.
5. *Form perception* (P). The ability to perceive pertinent details in objects or in pictorial or graphic material.
6. *Clerical perception* (Q). The ability to perceive pertinent details in verbal or tabular material.
7. *Motor coordination* (K). The ability to coordinate eyes, hands, and fingers rapidly and accurately to make precise movements quickly.
8. *Finger dexterity* (F). The ability to move the fingers and manipulate small objects with them rapidly and accurately.
9. *Manual dexterity* (M). The ability to move the hands easily and skillfully.

Combining scores provides a composite score that is cross-referenced with specific occupational areas to find a general aptitude for a field.

The combined G, V, and N scores relate to cognitive abilities. A functional "performance" score is obtained by combining the S, P, Q, K, F, and M scores. Although comparing results from instruments designed for different purposes is risky, it is interesting to note the similarity in criminal profiles obtained by the GATB and Wechsler IQ tests. Here again criminals tend to score significantly higher than noncriminals on the performance (functional) test than on the verbal (cognitive) test.

Minnesota Multiphasic Personality Inventory The MMPI, developed in the 1930s, is one of the most widely used personality inventories in corrections. It consists of 550 affirmative statements, to which the test-taker responds with "true," "false," or "cannot say." An MMPI-based typology of criminal offenders is one of five psychological classification systems used by the Federal Bureau of Prisons (Van Voorhis 1988).

The MMPI has scales relating to the following ten different clinical disorders:

- Hypochondriasis (Hs)
- Paranoia (Pa)
- Depression (D)
- Psychasthenia (Pt)
- Hysteria (Hy)
- Schizophrenia (Sc)
- Psychopathic deviate (Pd)
- Hypomania (Ma)
- Masculinity-femininity (Mf)
- Social introversion (Si)

Three additional control scales are built into the inventory. The Lie (L) scale assesses the person's tendency to try to "look good." The Validity (F) scale is intended to reveal confusion and carelessness. The Correction (K) scale is the most subtle: A high K score suggests that the respondent either is highly defensive or is attempting to "fake good." A low K score suggests

Perspectives from the Field

On Rules and Crisis Intervention

Charles L. Miller

Chuck Miller spent six years as a police officer before entering the corrections field. His corrections experience includes supervision of maximum security and death row sections and command of the SWAT team at the Idaho State penitentiary. A certified self-defense instructor, he holds an M.S. degree in human relations from Abilene Christian University, Texas.

The supervision of a high-security prison unit will provide numerous opportunities to practice and experiment with different aspects of crisis intervention. A crisis may occur at any time and for any reason. The key to good crisis intervention in an institutional setting begins long before a crisis occurs. The counselor involved with the crisis intervention must have a great deal of credibility and must demonstrate a willingness to enforce the rules of the institution consistently, equally, and fairly and at the same time demonstrate genuine concern for the welfare of the inmates.

My experience leads me to the belief that inmates have an unrecognized desire to be controlled. While they try all sorts of devious things to circumvent the rules and may even riot when rules become too oppressive, they desire some sort of structure. A great many of them desire rules to make up for the self-control that they personally lack. Lack of self-control probably got them into prison in the first place. They lack the controls necessary to live within the boundaries established by society and its laws. Many come to see the prison rules as a sign of caring on the part of those who enforce them.

I remember a young man I dealt with when I was a street cop. Ted had served time in a juvenile facility and had been released to live with his sister. His sister lacked the ability or desire to enforce any rules. Ted soon found himself in all kinds of trouble with the law again. The funny thing is that it seemed as though he wanted to be caught. He either turned himself in or made it extremely easy for us to catch him. The upshot was that he was returned to the juvenile facility.

About nine months later I was sitting in a coffee shop on a break when Ted walked in with a friend who had been incarcerated with him. They sat down with me and we talked about a number of things. I asked Ted if he hadn't been trying to get caught for his crimes and returned to the institution nine months before. He proudly explained that he was. I asked him why—wasn't it a prison? I'll never forget his answer: "I liked it there because the people there cared enough about me to tell me what I could and couldn't do." His friend chipped in "Yeah, that's right." It appeared that Ted had become institutionalized at an early age—unable to function in open and free society as a result of his juvenile incarcerations.

Ted proved me wrong for a while. He married an older woman who kept him in line. But she left him, tired of playing mother as well as wife, after he came home stoned one day.

I next saw Ted as an inmate in prison. He was a model inmate who never caused any trouble. Ted is on parole now and seems to be doing well. What will happen when he is no longer supervised will be interesting.

Another way that a person demonstrates genuine caring is through the art of listening. Far too often we see counselors acting before they have really listened. When a crisis threatens we often see them taking strong security actions or opening their big mouths to make matters worse. We could all be more effective and demonstrate more caring if only we would listen.

Listening is a skill that must be worked on. It is more than simply hearing what a person says. The listener must demonstrate that he or she understands the implications of what is being said. I have always tried to be a listening supervisor. I have found that at those times when I have not taken the time to really listen, the level of tension on the tier increases. I have never been an inmate, but I can understand how their frustrations and impotence to change their environments can lead to violence. Many potentially dangerous crisis situations can be averted by empathetic listening.

To sum up: Crises in prison occur with disquieting frequency. They occur when inmates are thrown off emotional balance by the frustrations of inmate life. The best way to deal with crises is to anticipate them by being sensitive to precipitating conditions and by listening empathetically to complaints. When they do occur, remain calm and project self-confidence. Listen to the complaint and examine with the inmate(s) what can be done about it. However, never promise anything you can't produce—and produce what you have promised. Through conscious efforts to show a caring attitude, a great number of potentially major incidents can be defused.

---

either an attempt to "fake bad" or a tendency to be overly self-critical.

Human Synergistics Lifestyles Inventory People taking the Human Synergistics Lifestyles Inventory (HSLI), developed by Dr. C. Lafferty, are given a series of paired statements and asked which in each pair is more descriptive of them. Each statement is repeated often, with alternative pairings. The responses generate a profile of lifestyle preferences, among them the following:

1. *Humanistic.* Enjoys helping, developing, and teaching others. Regards people as inherently good and accepts them unconditionally. Likes people and understands them. Needs open, warm, and supportive relationships.
2. *Affiliative.* Cooperative, friendly, and open with others. High need for relationships with many friends. Wants to like and be liked.
3. *Approval.* Overly concerned with being liked. Bases own opinion of self and things on what others think.
4. *Conventional.* Conformist, taking few risks, covering mistakes, and following rules.
5. *Dependent.* Does what is expected without question. Compliant and eager to please. Highly influenced by others.
6. *Avoidance.* Tendency to stay away from any situation that may pose a threat. Need to protect self-worth rather than experience life and growth.
7. *Oppositional.* Needs to question things, including resisting authority. Critical tendencies may be a reaction against the need to be close to others. Behavior can be antagonistic, causing defensiveness in others.
8. *Power.* Tends to be hard, tough, bossy, and aggressive. Needs to gain influence and control over others to maintain personal security. Authoritarian and dictatorial as a leader.
9. *Competitive.* Self-worth based on winning. Turns many situations into contests. Strong need for commendation and praise. Can be self-defeating because failure is unacceptable.
10. *Competence.* Driven need to appear independent and confident. High expectations for self to the point that they are unreasonable. Failure to meet perfectionist standards results in self-blame.
11. *Achievement.* Feeling that personal effort makes the difference in the outcome. Need to set own standards of excellence and pursue set goals. Willing to take some risks if they may produce positive results.
12. *Self-actualizing.* Concerned with personal growth and development. Responsible, confident, relaxed, and unique. Motivated by internal need to accomplish set goals. Perceptive and understanding of others, accepting life in all its fullness.

Individuals scoring high in areas 1, 2, 11, and 12 tend to have a realistic view of self. Such people are extremely rare within prison walls. Individuals scoring high in areas 3, 4, 5, and 6 are insecure, but mask it to gain approval. They avoid risks and are easily influenced. High scorers in areas 7, 8, 9, and 10 keep people at a distance and are unable to deal with their feelings and emotions. They deeply distrust others. This group is heavily represented in institutions.

The Lifestyles inventory is also useful in identifying oppositional aspects of respondents' personalities. An individual who scores high on opposing lifestyle areas—for example Humanistic/Oppositional, Affiliative/Power, or Approval/Competitive—is attempting to meet competing and incongruent needs. Such attempts will probably result in debilitating intrapersonal conflicts and stress.

Myers-Briggs Type Indicator (MBTI) Developed in 1962, the MBTI is based on psychoanalyst Carl Jung's theories of judgment and perception. Jungian theory proceeds from the premise that from an early age, people are predisposed to react to the world in different ways. These preferences of interaction will direct the use of judgment and perception and influence both what people direct their attention to and the conclusions they draw from their interactions.

The MBTI identifies four separate preference categories that interact to provide sixteen separate groupings or "types" of individuals. The following are the four categories:

1. *Extroversion-Introversion* (EI). This category reflects the individual's basic attitudes or orientation. An extrovert is oriented to the outer world and tends to focus perceptions and judgments on people and things. An introvert is oriented inwardly and tends to focus judgments and perceptions on concepts and ideas.

   Extroverts (E) have a breadth of interests; they like variety and action and are often impatient with long slow tasks, preferring to get the task accomplished so that they may see the results of their efforts. They tend to be faster, often acting quickly, sometimes without thinking; because of this spontaneity, they dislike complicated procedures. Since they are people-oriented, they are interested in how other people would accomplish a task; they enjoy the company of others, are good at greeting people, and communicate well.

   Introverts (I) like to know why they are doing their jobs and dislike sweeping statements. Where extroverts have a breadth of interest, introverts have a depth of concentration that lends itself to detail work and uninterrupted work on a single project. They prefer quiet environments where they may work contentedly alone; they like to mull things over before they act (and sometimes fail to act). Being introspective and preferring their own company, they tend to have trouble remembering names and faces and experience some problems in communicating.

2. *Sensing-Intuition* (SN). The SN category relates to the individual's perception functions: The sensing process is dependent on observable objects and occurrences, which are processed through the senses. Intuition is based on "gut feelings" about relationships, things, and occurrences and is beyond the scope of the conscious mind.

   The *sensing* (S) preference relies heavily on facts; persons with this orientation seldom make errors of fact and are good at precise work. Sensing people prefer to deal with the immediate, real, practical facts of experience and life. They dislike problems that do not have a routine solution; because they are seldom inspired, they rarely trust inspiration. They prefer established routines using skills they have already learned. They tend to work steadily through a task to reach a conclusion, with a realistic idea of the time needed to finish the task. Although patient with routine details, when the details of a task become complicated, sensing types become frustrated and impatient.

   Intuitive (I) individuals like solving problems and prefer to perceive the possibilities, relationships, and meanings of experiences. They strongly dislike routine details and repetitive tasks, especially when they will take a long time to get right; however, they are challenged and patient with complicated, nonroutine situations. The intuitive enjoys learning new skills, but not necessarily using them. They tend to pursue a task for a short period with high enthusiasm and energy and then slack off. The intuitive person follows inspiration, good or bad, often makes errors of fact, and often jumps to conclusions.

3. *Thinking-Feeling* (TF). The TF category is the judgmental index. Thinking allows the individual to reflect on the probable consequences of choices made. Feeling, in contrast, will provide the basis of personal or social values.

   The *thinking* (T) type relies on logic and analysis to make objective and impersonal decisions while considering both the causes of events and where decisions may lead. Thinking types are relatively unemotional and uninterested in the feelings of others. They make decisions on an impersonal basis, sometimes ignoring the wishes and hurting the feeling of others without knowing it. Because they are able to reprimand people and fire them when necessary, they seem hardhearted. Although thinking types relate well only to other thinking types, they do have a need to be treated fairly.

   A *feeling* (F) person subjectively weighs the values of choices and how the choices matter to others when making judgments and decisions. Decisions may therefore be influenced by their own or other people's likes and wishes. They tend to be very aware of other people and their feelings and enjoy pleasing others even in small, unimportant ways. Thus they relate well to most people. Feeling people are sympathetic and dislike telling people unpleasant things; they also require occasional praise. They have a strong preference for harmony; their efficiency can be badly disturbed by discord.

4. *Judgment-Perception* (JP). This category relates directly to the extroverted—how a person deals with the outer world. A person who prefers to use judgment in these dealings will assign either the thinking or the feeling process to situations. However, if the individual reports a perception preference, the perceptive functions of sensing and intuition will dominate in relating to outer world activities.

   A *judging* (J) type tends to rigid organization and prefers to live in a decisive, planned, and orderly way in order to control events. Judging persons work best when they can plan their work and follow the plan; once they have reached a judgment, they tend to be satisfied. They want only the essentials needed to accomplish a task so that things may be settled and wrapped up; as a result, they may decide things too quickly, may not notice new things that need to be done, and may dislike to interrupt a current project for one with a higher priority.

   Perceptive (P) persons are spontaneous and flexible, attempting to understand life and adapt to its changing situations. They may have problems making decisions and may postpone unpleasant tasks. They do not mind leaving things open for alteration. They tend to be curious, welcoming new perspectives, but curiosity causes them to start many new projects they have difficulty finishing. When beginning a new task, they want to know all about it.

Each of the sixteen possible groups or types is derived from factor analyses of the category scores. Each type has particular characteristics depending on which of the bimodal attributes are dominant, auxiliary, tertiary (meaning "third most important"), or inferior functions.

Each letter indicates preferences in a fixed order; the first letter indicates the E-I preference; the second refers to the preference for the perceptive function (S-N), the third for the judgment function (T-F), and the fourth (J-P) for a function that is typically extroverted, thus the other preferred function will be introverted. By identifying each function, we are more readily able to understand the dynamics of behavior.

The dominant function is the function that is most used, most developed, and most allowed the freedom to shape the life of an individual. The individual may use auxiliary functions as the need arises and on occasion will resort to tertiary and inferior functions.

For example, an ENTJ is an extrovert whose dominant method of relating to the external world is as a thinking type. The J points to the third letter, which is the judgment function, thinking and feeling, in this case T. The P on the other hand points to the second letter, which is the perception function, sensing and intuition, thus an ENFP would take an intuitive (N) approach as the dominant method of relating to the external world.

In the case of the first example, ENTJ, since the dominant function is extroverted T, the auxiliary function would be introverted intuitive (N). The third function is the opposite of the second and thus would be sensing (S); the inferior function is therefore the opposite of the dominant function and is feeling, F. By using the same logic, the ESFP functions would be S (dominant), F (auxiliary), T (tertiary), N (inferior).

This may be translated into a client profile that depicts the client as decisive, ingenious, and good at many things. ENTJ clients are usually good at whatever they attempt and well-organized, relying on reasoning, logic, and analysis to control their world. Sometimes they are more confident than their experience warrants. They tend to use their intuitive function to look at the possibilities and relationships beyond what is known. The intuitive function hones the thinking function, but tends to negate the sensing function. It is often necessary for the ENTJ to rely on a sensing type to provide relevant details. Feeling is the least-developed process; the ENTJ may consciously manipulate others without regard for their feelings.

The introspective dynamics differ in identifying the dominant and auxiliary functions. Recall that the J-P index points to the visible and extroverted function. Thus if the attitude (E-I) preference is introverted, and the J-P index points to the extroverted function, the other preferred function will be introverted. Thus an ISFP would have a dominant preference of feeling. P points to the perception functions S-N. Since the J-P index points to the extroverted, that is, the visible outer-world function, S in this case, the other preferred function, F, must be introverted. Insofar as the E-I attitude is introverted, the dominant preference must also be introverted. The dominant function then is F; using the same formula and logic described for the extrovert, we can determine that the auxiliary preference is S, the tertiary N, and the inferior is T.

Any further explanation of the MBTI is beyond the scope of this book, but it can be helpful in identifying and understanding clients' personalities. Once this is achieved, the counselor can assist the client to develop tertiary and inferior personality functions in a wholesome direction. In the case of an ENTP client, for example, by helping the client to deal with routine assignments until completed and to identify flaws in logic that are being used to justify aberrant behavior, the counselor may help the client to an enhanced personality (For more information, see Myers and McCaully (1985) and [an abbreviated version] Keirsey and Bates (1984)).

All test results, information from the presentence investigation report, reports submitted by custodial and other staff, and criminal history are consolidated by the classification committee into a comprehensive profile of the inmate.

Risk and Needs Assessment

Once all the data have been gathered, new inmates are given a classification interview where the factors that establish their risk and custody level are explained to them. The psychological, educational, and vocational needs that have been identified during the assessment period are also explained. Inmates are told how to get into available programs.

The final step is to establish any override considerations. An override means that unusual factors not addressed in the classification instruments are considered important enough to override the normal custody level in favor of some other option. Areas of concern related to security and maintenance of order include gang or organized crime affiliations. Areas of concern related to custodial safety include any suicidal gestures, the protection of inmates known to be informants, and protection of those whose crimes make them targets for abuse, such as child molesters.

The override option provides for both objective and subjective considerations not addressed in the classification instruments. Overrides must be exercised carefully and justified in writing by the committee. If a classification instrument is overridden often, either the classification committee is not using the instrument properly or the instrument itself is defective. Either condition may result in judicial action to correct the problem.

In the years since the *Morris* decision, several classification models have appeared. The *actuarial prediction model* summarizes statistical data in an effort to predict future behavior. *Consensual classification* is an incremental process conducted by prison administrators that weighs classification criteria for implementation with individual inmates. *Clinically-based systems* employ psychological test data as predictors of behavior and adjustment. The additive model combines both actuarial and statistical data to provide cut-off scores along a continuum.

Decision-tree models are sequential: Each decision is based on the evaluation immediately preceding it. Figure 10-3 illustrates the decision flow. It has not been extended to the ultimate decision, but you can see the beginnings and progression of the decision flow. "Further decisions" are based on the criteria met at each level and will lead the decision makers to the custody level appropriate for a given inmate.

A common feature of the models is the relative simplicity of the instruments used to deal with a complex problem. The issues they address are of the utmost importance given the risk an inmate may present to society and the institution, as well as the needs of the inmate, which should be met in a way that minimizes that risk.

Two risk and needs models offer a closer look at the classification process. They are the National Institute of Corrections Model for Custody and Need (NIC) and

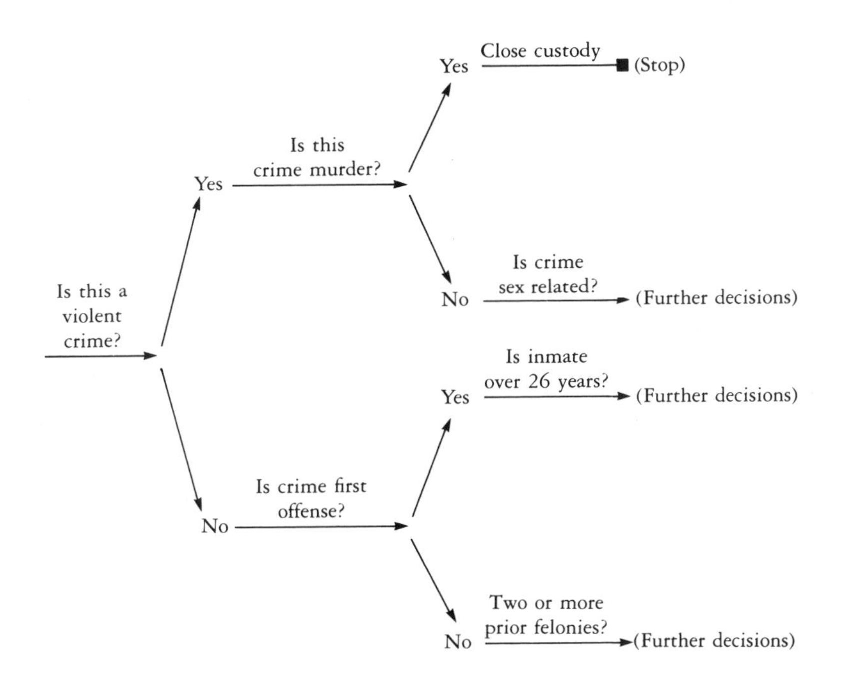

Figure 10-3 Custody classification decision tree

the Adult Internal Management System (AIM), both reproduced with score sheets in Appendix B.

The NIC Model

Custody Classification The NIC instrument identifies eight areas of assessment that, when properly scored, provide for objective custodial placement. To accurately assess a new inmate, the classification committee must refer to the detailed manual that accompanies the instrument. For the present purpose, a brief explanation is sufficient. As we go through the custody classification sections we will apply them to Bill Bloggs using the information contained in his PSI report in Chapter 6.

1. *History of Institutional Violence.* Assault and battery is defined as any overt act toward another person, including another inmate, in which contact was made and injury attempted. If a weapon was used or a serious injury occurred, this section is scored 7. If there have been two similar offenses, only the more serious is scored. Bill Bloggs had no such history. Therefore, unless he assaulted someone at the reception center, he would have a score of 0.
2. *Severity of Current Offense.* A severity of offense scale is provided on the reverse side of the instrument. Although an inmate may be committed for several offenses, only the most severe is scored, for a maximum of 6 points. Bill would get 6 points because he committed armed robbery.
3. *Prior Assaultive Offense History.* This section reflects an offender's propensity for frequent violent behavior. All attempts to commit battery (simple assault) are scored regardless of the degree of contact or injury. Maximum score is 6. Bill's assaultive history is minimal, but shooting a police officer to avoid capture is extremely serious and indicates that Bill can be dangerous when cornered. An assessment of 6 or 4 points would be discretionary, though in light of the seriousness of the assault, 6 points seems appropriate.
4. *Escape History.* Any documented escape or attempt within a given time frame is scored. Any adjudication by an institutional disciplinary hearing committee is sufficient for assessment whether or not there was a court prosecution. Maximum score is 7. Bill has no escape history. Assess him 0 points.

The first four areas, the custody score, are the primary indicators of the risk an inmate presents to the security of the institution and the welfare of other inmates and staff. The maximum score is 26. A score of 10 or more requires that the inmate be classified to close custody supervision. A score of 9 or less requires that the last four classification criteria be scored. Because Bill has had 12 points assessed against him, he will be placed in maximum custody. If he had 9 or fewer points, he would be scored on the following:

5. *Alcohol/Drug Abuse.* Abuse causing occasional legal and social adjustment problems is defined as any abuse that has resulted in up to five misdemeanor convictions or interruption of employment within the last three years. Six or more alcohol or drug convictions at any time or commitment to jail or treatment facilities for substance abuse within the last three years is considered serious abuse. Maximum score is 3. Because Bill has no history of drug or alcohol abuse, he would get 0 points.
6. *Current Detainer.* A detainer is a legal hold that another jurisdiction has placed on an inmate. Before releasing the inmate on parole or at the expiration of sentence, the institution notifies the jurisdiction that holds the detainer to make arrangements to transfer the inmate to that jurisdiction. Maximum score is 6. Bill has no current detainers. He gets 0 points here.
7. *Prior Felony Convictions.* Prior felony convictions do not include the current offense. Maximum score is 4. Again, Bill is not assessed any points since the current offense is his first.
8. *Stability Factors.* Each item should be verified before scoring. This is the only area in which the scores are cumulative, leading to a possible score of -4. Bill would get the maximum points for stability factors. He was older than 26 at the time

I ——— Heavy ———	II	III Moderate	IV ——— Light	——— V
Aggressive	Sly	Not excessively aggressive or dependent	Dependent	Constantly afraid
Confrontational	Not directly confrontational	Reliable, cooperative	Unreliable	Anxious
Easily bored Hostile to authority	Untrustworthy Hostile to authority	Industrious Do not see selves as criminals	Easily upset Clinging	Passive Seek protection
High rate of disciplinary infractions	Moderate-to-high rate of disciplinary infractions	Low rate of disciplinary infractions	Low-to-moderate rate of disciplinary infractions	Moderate rate of disciplinary infractions
Little concern for others	Con artists, manipulative	Concern for others	Self-absorbed	Explosive under stress
Victimizers	Victimizers	Avoid fights	Easily victimized	Easily victimized

Table 10-4 Characteristic behaviors by group

of his offense (-2), he is a high school graduate (-1), and he had been employed for more than six months at the time of his arrest (-1). If this section were scored no matter what the primary score, Bill would have a total of 12 - 4 = 8 points, putting him in medium rather than maximum custody. The classification committee might well decide to override the custody classification score and place him in medium custody.

If the score in sections 1 through 4 was 9 or less, that score is totaled with the scores in sections 5 through 8. If the final score is 7 or more, the inmate will be assigned to medium custody. If the score is 6 or less, the assignment will be to minimum custody.

Needs Classification Identification of inmate needs is based on all gathered data plus the inmate's own perceptions of his or her programming needs. During initial assessment interviews and testing, staff should elicit from inmates their ideas of what they need to become productive citizens in terms of their educational, vocational, and medical needs, mental abilities, psychological problems, and substance abuse problems. The NIC instrument reflects the fact that how an individual perceives his or her own needs is somewhat subjective. For this reason, it is imperative that a high-quality classification interview be conducted by someone thoroughly trained in the process. (See "Initial Inmate Classification Assessment of Needs" in Appendix B.)

Following the risk and needs classifications, the classification committee will summarize the findings, including the custody level and score, any override considerations and justifications for them, a final custody level assignment, and program and job assignment recommendations. (See "Initial Classification Summary" in Appendix B.)

Adult Internal Management System

Herbert C. Quay has created a classification system that differs substantially from the NIC model. Dr. Quay's model relies on behavior patterns as observed by correctional staff; it integrates the documented behavioral history addressed by the NIC model. This system of classification was adapted from an earlier model designed by Quay for use in the Florida juvenile corrections system and has been used in the federal prison system as well as in some states.

The Adult Internal Management System (AIMS) model sets behavioral criteria for five groups of inmates. (See Table 10-4.) Groups I and II ("heavy"),

Group III ("moderate"), and Groups IV and V ("light"). The terms heavy, moderate, and light allude to prison argot that describes a perceived risk, threat, or the propensity to victimize other inmates or to be victimized. The basic idea behind the AIMS model is that classifying inmates according to behavioral characteristics can greatly enhance treatment choices.

The unspoken assumption behind custody classification based on type of crime is that those who commit similar crimes are similar in terms of general behavioral traits. Under the risk classification model we have already examined, we might find all five of the AIMS groups represented in each custody level. Those who have been employed in correctional facilities can attest to the fact that at each custody level there are a wide variety of behavioral types. At each level there are those who are victimized and those who victimize. The vast majority of inmates, however, are found between these extremes. Also, within each custody level, it is necessary to provide programs that are duplicated at other levels. AIMS classification is an attempt to discriminate more meaningfully among inmates so that

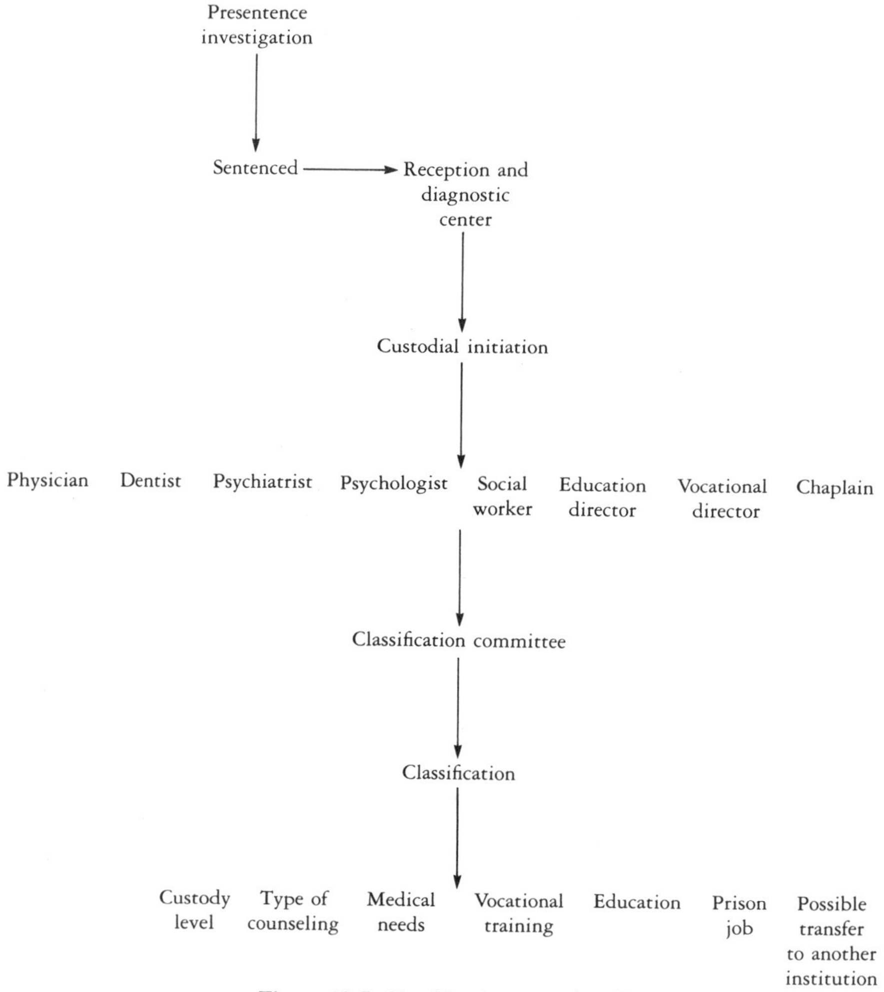

Figure 10-5 Classification procedure flow

victimizers are not mixed with victims and so that programs are not duplicated unnecessarily. This should result in both a reduction of prison violence and an increase in program effectiveness.

Correctional Adjustment Checklist Quay has devised two simple checklists—the Correctional Adjustment Checklist (CACL) and the Checklist for Analysis of Life History (CALH)—that when transferred to appropriate scoresheets provide a raw classification score. (Both are in Appendix B.) The raw score is then converted through the use of conversion tables into what statisticians call T-scores; raw scores that have been mathematically standardized to be able to compare scores that are dissimilarly distributed. In Quay's own words (1984:34): "The intent of the checklist is to cover as adequately as possible the domain of behaviors that might forecast adjustment and program participation in correctional settings."

To develop the CACL Quay solicited behavioral descriptions from professional correctional practitioners and from mental health professionals with correctional experience. He also incorporated descriptions developed from his own research with juveniles. The CACL, which contains forty-one behavior descriptions, tends to identify behavioral extremes of aggressiveness or submission.

In practice, line correctional personnel—the staff that has the most contact with inmates—complete the CACL. The form is then submitted to the classification staff for scoring. The scores place inmates in either the "aggressive-manipulation" group (Groups I and II) or the "passive-inadequate" group (Groups IV and V). Group III inmates are not identified by the CACL instrument because their behavior is generally acceptable in a prison environment.

Checklist for the Analysis of Life History The source of data for the Checklist for the Analysis of Life History (CALH) is the presentence investigation report. Quay asserts that descriptions that should be readily available from the PSI report and from the casework interview can be used to gauge the likely degree of institutional adjustment and program participation of the inmate (1984:36). The classification staff uses the CALH scores to assign inmates to groups.

After completing both the CACL and the CALH raw-score forms, the classification committee transfers the data to the Classification Profile for Adult Offenders and converts the raw scores to T-scores. (See the last two forms in Appendix B.) The T-scores are then combined to provide a final classification of the inmate.

The AIMS classification method provides an excellent management tool for the differential assignment of inmates to programs; it discriminates well among inmate behavioral types. Group I inmates create serious disciplinary problems more often than those in other groups, and Group III inmates rarely make violent disturbances and present fewer management problems.

However, it is not advisable to do away entirely with the risk classification tools provided by the NIC model. For example, an inmate convicted of homicide having no previous contact with the criminal justice system would be classified as a close custody inmate under the NIC model, yet the same inmate could qualify as a Group III inmate (the minimum custody level) under the AIMS criteria. Given current public attitudes to incarceration, it is extremely doubtful that initial assignment of a convicted murderer to minimum custody could be justified.

Figure 10-5 demonstrates the classification process starting from the presentence report to the initial classification of an inmate to custody level, job assignments, and programs aimed at institutional adjustment and personal improvement.

Summary

In this chapter we have looked at what prison classification is and why and how we classify inmates. Classification is the differential assignment of inmates to maximum, close, medium, or minimum levels of security. The determination of custody level is influenced primarily by the risk that the inmate presents to the safe and orderly operation of an institution. The classification level affects an inmate's access to counseling, educational, vocational, and recreational programs; program access varies inversely with security and custody levels—as security is increased, program access is decreased. Professional organizations such as the American Correctional Association and the National Institute of Corrections have been influential in setting standards for classification and creating models for implementing those standards.

The influence of the judiciary and the human sciences has resulted in some classification procedures that go beyond the concern for institutional security. Testing and assessment tools have been developed that can be used by correctional administrators to evaluate inmates in terms of their personalities, needs, and potentialities. We briefly examined the GATB, WAIS, MMPI, HSLI, and MBTI instruments.

Of the numerous classification methods in use, most are hybrids of the two models (NIC and AIMS) presented here. As new data become available through research, we will see more efficient and effective classification systems, just as evolution occurs in the more advanced fields.

References and Suggested Readings

Allen, H., and C. Simonsen. 1981. *Corrections in America.* New York: MacMillan.

American Correctional Association. 1981. *Classification.* College Park, Md.: ACA.

American Correctional Association. 1982. *Classification as a management tool: Theories and models for decision-makers.* College Park, Md.: ACA.

American Correctional Association. 1990. *Standards for adult correctional institutions.* 3rd ed. Laurel, Md.: ACA.

Farrington, D. 1988. Predicting individual crime rates. In *Prediction and classification*, edited by D. Gottfredson and M. Tonry. Chicago: University of Chicago Press.

Jeffery, C. 1979. *Biology and crime.* Beverly Hills, Cal.: Sage.

Keirsey, D., and M. Bates. 1984. *Please understand me: Character and temperament types.* Del Mar, Cal.: Prometheus Nemesis. (P.O. Box 2748, 92014; phone 619/632-1575)

Korn, R., and L. McCorkle. 1959. *Criminology and penology.* New York: Holt, Rinehart, Winston.

Lewis, O. 1967. *The development of American prisons and prison customs, 1776-1845.* Montclair, N.J.: Patterson-Smith.

Morris, N., and M. Miller. 1987. Predictions of dangerousness in the criminal law. In *Research in Brief, March 1987.* Washington D.C.: National Institute of Justice.

Myers, I., and M. McCaulley. 1985. *A guide to the development and use of the Myers-Briggs type indicator.* Palo Alto, Cal.: Consulting Psychological Press. (577 College Ave., 94306)

National Institute of Corrections. 1984. *Prison classification: A model systems approach.* Washington, D.C.: GPO.

Quay, H. *Managing adult inmates.* College Park, Md.: American Correctional Association.

Steadman, H. 1987. How well can we predict violence for adults? A review of the literature and some commentary. In *The prediction of criminal violence,* edited by F. Dutile and C. Foust. Springfield, Ill.: Charles C Thomas.

Steel, B., and M. Steger. 1988. Crime: Due process liberalism versus law-and-order conservatism. In *Social regulatory policy: Moral controversies in American politics,* edited by R. Tatalovich and B. Daynes. Boulder, Colo.: Westview Press.

Van Voorhis, P. 1988. A cross classification of five offender typologies: Issues of construct and predictive validity. *Criminal Justice and Behavior* 15:109-124.

Chapter 11

Group Counseling in Institutional Settings

When the prison gates slam behind an inmate, he does not lose his human quality, his mind does not become closed to ideas, his intellect does not cease to feed on a free and open interchange of opinions; his yearning for self-esteem does not end; nor his quest for self-realization conclude. If anything the needs for identity and self-esteem are more compelling.

Justice Thurgood Marshall

The Power of the Group

Jails and prisons were never meant to be and never can be nice places. They exist to punish lawbreakers and to separate them from society. They are prime examples of what Goffman (1961) has called "total institutions"; institutions like mental hospitals or army training facilities where large groups of people live together under tightly restricted and scheduled circumstances under the control of a central authority. Inhabitants of total institutions are either "managers," who control, or "subjects," who are controlled. It is the function of the managers to restrict social interaction between the subjects and the outside world. This authoritarian and coercive situation results in two antagonistic subcultures within the institution. Social distance between the controllers and the controlled is great, and each group tends to become hostile to the other.

The Inmate Code

Hostility toward the managers is expressed in informal rules known as the inmate code, which includes the game-playing we discussed in the section on transactional analysis. One such rule is "Don't be a sucker," a rule that warns inmates against granting trust and overt respect to prison staff. This rule does not mean that inmates should openly defy prison officials and regulations, because overt acts of defiance may bring down the wrath of the managers on the entire group. Rather, it means never being openly friendly to officials unless you can use them for your own ends, never cooperating beyond what is necessary to avoid trouble, never volunteering for anything simply for the good of the institution, and never showing subservience.

Unfortunately, the inmate code extends to non-cooperation with those members of the prison staff whose function it is to help them. No wonder it has been said that trying to rehabilitate criminals in prison is like trying to help alcoholics maintain sobriety in a brewery. Institutional counseling is the ultimate challenge for the criminal justice helper.

The Origins of the Inmate Code Many criminals develop a set of values and attitudes in opposition to lawful behavior through the frequency, duration, priority, and intimacy of their associations with individuals of like mind. The individuals with whom they most associate, either by choice or of necessity, become their reference group, the group around which they orient their lives and against whose standards they evaluate themselves. In prison the reference group becomes more powerful because it is now the only group with which criminals are able to associate. Within this closed community, antiestablishment values are refined and reinforced; compliance with these values can be much more of a survival imperative than it ever was on the outside.

Prisonization Though not all inmates enter prison with antisocial attitudes, new inmates, like new immigrants, face a painful process of assimilation into a new culture from which it is difficult to remain aloof. Clemmer (1958) has called the process of assimilating the norms and values of the prison subculture "prisonization." The basic premise of prisonization is that people who share a common experience, especially an imposed experience, develop a sense of "we-ness" buttressed by legitimizing attitudes that are in opposition to the attitudes of those who are imposing the experience.

The first steps in the prisonization process are simple acts of behavioral conformity; they occur regardless of how the inmate feels about performing them. The inmate follows the examples of other inmates because conformity makes life easier, avoids conflicts, and enables the inmate to fit in without being conspicuous. Soon the inmate is speaking the language of fellow inmates and beginning to define the inmate world in their terms. As Clemmer (1958:299) points out, it requires only a subtle and minute change to make a stated attitude become a "taken-for-granted perception."

Although all inmates have to conform behaviorally, not all—perhaps not even most—will conform attitudinally in the sense that they will internalize the inmate code as right and proper. Ways to avoid attitudinal assimilation suggested by Clemmer are shorter sentences and more frequent contact with the outside world. Inmates with strong personalities and those who actively strive to remain aloof from the prison subculture do not succumb to prisonization to the same extent as more pliable individuals. Some take on the values surrounding them only for convenience, being fully aware that their conformity is a temporary condition of their confinement (Hawkins 1976). Well-run group counseling sessions can help these individuals to counteract the insidious process of prisonization and even perhaps help those who have already succumbed.

Group Counseling

The inmate code is a major obstacle to effective institutional counseling. Attendance at counseling sessions, Alcoholics Anonymous and Narcotics Anonymous meetings, and vocational and educational programs is not a violation of the inmate code. Indeed, much banter is heard in prisons about the need to "get into a program." Unfortunately, the concern for getting into a program is usually motivated more by a desire to impress the parole board than by a genuine concern for self-improvement (Berne's "HDIGO"). If the ultimate reward for participation—early release—were not a reality, inmates who attended such sessions would be violating the inmate code and branded as "suckers" or "ass-kissers." Inmates who attend sessions aimed at reforming criminal behavior patterns may therefore spend a great deal of time telling other inmates how they are exploiting the sessions for their own ends.

Group counseling is an effective way to combat the negative group pressures that hinder rehabilitation. The differential association theory of crime stresses the power of peer group pressure to lead the individual into conformity with antisocial values. Why not use the same pressure for the opposite purpose? Group counseling can be a kind of intellectual judo in which the strength of the group is used against itself. Group counseling uses peer pressure to combat the criminal values of many group members. As Cressey has put it, "If the behavior of an individual is an intrinsic part of groups to which he belongs, attempts to change the behavior must be directed at groups" (1955:117).

This is not an easy task. How does one change the attitudes of individuals in a group that, with the exception of the leader, consists of criminals? Although it is extremely difficult, and realistically there will be at least as many failures as successes, it is not impossible. Think about the gratifying success rate of Alcoholics Anonymous (AA) groups. Is it more difficult to rehabilitate the typical alcoholic than the typical criminal? Objectively the alcoholic seems to present the more difficult case. After all, there is no biological urge to commit crimes as there is for the alcoholic to drink. The criminal who desists from committing crime does not suffer painful physical withdrawal symptoms that are alleviated only by committing another crime. Nor are criminals physiologically punished for stopping their activities as alcoholics are. On the contrary, they run the risk of punishment for continuing with the activity.

Many criminals enjoy the thrills of the criminal lifestyle just as alcoholics enjoy drinking. But neither alcoholics nor criminals like the negative consequences of their activities. Significant emotional events in their lives, the loss of jobs, spouses, and self-respect, and the loss of long periods of freedom constitute powerful motivations for change.

Any motivations for change must be brought into full consciousness. They must then be carefully nurtured. In other words, dissonance and tension must be generated in those whose attitudes are to be modified by forcing them to confront the reality of their behavior. Many criminals are so present-oriented that they fail to consider what five years in prison actually mean. It is the group counselor's task, with the cooperation of the group, to bring each member to the realization that powerful motivations for change do exist in every one of them. If AA can achieve respectable success rates in groups consisting of members who have all experienced the pleasures and the pains of alcohol, there is no reason that groups consisting of those who have experienced the pleasures and pains of crime could not enjoy similar success.

Group Dynamics

George Homans has defined a group as "a number of persons who communicate with one another often over a span of time, and who are few enough so that each person is able to communicate with all others, not at secondhand, through other people, but face-to-face" (1950:1). The prison community is not a group in this sense, but merely an aggregate of people in the midst of which the individual could feel terribly alone. None of us likes to feel alone; social animals that we are, we will often go to great lengths to become part of a group. Group counseling takes advantage of this human need by offering inmates a constructive alternative to the antisocial cliques that form in prisons.

Groups have dynamics of their own that are relatively independent of the individual attributes of their members. Much of sociology and social psychology revolves around how group life affects individual behavior. Numerous studies attest to the ability of groups to generate conformity to their norms, even among reluctant members. Group conformity is more likely if goals are shared; goals are more likely to be shared if they are democratically determined. As the group leader, the person who initiates the process, the counselor is in a position to strongly influence the goals. Inmates realize, of course, that the ultimate goal is to reeducate them into conformity with society's expectations. Therefore, they are not likely to choose topics that they perceive as being directly related to this end. As a group counselor, you must make haste slowly. Inmates will learn new values, unlearning old ones, only by a process of self-exploration that is of their own choosing.

Planning for Group Counseling

Goals and Operating Philosophy

The first task in planning group counseling is to formulate the specific goals that you want the group to pursue. Operate like a professor who has a certain core of knowledge to impart but who remains flexible enough to let the students dictate the pace of the class. Much interest and participation is lost in classes where professors refuse to follow a train of thought brought up by a student because "We have to finish Chapter 10 by Thursday." Activity in groups can be similarly stifled if you do not maintain an attitude of structured flexibility.

Selection of Members

Your next task is the selection of members from the pool of volunteers for group counseling. There is rarely a shortage (Juda 1984:48). Do not simply throw people together to see what will happen, an all-too-common practice in prisons (Rizzo 1980:29); Rizzo suggests a "loose homogeneity." The offenders' classification scales and their psychological profiles will obviously help you here. If the group is to concern itself with a specific problem like alcoholism, drug addiction, or sexual offenses, obviously inmates will be selected because they have problems in that area.

Each prospective member of the group should then be interviewed. The following is one of the ethical guidelines of the Association for Specialists in Group Work (ASGW):

> The group leader shall conduct a pregroup interview with each prospective member for purposes of screening, orientation, and, insofar as possible, shall select group members whose needs and goals are compatible with the established goals of the group; who will not impede the group process; and whose well-being will not be jeopardized by the group process (1980:1).

Corey (1980:102) suggests using the following questions to explore suitability in a half-hour interview with each candidate:

1. Why does this person want to join the group?
2. How ready is the person to become actively involved in the process of self-examination that will be part of the group?
3. Does the candidate have a clear idea about the nature and purpose of the group? Does he or she understand what is expected?
4. Might the person be counterproductive to the development of cohesion in the group? Might this group be counterproductive for the person?

The screening interview allows you not only to choose group members who will strengthen the possibility that the group will succeed but also allows you to become acquainted with individual clients. It also gives clients the opportunity to decide for themselves whether they really want to be part of the group. Thus the interview is a double screening process, yours and theirs. Otherwise, you and your clients are on a blind date, and those can sometimes turn out to be disastrous.

Components of Group Counseling

The best definition of group counseling is by Gazda, Duncan, and Meadows:

> Group counseling is a dynamic, interpersonal process focusing on conscious thought and behavior and involving the therapy functions of permissiveness, orientation to reality, catharsis, and mutual trust, caring, understanding, acceptance, and support. The therapy functions are created and nurtured in a small group through the sharing of personal concerns with one's peers and the counselors. The group counselees are basically normal individuals with various concerns which are not debilitating to the extent of requiring extensive personality change. The group counselees may

> utilize the group interaction to increase understanding and acceptance of values and goals and to learn and/or unlearn certain attitudes and behaviors (quoted in Mahler 1973:101).

Let us analyze the components of the definition to get a sense of the process of group counseling, what it is, and how it should be conducted.

"Group counseling is a dynamic, interpersonal process": The process is active, productive, forceful, and energetic. It is not static, but full of continuous verbal movement toward purposeful goals. It can be dynamic only if real concerns are put before the group for open discussion within the group.

"Interpersonal": It is an activity for two or more people. Advocates of group counseling feel that members learn and unlearn attitudes, values, and perceptions better in a group because it is more like their natural interpersonal world. Relating to peers is more consistent with normal socialization than relating to a counselor in a situation that can be like the teacher/student relationship. Most of all, "interpersonal" means sharing.

"Focusing on conscious thought and behavior": The topics explored are problematic attitudes and behaviors of which the group members are fully aware. Group counseling is not group therapy. Group therapy is more likely to deal with unconscious motivations; it is usually conducted by individuals with advanced degrees in psychiatry, psychology, or psychiatric social work. The difference is like the distinction between psychotherapy and individual counseling: Like psychotherapy, group therapy goes into great depth; it is a process that may last months or years. Group counseling is short by comparison and may be conducted by individuals with minimal specialized skills. The most successful group counseling in the world is conducted by the concerned amateurs of Alcoholics Anonymous. The personal attributes of the counselor are more important to success than the depth of the counselor's knowledge of the complexities of mental health.

"Permissiveness, orientation to reality, catharsis, and mutual trust, caring, understanding, acceptance and support": These are attributes that the counselor must strive to foster in the group. This is not easy with a prison group. Permissiveness does not mean that the members are allowed to act out, to bully weaker members, or to be otherwise disruptive. It means that the group should be democratic in its choice of problems to discuss, that no one member be allowed to monopolize the floor, and that no relevant topic be denied a hearing.

Neither does "permissiveness" mean that the group is run without ground rules. As with the formulation of treatment plans in community corrections, the rules should be determined by the group. However, group counseling is a guided experience: During the initial screening interview, the counselor will state expectations about what will go on in the group. The counselor basically wants group members to examine their impulses in an atmosphere of acceptance to help them make connections between those impulses and their criminal behavior. Groups function much more effectively if each member has been given an opportunity to participate in the formulation of group expectations. A democratic group structure outlining purposeful goals goes a long way toward creating a feeling of "we-ness" in the group. The essential elements of group interaction—each individual "I," the "we" of the group, and the "it" of the goals—must form an integrated "I-we-it" triangle if the process is to be useful (Anderson 1984:13-15).

Take care, however, that democratic decisions about group topics and issues are not at odds with institutional requirements, are not socially unacceptable, and are not unfit for some individual members of the group. As Bennett, Rosenbaum, and McCullough put it (1978:89): "We cannot continue to coerce offenders into conformity. We must provide those experiences necessary to individual adjustment and a meaningful life. For most people this comes through opportunities for intellectual and emotional growth. Why not for offenders?" Why not indeed?

"Orientation to reality": All group members must be aware that the goals of the group are directed toward the rejection of unrealistic and irresponsible values and behavior and the substitution of realistic and responsible values and behavior. "Realistic and responsible"

here are consistent in meaning with Glasser's usage in reality therapy. The general goals of a prison group are improved self-awareness, genuine problem-sharing, an awareness of the self-defeating nature of a criminal lifestyle, improved coping skills, and an understanding of the benefits and possibilities of the straight life. Specific goals are determined by the makeup of the group (for example, alcohol abusers, exhibitionists, and so forth).

"Catharsis" (the release and ventilation of repressed emotions associated with painful experiences): Psychoanalysts feel that much guilt, anger, aggression, and hostility are the result of repressed emotions. If these pent-up emotions can be liberated—brought into consciousness and explored—then much of the negativism they generate will dissipate.

"Mutual trust, caring, understanding, acceptance, and support": These attributes are conspicuously absent among prison inmates at anything beyond a superficial level, but they are not impossible to generate in a prison setting. Inmates do not possess these attributes because they have rarely encountered them. If you can foster such an environment, if you can demonstrate acceptance, understanding, and caring, some of it is likely to rub off. Here is one inmate's report of her experience in group counseling: "I have felt needed, loving, competent, furious, frantic, anything and everything, but just plain loved. You can imagine the flood of humility, release that swept over me. I wrote with considerable joy, 'I actually felt loved.' I doubt that I shall soon forget it" (quoted in Jarvis 1978:197-198).

"The therapy functions are created and nurtured in a small group": Size of the group is an important consideration. Too few members, say three, may be comfortable for the leader to handle, but it is not a very practical group in terms of the efficient management of time and resources. Groups this small also have the almost inevitable disadvantage of two members forming an alliance against the third. Too many members renders the group unmanageable; the group begins to act like a class in school, directing communications primarily at the counselor. This tendency defeats the whole purpose of a group. The more people there are in a group, the easier it becomes for some members to avoid discussing their problems. Even if no one wanted to hide, there is just so much air time, and the multiplicity of topics may prevent concentration on something important. The accepted optimal group size is between four and eight members (Ohlsen 1970:58).

Even a group of this size can be intimidating for the new counselor. In a one-on-one situation the counselor has the feeling of being in control, but it is not unusual for inmate groups to test new counselors by ganging up on them. Having a vested interest in maintaining their current self-concepts, demonstrating independence and noncooperation, and displaying bravado, group members often feel that the best defense is offense. Self-assured counselors deal with this obvious game-playing by letting the group know that they know what is going on and asking the members why they feel they have to do it. It is unwise to go on the defensive; toss the ball right back at the group, without emphasizing your moral superiority. The self-confident bull rules his pasture without snorting and bellowing.

"Through the sharing of personal concerns with one's peers and the counselors": The exchange of self-disclosure and feedback among members of the group is the essence of group counseling. The success or failure of the group depends almost entirely on how meaningful are the self-concerns expressed and how helpful the feedback.

But in prison inmates often have to shut off their emotions. Inmates are supposed to "do their own time." To reveal personal concerns is to open oneself up to abuse, derision, or even blackmail. Consequently, inmates may go to great lengths to lead the group away from themselves toward others or onto general topics. Such ploys may appear in any group, but they are especially likely in the prison setting. You must confront members about them, at the same time recognizing the motivations behind them. A prison group is not an encounter group for which members have paid considerable sums of money for "self-actualization." You will be setting yourself up for failure if you do not recognize the special problems of self-disclosure within a prison setting.

There are several ways to handle the lack of self-disclosure within the group. It is wise not to expect or to attempt to facilitate self-disclosure at all during the first session. Just give the group members an opportunity to warm up to intergroup communication by venting general nonthreatening concerns. Inmates must sense at least a modicum of acceptance before they will risk self-disclosure.

Nicholson (1981) wisely suggests that the first session begin with an explanation of Berne's theory of structural analysis. Its easy terminology and simple diagrammatic presentations of PAC interactions provide a useful framework from which all participants can analyze what will go on in future sessions. The ego states and their transactions can be drawn on a blackboard and explained. You will be surprised how easily group members will pick up on game-playing and how this powerful anchor of shared discourse will facilitate understanding.

After one or two getting-acquainted sessions, you may tell the group something like the following: "You know, we've been talking for quite some time together now, but I haven't heard anyone touch on the topics of 'self' or 'I' yet. Will somebody volunteer to explore with us the question 'Who or what am I?'"

The first attempt at self-disclosure should be positively reinforced by nonthreatening and nonjudgmental feedback from the counselor. Feedback should reflect the feelings of the discloser, making sure that the reflection is based on accurate perceptions rather than on inferences. If, for instance, Frank responds to your request to explore the question "Who am I?" by saying, "I suppose that by society's standards I'm a failure, a no-good screw-up," he is making a statement about his perceptions of how others view him. Do not imply that he perceives himself that way by asking him why he is a "screw-up." Instead, ask him if he agrees with that perception and why he does or does not. This feedback could lead to an animated group discussion of the attitudes held by group members.

As a member of the group, the counselor should be prepared to model self-disclosure and to answer uncomfortable questions honestly. It is not unusual for inmates to test the counselor by asking pointed questions like "Did you ever steal anything?" Everybody has stolen something at one time or another, even if it was only a candy bar or a company pen. Do not try to give the impression that you are a "goody two-shoes" by denying that you have, thereby modeling dishonesty. You might take advantage of such a question by describing how guilty you felt afterwards and asking other members of the group how they feel when they steal and how they felt when others have stolen from them. You can also use the opportunity to describe your ideas of responsibility, emotional maturity, respect for self and others, and how your values have enabled you to lead a basically happy life—but be careful not be preachy, trying to impress the group with your moral superiority.

"The group counselees are basically normal individuals with various concerns which are not debilitating to the extent of requiring extensive personality change": Respect the humanity of group members. Do not think of them as sick, evil, beyond help, or radically different from yourself. They are unloved people with deficiencies that prevent them from functioning in a socially acceptable way. Inmates who do have crippling concerns do not belong in group counseling. Think of all group members as possessing wholesome potential that needs only to be recognized. The distortions of reality you encounter are the result of faulty thinking rather than pathological blockages. Your task is to reeducate inmates toward responsibility, not to psychoanalyze them.

"The group counselees may utilize the group interaction to increase understanding and acceptance of values and goals and to learn and/or unlearn certain attitudes and behaviors": These are the goals of any counseling session, group or individual. A group is a guided effort to change a failure identity into a success identity through self-disclosure and feedback. The only difference is that group counseling makes use of peer feedback and modeling.

Topics and Strategies for Group Counseling

Your goal of group counseling is to guide your clients toward change by exploring their values, attitudes, and behaviors. There are specific strategies for doing this.

The Cost of a Criminal Lifestyle

From the perspective of some criminals crime is a rational pursuit because there is a logical fit between the ends to be attained and the means used to achieve them: Crime gets criminals what they want at a price they think they can afford. This first group exercise is designed to challenge that perception of rationality. From any objective viewpoint (going beyond the subjective perception of immediate rationality), for all but the kingpins, crime simply does not pay in the long run.

You can help a group of property offenders discover this for themselves by having them inventory their estimated gains from the crimes for which they are in prison. You might go even further by asking them to list their gains from undetected crimes committed between the current arrest and any previous arrest. They should list actual cash gains and the "fenced" value of any property taken. An offender who did forty months in prison for three burglaries compiled the following list, which covered ten other break-ins for which he was not caught:

Cash	$400
Stereos	150
TVs	75
Jewelry	200
Tools	20
Miscellaneous	180
Total	$1,025

After the lists are completed, divide the monetary total by the amount of time spent in prison (take along a calculator). The person in the example received a "paycheck" from his criminal activity of $1,025, for which he did forty months in prison. Therefore, his earnings were $1,025/forty months = $25.62 per month, $0.82 per day, or $0.10 per hour. You will be surprised at just how surprised the group members will be when they discover how much per hour they have been "working" for. Few of your clients, if any, have ever

Table 11-1 What do I gain and lose from a life of crime?

Benefits	Costs
Lots of leisure (not working)	No regular paycheck, little money to spend
The excitement and thrills	The boredom of sitting in a cell
The street reputation	The worry caused to my parents
Doing what I want, being free to be my own man	Having the screws decide almost all I do and when I should do it
Lots of girls think I'm cool	No women in the joint
The laughs	Police hassle and arrest
Putting one over on the system	Can't get a job because of record
Money for nothing	The whole prison experience
	Appearing in court and paying fines
	This prison is a long way from home, so I rarely see my parents
	My wife divorced me and married another guy while I was away

thought along these lines. Discussion of how smart it is to work for ten cents per hour is likely to be animated.

You can drive the point home by calculating the possible gains if that person had spent forty months in noncriminal activity. Ask what portion of the prison sentence the group member could reasonably have worked at a regular job on the outside. If the offender doing forty months would have worked only one quarter of the time, multiply this time by the take-home pay he would have received at minimum wage (about $400 per month): $400 times ten months = $4,000. Add to this approximately $100 per month in unemployment benefits that might have been available and the total is $7,000. Hardly a princely sum, but considerably more than $1,025. Even if you add to the fruits of a criminal lifestyle prison wages for those lucky enough to have a prison job (about 35 cents per hour) the contrast is still dramatic.

Other less tangible but sometimes more important costs and benefits of a criminal lifestyle can be discussed in the group.

To start this discussion rolling, have each member divide a sheet of paper into two equal columns labeled Benefits and Costs. You might consider dividing the group into two sections, one to brainstorm about the benefits of crime and the other to do the same about the costs of crime. They might arrive at something like Table 11-1.

Almost invariably members will be able to think of a lot more costs than benefits. Discuss this discrepancy with them, as well as the inconsistency of such items as "being free to be my own man" on the one hand and having every movement dictated by the "screws" on the other. You may even invite them to rate each item on a scale of 1 through 10 according to how positive they consider each benefit and how negative they consider each cost of crime. They can then sum the columns to arrive at their own numeric evaluation of their lifestyles. Since they will have listed the items themselves, as well as deciding what numeric score to assign to them, this exercise can be a powerful tool in getting your group members to realize how destructive their lifestyles are.

Role Reversal and Empathy Training

Criminals rarely think of the feelings of their victims. One way to encourage such thought is to ask them to list feelings they think the victims may have experienced as a consequence of their latest crimes. The lists might contain such feelings as anger, revenge, fear, and outrage. Ask the group members if they feel that these responses would be justified. This exercise should not be conducted in the spirit of "How would you like it . . . ?" Most members will have long ago become inured to such moralizing.

Most group members will have been victims of crimes themselves in the past; ask them to recall how they felt about their victimizers. Also have them explore the feelings they had when family members or close personal friends were victimized. The discussion should lead to the general conclusion that even criminals value justice and "law and order" when the offender/victim roles are reversed.

Sentencing Exercises

You can further emphasize their beliefs in conventional morality by engaging in the kind of sentencing exercises students do: Give the group hypothetical criminal cases and let them decide on appropriate penalties. Inmates will present arguments like those of probation officers at sentencing staffings (meetings at which officers decide together on a sentencing recommendation) and are often more punitive in their sentencing decisions. What group members will be doing in these exercises, without fully recognizing it, is reflecting on their anticriminal and prosocial values.

Reattributing Responsibility and Increasing Self-esteem

Generally when something good or praiseworthy happens to us, we all locate the causal agent in ourselves: "I was able to reach this goal because I'm a pretty dependable person." When something bad or blameworthy happens to us, we tend to attribute it to circumstances beyond our control: "I'm branded a criminal because I was never given a chance. My parents beat me and never took an interest in me.

Nobody'll give me a job, so I have to steal." In the first instance, we take a free-will perspective by offering "reasons" located within the self for having accomplished something. In the second instance, we take a determinist position by offering "causes" external to ourselves that guarantee "it could not be otherwise."

Such attributions of responsibility are normal. They function as defense mechanisms to protect our self-images. Like all other defense mechanisms, however, they can become pathologically destructive if we deny all responsibility for the negative things that happen to us. Unfortunately, many criminals are remarkably creative in exaggerating the power of outside circumstances to justify their criminal behavior and their inability to follow the straight and narrow. Your task is to demonstrate the irrationality and lack of responsibility inherent in this attitude. We are not dead leaves blown about by environmental winds. We do have a hand in what happens to us, and we can bring those events under our control.

In order to explore this way of thinking with your group, ask them to draw a large four-celled square like the one in Figure 11-2. Instruct them to list in the windowed cells (1) the good things in their lives that are the results of their own actions, (2) the good things in their lives that are the results of circumstances outside their control, (3) the bad things in their lives that are the results of their own actions, and (4) the bad things in their lives that are the results of circumstances outside their control.

The odds are that you will see the great majority of responses in the upper-left and lower-right cells of the square. Ask members to volunteer reasons why they have placed a given event in a given cell and then open up those reasons for discussion. You can steer the discussion to the concept of human autonomy, guided by the insights of Ellis's rational-emotive therapy. Emphasize that the subjective reality of free will is extremely useful for individuals if they are to believe that they are capable of initiating actions that will lead to self-improvement.

Individuals who insist that they are the directors of their own lives, that they alone are responsible for what they will become, and that they can overcome almost anything through sheer acts of will are people who will achieve far more than their less active peers who seek excuses for their failures.

Of course, things do happen to us that are beyond our control. Individuals who blame themselves for events that are clearly outside their power to influence suffer from low self-esteem (Ickes & Layden 1978). The objective of this exercise is not to move everything

MY LIFE

	Good things that have happened to me	Bad things that have happened to me
The result of my own actions		
The result of circumstances beyond my control		

Figure 11-2 Reattributing responsibility (Adapted from McGuire & Priestly (1985)

into the top two cells; it is to explore ways in which some of the bad events could have been brought under the individual's control. The exercise is also designed to enhance the self-esteem of those who masochistically attribute all negative events to themselves and who may tend to attribute the positive events in their lives to outside influences. The idea is expressed in Reinhold Niebuhr's Serenity Prayer: "God grant me the serenity to accept the things I cannot change, courage to change the things I can, and wisdom to know the difference."

Difficult Group Members

Despite everything you do to gather a relatively homogeneous group, you will probably run into members who will be disruptive in one way or another, though their behavior may not be intended to be disruptive or noncooperative. In order to prevent such members from hindering the progress of the other members of the group, you must deal quickly with disruptive behavior. Even if noncooperative behavior affects only the person not cooperating, you should deal with it. Some of the more usual types of difficult members are described below. Although we begin with the resister as a separate type, all other types are also resisters in one or more respects.

The Resister

Since all group members have volunteered and all have had the opportunity to screen themselves out of the process, you can assume that the resister is experiencing ambivalence about the process. This member has made a commitment in theory to self-exploration but finds it difficult in practice. Since we have dealt at some length with resistance in Chapter 9 we will not explore it in detail here. Most authorities on group counseling feel that resistance is easier to deal with in a group than with an individual, particularly if you have given the group a common discourse for identifying resistance, such as TA's structural analysis. For instance, Bry states:

> The first and most striking thing in handling resistance in groups is that frequently resistance does not have to be "handled" at all, at least not by the therapist. The group is remarkably effective in dealing with this phenomenon. Early in the experience of each group considerable effort is directed toward demonstrating what resistance is and how to become sensitive to its appearance in others as well as oneself. The group members as well gradually develop ideas as to how to deal with resistance and how to use it productively. In cases of protective talking, sooner or later a group member usually gets sensitive to its resistance character and starts complaining about the "beating around the bush" (1951:112).

The "Expert"

The "expert" knows the answer to everyone's problems and dispenses advice liberally on how to deal with them. This behavior can be intimidating to the group leader if the advice-giver really is an expert, or if everyone thinks so. I once had a physician in a group of child molesters who knew what was wrong with everyone but himself. Since he was an M.D. and I had only a master's degree at the time, I was awed. I felt myself relinquishing the group direction to him. Rather than trying to understand his motivations, I eventually confronted him with a reminder that I was the group leader, he was an offender, and that I had dealt with "hundreds" of sex offenders. In other words, I reduced myself to his level by puffing up my sense of importance as an "expert" in my own right. This was a poor way of handling the situation; I was a bull bellowing that this was my pasture.

An empathetic recognition that this man's conviction as a child molester had severely damaged his self-respect and that he was trying to regain some of it by demonstrating his superiority would have led to a more sympathetic and understanding resolution to the problem he posed to the group. It is likely that he used advice-giving to divert attention from his own problems, from letting others help him to face his painful situation. Perhaps he even felt that his advice would be genuinely helpful.

We all know how unwelcome unsolicited advice is. The group is not meeting for exchange of advice but for self-exploration. When a group member offers advice to another member, you might say: "Charlie, it's obvious that John's problem is of concern to you, and you're concerned enough to offer some suggestions about what he might do." Without pausing, you could then address John: "John, when you have difficulty in coping, do you like to have someone who cares enough to suggest what you might do?" "Do you feel that Charlie's suggestion could be of use to you?" You have interpreted Charlie's advice as a genuine attempt to help John with his problem; you have not put him down. You have also given John an opportunity to respond to Charlie's advice-giving, plus a chance to explore his problem further. John will put Charlie in his place if he feels he needs to; that is part of the group process of getting feelings out into the open. It is important that any necessary putting-down be left to the group members rather than to the group counselor. Only after "experts" are confronted with the unacceptability of their behavior will they start to explore their own problems.

The Monopolizer

The monopolizer, like the resister and the expert, tends to be a self-centered recognition-seeker who wishes to rule the group pasture. Like the expert, the monopolizer may really feel that he or she is the only one present with anything meaningful to contribute. However, monopolizing may also be a conscious tactic to steer the group away from uncomfortable topics to topics of the monopolizer's choosing. Either way, the effect on the group is negative.

Bry's statement about the resister is likely to apply here. Sooner or later someone will pipe up with "Why don't you give somebody else a chance to speak?" Once that happens you can say something like: "Debbie, you feel angry at Sue because you feel that she's not interested in what others have to say and may be avoiding topics that are not comfortable for her. Am I right?" If Debbie indicates that you have accurately reflected her feelings, you might go on to say to Sue: "Sue, do you see yourself as monopolizing the conversation? Wouldn't you really like to listen to what others have to say and perhaps learn more about yourself and about others?" Monopolizers lack the important skill of listening. They need feedback from the other members about how their behavior is affecting others, even if the feedback causes a temporary sullen withdrawal from participation.

The Withdrawn Member

The withdrawn group member either is engaging in passive resistance or is lacking in confidence or the verbal skills to express himself or herself effectively. This person hides, quite content to let the monopolizer or anyone else have the limelight. The counselor should resist calling on such a person as a teacher calls on a student in a classroom, but the withdrawn member is fair game for other members to call on. Be ready to help the person out on such occasions so that being on the spot does not become too painful.

You might decide that you have made a mistake in allowing the withdrawn person to participate in the group or that the person has made a mistake in deciding to participate. That person's presence, however, can be taken as a sign that he or she desires counseling. You can determine this using a session evaluation form containing the question: "Would you like an individual session with me?" If the answer is yes, the person can transfer from group to individual counseling. If it is no, every effort must be made to include that person in the group discussions.

The Masochist and the Sadist

Masochists are persons with low self-esteem and ingrained dependency needs who purposely set themselves up as targets for the displaced aggression of others. They doubt their ability to be loved, respected, or accepted by others. Since they desire companionship and relationships, however, they feel that the only strategy available to them is to make themselves the victims of bullying, teasing, bad jokes, and sarcasm. They often become welcome targets for sadistic members of a group, and others may quickly follow the sadist's lead to avoid personal exploration.

Both the masochist and the sadistic bully must be quickly identified. The feelings of both parties should be reflected so that other group members can suggest better methods for each to relate to others. Under no circumstances should you allow a group member to be a constant target for unproductive criticism and hurtful comments. When other group members realize that such bullying is not acceptable to you, they will rally to the defense of the masochist. They can be relied on to put the offending party down. Allow them to do this for as long as seems useful—he or she needs it—but if violence threatens to replace the spoken word, as may well happen with a bully, you must bring the put-down to an end. You may offer the offending party an "out" by suggesting that he or she perhaps really didn't mean to be hurtful: "Isn't that true, Mike?"

Advantages and Disadvantages of Institutional Group Counseling

There are, then, both theoretical and practical reasons why group counseling may be superior to individual counseling in an institutional setting, though not for all clients—some clearly benefit more from individual sessions. Likewise, many corrections workers are more comfortable conducting private rather than group sessions.

Some Advantages

1. Shortages of time and personnel make groups an efficient way to counsel individuals with similar problems.
2. Groups with prosocial purposes offer inmates a constructive alternative to the antisocial inmate cliques that form naturally in response to the need of humans beings for social interaction.
3. When group members share problems, much is learned about alternative coping strategies.
4. These alternative strategies can be tried out in the abstract in the group by involved discussions with others who have experienced them.
5. Well-led, democratic groups encourage a feeling of "we-ness."
6. The sense of belonging can enable group pressure to change the attitudes of individuals in the direction of the group's purposes—to change antisocial attitudes into prosocial attitudes.
7. Unlike one-on-one counseling with a representative of the "system," group counseling lessens the possibility that an inmate will be intimidated by a perceived authoritarian relationship.

Disadvantages

1. Some offenders may be reluctant to explore intimate feelings with peers, although they may desperately want to. Some feel much more comfortable speaking in private with an authority figure. You can handle this including the invitation for individual sessions in your evaluation forms. Concerns that have surfaced in the offender's mind during a group session can then be voiced in private.
2. Time can be wasted pursuing meaningless topics; unfortunately, we can realize they are meaningless only after they have been fully expressed. Only experience will tell you when to redirect the session along more meaningful avenues. However, this lost time is more than compensated for by the time saved in counseling a number of individuals at once.
3. There is a danger that the means become accepted as the goals. If discussion is generated without reference to where the discussion is leading, little is accomplished. The discussion is the means, not the goal. Group counseling must always be directed to realistic goals.
4. Some group members may take advantage of the numbers in the group to hide, like students who select large classes and then sit at the back to avoid class participation; they miss out on much of the educational experience. Likewise, the offender who hides misses out on much of what could be personally meaningful. Evaluation forms can help the counselor determine if a given person is a hider or someone who really wishes to address problems but who is shy.

Perspectives from the Field

A Man Called August

Steven Taylor, Ph.D.

Taylor is the director of the Center on Human Policy and professor of special education and sociology at Syracuse University, New York. This story is reproduced with the kind permission of Dr. Taylor. It has been published in ***Institutions, Etc.****, Vol. 7, 1984, and in the* ***Academy of Criminal Justice Sciences Today,*** *May 1986.*

This is a story—a true one—about an ugly institution, an amoral bureaucracy, personal tragedy, and the indefatigability of the human spirit. It is a story about a man named August.

I first met August in March 1979. He was living then at a place called Craig "Developmental Center," an institution for the so-called mentally retarded in Sonyea, New York. Sonyea is a road sign found on a stretch of highway located between Auburn and Attica prisons in upstate New York. August had lived there since 1941.

August seemed to be the kind of fellow who gave severely and profoundly retarded people a bad name. He was certainly one of the most retarded people I had ever met. He couldn't speak, use the toilet, dress himself, or do much of anything at all. He also had quite a few troubling behaviors. Staff at the institution variously described him as "aggressive," "regressive," the "worst case," and "the most severe behavior problem." In short, August was the prototypical "wild man," a lost member of the human family.

August wasn't always this way. We'll probably never know August's side of the story. But the institution's side is well-documented in volumes of case records, ward logs, and professional evaluations maintained over the past forty years.

Born in New York City in October 1936, August's early years had been far from trouble-free. Doctors suspected that he had suffered brain injury at birth, and at nine months of age he incurred a severe head injury in a fall from his crib. As bad as all of this might seem, his real troubles were only starting. In the fall of 1940, his twenty-six-year-old mother was killed as she attempted to rescue August from the path of an oncoming truck. One year later, August, scarcely five now, found himself at what was then Craig State School, hundreds of miles away from his New York City home.

August's first several months at the institution were rather uneventful, at least from the institution's perspective. An entry from the ward notes on October 31, 1941, reads: "On ward in good condition. Gets along well with other boys." Then something happened.

By mid-January of 1942, August was striking out at his peers on the ward. By 1948, he was digging his rectum and smearing feces, and by 1949 he was continually ripping off his clothes.

Remember the 1950s and '60s? August's memories of the period are probably hazy at best: "He is constantly under heavy sedation."

The drugs took their toll. By 1958, August began to experience "extrapyramidal disorders," a drug-induced pseudo-Parkinson's disease involving twitches, tremors, difficulty ambulating, and loss of balance. To this day, August walks with an unsteady gait. Yet the drugs did not do what they were supposed to do: namely, control his behavior, reduce his aggression, or eliminate his untidy personal habits.

So the institution turned to a time-proven device for controlling unruly inmates, the straightjacket, euphemistically called the camisole. August spent the '50s and '60s in restraint: "Occasionally, patient has days and short periods of time out of restraint."

By the early 1970s, the man seemed to have been broken, a real-life R. P. McMurphy. He lost weight, looking "emaciated and run down," became "dull and lethargic," and began "falling frequently." He still occasionally assaulted fellow inmates and staff. However, he slowly turned inward, becoming asocial rather than antisocial, isolating himself.

They extracted his infected teeth around this time, and he lost one ear to the surgeon's knife. The records don't say much about this. What is it about institutions that we can find out more about a man's bowel than how he lost his ear?

Some time around the spring of 1972, they say August took a liking to the shower room on his ward. The records don't say a lot about this either; three months' worth of ward notes for this period are missing completely. August spent the next seven years of his life in the shower room.

The advocates got August out of the shower room. I'm sure you know the type: naive and idealistic, smug and self-righteous, pushy and arrogant. Advocates seemed to be getting their way back in 1979.

The day I first met August was his second day out of the shower room. August looked like what they called the "living dead" at Auschwitz and Treblinka. He lay on the floor, grunting and groaning, with an agonized look on his face. He didn't seem to be interested in having visitors, no eye contact, no sign of recognition.

Within days, August became a plaintiff in a federal lawsuit against Craig's director and the commissioner of New York's Office of Mental Retardation and Developmental Disabilities. After fighting the suit for five years, the state finally agreed to settle the case this past April. It probably just wasn't worth all the time and embarrassment. I saw August last August, for the fifth time. He's out of the institution now. August lives in a small home with six other people. It's not perfect. The house is located not far from Craig and formerly was the groundkeeper's residence. It's not part of the community, but it's not the institution either.

August spends his days at the Medicaid-funded "day treatment center." He sits at a table sorting blue and yellow pieces of paper, putting pegs in a pegboard, and otherwise wasting his time. For doing this day in and day out, August gets oyster crackers and some kind words.

August is a changed man. I knew this when he reached out his hand to shake mine.

August will never receive a college diploma. He's developed some skills and never causes any trouble, though. He's toilet trained, eats with a fork and spoon, and not only keeps his clothes on, but dresses himself.

Perhaps the biggest change in August is his sociability. He never used to smile at anyone else. Now he thrives on human contact. This wild man, this aggressive and then asocial individual, spent the better part of an hour holding my hand, patting me on the back, and taking my hand and stroking the side of his head with it. The supervisor of August's home says that everyone likes working with August: "He's loving, kind, and gentle."

A lost member of the human family has come home.

So, what are the lessons of August's story? The first has to do with what sociologists call the self-fulfilling prophecy. If we view people as animals and treat them that way, then surely they will act like animals. This goes for people we label mentally retarded as well as juvenile delinquents and even hardened criminals.

The second lesson is that all people, even the so-called profoundly retarded, can learn to grow if given the opportunity. August was the "worst case," the "most severe behavior problem" at the institution. If August can learn skills and live in a small home, then no person need live in an institution for the mentally retarded.

The next lesson relates to the nature of change. August's life did not improve because the bureaucracy became more humane or just. To be sure, some decent people made changes in August's life possible. Yet the bureaucracy resisted change at every step. It took a lawsuit to get August out of the shower room.

The last lesson is a more sobering one. It concerns the durability of institutions. Craig was not always an institution for people labeled mentally retarded. Before that, it was a facility for people with epilepsy. We no longer put people with epilepsy in institutions. One hopes that the day when we will stop segregating people with mental retardation is not far away.

The place called Craig seems to be a dying institution. While one building is earmarked for the mentally retarded, most of the institution is being converted to the Groveland Correctional Facility.

As retarded as they say he is, August knew it was a prison all along.

Summary

Time and cost considerations make group counseling in institutions attractive. This does not mean that group counseling is "second best" to individualized counseling. Group counseling can actually be more beneficial for some clients than individual counseling. Group counseling uses the power of the group to achieve its aims. It offers inmates a constructive alternative to the antisocial cliques that develop in prisons and can offset the power of the inmate code. Through the process of sharing, inmates can learn about alternative coping strategies from others who have "been there." A properly run group can develop a feeling of "we-ness," which is not always possible in individual counseling.

Exercises derived from the insights of TA, RET, and reality therapy can be used to stimulate discussion; the "counting-the-costs" exercise is often particularly beneficial. It is important that you plan topics for discussion in your counseling strategies; it is too easy to mistake discussion that is animated but irrelevant for progress. Group counseling must have a goal to direct it. However, any relevant topic raised by a group member should be explored. As a member of the group, the counselor is fair game for discussion.

In almost any group setting there will be members who are disruptive. You can minimize their effect through the proper selection of members based on assessment information and one-on-one interviews, but disruptive members will always slip through. Group members themselves will take care of much of the disruption, but the counselor has the ultimate responsibility of dealing with disruption. Disrupting members should be dealt with in a dignified and caring way, but disruption may be a signal that the person doing the disrupting should not be in the group and should be offered individual counseling. Finally, the story of August illustrates how even the most intractable of individuals can improve significantly if treated with warmth and caring.

References and Suggested Readings

Association for Specialists in Group Work. 1980. *Ethical guidelines for group leaders.* Falls Church, Va.: ASGW.

Anderson, J. 1984. *Counseling through group process.* New York: Springer.

Exercise in Group Counseling

One of the best exercises for getting the feel of group counseling is to repeat the exercise in retribution of responsibility. Since social psychologists tell us that almost everybody has the tendency to systematically bias causal attributions, this exercise will be more realistic for you than exercises such as counting the cost of criminal lifestyle because you will be dealing with real issues rather than role-playing. The instructor may wish to act as the group leader, or he or she may wish to assign this task to someone. Just as in a real group situation, the group leader can begin the process by asking one of the other members to volunteer to explain a life event and to state where he or she has placed it in the 2 X 2 square. The discussion among group members can then begin to explore whether that event (good or bad) could have been brought more under the control of the individual.

This is obviously a time-consuming exercise, and it is likely that not everyone in the class will have the opportunity to offer a life event or serve as the group leader. Given the time constraints, I feel that it is preferable to go into some depth with one or two individuals rather than to try to cover everybody superficially. Therefore, the instructor may wish to examine everyone's summary of life events prior to the exercise, select one or two of the most interesting ones, and ask those people to volunteer.

Bennett, L., T. Rosenbaum, and W. McCullough. 1978. *Counseling in correctional environments*. New York: Human Sciences Press.

Bry, T. 1951. Varieties of resistance in group psychotherapy. *International Journal of Group Psychotherapy* 1:106-114.

Clemmer, D. 1958. *The prison community*. New York: Holt, Rinehart & Winston.

Corey, G. 1983. Group counseling. In *Being a counselor: Directions and challenges*, edited by J. Brown and R. Pate. Monterey, Cal.:Brooks/Cole.

Cressey, D. 1955. Changing criminals: The application of the theory of differential association. *American Journal of Sociology* 61:116-120.

Goffman, E. 1961. *Asylums*. Garden City, N.Y.: Anchor.

Hawkins, G. 1976. *The prison: Policy and practice*. Chicago: University of Chicago Press.

Homans, G. 1950. *The human group*. New York: Harcourt, Brace & World.

Ickes, W., and M. Layden. 1978. Attributional styles. In *New directions in attribution research* (vol. 2), edited by J. Harvey, W. Ickes, and R. Kidd. Hillsdale, N.J.: Lawrence Erlbaum Associates.

Jarvis, D. 1978. *Institutional treatment of the offender*. New York: McGraw-Hill.

Juda, D. 1984. On the special problems of creating group cohesion within a prison setting. *Journal of Offender Counseling, Services and Rehabilitation* 8:47-59.

Mahler, C. 1973. Group counseling. In *Group counseling: Theory, research, and practice*, edited by J. Lee and C. Pulvino. Washington, D.C.: American Personnel and Guidance Association.

McGuire, J., and P. Priestly. 1985. *Offending behaviour: Skills and stratagems for going straight*. London: Batsford Academic and Educational.

Nicholson, R. 1981. Transactional analysis: A new method of helping offenders. In *Correctional counseling and treatment*, edited by P. Kratcoski. Monterey, Cal.: Duxbury Press.

Ohlsen, M. 1970. *Group counseling*. New York: Holt, Rinehart & Winston.

Rizzo, N. 1980. Group therapy: Possibilities and pitfalls. *International Journal of Offender Therapy and Comparative Criminology* 24:27-31.

Chapter 12
Dealing with the Alcoholic Client

If you treat an individual as he is, he will stay as he is. But if you treat him as if he were what he ought to be, he will become what he ought to be and could be.

Wolfgang von Goethe

Although we might talk in very general terms about causes of criminal behavior, all theorists should acknowledge that these are all subject to the deadening qualification "all other things being equal." It is true, but not helpful, to describe criminal behavior as irresponsible. It is also true that irresponsible behavior is highly associated with the lack of warm reciprocal love attachments to others and that this deficiency can often be traced to early emotional deprivation.

But criminal behavior is located somewhere in a dense and messy causal maze, and many are the specific pathways trodden by those who arrive in your office. Many clients have substance abuse problems, a few have chemical imbalances, some are normally responsible people who have succumbed to the pressures of the moment. Without specific intervening variables functioning as proximate causes (the determinant most immediately preceding an event), the more general ultimate causes (determinants that are fundamental and usually the furthest removed from the present) would have remained dormant. Although proximate causes may be quite difficult to work with, they are certainly more amenable to identification and treatment than are ultimate causes.

This book does not offer an exhaustive typology of the characteristics of such offender types as the murderer, the robber, or the check forger. A useful treatment of such typologies can be found in Clinard and

Quinney (1973). We are concerned here with general patterns of behavior and personal characteristics that may dispose people to commit any number of different crimes. The five problem groups that are the most common or that present the greatest treatment challenges in corrections are alcoholics, drug abusers, sex offenders, schizophrenics, and the intellectually deficient.

"Normal" clients largely bring substance abuse problems on themselves by choosing to take behavior-altering substances into their bodies. Alcoholism, the subject explored in this chapter, is perhaps the most common problem among criminal justice clients. Chapter 13 deals with drug abuse, the second most likely problem area for a criminal justice worker. The following two chapters deal with clients whose problems are within themselves rather than within a pill or a bottle: the sex offender, the schizophrenic, and the intellectually deficient.

The Scope of the Alcoholism Problem

An estimated one-third of all arrests are for alcohol-related offenses, and about 75 percent of robberies and 80 percent of homicides involve a drunken offender or victim or both (Masters & Robertson 1990:274). Alcohol is at the same time the most deadly and the most popular of chemical comforters. We drink to be sociable, to liven up our parties, to feel good, to sedate ourselves, and to anesthetize the pains of life. Fishman (1986:14-19) estimates that between 10 and 13 million Americans suffer from alcoholism and that about one out of every ten Americans will develop a serious alcohol-related problem at some point. Males are at much greater risk for alcoholism than females. Failkov's review of the literature (1985:248) shows that the lifetime expectancy rate for alcoholism among males ranges between 3 and 5 percent, but only between 0.1 and 1.0 percent for females. The greater risk for males has been attributed both to greater social pressure for males to drink and to differences in neurophysiological processing of alcohol (Hoffman & Tabakoff 1985). The cost of alcohol abuse to society in terms of crime, health, and family and occupational disruption is staggering.

Alcohol is a depressant drug that affects behavior by inhibiting the functioning of the higher brain centers, the locus of our rational thought processes (the conscience, or the superego). The more alcohol we ingest, the less inhibited our behavior becomes as the rational neocortex surrenders control to the emotions of the more primitive limbic system. Raw emotions are then allowed expression without first being channeled by reason. With the superego brake released, husbands beat up wives, fathers molest their daughters, young men demonstrate their bravado by assaulting strangers and breaking into gas stations, and friends sometimes kill one another. The rate at which this surrender to raw emotionality occurs depends on a number of variables such as the alcohol content of the drinks and the number, the speed with which they are drunk, the weight of the drinker, the amount of food in the stomach, and even the time of day.

The Problem Drinker and the Alcoholic

The difference between a problem drinker and an alcoholic is not an easy one to discern. Certainly, both types drink themselves into a stupor with regularity, and the negative consequences to themselves and to others are equally serious. One way of differentiating them might be in terms of their motivation to drink: Problem drinkers are not physically addicted to alcohol; they drink to achieve the euphoria that enables them to escape a threatening reality. Problem drinkers may or may not become alcoholics (physically addicted to alcohol) after years of excessive drinking. The roots of their problem may be psychological or social or both, but they certainly have a psychological dependence on alcohol.

Full-blown alcoholics have a physical dependence on alcohol. The American Psychiatric Association's DSM-III-R (APA 1987:173), terming this "Gamma alcoholism," characterizes it as the inability to stop drinking while physical and financial resources remain viable once a drinking bout has begun. The body has developed a metabolic demand for a particular substance and rebels violently when that substance is denied to it. Alcoholics use alcohol not necessarily or normally to assuage psychological pain, but to avoid the terrible physiological pains of withdrawal (which can be more life-threatening than withdrawal from narcotics). Often the social and psychological difficulties of alcoholics follow from their alcoholic condition rather than causing it, unlike problem drinkers, whose problems led them to seek solace in the bottle. Approximately 10 percent of those who drink become alcoholics (Mendelson & Mello 1986:13).

Alcoholic Stages

Jellinek's authoritative studies (1960) suggest that alcoholism is a progressive disease that occurs in predictable stages. We will concentrate on the four primary stages, although each can be broken down more minutely.

1. The first stage, the *prealcoholic symptomatic stage,* begins with the first drink, whether taken for social or other reasons. The age of onset for males is in the late teens to early twenties, for females somewhat later (APA 1987:174). Though drinkers may occasionally overindulge and make fools of themselves, they find it a small price to pay for the pleasure they experience. Not only does drinking give them pleasure, but they find that it increases their confidence and sociability and diminishes their tensions. Unfortunately, many of us come to view alcohol as a magical tonic to which we turn more and more often as a morale booster and a tension reducer.
2. The *prodromal stage* begins when heavy drinkers suddenly begin to experience amnesiac ("blackout") episodes. They wake up after a bout of drinking unable to recall what they did the night before. This stage also marks the onset of secret drinking, a preoccupation with planning for the next drink, and gulping rather than sipping drinks. Drinkers in this stage show some anxiety about their growing reliance on booze, but they quickly submerge it in a sea of more alcohol. Their drinking increasingly becomes more a private than a social activity.
3. In the *crucial stage* individuals begin to lose their grip on alcohol as it tightens its grip on them. They can still control when they will drink but not how much they will drink once they start. No longer social drinkers, they have become antisocial drinkers. Faced with impaired efficiency on the job and in the bedroom, they begin to experience occupational and marital problems, even dismissal and divorce. The threat of impending problems may lead drinkers to foreswear drinking for long periods of time, for they can still exercise their willpower at this point. However, because they are psychologically predisposed to turn back to drink, they easily revert.

   If they do turn back to the bottle at this stage they have probably crossed the line from psychological to physical dependence. They now engage in many prolonged drinking binges ("benders"). They become oblivious to their responsibilities, to their personal health and safety, and to the welfare of their families. Their lives become an all-consuming quest for alcohol. Many alcoholics at this stage, however, can abstain from alcohol for some time after the bender is terminated.
4. In the *chronic stage* the drinker "hits bottom." This stage is characterized by almost continuous drinking. The drinker's physiology will be so altered at this point that it takes only about half the amount of alcohol previously needed to maintain the drunken stupor, and he or she cannot stop drinking once it has started. At this stage, drinkers drink now mainly to avoid such withdrawal symptoms as nausea, vomiting, hallucinations (the "pink elephant"), and delirium tremens (the "DTs" or the "shakes"). Among the many health problems for which the alcoholic is now at risk are hepatitis, gastritis, anemia, pellagra, cerebellar degeneration, the Wernicke-Korsakoff syndrome, and cirrhosis of the liver. In short, the chronic alcoholic is a physical and psychological mess.

It should be emphasized that these stages are another example of the "ideal type" method of examination. Jellinek's stages proceed in predictable fashion from the social drinker to the skid row bum, yet only about 5 percent of alcoholics go all the way to skid row (Stencel 1973:989). Most alcoholics have families and jobs and may have little or no contact with the law. There seem to be social and psychological differences between those alcoholics who maintain a fairly conventional lifestyle and those who do not. In a statement with which control theorists and reality therapists would heartily concur, the President's Task Force on Drunkenness concluded that the chronic drinker "has never attained more than a minimum of integration in society . . . he is isolated, uprooted, unattached, disorganized, demoralized, and homeless" (1967:11-13). We do not know to what extent these differences are consequences rather than causes of chronic alcoholism, but the task force report once again emphasizes the tremendous importance of reciprocal love relationships for healthy human functioning. It is this type of alcoholic with whom you are most likely to come into contact in corrections work.

Some Causes of Alcoholism

The conclusions of the task force point to possible social-psychological precursors of alcohol abuse, an explanation that fits nicely into anomie theory. We can think of alcoholics who get into trouble with the law as anomic retreatists from the American goal of material success. Such people may have been denied access to the means of attaining it or perhaps do not have the fortitude to take advantage of the opportunities that they have had. Native Americans represent a group with high anomie and high rates of alcoholism, while Jews have both low anomie and low alcoholism rates (Winick 1986:355).

Reichman (1978) views alcohol not only as a self-prescribed remedy for the anxiety and bitterness of the lack of social mobility in a competitive society, but also as a tool to help the drinker deal with identity conflicts. An alcoholic booster makes the drinker feel more confident and "successful." Thus, success identity needs are being met, however destructively. Nevertheless, the alleviation of stress and the enhancement of feelings of self-worth, however temporary, reinforce drinking for alcoholics. For the heavy drinker who has not yet felt the agonies of full-blown alcoholism, alcohol is often associated with the desirable; think of the stereotypical themes of success, macho masculinity, and sensuality implicit in the names of some of our popular alcoholic concoctions such as Manhattans, Margaritas, piledrivers, and boilermakers.

While explanations like this give reasons why people drink excessively, they do not tell us why some become alcoholics and others do not, even among those whose drinking patterns in terms of amount and frequency are similar. If we are to devise effective treatment programs for alcoholism we must understand "clinical phenomena like loss of control, craving, tolerance, and physical dependence" (Goedde & Agarwal 1989:349). Studies that follow this advice tend to look at the genetics of alcoholism rather than social learning.

This does not mean that researchers posit the existence of a single gene for the syndrome we call alcoholism. Genes code for physiological processes that, in interaction both with other genes coding for other processes and with environmental stimuli, increase or decrease the probability of certain biological outcomes and behaviors. The heterogeneous nature of alcoholism makes it highly unlikely that a single genetic marker will ever be found to identify those who are at risk for alcoholism.

Accumulating data point more and more to the conclusion that physical addiction to alcohol (as opposed to psychological dependence) is genetically related to differential enzyme functioning (Rosenfeld 1981; Goedde & Agarwal 1989). Enzymes are protein molecules that catalyze the chemical conversion of molecules into other types of molecules. Ethyl alcohol is broken down in the liver by enzymes into acetaldehyde (AcH) molecules. AcH produces such unpleasant reactions to drinking as nausea and headaches, if it is not itself converted by other enzymes into other molecules that are excreted in the urine. Those people whose metabolisms convert alcohol rapidly but allow for the buildup of AcH will quickly be sensitized to its unpleasant effects. This natural punishment for drinking makes them less likely to overindulge. AcH, the first metabolite of alcohol, is thus a built-in guardian against alcoholism. In fact, disulfiram (Antabuse) is used to treat alcoholics because it supports high levels of AcH by retarding further metabolic reactions.

In alcoholics, enzymes apparently convert AcH into a morphinelike substance called tetrahydropapaveroline (THP), which is highly addictive. This may explain why the vast majority of those who drink over a lifetime never become addicted. Perhaps alcohol itself is not inherently addictive, but the biosynthetic byproducts of alcohol are; these are produced differentially according to the functioning of the individual metabolic system—a functioning that is under genetic control. This is not the complete story of the etiology of alcoholism. It only states that among those who do turn to drink, some have an inherited predisposition to become addicted. (See Applewhite [1981] and Taylor [1984] for a more extensive treatment of this.)

Assessment, Treatment, and Counseling

In view of the high social and financial costs of alcoholism and problem drinking, it is imperative that you make every effort to identify clients with these problems. Most alcoholics and problem drinkers will not admit to a problem and are convinced they can control their drinking. They do not wish to admit, even to themselves, that they have relinquished control of their lives to alcohol. Alcoholics have the choice of either rejecting alcohol or rejecting reality. In order to maintain consistency between their evaluation of themselves as in control of their lives and their continued use of a substance that they find rewarding, they often choose to reject reality. In contrast, some clients will overemphasize their drinking, hoping that you and the judge will regard it as a mitigating factor when considering sentencing alternatives.

Identifying Alcoholics

The ability to identify the alcoholic and the problem drinker is an indispensable art for all criminal justice counselors. The most obvious indicator of a drinking problem is a record of alcohol-related arrests (for example, drunk driving or drunk and disorderly). Inquire into the client's drinking patterns: the frequency and amount of alcohol consumed weekly, the frequency of legal problems due to drinking, and the amount of time and money spent on drink. If you discover such patterns, they will help you convince the client that he or she does have a drinking problem. Point out to the client that continuing to deny it in the face of such evidence is irrational and unacceptable. On no account respond to alibis designed to convince you that factors other than drinking are responsible for irresponsible behavior. To do so will result in an argument over the merits of the alibi, thus possibly reinforcing the alibi, since the more a person defends a position the more difficult it becomes to relinquish it.

Among the screening tools you can use to help identify the alcoholic client is the Michigan Alcoholism Screening Test (MAST) (see Appendix C). By no means should you rule out alcoholism if the scale score is negative for alcoholism; use the twenty-four-item questionnaire only as a corroborative diagnostic aid. Because clients can certainly lie on the questionnaire, verbal and nonverbal cues, such as alcohol-related arrests recorded in the file, may be more valuable with clients reluctant to disclose the requested information. It is best to administer the questionnaire in person so that you can clarify the items if necessary. Each question is answered yes or no.

The client's general appearance and behavior during the interview can give useful cues: An emaciated figure with a swollen abdomen, a flushed or sallow complexion, sunken eyes, dilated pupils, and generally poor hygiene are markers of the insomnia, poor nutrition, frequent sickness, and dehydration that often accompany alcoholism, as are tremors of the face and hands, poor concentration, memory impairment, and confabulation (the tendency to invent names, places, and stories to cover up memory loss). The more serious the drinking problem, the more obvious these signs will be, though their absence or your failure to perceive them do not exclude the possibility of a drinking problem. If there is a record of alcohol-related offenses or the present offense is alcohol-related, the client by definition has a problem.

Treatment for the alcoholic or problem drinker is complex, perhaps including both medical treatment and psychosocial counseling. Much will depend on how much the client is drinking when you first meet. If the client is in the chronic stage of alcoholism, hospitalization for detoxification ("drying out") will be necessary. More likely, detoxification took place in the jail or at a hospital after the client's arrest, and you will not have to concern yourself with it. If it did not, make every effort to secure inpatient medical treatment for your client. Detoxification in a medical environment is a necessary prerequisite to any future treatment. If the client is not insured and if welfare authorities cannot provide it, organizations like the Salvation Army and the Volunteers of America are often successful in securing the necessary treatment. Although these organizations do not accept clients for detoxification (not being medical facilities), they both run valuable in-house programs for recovering alcoholics on a free or sliding fee basis. Detoxification is not a treatment of alcoholism, which is a long and difficult process; it is a treatment for intoxication preparatory to treatment for alcoholism.

Perhaps the best nonresidential program for alcoholics is Alcoholics Anonymous (AA). This organization of recovering alcoholics is a supportive group whose members will go to great lengths to assist one another. They will nurse fellow members through hangovers, depressions, and periods of craving for alcohol, and they may even give them room and board. However, some think AA can be of little use to individuals who refuse to admit their problem and who are not motivated to do something about it. In fact, the first of AA's famous Twelve Steps (to recovery) says: "We admit we are powerless over alcohol—that our lives had become unmanageable." Voluntary affirmation, while obviously a plus, does not necessarily mean that you should dismiss AA as a treatment option if your client refuses to recognize the problem or is unmotivated.

Counseling Alcoholics

Alcoholic group counseling has certain advantages over individual counseling. Each member of the group, including the leaders, knows where all other members are coming from. All the requisites for successful counseling outlined by Carl Rogers are at least potentially present in a gathering of similarly situated individuals. Positive regard for fellow members is an integral part of the quasi-religious philosophy of AA. Alcoholics are led to the "conversion" experience in a fellowship of individuals like themselves who are in various stages of alcoholic recovery.

Empathy in the Rogerian sense is also present. No one is allowed to skirt the issue; alcoholic clients cannot reasonably tell their bottle-wise compatriots that they "just don't understand," as they could nonalcoholic corrections counselors. Fellow AA members will give your clients not only support but also visions of the possible. They are role models whose presence emphasizes much more strongly than the counselor could that recovery is possible. Methods of dealing with specific alcohol-related problems are drawn from the experiences of those who have already successfully dealt with them. When the solution to a problem is offered by a peer, it is likely to carry more weight than if it is offered by "the Man," whom many clients instinctively resent.

Genuineness is another Rogerian principle that is a hallmark of AA treatment. The AA program insists that its members honestly confront their problems, their shortcomings, their responsibilities, and their realities. Manipulation and game-playing are quickly rejected: "You can't con the cons." Members are encouraged to share with the group their fears, anxieties, hopes, and self-evaluation. This self-disclosure gives the client an opportunity to share genuine feelings with others and to build self-esteem and a group identity—qualities sorely lacking in the lives of alcoholics.

The enhancement of self-esteem and the development of a success identity and spirit of "can-doism" are of great importance for recovering alcoholics. These attributes are part of a more general attribute that people bring with them to any situation, namely character. Character implies willpower and a strong sense of responsibility, terms that are not liked by those who hold strongly to the disease model of alcoholism. For them, willpower and a sense of responsibility are moral terms that the self-righteous use to explain alcoholism and that have no meaning in the treatment of a problem over which the alcoholic has no control. (Paradoxically, these same people expect recovering alcoholics to exert lifetime self-control and abstinence from alcohol.)

But that amorphous quality we call character does affect treatment outcomes, as it affects everything else we do in life. Baeklund, Lundwall, and Kissin (1975:305) state it well when they write about their experiences in treating alcoholics: "Over and over we were impressed with the dominant role the patient, as opposed to the kind of treatment used on him, played both in his persistence in treatment and his eventual outcome." Fingarette, who calls the disease model of alcoholism a myth, supports them: "The consensus of scientific researchers is that willpower and personal strengths do affect the course of a heavy drinker's efforts to control his drinking" (1988:72). So we return to a central thesis of reality therapy: individuals—alcoholic, drug addict, criminal, or whatever—can only change their destructive behavior by resolving to accept personal responsibility for that behavior. AA is one vehicle that may help the alcoholic to develop that resolve. "The alcoholic must regain control over his life to satisfy his needs. AA, by itself, cannot satisfy his needs, but it is a way—probably the best way we have available—to get the process started" (Glasser 1984:132).

Glasser views diseases as falling on a continuum in terms of the amount of control we have over them. At one end of the continuum is a disease like Huntington's chorea that is totally genetic. It matters not one iota how healthy, fit, and strong you may otherwise be or what you do to avoid it, if you have the gene for Huntington's chorea you will eventually get it. Further down the continuum is cancer. Though cancer is a genetic disease, we can lessen our chances of getting it by altering our environment (eating right, not smoking). Further along the continuum are the cardiovascular diseases that may be under genetic and environmental control equally. Living a healthy life dramatically reduces our risk of such diseases, even given a genetic predisposition. At the other end of the continuum is alcoholism. Glasser concedes that alcoholism is a disease, but asserts that we have considerable control over it. Even if we have a genetic predisposition, if we learn to resist the temptation to drink, the disease cannot manifest itself. Glasser's approach appears to be an eminently sensible compromise between the disease and nondisease models of alcoholism.

Whether alcoholism is or is not a disease is a medical question. Because the Supreme Court ruled that the Veterans Administration (VA) may deny certain benefits to alcoholics because their behavior was thought to be the result of "willful misconduct," we sometimes hear that the Supreme Court has ruled that alcoholism is not a disease. The Supreme Court is no more qualified to make such a judgment than we are. The Court simply ruled on a matter of law that had to do with the benefit guidelines of the VA.

It is probably best to prod all alcoholic or problem drinkers caught up in the criminal justice system into AA. Half of those who regularly attend AA meetings with serious intent are rehabilitated, Chafetz and Demone found (1972). The success rate for criminal justice clients is not likely to be this high, because client motivation is a crucial variable, and the success rate cited by Chafetz and Demone was for those who put themselves into the program.

As a corrections worker you can only help by doing your best to generate this motivation. You can make attendance at AA meetings a condition of probation or parole. Experiencing the warm support and caring of fellow travellers may well motivate the reluctant client. Insisting that the client attend AA is an instance of the constructive use of authority. Be aware, though, that traditional AA programs have a strong religious component: six of the twelve steps make reference to God. A 1982 United States Court of Appeals case (*Owens v. Kelly*) found that under the First Amendment's freedom of religion clause, probationers cannot be compelled to engage in a program whose religious content violates their religious beliefs. Although little or no religion is dispensed in the typical AA meeting, a client bent on frustrating your treatment efforts may legally use the religious content of the Twelve Steps to refuse to participate in AA.

An alternative to AA meetings is an in-house alcohol program, which has the advantage that officers can closely monitor attendance, participation, and progress. In-house meetings and group counseling sessions are best led by volunteer members of AA or community corrections workers who are thoroughly versed in alcohol counseling.

The Lucas County (Ohio) Adult Probation Department has an in-house program called STOP (Sobriety Through Other People). STOP clients are required to (1) attend one in-house AA meeting and at least three others outside the department, (2) attend biweekly in-house group meetings, (3) submit to weekly urinalysis, and (4) meet with the program coordinator once per month. Latessa and Goodman (1989) compared 102 STOP probationers with a control group of 101 other probationers matched for sex, race, and supervision level. STOP clients had more serious criminal histories, much more serious substance abuse problems, and a higher rate of absconding and of technical probation violations. The bright spot was that the STOP clients had 9.2 percent fewer arrests than regularly supervised clients—a relatively small difference but notable given that alcoholic offenders are particularly susceptible to frequent arrests. As the authors conclude: "The STOP program has demonstrated it is possible to select special-need offenders and deliver increased services in an effective manner" (Latessa & Goodman 1989:42).

A new organization for alcoholics suited to people who object to the quasi-religion of AA is called Rational Recovery (RR). Though broadly based on AA, it stresses self-reliance rather than reliance on "a power greater than us." The theoretical underpinning of RR is rational emotive therapy. The idea of admitting "we are powerless over alcohol," as is done in AA, is an idea (a MUSTurbation) that RET adherents do not accept. RR members blame their drinking on addictive thinking, not booze, and work to correct this faulty thinking. Further, they do not believe that it is necessary or advisable to attend meetings for the rest of their lives and declare themselves "recovered" rather than "recovering"; that is, they work to defeat an acute disease syndrome rather than being engaged in a constant battle with a chronic disease syndrome.

Neither AA nor RR should be viewed as "inferior" or "superior" to the other; they are alternative paths to the same goal. Those who are philosophically drawn to RET theory will prefer RR, and those more attuned to the ideas of client-centered therapy will be drawn to AA. AA has been emphasized here because it is far better known and has a much longer history.

Antabuse Treatment

Antabuse treatment, a kind of aversion therapy, can be a very useful adjunct to other treatments. Antabuse, administered under medical supervision because it can have harmful, even fatal, effects for people with heart problems, is begun after detoxification. The drug is usually given for several consecutive days along with small doses of alcohol. The unpleasant feelings that accompany drinking alcohol while the AcH level is high act as negative reinforcers. It is hoped that associating highly unpleasant consequences with alcohol ingestion will be sufficiently aversive to condition the patient from future abuse. Antabuse treatment is voluntary; you cannot require it as a condition of supervision. Clients who do choose to take Antabuse are taking treatment seriously; in effect they have made the decision not to drink during the period that this highly aversive drug remains effective. (Antabuse is eliminated from the body very slowly, leaving the body sensitive to alcohol for six to ten days after the last dose.)

Like most other conditioned responses, however, the effects of Antabuse will be extinguished with time. It does provide a strong, immediate reason not to drink and thus buys time for other types of treatment. It appears to be quite successful when supported by psychosocial counseling. Billet (1974) reports that 64 percent of a sample of patients who were given Antabuse while undergoing a comprehensive psychosocial rehabilitation program showed "marked improvement." Only 31 percent of those who were in the same program but who did not receive Antabuse showed a similar level of improvement.

The increasing evidence that alcoholism has a strong biological basis is not cause for despair. Schuckit, one of the leading researchers in the biology of alcoholism, has written: "It is unlikely that anyone is predestined to alcoholism or that all those predisposed exhibit the same mechanism of risk" (1989:297). Even those genetically identified as at risk will obviously not succumb to the disease if they never drink, and those who have succumbed can be spared its further ravages if,

Perspectives from the Field

Tough Love and Alcoholics

Sandra Tebbe

Tebbe is a probation officer who specializes in working with alcoholic clients. She holds master's degrees in both sociology and rehabilitation counseling and is a Certified Alcoholism Counselor. In the past she has also counseled compulsive gamblers on probation.

Alcoholics usually will not recognize that they have a drinking problem. Many don't want to recognize it because they enjoy their alcoholism and find satisfaction in the "loving" concern of those around them. They use this "love" as a means of manipulating their way through a drunken lifestyle. The alcoholic's skillful maneuvers and manipulations do not stop when he or she commits a crime. Most alcoholic probationers come under supervision expecting the same "loving" concern and the same ignoring, overlooking, and excusing that they are accustomed to.

To help the alcoholic offender you have to be willing to be rejected. That's what "tough love" is all about: caring enough about clients to hold them totally responsible for their behavior, regardless of whether they like you or not. Tough love is making each decision carefully to assure that you are not enabling the probationer to continue drinking. This will not make you popular, and it certainly won't make you loved. It is all too easy to ease up a little, to give them some slack, so that they will like you. But you are not the issue. You demonstrate your love for them by holding them responsible for the defeat of their alcoholic conditions.

I started working as a probation officer three years ago. For the past year-and-a-half I have coordinated a special state-funded, in-house alcohol program. This program has one of the highest levels of supervision in community corrections and provides for strict and unambiguous correctional consequences for every misbehavior. It has been a good program to learn what tough love is all about.

I am often asked, "How can you spend so much time working with alcoholics without getting burned out?" I entered the probation profession at a young age and with idealistic attitudes. It didn't take me long to learn how to adapt and survive. Counseling alcoholics means learning how to let go. It doesn't mean that you stop caring, it means that you must learn that you can't do it for someone else. It's the realization that you can't control another person's life or fix its defects. Only they can do that. You have to respect their capacity for control and choice and allow them to learn from the natural consequences of their behavior.

Most alcoholics have had someone to enable, or make possible, their drinking behavior from the very start. This is one of the reasons that the alcoholic's family, and most everyone else influenced by him or her, becomes "sick." Enabling is usually in the form of continually making excuses for and rescuing the alcoholic from distress. Unfortunately, it is not until alcoholics experience the real pains of their disease that they get around to making a decision to change their lifestyles.

You can easily fall into rescuing behavior with your alcoholic clients, but you are not doing them any favors if you continue with the enabling patterns they have come to expect. You are not being "nice," "neat," or "loving" to those who need tough love by allowing them to manipulate you and to continue to ruin their lives. Confront them, challenge them, educate them, help them!

Alcoholics will almost always deny thier alcoholism. Take Jim, a high-risk probationer of mine. He had been in prison for threatening the life of his baby when police arrived at his home on a domestic dispute call. During the alcohol screening period, Jim stated over and over that he was not an alcoholic: "I don't have to wake up to a drink every day like the drunks on the street. I'm not a weak man. There's lots of times I don't drink."

Jim's defensiveness was a reaction to the many myths associated with alcoholism. Many people think of alcoholics as weak, low-class moral degenerates who lack willpower. My job as his probation officer was to educate him about his disease so that he would open up his mind to treatment. Jim learned through my efforts and through mandatory participation in AA that alcoholism is primarily a physiological disease and that he became addicted because his body is incapable of processing alcohol normally. He also learned that alcoholism is a disease that affects all classes and races. Jim's many family and financial problems did not cause his alcoholism. Rather, his alcoholism undermined his ability to cope, and this inability then exacerbated his problems.

Once Jim learned about his disease he was better able to deal with it. Jim had to realize that to admit his alcoholism was not to admit that he was a weak or bad person. Through small-group participation and AA attendance, Jim found comfort and support from others with the same problem. These folks "tough loved" Jim into sobriety. Jim has been sober for two years now. He has chosen a new life for himself. Although all of his other problems have not disappeared, he is learning how to cope with them without alcohol.

Jim was relatively easy to deal with as alcoholic probationers go. Often I find that supervising alcoholic probationers means long periods of time waiting for them to "hit bottom." "Hitting bottom" means that the alcoholic comes to realize that he or she has gone about as low as possible and that he or she must change or be forever lost. A few months ago, one of my probationers hit bottom while sitting in the county jail. John was doing thirty days for his second probation violation, a violation that I could have easily ignored. He had continually denied having a drinking problem, refused to go to AA meetings, and was resentful of authority.

This time, however, something was different about John when I visited him in jail. For the first time he didn't attempt to rationalize his behavior or blame it on someone else. He was physically sick from withdrawal, homeless, and his wife had left him (a natural consequence of his behavior) because she couldn't handle his drinking anymore. With a broken spirit, John started to take a hard look at himself and finally asked for help. John is now doing something about his problem. He is one of several sober probationers in the program. John is one of the many probationers who have learned to love and respect themselves through an officer's use of tough love.

With the help of caring others, they can move toward sobriety "one day at a time."

Summary

This chapter addresses the most common problem you will encounter in corrections: alcoholism and problem drinking. The alcoholic and the problem drinker can be differentiated in terms of the physiological dependency of the alcoholic. Jellinek's four stages of alcoholic progression—prealcoholic, prodromal, crucial, and chronic—are not universal for all problem drinkers. Only about 5 percent of all alcoholics ever hit bottom and arrive at skid row.

The latest scientific evidence on the cause of alcoholism points strongly to the role of the production and metabolism of acetaldehyde (AcH). Antabuse, a drug used in treating alcoholism, functions to maintain high levels of AcH in the bloodstream. This causes the alcoholic to experience the "punishing" physical feelings associated with high alcohol intake. Antabuse is administered to chronic alcoholics in association with intensive psychosocial counseling.

The most successful program for counseling alcoholics is Alcoholics Anonymous (AA), which gives members all the components of a successful counseling relationship as outlined by Rogers: positive regard, genuineness, and empathy. Rational Recovery (RR) is a relatively new alternative to AA that stresses individual responsibility and character.

References and Suggested Readings

American Psychiatric Association. 1987. *Diagnostic and statistical manual of mental disorders* (3rd ed.-revised). Washington, D.C.: APA.

Applewhite, P. 1981. *Molecular gods: How molecules determine our behavior*. Englewood Cliffs, N.J.: Prentice-Hall.

Baeklund, F., L. Lundwall, and B. Kissen. 1975. Methods for the treatment of chronic alcoholism: A critical approach. In *Research advances in alcohol and drug problems*, edited by R. Gibbons, Y. Israel, et al. New York: Wiley.

Billet, S. 1974. Antabuse therapy. In *Alcoholism, The total treatment approach*, edited by R. Cantanzaro. Springfield, Ill.: Charles C Thomas.

Burnett, M. 1979. Understanding and overcoming addictions. In *Helping clients with special concerns*, edited by S. Eisenberg and L. Patterson. Chicago: Rand McNally.

Chafetz, M., and H. Demone. 1972, *Alcoholism and society*. New York: Oxford University Press.

Clinnard, M., and R. Quinney. 1973. *Criminal behavior systems: A typology*. New York: Holt, Rinehart & Winston.

Failkov, M. 1985. Biologic and psychosocial determinants in the etiology of alcoholism. In *Alcohol and the brain: Chronic effects*, edited by R. Tarter and D. Van Theil. New York: Plenum Medical.

Fingarette, H. 1988. *Heavy drinking: The myth of alcoholism as a disease*. Berkeley, Cal.: University of California Press.

Fishman, R. 1986. *Alcohol and alcoholism*. New York: Chelsea House.

Glasser, W. 1984. *Control theory*. New York: Harper & Row.

Goedde, H., and D. Agarwal. 1984. Editorial remarks: Biomedical and genetic aspects of alcoholism: Current issues and future directions. In *Alcoholism: Biomedical and genetic aspects*, edited by H. Goedde and D. Agarwal. New York: Pergamon Press.

Hoffman, P., and B. Tabakoff. 1985. Ethanol's action on brain chemistry. In *Alcohol and the brain: Chronic effects*, edited by R. Tarter and D. Von Thiel. New York: Plenum Medical.

Jellinek, E. 1960. *The disease concept of alcoholism*. New Haven, Ct.: Hillside Press.

Keller, M., and C. Gurioli. 1976. *Statistics on consumption of alcohol and on alcoholism*. New Brunswick, N.J.: Rutgers Center of Alcohol Studies.

Latessa, E., and S. Goodman. 1989. Alcoholic offenders: Intensive probation program shows promise. *Corrections Today* 51:38-42.

Masters, R., and C. Robertson. 1990. *Inside criminology*. Englewood Cliffs, N.J.: Prentice-Hall.

President's Commission on Law Enforcement and Administration of Justice. 1967. *Task force report: Drunkenness, annotations, consultant's papers, and related materials*. Washington, D.C.: GPO.

Reichman, W. 1978. *Alcoholism and career development*. New York: Baruch College, City University of New York.

Rosenfeld, A. 1981. Tippling enzymes. *Science* 81 (February): 24-25.

Schuckit, M. 1989. Biomedical and genetic markers of alcoholism. In *Alcoholism: Biomedical and genetic aspects*, edited by H. Goedde and D. Agarwal. New York: Pergamon Press.

Stencel, S. 1973. Resurgence of alcoholism. *Editorial Research Reports* 2 (December): 990-991.

Taylor, L. 1984. *Born to crime*. Westport, Conn.: Greenwood.

Winick, C. 1986. The alcohol offender. In *Psychology of crime and criminal justice*, edited by H. Toch. Prospect Heights, Ill.: Waveland Press.

Chapter 13
The Drug-abusing Client

To start thinking about drugs, we need to pose a question of social philosophy: what kind of society do we want? Is it a society in which drugs are necessary for satisfaction and happiness, or is it a society where they are not necessary?

Maureen Kelleher, Bruce MacMurray, and Thomas Shapiro

The Scope of the Problem

Although alcohol is a mind-altering drug like other drugs, it was discussed separately because the attitude of American society is different toward alcohol and nonalcoholic drugs. Alcohol is a legal, socially acceptable form of drugging oneself; marijuana, heroin, LSD, and cocaine are not. Respectable middle-class people drink; criminals, hippies, street people, and ghetto types take drugs. Contrast the positive names for "our" booze with the negative tags ("weed," "acid," "scag," and the generic "dope") for "their" drugs.

Drugs are related to crime in three ways: psychopharmacological, economic-compulsive, and systemic (U.S. Department of Justice 1991:17). Drug-induced changes in mood and cognitive functioning can instigate crime, but in truth the psychopharmacological effects of drugs, unlike alcohol, have less influence on crime than the economic-compulsive and systemic connections. Economic-compulsive crimes are committed to obtain money to buy drugs, which are expensive because they are illegal. Systemic crimes are part of doing business in the drug culture. For instance, about 80 percent of the homicides in the District of Columbia in 1988 were drug-related, a staggering increase from the 1985 estimate of 21 percent (U.S. Department of Justice 1991:17).

Systemic drug-related crime is more a social and political than a corrections issue. We are concerned with the demand side—the users and minor pushers. Data from the National Institute of Justice's Drug Use Forecasting (DUF) research program (Figure 13-1) forcefully demonstrate the link between drug use and crime in twenty of our largest cities. More than half the arrestees in all cities tested positive for at least one illegal drug. Although the drugs used vary considerably by city, cocaine (including crack) is by far the drug abused most frequently. These data bring home forcefully just what the criminal justice worker has to deal with in terms of the supervision and treatment of clients, not only in the community but also inside prison: "Drug use has become a major problem with a variety of ramifications, including threats to prison order, violence among inmates, and corruption of guards and other employees" (Malcolm 1989:10).

City	% Positive Any Drug	Range of % Positive				% Positive					
		LOW	DATE	HIGH	DATE	2 + Drugs	Cocaine	Mari-juana	Amphet-amines	Opiates	PCP
Philadelphia	80	79	8/88	84	4/89	30	70	19	0	8	1
San Diego	80	66	6/87	85	1/89	50	45	37	30	17	6
New York	79	76	4/89	90	6/88	36	67	24	0	20	4
Chicago	75	71	11/89	85	7/88	46	59	38	0	27	10
Houston	70	61	1/88	70	7/89	18	57	21	**	6	0
Los Angeles	70	63	10/89	77	4/88	28	54	19	0	16	5
Birmingham	69	60	11/89	75	7/88	21	50	18	0	6	0
Dallas	66	57	12/88	72	6/88	20	44	32	0	7	0
Cleveland	65	62	11/89	70	8/89	22	49	26	0	4	1
Portland	64	54	1/89	76	8/88	21	24	40	13	10	0
San Antonio	63	49	12/89	63	3/90	26	30	39	2	17	1
St. Louis	62	56	10/88	69	4/89	18	48	26	0	4	2
Ft. Lauderdale	61	61	3/90	71	3/88	18	47	27	0	**	0
New Orleans	60	58	1/88	76	4/89	22	51	20	**	6	3
Phoenix	60	53	10/87	67	1/88	20	27	38	9	5	**
Indianapolis	60	50	2/89	62	9/89	19	22	48	0	3	0
Washington, D.C.	59	57	11/89	72	2/89	24	49	12	**	15	6
Denver	59	DATA NOT AVAILABLE				16	30	37	1	3	**
San Jose	58	58	2/90	65	8/89	23	32	26	8	8	8
Kansas City	57	54	11/88	64	5/89	12	38	26	**	2	**

Figure 13-1 Drug use by male arrestees

Source: National Institute of Justice/Drug Use Forecasting Program

* Positive urinalysis, January through March 1990. Drugs tested for include cocaine, PCP, opiates, marijuana, amphetamines, methadone, methaqualone, benzodiazepines, barbiturates, and propoxyphene

**Less than 1%

Some Causes of Drug Abuse

Drugs affect brain functioning in one of four ways: (1) They inhibit or slow down the release of chemical neurotransmitters, (2) they stimulate or speed up their release, (3) they prevent the reuptake of transmitters after they have stimulated neighboring neurons, or (4) they break down the transmitters more quickly. Depending on the drug taken, the individual's behavior or feelings may be speeded up or slowed down, intensified or reduced, or stimulated or mellowed. In short, drugs help change an undesirable mood to a more desirable one.

People turn to drugs for the same reasons that they turn to booze. They take them initially to be sociable and to conform, to induce pleasure, to escape psychic stress or chronic boredom. They abuse and become dependent on drugs because they find little pleasure, comfort, solace, or meaning in their lives. People who daily confront more pain than pleasure seek all the artificial comfort they can get. Addicts become emotionally attached to their substances the way most of us become attached to other people because their experiences have usually not prepared them for intimate relationships with people. "In almost all addict families, there was a disturbed relationship between the parents, as evidenced by separation, divorce, open hostility, or lack of warmth" (Chein et al. 1964:273). A similar sentiment is expressed by Burnett (1979:354): "Drug abusers often complain of lack of love and warmth in their homes. An absence of parent 'stroking' in the home will lead to low self-image, which contributes to the susceptibility to drug abuse." Lacking an inner sense of warmth and self-esteem, addicts think of their pharmacopoeia in terms not of what it does "to" them, but of what it does "for" them. We have to break through all their rationalizations, projections, and denials to make them understand the profound difference between "for" and "to."

Jellinek's four stages of alcoholism also apply to the transition from casual drug usage to full-blown addiction. Some drugs are physically addictive, while some are only psychologically addictive, meaning that there are no painful physiological symptoms associated with withdrawal. This somewhat artificial distinction between physical and psychological addiction does not necessarily imply that the former is more serious than the latter. Barbiturates, such as Seconal and phenobarbital, are considered physically addictive; cocaine is not. Yet cocaine may be the most addictive drug there is, judging by the number of successful athletes, entertainers, and professional and business people—people more likely to be in good control of their lives—who become addicted (Glasser 1984:140). And cocaine is probably the most difficult of addictions to treat successfully.

Addiction is not an invariable outcome of drug usage any more than alcoholism is an invariable outcome of drinking. In fact, most people who experiment with drugs during adolescence do not become addicted (Marlatt et al. 1988). The danger of addiction, however, is considerably greater with illegal drugs than with alcohol.

Drug Classification

As a criminal justice counselor, you should become familiar with the effects of all types of illegal drugs. What follows is a brief description of the different classes of drugs, with an emphasis on heroin and cocaine, the two drugs that cause the most problems in terms of their association with crime (and therefore the criminal justice system) and treatment. A listing of many of the drugs and their street names is presented in Appendix C.

The Depressants

The depressants include the barbiturates/sedatives and the narcotics/opiates. All drugs in this category can cause physical and psychological dependence, and all produce tolerance (the tendency to require larger and larger doses over time to produce the same effects). Depressants range from the relatively mild analgesic sedatives to such insidious narcotics as heroin. This class of drugs tends to appeal to individuals whose coping style leans toward isolation, withdrawal, and indifference.

Taking one of the stronger varieties in this category, such as heroin or Dilaudid (a cheaper and increasingly popular substitute), wafts the individual into a euphoric state of sweet indifference, a state that heroin users describe as the "floats." Intravenous injection of heroin ("mainlining") is the most popular way to take the drug for hardcore addicts. This produces the famous "rush," a warm skin flush and orgasmic feeling. After the initial rush, the addict drifts off into a private carefree world for three to twelve hours. Needless to say, the problems are still around after the effects wear off, not the least of which is the problem of securing the next rush. A heroin addict who had a $300-per-day habit once challenged my characterization of him as lazy. He said, "Man, we addicts work harder than anybody you know. You try to hustle the streets to come up with that kind of bread every day."

This "hustle" is the main reason for the close association of heroin addiction with criminal activity. Because the euphoric state achieved under the influence of heroin is not conducive to effort, criminal or otherwise, narcotics users are significantly less likely to commit violent crimes than are users of alcohol or stimulants, particularly methamphetamine and cocaine. In fact, Hartman (1978:404) reports: "In those countries where free narcotics are supplied to habitual abusers, the crime rate is said to be lower for this group of people than for the general population." This reduction of economic compulsive and systemic drug-related crime is the primary argument for those who advocate the decriminalization of many drugs.

Heroin, a derivative of the powerful painkiller morphine, is a white or brownish powder that is usually dissolved in water and injected. It has been reliably established that the brain has its own painkilling substances, the endorphins (for "endogenous morphinelike substances"). These natural analgesics provide clues to the addictive process. Some individuals may become heroin addicts because they have insufficient natural endorphins to anesthetize them to the pains of life (Applewhite 1981:132). The lack of normal amounts of nature's "tonic" precipitates a search for artificial substitutes to make up the deficit.

This assumption is deceptively similar to the AcH explanation of alcoholism. However, the evidence relating AcH and alcoholism is compelling, whereas the evidence for an endorphin-deficiency theory of opiate addiction is practically nonexistent. Whereas alcoholism tends to be fairly distributed across class lines, heroin addiction tends to be concentrated at the lower levels of the class structure. A hereditary predisposition to drug addiction would predictably be fairly evenly distributed among the class strata, assuming that experimental usage is itself not class-based.

Restak offers a more plausible biological explanation of heroin addiction. He says that the frequent injection of heroin affects the body's natural capacity to release endorphins much as giving individuals too much thyroid extract will eventually cause the body to cease its own thyroid production. An addict's assumed lower level of natural endorphins is therefore a consequence rather than a cause of addiction (Restak 1979:344-355).

The Stimulants

The stimulants, primarily amphetamines and cocaine, have effects opposite to those of the depressants. They mimic the activity of the sympathetic division of the autonomic nervous system, meaning that they increase arousal and a sense of well-being. They are the drugs of choice for individuals who seek excitement and adventure—the bored, the driven, and the chronically underaroused (Grabowski 1984). Stimulants include everything from $3.95 over-the-counter diet pills to $100-per-gram cocaine. Although heroin addicts are rarely professional or even middle-class persons, cocaine addicts used to be almost exclusively middle-class and professional (physicians, lawyers, businesspeople). This is no longer the case (see Figure 13-1). Over the last six or seven years cocaine has become dramatically more popular. The Drug Enforcement Agency (DEA) estimates that about 5,000 people each day try cocaine for the first time. The magic of the free market system has combined with the glamour of cocaine's association with the rich and powerful to democratize its use.

Along with the depressant alcohol, amphetamines and cocaine have the most immediate association with violent criminal behavior (Hartman 1978:412). Holden (1989:1378) has characterized cocaine as "the most powerful reinforcer known," and Bogdanovich (1985:143) gives a dramatic description of its effects:

> Cocaine gives an icy-cold high that freezes your heart and makes you believe that you are all-powerful, invincible, and righteously correct in all of your appetites and impulses. It is the most self-deceiving of drugs, and the most insidious, quietly turning every user into a Mr. Hyde. If grass is the drug of peace, cocaine is the drug of war.

Cocaine is the powdered derivative of the South American coca plant. Although officially classified as a narcotic, it is actually a very strong stimulant. Cocaine users, who spend about $30 billion a year for the drug, have about a 50-50 chance of becoming addicted; compare this with the approximately 10 percent chance that frequent drinkers will become alcoholic (Lister 1986:13). Addiction appears to be a function of the frequency and amount of intake rather than biological predisposition.

Cocaine works by blocking the uptake of the neurotransmitters dopamine and norepinephrine at the synaptic neuroterminals, thus keeping the body in an extended state of arousal. Being highly soluble in fatty tissue, cocaine is quickly taken up by the brain, producing the euphoric rush. When cocaine is taken intravenously, this rush takes only about fifteen seconds. The strongest and fastest rush comes from smoking "freebase" (the cocaine alkaloid freed from its acid salt to produce pure cocaine).

A form of smokeable cocaine, known as "rock" or "crack," has been hitting the streets with a vengeance over the past few years. Crack is manufactured by combining cocaine, baking soda, and water. The mixture is heated, allowed to cool, and broken into tiny pieces resembling gray slivers of bar soap. Without the elaborate and sometimes dangerous preparations necessary to produce freebase cocaine, crack produces the same sort of high, and its relatively low price makes it attractive to those who formerly resisted the more expensive powdered cocaine. In 1986 Lister estimated that crack prices ranged from $5 to $25 for 300 milligrams as opposed to about $120 for a gram of freebase (Lister 1986:13); prices have decreased considerably since. After crack is smoked in cigarettes or through a water pipe, the high, which lasts about fifteen minutes, comes within ten seconds. With all these "advantages," probation and parole officers can expect an increasing number of clients who smoke crack, a drug predicted to become the most abused drug in the United States. (Figure 13-1 suggests that it already is, at least in our biggest cities.)

Cocaine addiction is extremely difficult to treat because use of the drug is so rewarding. Quickly, powerfully, and directly it affects the brain's pleasure receptors. Addicts who have been involved with other drugs will tell you that cocaine is by far the most desirable. A client of mine once spent nine days locked in her room living on cocaine and water. It cost her $5,000, which she had obtained by selling the stuff to her middle-class friends. Cocaine addiction is also very difficult to treat because stopping after prolonged use causes a devastating "crash," about four days of intense anxiety, irritability, and depression. After prolonged cocaine use, the natural activation of the brain's pleasure centers does not occur, making the brain dependent on cocaine to feel any pleasure at all (Visher 1990:3).

Although the amphetamines and cocaine quickly produce tolerance, requiring increasingly greater amounts to obtain the same effects, they do not produce physical dependence—but the psychological dependence is very strong. The depression and fatigue resulting from the overstimulation of the nervous system create a tremendous desire for more cocaine. Since smoking cocaine produces a quicker and stronger high than snorting it, its effect is of shorter duration, and the crash is more devastating. If more cocaine is not immediately available, addicts will take barbiturates to help ease the crash.

Methamphetamine (Speed)

Methamphetamine or "speed" is the most dangerous of all drugs in terms of its psychopharmacological association with violence. Compounding the violent effects associated with speed itself is the fact that it is the drug of choice after alcohol among alcoholics (Cadoret, Troughton & Widmer 1984). A favorite with the hippie subculture of the sixties, it is still very much around. Speed operates on the limbic system to accelerate the visual, tactile, auditory, and olfactory impulses. The intensification of these senses was tailor-made for the free-love philosophy of the hippie generation, for it generates hypersexuality.

When "speed freaks" become "wired," they have boundless energy and alertness. The effects feel so good that they often go on what is called a "run." A run consists of several days on speed without sleep. Speed is considerably less expensive than cocaine, so a run of five days will cost only about $150. The price paid for the run is that the longer it lasts, the more the feelings of well-being turn to hyperactive aggressiveness. Accentuated sensitivity to stimuli, intermixed with fatigue, can easily produce psychoticlike reactions, especially if the run is carried on, as it usually is, with several others, all similarly hypersensitive. Love and beauty and clever conversation increasingly turn to paranoia, ugliness, hostility, and violent disagreement as the run is extended and the supply of speed peters out.

Speed freaks are especially dangerous after the run is over. Deep depressions, badly frayed nerves, and a desperate need for sleep make them argumentative and susceptible to explosive violence. Any confrontation worsens the depression and sends them on a desperate search for more speed to alleviate the feeling. They will do almost anything to get the next fix and start the vicious cycle again.

A more potent, more addictive form of methamphetamine called ice has recently been added to America's ever-growing illicit pharmacopoeia. Ice is chemically identical to methamphetamine, but is crystalline rather than powdered. It is becoming popular among users of stimulant drugs because it is even cheaper than crack, its high is intense and long-lasting (from seven to twenty-four hours), it can be smoked rather than injected, and because it is virtually odorless, reducing the chance of detection (Nugent 1990a:4).

The Hallucinogens

The hallucinogens are mind-altering drugs such as marijuana and lysergic acid diethylamide (LSD). Smoking marijuana is so common today that we pay little attention to it. Perhaps nine out of ten criminal justice clients under forty years of age have tried or continue to smoke it. Its quasi-acceptance can be discerned in PSI reports, which often contain such statements as "With the exception of marijuana, the defendant denies any drug usage." To my knowledge, no client is ever ordered into treatment for a marijuana habit. Most criminal justice workers seem to consider it relatively innocuous. They fail to realize the greater potency of the modern product. Whereas the marijuana of the sixties and early seventies contained about 5 percent of the mind-altering cannabinoid THC, today's contains about 25 percent. Unlike alcohol, which is water-soluble and quickly metabolized and excreted, cannabinoids are fat-soluble. They penetrate the fatty areas of the body—notably in the brain and the gonads—and remain there for long periods. Since only about 10 percent of the THC crosses the blood-brain barrier to produce the marijuana "high," the other 90 percent of this powerful chemical continues to damage the body. Marijuana is anything but harmless. It has a wide range of insidious physical and psychological effects.

LSD is a more immediately dangerous hallucinogen. In its unadulterated form, LSD is a clear, odorless, and tasteless liquid. It is sold soaked in sugar cubes, in tiny pills, or on saturated blotting paper (microdots). LSD has been called psychomimetic because its effects sometimes mimic psychosis. In a very few cases LSD usage produces a psychotic break. It could be, however, that these few people were predisposed and that LSD functioned as a catalyst.

After a period of decline, LSD usage appears to be increasing again. Today's LSD, however, is only about half as potent as it was during the hippie period. It is a drug primarily favored by those who seek intellectual adventure, the inward-lookers who seek to increase awareness rather than escape it. It causes hyperawareness and a greatly enhanced appreciation of perceptual stimuli. Among the lower classes and habitants of the ghettoes, where drug use is an attempt to decrease the awareness of the reality of life, LSD has found little acceptance. LSD does not cause physical dependence, but psychological dependence may occur, and the drug produces tolerance rapidly.

Drug Abuse Treatment

Everything said in the previous chapter about alcoholism treatment applies in general to drug treatment. Attempts to rehabilitate drug abusers have been impeded by the pessimistic attitude, "once an addict, always an addict." This attitude may be partly a function of society's more negative perceptions of drug addicts than of alcoholics. The corrections worker should not share these attitudes.

Like alcoholics, drug abusers and addicts are reluctant to admit that they have the problem unless they feel you might consider it to be a mitigating factor in sentencing. If drug abusers do not admit their dependency during the initial interview, they will do whatever they can to hide it while under supervision. It is important that you identify any drug problem at your first contact.

The obvious first step is to check the record for a history of drug-related arrests or previous drug treatment. Ask the client about them. This may lead to an admission of current usage. Chronic drug abusers, like alcoholics, tend to look disheveled because their personal hygiene and nutritional habits are subordinated to the habit. If you suspect narcotics usage, look for tracks on their hands and arms, which they conceal by wearing long sleeves even in summer. Does the client wear sunglasses to conceal constricted and fixed pupils? Is the client drowsy and "laid back?" A runny nose or watering eyes may indicate that the client is overdue for a fix. Does the client scratch a lot and complain of frequent sickness? Does the client have difficulty concentrating and often arrive late or miss appointments?

The abuser of stimulants is harder to detect from behavior in your office. Unlike the narcotics addict, the stimulant abuser may be excited, hyperactive, and talkative and then degenerate into hostility and irritability, particularly if you state that you suspect the client of drug abuse and order a urinalysis. All clients whom you suspect of drug abuse should be made to undergo urinalysis regularly. Regular urine testing in conjunction with intensive supervision is more effective in reducing recidivism among probationers and parolees than intensive supervision without urine testing (Speckart, Anglin & Deschenes 1989; Anglin, Speckart & Deschenes 1989).

A new drug-testing kit that is less intrusive than urinalysis can be used in the probation and parole officer's office. These matchbox-size kits currently cost $7 each, but the price is expected to drop considerably soon. Each test is designed to detect a specific drug, with kits currently available for heroin and cocaine. Officers simply wipe the palms of a person's hands with the test material, and, if the target substance is present, it will change color. These kits can detect the smallest trace of their target substances and should prove more cost-effective and efficient than urine testing (NCTAP 1990:1).

Therapeutic Communities

Addicts have the same treatment options as alcoholics. They can obtain detoxification and initial counseling as inpatients, or they can be part of the communal living of a therapeutic community of role models, recovered and recovering addicts. The use of therapeutic communities in the treatment of drug abuse has been popular since 1959 when Synanon was established. They are relatively successful as resocialization experiences (Winick 1986).

In such settings addicts are given support, feedback, and information in an accepting, caring, honest, and empathetic way. They learn that if tensions and stresses arise a refocusing of the primary stress in their lives (addiction) will place other tensions and stresses in proper perspective. They will gather reservoirs of self-esteem with renewed feelings of self-control. They will, through the example of others, learn self-forgiveness by focusing anger and negative talk on the substance that holds them in its grip rather than on themselves, and thus acquire a sense of self-worth. As with treatment for alcoholism, of course, the degree of success will also depend heavily on the personality attributes addicts bring to the therapeutic process.

Therapeutic communities generally provide comprehensive social, psychological, educational, and vocational programs aimed at helping the client to

Case Study

Confessions of a Reformed Addict

Anonymous

"Anonymous" is a former student who found love, both tough and tender, to be the answer to her many addictions. She is now a drug abuse counselor—a good one.

We all know what drug and alcohol addiction is, but I was addicted to just about everything that kicked my pleasure centers into gear—booze, drugs of all kinds, food, tobacco, and sex. You might say that I have an addictive personality. This is no story about a ghetto child, for I'm the product of an upper-middle-class background.

At my "sweet sixteen" stage of life I discovered men. I was fresh out of a private Catholic girl's school, and men, a lot of them, was what I wanted. I would go out to the Naval air station in Lemore, California, to dance, drink, and find a man who would go to bed with me while the rest of my chums were at a high school football game or at some other "square" function.

I was drinking heavily by the time I was eighteen and was also beginning to turn on to various drugs. When I graduated from high school I didn't go on to college like most of my friends, I went to a home for unwed mothers. We were counseled there for our promiscuous ways, but the subject of drug and alcohol abuse was never addressed. This was 1968, and nobody thought about addiction among "young ladies." After all, heroin addiction belonged in the ghetto, and alcoholics were all dirty old men rolling in the gutters of skid row.

At this period in my life I sought men out only for sex; "meaningful relationships" were for squares. Besides, who would want to love a 280-pound woman anyway? (Food was another of my addictions). Not too many wanted to sleep with one either, so I found myself "buying" a man for a gram of coke or a few drinks. I didn't really get pleasure from sex, and often I would actually get physically sick thinking about what I was doing. I realize now that I just wanted someone to hold me, and if sex was the price, so be it. This is not much different from being willing to suffer hangovers and withdrawal pains from my other addictions.

Throughout the late sixties, seventies, and early eighties, sex, drugs, and rock n' roll were a way of life for me. I was desperate for love, but thought I could only get it from stuffing myself with food, booze, pills, or penises. I spent my entire inheritance of $250,000 (I told you I was no pauper) in the mad service of these addictions. It's a horrible feeling to wake up in the morning thinking that the only things that would make the new day bearable were my addictions. This lifestyle cost me my health, the respect of my family, my self-respect, and the opportunity to get an education and lead a normal life. I can't even bear children now because the venereal diseases I've had have destroyed this capacity.

One event in my life was instrumental in turning it around for me. I was in an automobile accident in which both the driver and myself were drunk and high. I received a broken jaw and a few other things, but was out of the hospital and back running the bar I owned within six weeks. But by now the cops were on to me. I was doing a little drug dealing from my bar, and was stupid enough to sell $1,800 worth of coke to an undercover officer. I was busted the next day and held in jail until my trial date. Here I spent three months without drugs, alcohol, sex, or excessive amounts of food.

The judge sentenced me to five years probation, a $4,000 fine, and 120 hours community service. I also was ordered to pay back the "buy money." My probation officer was a real "knuckle dragger," an ex-cop. He made it plain to me that his only job was to put me back in jail if I fucked up. Anyway, I did my community service hours and visited my PO weekly. I began to see him as the caring father that I never had. I actually enjoyed the discipline of doing my community service and following my PO's orders. He and I became as friendly as a probationer and her officer could be. He was a very positive influence in my life, and it was he who got me interested in enrolling in college and pursuing a career in criminal justice.

I am now off probation, have my degree in criminal justice, and am married to a very loving man. I have not touched either alcohol or drugs since I was busted, have given up smoking, am down to a respectable weight of 165 at 5' 6", and my husband is the only man I've had sex with, or wanted to have sex with, in the past six years. I still see and talk with my probation officer, and I still volunteer at the agency I did my community service with. I want to devote my life's work to helping those poor lost souls on the same mad path to hell that I once walked, a path now made even more dangerous by the appearance of the AIDS virus. There is a life after addiction if only you can find love and give it in return. I first found it in the cold stare of my probation officer, and then in the arms of my loving husband and the soft smiles of his two children.

---

reenter society as a more responsible individual. The assumptions and dynamics of these programs are like those for alcoholism. Unfortunately, drug addicts are more difficult to deal with than are alcoholics, especially during the first few crucial days when the drugs still in the system cause feelings of anxiety, fear, and paranoia. At this time, addicts need a calm, quiet, and supportive environment, as isolated as possible from outside contacts. Any phone contact from fellow users on the outside can trigger the urge to run from the facility back into the arms of drugs.

Nonresidential Options

Among the many nonresidential treatment options is Narcotics Anonymous (NA), a group therapy program modeled on AA. It too is usually staffed and run by ex-addicts. All the AA advantages of peer group counseling and association exist in NA.

Finally, addicts can avail themselves of antagonistic drugs (pharmacotherapy). Opponents of pharmacotherapy argue that this is not a treatment because it merely substitutes one drug for another. Advocates of pharmacotherapy respond that it enhances and augments, not replaces, traditional treatments and is more cost-effective (Nugent 1990b:6). Nugent argues that "Drug users are often emotionally unstable; pharmacotherapeutics regulate them, making them more receptive to counseling and rehabilitation." The procedure is in fact the same as for depressives, schizophrenics, and other syndromes associated with chemical imbalances in the brain; we try to stabilize first their brain chemistry and then their lives.

The best-known and most widely-used drug therapy is methadone maintenance. Some authorities feel that this method should be used only after psychotherapeutic methods have failed because methadone creates its own dependence, and methadone-related deaths have been reported (Brown, Benn & Jansen 1975). However, methadone maintenance is extremely successful in blocking the withdrawal pains of heroin without producing any rewarding euphoria or rush of its own. Withdrawal from methadone is not nearly as severe as heroin withdrawal, and the symptoms do not appear for about twenty-four hours after the last dose, as opposed to about five hours for heroin. Best of all, the heroin addict on a methadone program can function normally. Although addicts retain their physical dependence on a narcotic (methadone), they defeat their psychological craving for heroin and no longer have to engage in criminal activity to avoid withdrawal. Addicts typically report to a clinic daily to drink their methadone mixed with orange juice. Kaplan (1991:3) states that: "Methadone maintenance 'works' for around 30 or 40 percent of the addicts who undergo treatment. Moreover, the arrest rate of addicts drops dramatically when they enter methadone treatment."

Narcotic antagonists such as Cyclazocine and Naloxone are available to offset a psychological craving for heroin. They do not possess the narcotic-like properties of methadone, but they do produce rapid detoxification. These antagonists block the pleasurable effects of heroin and, like Antabuse, should be used in conjunction with intensive counseling designed (as always) to enhance clients' self-esteem, get them to exert control over their own lives, and encourage them to behave responsibly.

Disipramine, a drug that has been used experimentally in the treatment of cocaine addicts, has been claimed to keep addicts from craving the drug for up to nine months; other methods have reported records of only fifteen days (Hazleton 1984). The newest antagonistic drug is buprenorphine, which can be used to treat addiction to both cocaine and heroin and possibly other drugs. One of its advantages is that it is nonaddictive. Unlike methadone and other therapeutic drugs, buprenorphine is not likely to create an illicit drug market because its opiate effects are weak (Nugent 1990b:6). (You should be familiar with medical facilities that dispense antagonistic drugs in case you are faced with a particularly intractable client.)

Do not be put off by the argument that these drugs "only treat symptoms, not the cause." The symptoms are precisely what we are most immediately concerned with. Much of medicine is concerned with treating symptoms while the body's natural defenses are marshaled to attack the cause. In fact, apart from the infectious diseases, medicine has very few "cures." Heart disease, diabetes, and arthritis, like alcoholism, are never cured. Drugs can minimize the destructive effects of the symptoms associated with these medical problems; they help people to cope.

Further, do not be disheartened by those who tell you that it is "impossible" to wean substance abusers successfully. Many troops returning from Vietnam were able to kick their habits regardless of whether or not they were treated. Robins et al. (1980) found that 43 percent of a sample of 600 returning soldiers reported an addiction to heroin in Vietnam. Although some reported occasional use back home, only 12 percent of those reporting addiction in Vietnam relapsed to addiction back in the United States. "Removed from the pressures of war and once more in the presence of family and friends and opportunities for constructive activity, these men felt no need for heroin" (Peel 1978:65). This is an instructive statement about the power of attachment, commitment, and involvement to generate responsible behavior.

To those who assert that the voluntary acquiescence of the client is "absolutely necessary" for successful treatment, it should be said that the majority of chemically dependent people who have been successfully treated have been to some extent forced into treatment. They did not necessarily want to discontinue their chemical usage, but crises in their lives forced them to accept help. Certainly, being caught up in the criminal justice system because of substance abuse should be crisis enough to generate at least some motivation in the client. As a corrections worker who is probably not trained in substance abuse techniques, you are not likely to be directly involved in treating alcoholics or drug abusers, but you will need to be a knowledgeable broker of the treatment programs in your community, insisting on frequent urine testing of clients not in residential treatment, and above all, holding clients strictly responsible for remaining alcohol- and drug-free. Treating offenders with substance abuse problems is a team effort; you do your part by effective client monitoring and effective liaison with treatment agencies.

Summary

Drug users bear the additional burden of the illegality of their practices; crime is associated with drug addiction largely because of the high cost of drugs. Many more drug users become addicted than do users of alcohol.

The depressants such as heroin tend to be used most by those people who desire to escape from the pains of life. It is extremely difficult to overcome the heroin habit, but Peel's statement about the soldiers who used heroin in Vietnam but who kicked it on their return to the United States says much about the value of attachment, commitment, and involvement.

Whereas the users of depressants are "laid back," stimulant users are hyperaroused and sensitive to their environments. Methamphetamine users are especially prone to violence when they are "wired." Cocaine appears to be the most popular and rewarding drug of all, and the emergence of crack in recent times has removed class boundaries from the use of cocaine.

The hallucinogens, such as marijuana and LSD, are not quite so problematic for the corrections counselor. Because they are relatively cheap, they are affordable without criminal activity, and their effects do not ordinarily make their users prone to violence.

The assessment and treatment of drug addicts is much like that of alcoholics. Narcotics Anonymous functions much like AA, and there are narcotic antagonistic drugs much like Antabuse. Methadone (for heroin addiction) is the best-known of these drugs. Do not fall for the "only treating symptoms" or the pessimistic "once an addict, always an addict" arguments. The symptoms of alcoholism and drug addiction are what we are most immediately concerned with, and pessimism has a way of becoming a self-fulfilling prophecy.

References and Suggested Readings

Anglin, M., G. Speckart, and E. Deschenes. 1989. *Reexamining the effects of probation and parole on narcotics addiction and property crime.* Final Report, National Institute of Justice. Washington, D.C.: U.S. Department of Justice.

Bogdanovich, P. 1985. *The killing of the unicorn: Dorothy Stratten 1960-1980.* New York: Bantam.

Brown, B., G. Benn, and D. Jansen. 1975. Methadone maintenance: Some client opinions. *American Journal of Psychiatry* 132:623-628.

Burnett, M. 1979. Understanding and overcoming addictions. In *Helping clients with special concerns,* edited by S. Eisenberg and L. Patterson. Chicago: Rand McNally.

Cadoret, R., E. Troughton, and R. Widmer. 1984. Clinical differences between antisocial and primary alcoholics. *Comprehensive Psychiatry* 25:1-8.

Chein, I., G. Gerhard, R. Lee, and E. Rosenfeld. 1964. *The road to H: Narcotics, delinquency and social policy.* New York: Basic Books.

Glasser, W. 1984. *Control theory.* New York: Harper & Row.

Grabowski, J. 1984. *Cocaine: Pharmacology, effects and treatment of abuse.* Washington, D.C.: National Institute of Drug Abuse.

Hazleton, L. 1984. Cocaine and the chemical brain. *Science Digest* 92:58-66.

Holden, C. 1989. Street-wise crack research. *Science* 246:1376-1381.

Kaplan, J. 1991. *Heroin.* National Institute of Justice Crime File (NCJ # 97225). Washington, D.C.: U.S. Department of Justice.

Liebowitz, M. 1983. *The chemistry of love.* New York: Berkley Books.

Lister, J. 1986. Cocaine smoking: The use of crack, America's new drug craze. *Payada* 1:13-14.

Malcolm, A. 1989. Explosive drug use in prison is creating a new underworld. *New York Times* (December 30, 1989): 1.10.

Marlatt, G., J. Baer, D. Donovan, and D. Kivlanhan. 1989. Addictive behaviors: Etiology and treatment. *Annual Review of Psychology* 39:223-252.

Narcotics Control Technical Assistance Program. 1990. Future drug testing kits. *NCTAP News* 4:1.

Nugent, E. 1990a. Ice: The new cold war. *NCTAP News* 3 (January): 1-4.

Nugent, E. 1990b. Pharmacotherapy. *NCTAP News* 3 (April): 6-7.

Peel, S. 1978. Addiction: The analgesic experience. *Human Nature* 1 (September): 61-66.

Restak, R. 1979. *The brain: The last frontier.* New York: Warner.

Speckart, G., M. Anglin, and E. Deschenes. 1989. Modeling the longitudinal impact of legal sanctions on narcotics use and property crime. *Journal of Quantitative Criminology* 5:33-56.

U.S. Department of Justice. 1991. *Violent crime in the United States.* U.S. Department of Justice, Washington, D.C.: Bureau of Justice Statistics.

Visher, C. 1990. Incorporating drug treatment in criminal sanctions. *NIJ Reports* (Summer): 1-7.

Winick, C. 1986. The drug offender. In *Psychology of crime and criminal justice.* Prospect Heights, Ill.: Waveland Press.

Chapter 14
The Sex-offending Client

Sex offenders had better not be viewed as horrible, villainous criminals who have to harshly punished. . . . They can, rather, be diagnosed either as relatively healthy individuals who are rash enough to get into occasional difficulty or as more seriously disturbed persons whose sexual behavior puts them in frequent conflict with the law.

Albert Ellis

Sex and American Society

Sexual offenses encompass such a wide range of behaviors that one may reasonably question the wisdom of placing all of them in a single category. The exhibitionist is as different from the rapist as the check forger is from the armed robber. If you live in one of the many states that still have antisodomy laws, you might even be guilty of felonious behavior for which you could be imprisoned if you engage in oral or anal sex, even with your consenting spouse. We will concern ourselves here only with those sexual offenses that involve a true offender/victim relationship, such as rape and child molesting—behavior that is almost universally considered a serious breach of lawful behavior, not merely a mild deviation from acceptable behavior.

The sex offender (almost invariably male) and his behavior have to be viewed in the context of his culture. Few things interest Americans more than sex; American culture is shot through with sexual themes. Billions of dollars are spent every year on cosmetics, hair styling, breath mints, and health spas to make us appear sexually attractive. Women's ears are pierced, lips painted, underarms sprayed, necklines lowered, and skirts raised; and young men advertise their wares by pouring themselves into shrunken jeans. Goaded by the wizards of Madison Avenue, many of us have fallen prey to the notion that we are less than good Americans if we are not supremely sexual beings.

Counteracting this pressure toward sexual expression is a highly puritanical strain in American culture. It has been said somewhat exaggeratedly that, with the exception of John Calvin's Geneva, the United States has the most moralistic criminal code that the world has ever seen (Morris & Hawkins 1969:15). Robinson makes clear the sensitivity of the American legal system to sexual behavior, extending even into the marital bed: "The laws [pertaining to sex] have few parallels in the modern world outside of the Soviet Union and some of its satellites. Western European nations have generally abandoned similar legislation, in some cases as long as a century ago" (Robinson 1987:251). Thus, Americans are simultaneously pushed toward sexual expression by a permissively erotic market and pulled back again by a restrictive code of sexual morality. It is against this background that the sex offender is defined and punished.

The Public Image of the Sex Offender

Americans do not like sex offenders. We are convinced that the sex criminal is "insane or mentally retarded; that he is brutal, depraved, immoral, and oversexed. He is a social isolate who spends his time reading dirty books or haunting dirty movies; a godless, brainless fellow, a 'dirty old man,' crippled or disfigured, dope addicted, and incurable" (Cohen & Boucher 1972:57). The general public sees the sex offender as an inhuman species apart, either a "super male" in an interminable state of tumescence or a pathetic and evil old man searching for sensuality in the unwilling arms of a child. Although such descriptions may sometimes be true, the criminal justice worker cannot afford to harbor such stereotypes.

No common characteristic distinguishes all sex offenders. A sex offender can be anyone from a sexual sadist who uses his penis to degrade his victim to the unassuming church deacon who "playfully" touches a neighborhood child where he should not. There are certainly differences between the sex offender whose passion for his new date exceeds her expectations and the rapist who attacks with equal intensity the nubile homecoming queen and the octogenarian cripple—differences that will affect your recommendations and treatment strategies. Likewise, we should not treat equally the father who, because of some extreme circumstances, sexually molests his daughter on a single occasion and the father who feels that he has the lordly "right of the first night" with a succession of his offspring.

Rape and Rapists

The Federal Bureau of Investigation defines forcible rape as "the carnal knowledge of a female forcibly and against her will" (FBI 1991). The agency reported 100,433 rapes in 1990, a 6.3 percent increase from 1989. Rape is perhaps the most underreported of all crimes, probably because of the fear and embarrassment of its victims. There is no doubt that rape is an excruciatingly traumatic event, the effects of which may last long after any physical scars have healed. This can be true even if the perpetrator is an acquaintance, boyfriend, date, or even spouse of the victim.

Views of the rapist in the professional literature vary widely; many of the opinions are strongly colored by such nonobjective factors as personal morality and sexual politics. Each view, of course, fits some rapists. No view fits all rapists. Some regard rape as symptomatic of dark psychological disturbances. Others see it simply as part of a complex of cultural values that emphasize masculinity, aggression, and sexual violence. Drzasga exemplifies the first view, explaining rape as an act performed by "degenerate male imbeciles" seeking to satisfy "sadistic and aggressive desires for sexual dominance" (1960:57). From this perspective, rape is a violent rather than a venereal act, substituting the penis for the gun or knife.

This view may be accurate for some rape cases, but to ascribe such motivations across the board is to commit what philosophers call the logical fallacy of affirming the consequent: Having observed the consequences of an action, we infer that they were the motivations of the actor. We may observe that the rapist in asserting his dominance over his victim humiliates, defiles, and degrades her, but there is no basis for assuming that he attacked her in order to accomplish that.

The common assertion that "there is nothing sexual about rape" may be politically correct, but it ignores the fact that if intercourse was accomplished, the sexual component is the only component of the act of which we can be sure—everything else is conjecture. We have no access to a rapist's motivations, which even he may not really understand. Lee Ellis supplies voluminous evidence (1991) to support his countervailing contention that "rape is sexually motivated, and [the] aggressiveness and dominating behavior exhibited by rapists largely reflect tactics rather than goals."

Many imprisoned rapists will eventually tell a counselor that their motivations were to degrade and defile their victims, but do they do this because those were indeed their motivations? Or do they do it because they have learned that the way to obtain parole points is to tell officials what they think officials want to hear? "Confess your crime, confront your crime, understand the motives for your crime, and show remorse for your crime"—these are the conditions of the parole game that inmates soon learn. Can it really be only coincidence that sophisticated criminals always seem to explain their behavior in accordance with prevailing academic theory?

The majority of rapes are motivated by misdirected sexual desires rather than by disturbed, sadistic psychological motivations far removed from sex, though it is true that male dominance feelings are an integral part of sexual relations, consensual or not. Perhaps rape is best viewed as a fusion of sex and aggression, with sex primary in some cases and aggression in others. As a criminal justice worker, you will be doing your clients a disservice if you succumb uncritically to interpretations that sound esoteric but may well be empty. Perhaps the best way to view someone who is accused of rape is Albert Ellis's: unless there is evidence to the contrary, think of him as a psychologically healthy individual who has committed an odious crime.

The other dominant interpretation of rape, which is more sociological, is exemplified by Ploscowe. He sees rapists as "men who are simply following the pattern of racial and cultural behavior with which they are familiar" (1968:205). A similar view is voiced by Robertson, who says that although rape is "socially regarded as intolerable, it has its origins in approved patterns of interaction between the sexes" (1987:259). These two male theorists are supplemented by feminist theorists Clark and Lewis, who view rape as indicative of a general hatred of women that characterizes the behavior of "normal" adult men (1977:140). A harsh view of men in general and lower-class men in particular, this interpretation sees rape as little more than an occasional and unfortunate manifestation of a general principle defining the relationship between the sexes.

Most rapes involve offenders and victims who are acquainted with one another. Many men convicted of rape under these circumstances are indeed enamored of traditional masculine values. They value sexual prowess and tend to hold the "whore/madonna" image of women. They have difficulty understanding how their victims could be so ungrateful as to accuse them of rape. They feel that once they have overcome a woman's initial protestations in a forceful "masculine" way, just like romantic heroes in the movies, she should melt into their arms. In the world of veiled sexual messages, it is common knowledge that "no" really means "yes."

Here is an excerpt from a PSI in which the processing officer is commenting on the statement of a defendant convicted of raping his sister-in-law. This defendant came home drunk one night (rape is often associated with alcohol), dragged his seventeen-year-old sister-in-law into his bedroom, told his sleeping wife to get up and get out, and raped his victim.

> It is clear from the defendant's explicit statement that he does not deny the charge. On the contrary, one almost gets the impression that he rather enjoyed writing his statement, which depicts him as an accomplished lover and mentor to the sexually naive. "How can this be rape?" he asks in an aggrieved tone of voice. He believes that his amorous designs were pursued fully in accord with the rules of the game, i.e., in the "masculine" way of his subculture. For him the crime was little more than an "assault with a friendly weapon." It strains this officer's imagination to think of the defendant as venting his sexual passions on an unwilling girl whose mother was in the next room

fully aware of what was going on. Not only that, he had the audacity to ask his wife to vacate her bed so that he could do his thing in comfort.

Rapists like this young man use aggression as a means to an end, not as an end in itself. Many of them might not have gone on to complete the act if they did not harbor stereotypes of women as sexual playthings who "really" want to "be taken," even if they do put up token resistance. Many date and acquaintance rapes would not occur if males could rid themselves of such stereotypes. (Unfortunately, many of these stereotypes regarding casual and brutal sex are perpetuated in heavy metal and rap music.) Women would also do well to divest themselves of their own stereotypes of femininity. Many victims of date and acquaintance rape tend to be nonassertive types with traditional views of the relationship between the sexes. Counselors at rape crisis centers often state that many rapes would be avoided if women could forcefully assert their right to their own bodies.

Some rapists do become more aroused sexually when victims fight back and may even be impotent without such stimuli. If they prefer violent to consensual sex, their primary motive may well be to defile and humiliate. Such rapes tend to be stranger rapes and are thus more terrifying and physically injurious to the victim. Rapists of this type tend to have marked feelings of inadequacy and inferiority (Hartman 1978:230) or powerlessness (Thio 1978:139), to be highly sexed but socially inadequate (Ellis 1991), and, unlike the typical date or acquaintance rapist, to have histories of other violent crimes (Adler 1984:163).

Most studies of rapists concentrate on the violent rapist. We do know with relative certainty that among them violence is an important component of the sexual excitement they obtain from their crimes. This pattern is determined by comparing penile responses of convicted rapists with those of nonrapists when exposed to sexual stimuli with a strong violence content. Penile response is measured by a device called a penile plethysmograph, which is rather like a blood pressure gauge that fits around the penis. The penile plethysmograph measures the pressure of blood in the penis to ascertain how sexually excited subjects become when exposed to auditory and/or visual stimuli depicting various sexual situations. Violent rapists become significantly more aroused than nonrapists or nonviolent rapists when exposed to this material (Barbaree, Marshall & Lantheir 1979; Quinsey & Chaplin 1982).

Most men, of course, will show some penile response to a variety of sexual stimuli, even if they consider it deviant and would not engage in it. The value of the penile plethysmograph lies not only in the opportunity it offers to compare the responses of convicted rapists with those of "normal" males, but also to compare the penile responses of rapists to stimuli depicting violent sex with their responses to stimuli depicting nonviolent consensual sex. For instance, if a rapist achieves a 30 percent erection when viewing nonviolent sex and one of 80 percent when viewing violent sex, we can conclude both that he is more interested in violent than consensual sex and that he is probably dangerous. Likewise, if a man has a 90 percent erection in response to sexual stimuli involving young boys and only 5 percent to stimuli involving adult females, we can conclude that he is a homosexual pedophile—the penis, unlike its owner, finds it difficult to lie (Earls & Proulx 1987).

Such findings do seem to indicate that the violent rapist is "sick" in that he apparently needs violence in order to complete the sexual act. Strangely enough, rape is not listed as a sexual deviation in DSM-III of the American Psychiatric Association (APA). The APA apparently does not see any clear syndrome associated with rape that could be called "rapism" in the same way that they identify conditions like exhibitionism and pedophilia (Hartman 1978:279). Violent rapists may simply be violent men who take what they want, whether it be money or sex. Their sexual offenses appear to be part of a pattern of violent criminality. The criminal justice worker's primary concern should be the safety of the public. Individuals who exhibit patterns of violent behavior should be placed in custodial care for as long as the law allows.

Stranger versus Date/Acquaintance Rape

There are some remarkable differences between stranger and date/acquaintance rape that suggest that the offenses are committed by psychologically quite different men (Walsh 1983). Victims of stranger rape could be any age from fifteen to seventy. As might be expected, the age range of victims of date/acquaintance rape was much smaller (fourteen through forty-four). Stranger rapists had far more serious criminal histories, were of much lower class, and were much younger (an average of twenty-two versus an average of thirty-one). Of the victims of stranger rape, 80 percent were physically harmed, versus 33.3 percent of the date/acquaintance category; 73 percent of the stranger rapists used some kind of weapon, versus 21 percent of the others; and 66.7 percent were drug or alcohol addicts, versus 12 percent of the others. Like other such studies, these findings emphasize the qualitative differences among acts of rape and its perpetrators.

Unlike stranger rape, which almost by definition involves the perpetrator's expectation of violence, in date rape force is usually used only after other nonviolent tactics (verbal pressure, getting the victim drunk or high, threatening to terminate the relationship, false pledges of love and other deceits) have been tried (Koss & Leonard 1984). These data should not be construed as minimizing date rape; it can cause injuries that go beyond the physical. The betrayal of trust inherent in date rape may be psychologically more deleterious to the victim than the physical and psychological pains of stranger rape.

Assessment and Treatment

Public outrage at rapists and child molesters has made treatment rather than swift punishment for sex offenders an unpopular idea. However, the realization that most incarcerated sex offenders will eventually be released has generated a demand for treatment to ensure successful reintegration into the community (Gendreau & Ross 1987:381). From their review of studies of sex offender treatment programs, Gendreau and Ross are cautiously optimistic. Most studies did report a gratifying rate of success when comparing results for treated and untreated offenders. Although none of the studies dealt with the violent rapist, the general impression was that treatment was most successful for incest and heterosexual child molesters and least successful for homosexual child molesters (Gendreau & Ross 1987:383).

The assessment and treatment of sexual offenders is almost always conducted by mental health teams. If the sentencing judge feels that an offender's crime or record of sexual offenses warrants it, he will be referred to a diagnostic center or if there is none to individual psychologists or psychiatrists. Typically, the offender is given a series of tests such as the MMPI and IQ tests and a series of psychosocial interviews. The judge and the PSI investigator are given the results of these tests, a diagnosis, a treatment prognosis, and a sentencing recommendation. The diagnosis tends to be a reflection of behavior (e.g., a nonviolent child molester will be labeled a "passive-aggressive pedophile"), and the prognosis and sentencing recommendation entirely a function of the severity of the offense and the offender's criminal history (Walsh 1990).

Treatment for the violent rapist is extremely difficult, and the results are discouraging. Many treatments such as aversive conditioning (where an offender is shown sexually arousing pictures in conjunction with a punishment, such as an electric shock) have been drastically curtailed in the United States for civil rights reasons. Therapeutic castration appears to be the most effective form of treatment. A review of European literature dealing with 2,055 sex-offending castrates followed for as long as twenty years found extremely low recidivism rates ranging from zero to 7.4 percent (Bradford 1990). These findings offer strong support for those who favor theories of rape that emphasize hormonal factors (coupled with inadequate socialization) in the etiology of rape, e.g., Ellis (1989). Although therapeutic castration has been tried in the United States, it has been discontinued for civil rights reasons.

It remains to be seen how the courts will view chemical castration by the use of drugs such as medroxyprogesterone (Depo-Provera) for offenders with excessive sex drives that place them at risk for reoffending. These drugs reduce the level of the male sex hormone testosterone, thereby diminishing arousal or responsiveness to sexuality and violence. It has been reliably established that violent male criminals have significantly higher levels of circulating testosterone than nonviolent criminals (Kreuz & Rose 1972). Violent rapists have a high rate of recidivism (about 26 percent) regardless of whether or not they are treated (psychotherapy rather than surgical or drug intervention) (Maletzky 1987).

Whereas the convicted violent rapist is nearly always incarcerated, the date or acquaintance rapist tends more often to get probation. The date rapist on probation should be treated first in group counseling designed to correct "thinking errors," in which stereotypical images of women are brought out for discussion. Educating males to accept women as equals who have the right to say no can go a long way toward preventing a recurrence. Many men do actually believe that women "ask for it" if they accept dinner and a date and perhaps engage in a little mild petting. Egocentric thinking—believing that everyone thinks as we do—leads some men to the conclusion that, "Hey, I'm aroused and ready to go, she must be too." The kind of men who tend to believe these things are traditionally masculine males (Bernard, et al. 1985)—"Real men don't take no for an answer." Given this, it would not hurt to also explore thinking errors as they relate to the date rapist's conceptions of what a "real man" is. The questioning and challenging techniques of RET and a healthy dose of bibliotherapy should prove useful.

Exercises like the victim experience one in Chapter 11 can be fruitful, as can movies that reveal the psychological trauma that accompanies rape. It is better yet to have a rape victim speak to the group about how her experience affected her life. Select the victim carefully, however. A speaker who spouts trendy sexual politics and who defines rape as everything from violent sexual assault to sexual innuendos will wash all meaning out of the word. Nor do you want one who flays the group, and all men, because of her experience. Although the response is understandable, the group will react defensively and refuse to take her seriously, and the whole exercise will probably do more harm than good. Local rape crisis centers usually know of strong victims willing to talk dispassionately about their experiences.

Child Molesters

McCaghy (1967:78) defines a child molester as a male over the age of eighteen who manipulates the genitals of a child of thirteen or younger or has the child manipulate his. A child molester may or may not be a true pedophile (literally a "lover of children" whose sexually orientation is toward them). Most men convicted of molesting children apparently prefer adult sex but have opportunistically taken advantage of a child. Some take advantage of any form of sexual gratification immediately available, regardless of age, sex, or even at times species. Child molesters tend to be either in the teen years, the mid-to-late thirties, or the mid-fifties on (Hartman 1978: 213-214).

Teenage molesters tend to be socially withdrawn and of lower intelligence than the average teenager. They rarely attempt intercourse, tending to confine their sexual activity to kissing and manually manipulating the genitals. The victim is most often known to the offender, and the act can be viewed as a sexual curiosity in a teenager who is too self-effacing to attempt to satisfy it with consenting persons his own age.

Offenders in their mid-to-late thirties are usually married, and the victim is often a stepchild. Not infrequently, the molestation continues over time. The offender usually is able to maintain the ongoing "relationship" by telling his victim that the child's mother would get mad if she found out or that the child might be placed in a juvenile detention center or a foster home if the offense became known. The first molestation is likely to occur when the offender has been unemployed for an extended period of time, has been drinking, or finds that his normal sex life has soured. One study found that 34.3 percent of child molesters were unemployed at the time of their offense (Walsh 1985)—about five times the average unemployment rate for males over a six-year period in that jurisdiction.

The molester of fifty-five and older has usually had no prior contact with the law. He may be lonely because he has recently suffered the loss of his wife by death or

Case Study

Portrait of a Sex Offender

Marc was a tall, good-looking man with an IQ of 119, an attractive wife, and a five-year-old son. Nevertheless, his work record was extremely poor. He was mainly a casual laborer. He never kept a job long because he always seemed to get into an argument with his bosses and get fired or quit. After losing a job he would go on short drinking binges. Despite his quick temper, his wife said that he was never abusive to her or their young son.

I first met Marc after his conviction for gross sexual imposition. He had been driving around one rainy day after a minor drinking bout when he came upon two children—a girl age twelve and a boy age eleven—standing at a bus stop in the rain. Marc stopped and offered them a ride, which they accepted. The children later said they had accepted because they had just missed one bus, it was raining heavily, and they apparently felt safety in numbers.

After some small talk, Marc took the children into an alley and told them both to take their clothes off. The children refused and started to cry. Marc then called the children "little fuckers" and proceeded to force his hand up the dress of the girl and stick his fingers in her vagina. He also fondled the boy's penis and told them both to keep quiet. The young boy was able to escape and shout for help from a nearby construction gang, who apprehended Marc and held him for the police.

Marc told me that his initial motive was simply to get the children out of the rain. Once the children were in the car "I felt an overwhelming urge to expose myself to them." He admitted frequently exposing himself to children standing at bus stops in the past, and he had two prior convictions for such behavior. He admitted telling the young girl to remove her blouse: "It gave me a feeling of mastery. But I knew she wouldn't do it because of modesty." He denied touching the girl's vagina or the boy's penis.

My investigation led me to discover a rape conviction in another state that was not on Marc's FBI rap sheet. He reluctantly admitted this conviction to me, but said that he was wrongfully convicted. This turned out to be the truth, much to my surprise. He has been granted a full governor's pardon and $2,000 compensation for the three years he spent in prison for his conviction. Marc's wife informed me that he had told her that he had been frequently raped in prison, which he described as "a whorehouse where the only thing missing was the women." She felt that many of his sexual problems stemmed from his prison experience.

Marc had referred himself to a private psychiatrist after his arrest and bail. This psychiatrist wrote that Marc's pedophilia was of recent origin, and that with "intensive psychotherapy it would never reach a stage of chronicity." He felt that Marc's desire to expose himself to children was caused by "deep-seated resentment of his mother's early rejection of him." (He was essentially "thumbing his penis" at his mother.) The psychiatrist recommended that Marc be placed on probation and that the county pay for his therapy.

For my part, I reasoned that Marc had kidnapped, terrified, and sexually molested two children and that nothing less than incarceration could be justified. The judge reasoned otherwise, and placed Marc on probation on the condition that he continue treatment and spend sixty days in jail. Marc did not continue therapy with his psychiatrist. Instead he opted to attend group counseling at the court diagnostic and treatment center and individual counseling with me.

For a variety of reasons, not the least, I suppose, being his ability to make intelligent conversation, Marc's case fascinated and challenged me. During one session in which we were discussing his prison experiences, he told me that other inmates had ridiculed him about the size of his penis and how this used to devastate him. (He never even divulged to his psychiatrist that he had been incarcerated.) Further discussion led to his telling me that he had measured his erect penis at five inches.

I then changed directions somewhat to discuss the possibility that his urge to expose himself to children may have stemmed from an exaggerated concern for the size of his penis. To a young child, an erect adult penis seems gigantic. Marc acknowledged that perhaps he was trying to reassure himself about the adequacy of his penis by shocking his victims with its erect enormity to compensate for the cruel hazing he received about it from his fellow inmates.

Latching onto what I thought might be a crucial piece of information, I assigned Marc some rational-emotive therapy "homework." I instructed him to go to the public library and check out three textbooks on human anatomy and physiology. From these books, he was to look up information on the size of the normal erect penis. He signed a plan saying that he would do this the following morning. This assignment led to Marc's discovery that 90 percent of all males have an erect penis of between 5.5 and 6.5 inches, meaning that Marc was just half an inch short of being in the average range.

This discovery provided for a fruitful evaluation of just how irrational it was for Marc to get himself into so much trouble for the sake of half an inch of floppy flesh that no one but he and his wife would ever see if he didn't expose himself. He was guided to view his self-esteem in terms of his good looks, his high intelligence, and the love of his supportive wife and dependent child.

Over the next few months, Marc reported that he had experienced urges to expose himself again. However, he had not done so because he reminded himself of the irrationality of the act and of his responsibilities to his family. Marc successfully completed three years of probation without further trouble with the law. I monitored the daily arrest sheet for the two remaining years I spent in probation without ever seeing his name on it. I ran into his wife one day at a shopping center. She told me that everything was going fine, that Marc had been at his job for over a year, that he had drastically cut down on his drinking, and that there didn't seem to be any residual sexual problems. Marc's was the kind of case that made me feel glad and proud to have been a probation officer, and, for once, glad that my recommendation to the court had perhaps been wrong.

---

divorce. It is extremely rare for such offenders to use any kind of force; they usually promise rewards such as money or candy to persuade victims to do their bidding. As with teenage but not middle-aged molesters, actual intercourse is rare. They are usually deeply remorseful when their activity is discovered; they are the least likely of all to offend again.

Homosexual molesters tend more to be true pedophiles than their heterosexual counterparts. One study (Walsh 1985) found that 34.7 percent of the homosexual molesters were diagnosed as pedophiles, as opposed to 13.2 percent of the heterosexuals. They were also more likely to be strangers to their victims (26.5 percent versus only 4.8 percent of the heterosexual offenders). On the one hand, homosexual offenders were much less likely (4.1 percent) to use force or the threat of force to gain compliance than were the heterosexuals (19.2 percent). On the other hand, they were more than twice as likely to have a prior conviction for molesting (49 versus 22.1 percent)—but in 21.6 percent of those prior molestations, the victims were females. It may thus be more accurate to call these men bisexual pedophiles.

Rapists versus Child Molesters

Both rapists and child molesters are threatened by normal adult sexuality (Groth 1979:151). The difference is that the rapist attacks the source of the threat and the child molester retreats from it to safer substitutes. Many child molesters are shy and introverted (Quinsey 1986), which may prevent them from interacting sexually with mature adults. It is not unusual to see cases in which an offender has carried on an "affair" with a child for long periods of time (Walsh 1988). The emotional investment appears quite often to extend beyond sexuality. However misdirected the attachment, the child is valued as a person and a "lover." In contrast, the target for the rapist is an object or a symbol on whose body he seeks to satisfy his selfish needs.

Perspectives from the Field

Counseling Sex Offenders: The Thoughts of a SANE Counselor

Tula M. Starck

Starck is a Boise State University graduate in criminal justice. She has field experience in a community services program for offenders, in probation and parole, and as a counselor in a sex abuse program called Sexual Abuse Now Ended (SANE).

Only recently has the problem of sexual abuse been pulled from under the carpet where it had been swept by embarrassed families and law enforcement alike. In response to this belated house-cleaning, a comprehensive community-based treatment and prevention program for sex offenders and their victims was instituted in the Third Judicial District of Idaho. This program is called Sexual Abuse Now Ended, or SANE. I like to tell people that I'm a "sane" counselor.

Counseling sex offenders requires unusual people. The capacity for empathy must exist, but a tough outlook, the ability to recognize a con, and the capacity to confront clients are essential. Before beginning with SANE, I spent many months with probation and parole researching sex offenders' case files. I was accepted as part of the agency's family and would often accompany officers on home visits and sit in on their talks with their sex offender clients. I learned to expect anything and be outwardly shocked by nothing. I learned that the sex abuser and the sexually abused could be anyone. He or she can be your neighbor, your doctor, the skid row bum, the girl or boy next to you in the church choir, the introvert, or the extrovert.

After years of study, numerous lectures on sexual abuse, many research papers, and interviewing both abusers and the abused, I was still not adequately prepared for working with sex offenders on a daily basis. I had not counted on my own emotional involvement. I'd heard countless people make statements about abusers such as "Why not use a .22? It's cheaper!" A part of me used to agree with this "solution," but the bigger part of me believes that there's a salvageable part to every human being.

In my work with SANE I've discovered that there's no typical day. I've seen mothers bring in children from one to eighteen years of age. All forms of sexual misconduct have been perpetrated on these children. Some of these children react by abusing others, some live in fear, some don't speak. Almost all regard themselves as guilty and worthless. We work with these children in group and individual counseling. There is also counseling for nonoffending spouses. We have found that a high percentage of nonoffending spouses were themselves abused as children.

My main function with SANE is as a cotherapist working with adult male offenders. Each day I go over case files trying to understand the offenders I will be working with. I'm mostly looking for each client's defense mechanisms, the methods by which they deny, fog, or excuse their behavior. Their abilities to negate responsibility for their acts are amazing. Many tend to be powerless, low-self-esteem individuals who seek even more powerless individuals as targets for sexual assault. They use sex to boost their feelings of power and control. They drain their victims of self-respect and create a feeling of helplessness in them.

Group counseling is the best tool we have. New offending clients are confronted not only by the counselor but also by "veteran" clients who have come to recognize warped thinking patterns. New clients in these programs are angry, afraid, and defensive. But the program is working because the offenders have to attend as conditions of their probation or parole. They are given short-term and long-term goals on a daily basis. It's a painful process for them because they have to look at themselves realistically again and again. They must become aware of their responsibility and their dysfunctional thinking and behavior. They are confronted with their needs for instant gratification and excitement. When they lie, they are confronted with that lie. For the first time in their lives they are made aware of their responsibility for their actions and of the consequences those actions have for their victims. They have to pass through many stages. Only by passing each stage successfully can they get out of the program. Reading assignments and reports are mandatory. They must keep daily journals, which are inspected by the staff and are often read aloud during group sessions. A clarification process is the goal—a process in which the offender comes to understand his behavior by writing down a description of each act of abuse and why it was perpetrated. If the victim agrees to meet with the offender in the presence of the counselor, the victim shares his or her feelings and questions with the offender. It is hoped that both offender and victim benefit from these meetings—the offender by acknowledging total responsibility and the victim hearing this acknowledgment by losing his or her sense of guilt.

I hope to make the counseling of sexual abusers and victims my life's work. I have found it rewarding for two major reasons. First, I'm helping to fight this national ailment through education and counseling. Second, each day and each client present a new challenge. You won't get bored in this business.

The child molester rarely attempts sexual penetration; penetration, as the primeval symbol of conquest, is the ultimate aim of the rapist. Only 14 percent of my sample of child molesters vaginally or anally penetrated their victims, as opposed to 69 percent of the combined stranger and date/acquaintance rapists. Oral sex (61 percent) was the primary kind of sexual activity engaged in by the child molesters, with 25 percent having only manual sexual contact with their victims.

The rapists had significantly more serious criminal histories despite being significantly younger (average age twenty-eight versus an average of thirty-seven for the molesters). The child molesters were of significantly higher social class, ranging occupationally from laborers to ministers and physicians. The rapists were almost all in lower-status occupations, if working at all. Of the molesters, 72 percent had been married at some stage; 42 percent were married at the time of their offenses. The marriage figures for the rapists were 58 and 30 percent. Of the child molesters, 90 percent were related to or acquainted with their victims, as opposed to 61 percent of the rapists, and 63 percent had had previous sexual contact with their victims as opposed to 23.8 percent of the rapists. None of the molesters used a weapon; 30 percent of the rapists did. Clearly, a sharp line divides the rapist from the child molester.

Most child molesters (child rapists—strangers who attempt or accomplish genital intercourse—excepted) tend to have a strong stake in conformity. If the offense was not violent or if the offender has no previous record of similar behavior that would suggest an abiding interest in children as sexual targets, he can usually be considered a good probation risk. But considering how serious this kind of behavior is, a thorough investigation into the offender's background is imperative before any probation can be recommended.

Assessment and Treatment of Child Molesters

One in three women and one in ten men have been sexually assaulted by the age of thirteen by someone they know (FBI 1989). An estimated 70 percent of prostitutes and 80 percent of female drug abusers have been sexually abused by a family member (Rush 1980:5). Despite the urgency of the problem, there is a aura of "nothing works" pessimism surrounding the treatment of child molesters (Ellis 1986:415). Most probation and parole officers have neither the time or the training to counsel child molesters; even those criminal justice workers whose exclusive role is counseling find it difficult to treat them without more expert help. It is therefore particularly necessary to locate treatment options for sex offenders in your community.

The treatment options most often implemented by public and private agencies rely almost exclusively on behavioral/cognitive modalities such as group therapy, interpersonal communication skills, and psychoeducational programs (i.e., social and self-control skills) (Brecher 1978). Their efficacy in preventing recidivism is questionable. Numerous studies (e.g., Romero & Williams 1983) have failed to find statistically significant differences in recidivism rates between sex offenders on probation who received treatment and a control group who did not. This would seem to suggest either that the treatment modalities themselves are not successful or that treatment had been initiated without a proper assessment of the condition to be treated. Psychometric assessment by itself has limited utility for the assessment, classification, and treatment of sexual offenders (Hall et al. 1986; Hall & Proctor 1987).

Greer and Stuart (1983) believe that a "state of the art" sexual abuse treatment program would include the penile plethysmograph and the polygraph—tools for physiological assessment of sexual arousal patterns—in addition to psychosocial assessment and treatment. Several researchers have reported the superiority of penile tumescence measures to classify sex offenders, as well as in treatment (Marshall & Christie 1981; Avery-Clark & Laws 1984). The rationale for the use of these tools is simple: "All therapists concur that effective treatment can only begin when the full extent of the offender's history of sexual deviant behavior is known" (Lundell 1987:2), and that includes the range of his sexual proclivities.

Self-disclosure does not necessarily imply emotional catharsis, although that may follow. While it is axiomatic that the offender cannot be properly confronted (nor can he confront himself) until the full extent of his offending behavior is in the open, the effort to elicit full disclosure has other purposes. Additional victims may be identified via the disclosure process and invited to come in for counseling. It is well-known that untreated victims are candidates for future psychological problems and may commit similar offenses themselves (Smith & Monastersky 1986; Walsh 1988).

The SANE Therapeutic Program

One "state of the art" treatment program known as SANE (Sexual Abuse Now Ended) has gained national attention. SANE is a victim-oriented program based on restitution therapy. Treatment for the offender is regarded as a privilege designed to repair the damage done to the sexually abused victim. "Clarification" is the process by which the sex offender accepts and communicates to his victim his responsibility for his crime, thereby eliminating much of the guilt experienced by victims of sexual abuse. Through treatment of one to five years duration, the offender is taught to restructure the thought processes that have allowed him to commit his crime and to develop empathy for how his victim experienced his abuse. RET and group counseling are used to unlearn thinking errors and to learn more appropriate thinking patterns.

The SANE program does not accept offenders who are violent, show clear evidence of brain damage or psychosis, or deny the charge against them. Offenders who deny accusations of child molestation generally have higher recidivism rates than either treated or non-treated offenders who admit their offenses (Marshall & Barbaree 1988). It is of little use to confront offenders who deny the existence of anything to confront.

To start the program, the offender completes a demographic and sexual history questionnaire (augmented by his presentence investigation report) and a battery of psychological tests. One of SANE's consulting psychologists uses the tests to determine diagnosis, client amenability to treatment, appropriate treatment, and risk of recidivism. Clinical staff then ascertain whether the offender has given his therapists a complete account of his sexual history. The process is facilitated by periodic polygraph assessments. The offender then learns to recognize and diminish his arousal to deviant sexual activity as assessed through periodic penile plethysmograph testing, which should show a progressive decrease in penile blood volume when he is exposed to deviant sexual stimuli.

The offender only completes the program successfully when he (1) has revealed all victims, verified by his polygraph examinations, (2) has confronted the deviant arousal patterns revealed by plethysmograph tests, (3) is demonstrably more aroused by nondeviant sexual material than by deviant sexual material, and (4) has in the view of his therapist accepted full responsibility for his actions and has made "emotional restitution" to his victim or victims. (See the *Perspective* by Tula M. Starck.)

Summary

Few kinds of criminals arouse our passion for punishment more than the sex offender. Sex offenses are perhaps the most underreported of all major crimes, but we should not put all sex offenders into a common basket. The rapist and the child molester differ dramatically, as do stranger rapists and acquaintance rapists. The majority of rapists appear to be traditional males who hold onto the notion that no means yes. They rarely respect women as autonomous human beings who have an absolute right to their own bodies. Some rapists (usually strangers to their victims) do appear to require violence and victim degradation for their perverted satisfaction, but this type of rapist is rare in comparison with the acquaintance/date rapist.

Treatment of rapists in community corrections should center on discussions of sex roles, images of women, and the victim experience. The violent rapist is usually imprisoned. Treatment there must be more intense and is usually administered by psychiatrists and psychologists.

Child molesters are in the main weak and lonely individuals. Only occasionally is one a true pedophile. Child molesters tend to be concentrated in three age categories: the teens, the mid-to-late thirties, and the mid-fifties onward. There are usually some special conditions contributing to child molestation, such as mental deficiency, unemployment, and loneliness. Just as there are some major demographic differences between acquaintance and stranger rapists, there are major differences between rapists and child molesters. The biggest differences are the average ages of the two groups and the rapists' greater propensity to use force.

The treatment of child molesters is best accomplished within specialized sex abuse clinics. One such program uses physiological assessment tools—the penile plethysmograph and the polygraph—to assess, treat, and monitor the offender.

References and Suggested Readings

Adler, C. 1984. The convicted rapist: A sexual or a violent offender? *Criminal Justice and Behavior* 11:157-177.

Avery-Clark, C., and D. Laws. 1984. Differential erection response patterns of sexual child abusers to stimuli describing activities with children. *Behavior Therapy* 15:71-83.

Barbaree, H., W. Marshall, and R. Lanthier. 1979. Deviant sexual arousal in rapists. *Behavior Research and Therapy* 17:215-222.

Bernard, J., S. Bernard, and M. Bernard. 1985. Courtship violence and sex-typing. *Family Relations* 34:573-576.

Bradford, J. 1990. The antiandrogen and hormonal treatment of sex offenders. In *Handbook of sexual assault: Issues, theories, and treatment of the offender*, edited by W. Marshall, D. Laws, and H. Barbaree. New York: Plenum.

Brecher, E. 1978. *Treatment programs for sex offenders*. Washington, D.C.: U.S. GPO.

Clark, L., and D. Lewis. 1977. *Rape: The price of coercive sexuality*. Toronto: The Woman's Press.

Cohen, W., and R. Boucher. 1972. Misunderstandings about sex criminals. *Sexual Behavior* 2:24-35.

Drzasga, J. 1960. *Sex crimes*. Springfield, Ill.: Charles C Thomas.

Earls, C., and J. Proulx. 1987. The differentiation of francophone rapists and non-rapists using penile circumferential. *Criminal Justice and Behavior* 13:419-429.

Ellis, A. 1986. The sex offender. In *Psychology of crime and criminal justice*, edited by H. Toch. Prospect Heights, Ill.: Waveland Press.

Ellis, L. 1989. *Theories of rape: Inquiries into the causes of rape*. New York: Hemisphere Press.

Ellis, L. 1991. A synthesized (biosocial) theory of rape. *Journal of Consulting and Clinical Psychology* 59:631-641..

Federal Bureau of Investigation. 1991. *1990 uniform crime reports.* Washington, D.C.: U.S. Dept. of Justice.

Gendreau, P., and I. Ross. 1987. Revivification of rehabilitation: Evidence from the 1980s. *Justice Quarterly* 4:349-406.

Greer, J., and I. Stuart. 1983. *The sexual aggressor: Current perspectives and treatment.* New York: Van Nostrand Reinhold.

Groth, A. 1979. *Men who rape.* New York: Plenum.

Hall, G., R. Maiuro, P. Vitaliano, and W. Proctor. 1986. The utility of the MMPI with men who have sexually assaulted children. *Journal of Consulting and Clinical Psychology* 54:493-496.

Hall, G., and W. Proctor. 1987. Criminological predictors of recidivism in a sexual offender population. *Journal of Consulting and Clinical Psychology* 55:111-112.

Hartman, H. 1978. *Basic psychiatry for corrections workers.* Springfield, Ill.: Charles C Thomas.

Kreuz, L., and R. Rose. 1972. Assessment of aggressive behavior and plasma testosterone in a young criminal population. *Psychosomatic Medicine* 34:321-332.

Koss, M., and K. Leonard. 1984. Sexually aggressive men: Empirical findings and theoretical implications. In *Pornography and sexual aggression,* edited by N. Malamuth and E. Donnerstein. New York: Academic Press.

Lundell, R. 1987. *The utility of polygraph testing in the treatment of sex offenders.* Paper presented at the annual conference of the Association for the Behavioral Treatment of Sexual Abusers, Portland, Oregon.

Maletzky, B. 1987. *Data generated by an outpatient sexual abuse clinic.* Paper presented at the annual conference of the Association for the Behavioral Treatment of Sexual Abusers, Portland, Oregon.

Marshall, W., and H. Barbaree. 1988. The long-term evaluation of a behavioral treatment program for child molesters. *Behavior Research & Therapy* 26:499-511.

Marshall, W., and M. Christie. 1981. Pedophilia and aggression. *Criminal Justice and Behavior* 8:145-158.

McCaghy, C. 1967. Child molesters: A study of their careers as deviants. In *Criminal behavior systems: A typology,* edited by M. Clinard and R. Quinney. New York: Holt, Rinehart & Winston.

Morris, N., and G. Hawkins. 1969. *The honest politician's guide to crime control.* Chicago: University of Chicago Press.

Ploscowe, M. 1968. Rape. In *Problems of sex behavior,* edited by E. Sagarin and D. MacNamara. New York: Thomas Y. Crowell.

Quinsey, V. 1986. Men who have sex with children. In *Law and mental health: International perspectives,* vol. 2, edited by D. Weisstub. Oxford: Pergamon.

Quinsey, V., and T. Chaplin. 1982. Penile responses to nonsexual violence. *Criminal Justice and Behavior* 9:372-381.

Robertson, I. 1987. *Sociology.* New York: Worth.

Romero, J., and L. Williams. 1983. A comparative study of group psychotherapy and intensive probation supervision with sex offenders. *Federal Probation* 47:36-42.

Rush, S. 1980. *Best kept secrets.* New York: McGraw-Hill.

Smith, W., and C. Monastersky. 1986. Assessing juvenile sexual offenders' risk for reoffending. *Criminal Justice and Behavior* 13:115-140.

Thio, A. 1978. *Deviant behavior.* Boston: Houghton Mifflin.

Walsh, A. 1983. *Differential sentencing patterns among felony sex offenders and non-sex offenders.* Ann Arbor, Mich.: University Microfilms International.

Walsh, A. 1985. *Homosexual and heterosexual child molestation: The similarities, the differences, and societal reaction.* Paper represented at the annual meeting of the Idaho Sociology and Political Science Association.

Walsh, A. 1988. Lessons and concerns from a case study of a 'scientific molester.' *Corrective and Social Psychiatry and Journal of Behavior Technology, Methods, and Therapy* 34:18-23.

Walsh, A. 1990. Twice labeled: The effects of psychiatric labeling on the sentencing of sex offenders. *Social Problems* 37:375-389.

Chapter 15

The Schizophrenic or Intellectually Deficient Client

Our task now is to begin to understand that the causes of mental health problems are as varied as their manifestations. Some are physical. Some are emotional. Some are rooted in social and environmental conditions. Most are a complex combination of these and other factors, some of which are unknown.

President's Commission on Mental Health

Schizophrenics

Schizophrenia is the most widespread of the psychotic disorders, affecting perhaps as much as 1 percent of the population. It is estimated that 170,000 schizophrenics live at home with their families and 120,000 more have no permanent home (Department of Health and Human Services 1981:21-22). Every criminal justice worker is likely to have two or three clients who have been diagnosed as schizophrenic at any one time. With the increase in concern for patients' rights and the decarceration movement, the criminal justice system is absorbing many of the mentally ill (Hochstedler 1987). Schizophrenics are extremely difficult to supervise in a community corrections setting, and they often violate the conditions of their probation or parole and are consigned to prison—not a humane way of dealing with clients whose ability to function conventionally is seriously impaired.

Schizophrenics are not a homogeneous category of individuals. There are various subtypes that need not concern us here, but there are also differences in the degree of mental deterioration and in how they reached their condition. The most severely impaired schizophrenics are hospitalized; those with whom you will be dealing are able to function outside a mental institution. The most serious form of general schizophrenia is a process schizophrenia, which develops insidiously over a long period of time. These individuals early on show an inability to function normally, to make friends, to handle schoolwork, and to behave acceptably. Reactive schizophrenics may not have early histories of psychological and social dysfunction. Their descent into schizophrenia is usually marked by an acutely stressful experience (APA 1987:187). Bill Bloggs's "early stage of reactive schizophrenia" was no doubt related to the stress of his arrest and incarceration (sometimes termed "jailhouse psychosis"); being incarcerated, especially for the first time, can bring out symptoms of a mental disorder not previously in evidence (Gibbs 1987).

The "four As" are used by mental health professionals to identify schizophrenia (APA 1987): *autism* (living in a subjective fantasy world), *ambivalence* (simultaneous conflicting feelings), inappropriate *affect* (emotions that are not congruent with the situation), and loose *associations* (the connections of an experience or idea with an unrelated experience or idea). Although schizophrenia is most often diagnosed long before a client is seen by a community corrections worker, be on the lookout for evidence of the four As and when you encounter them, make a referral to the local court diagnostic and treatment center.

It is extremely difficult for the nonschizophrenic to comprehend the schizophrenic experience. The brain has an inherent need for structure, to make sense of the information coming into it from the outside in the form of electrochemical impulses. Think of the scariest and most vivid dreams you have ever had: In a dream state our neurons are active making random connections but not with external stimuli as they do when we are awake. The brain does the best it can to generate order from the chemical chaos of sleep by drawing on past experiences stored in its memory banks. But since the impulses are haphazard, darting from one memory to others that may be quite unrelated, the images they generate are not necessarily coherent. Both the dream and schizophrenic states are evoked from similar private realities. The difference—and what a remarkable difference—is that when we can wake up from a dream, we recognize that we were dreaming and begin to respond normally to stimuli from the outside world. Schizophrenics must remain in their incoherent private worlds trying to make sense out of a random neurochemical cascade (Walsh 1991a:120).

Causality

The causes of schizophrenia—and even its objective existence—have long been hotly debated. Radical environmentalists used to dismiss it as a myth or as a diagnostic "grab bag" used against poor people whose behavior was considered inappropriate. We have since learned that this dismissal was as premature as the dismissal of the idea of psychopathy as an identifiable entity. The most compelling evidence comes from radioisotope brain scans using positron emission tomography (PET). PET scans use computer imaging techniques like those of the more familiar CAT scans; injections of radioactive glucose isotopes reveal a biochemical map of neurometabolism as the glucose is converted into energy. CAT scans give information about brain structure, PET scans about brain functioning. This technique distinguishes the neurological maps of normal, schizophrenic, and manic-depressive individuals (Fincher 1981:142-143). These identifiable differences in brain functioning suggest that the condition we call schizophrenia has an objective physical reality.

An earlier clue to the chemical basis for schizophrenia came with the advent of such antipsychotic drugs as Thorazine. Thorazine works by blocking dopamine at the synapses that use it as a neurotransmitter. Schizophrenia may result from one of three conditions: (1) an excess of dopamine, (2) a deficiency of an enzyme called monoamine oxidase, which removes dopamine by oxidation after it has performed its excitatory function, or (3) an excess of dopamine receptors in the brain (Clare 1979). Any one of these would cause the hyperstimulation characteristic of schizophrenics. High doses of amphetamines can also produce symptoms mimicking psychosis by stimulating the secretion of dopamine (Konner 1982:98). If any of your clients shows schizophrenic symptoms, it may be a good idea to check for a history of excessive use of stimulants and hallucinogens.

As a cause of schizophrenia, an excess of dopamine receptors currently looks like the best bet. In comparing twenty deceased schizophrenics and twenty-eight deceased nonschizophrenics, Seeman and Lee (1981) found twice as many dopamine receptors in the limbic systems (the emotional area of the brain) of the schizophrenics as in the nonschizophrenics. This excess capacity would make the limbic circuitry more sensitive to the emotional content of the environment.

Linking the schizophrenic syndrome to brain structure and functioning and to genetic predisposition does not preclude a strong environmental input. The genetic endowment with which we enter the world (genotype) interacts with the environment to produce the organism we recognize as "me" (phenotype). Genes are not expressed in a vacuum; many require a particular environment to effect their predisposition. Regardless of genetic predisposition, schizophrenia occurs in the brain, which is particularly sensitive to input from the environment. One biologically oriented researcher, in stating that we must also search for such environmental factors, further states that "These factors are most likely found in the family and in the sociocultural environment in which the child becomes schizophrenic" (Freier 1986:154). A developmental picture common to schizophrenics is that they tend to come from homes lacking in security and love (Wilson & Kneisl 1983:425). Recall how the Harlows were able to manufacture schizophrenic behavior in their love-deprived monkeys.

It very well may be that early childhood experiences change the physical structures of our pleasure and pain centers to establish new thresholds for activation and shutdown. Liebowitz (1983:46-47) is among those who think that limbic thresholds for pleasure and displeasure are determined by early experiences. If our early experiences were loving, our pleasure centers will be easily activated. In contrast, "People in whom painful childhood experiences are constantly stirred up are experiencing bombardment of their displeasure centers, rendering them more vulnerable and more likely to experience new events as painful as well" (Liebowitz 1983:47). This analysis certainly fits with the withdrawal, isolation depression, and anhedonia (inability to experience pleasure) so characteristic of the schizophrenic. Again it underscores the insidious nature of deprivation of love.

Treatment

The treatment of schizophrenics is primarily medical, with the criminal justice worker acting as community resource broker and medication monitor. Schizophrenics are usually cooperative as long as they take their antipsychotic medication. The difficulty has always been to make sure that they take it. They are prone to "forget" their daily dose; some who may be willing to take it one day may not be the next day for fear they are being poisoned. This problem is compounded by the fact that a client cannot be required to accept medical treatment. Ambivalence about daily pill-taking may be circumvented if you can negotiate an agreement to treatment with the long-acting drug Prolixin (assuming the medical adviser concurs). This drug is injected every two or three weeks and is released gradually over time. A family member will usually be willing to drive the patient to the community health clinic for this treatment every two weeks or so.

Be alert for the old argument about "treating symptoms rather than causes." Drugs no more cure schizophrenia than insulin cures diabetes, but antipsychotic drugs do for schizophrenics what insulin does for diabetics: They stabilize biological functions and thus help the sufferer to cope. They enable schizophrenics to control desires to act out their delusions. They do not, however, help them to regain their zest for life or human warmth. Perhaps you can.

Schizophrenics whose disorder is relatively mild are sometimes able to stabilize their lives through a supportive marriage and the acquisition of work skills. Although you cannot play Cupid, you can try to obtain employment for schizophrenic clients in sheltered workshops, where they can learn work skills, gather self-esteem, and become somewhat independent in a setting that is not as demanding as a regular work setting. Such work shelters also provide instruction on such work-related activities as grooming, timekeeping, work habits, following instructions and orders, and getting along with other employees. Most cities have at least one workshop; the final decision about admissions belongs to their administrators. If you have a client who is a likely candidate for a work shelter, go with the client on a visit so that you can learn about the program and the criteria for admission.

Their perceptions of reality, however distorted, are as real to schizophrenics as your vivid dreams are to you while you are asleep. Schizophrenics find the common reality too painful and threatening, so they have a vested interest in maintaining their own. Do not argue with their reality, but do point out its disadvantages and compare it with your own reality in a gentle and reassuring way. On no account should you validate their reality by pretending to participate in it; nor should you accept their condition as hopeless.

Glasser feels that schizophrenics, like other "deviants," have not been able to fulfill their basic needs to give and receive love and to feel worthwhile. He also feels that they can be brought back to reality by a counselor who works by carefully graded increments to increase their level of responsible behavior. The techniques for treating schizophrenia, he says, are exactly the same as those used with nonpsychotic clients: The counselor must demand responsible behavior from the client regardless of the label: "We have found over and over again that we pay the biggest price whenever we slip on the side of being too undemanding or too accepting of deviant behavior" (Glasser 1975:163).

The Intellectually Immature Client

Intellectual functioning as measured by IQ tests, after a long period of neglect in terms of its relationship with criminal activity, is making a strong comeback (Hirschi and Hindelang 1977; Moffit & Silva 1988). Wilson and Herrnstein are persuasive in their opinion that "criminology acted rashly when, in the 1930s, it virtually ceased considering IQ as a significant correlate of criminal behavior, for it was just at that moment in the evolution of mental testing that the tests were beginning to yield solid data on the cognitive predispositions toward offending" (1985:159). Although many criminologists still believe that IQ tests are biased, ten years of research by geneticists and developmental psychologists led the National Academy of Sciences to insist that they are not (Linn 1982), as did the overwhelming majority of more than 1,000 experts surveyed by Snyderman and Rothman (1988). Given this new interest in IQ, and given that IQ scores are the psychological assessment measurements most readily available (and probably the most useful) to corrections workers, it is necessary to know what these scores have to tell us.

The most widely used IQ tests are the Revised Wechsler Intelligence Scale for Children (WISC-R) and the Wechsler Adult Intelligence Scale (WAIS). These scales (see Chapter 3) have subtests measuring verbal IQ (VIQ) and performance IQ (PIQ). PET scan studies have shown that the neurological processes engaged when subjects are administered the different IQ subscales are lateralized to opposite hemispheres of the brain (Chase et al. 1984; Duara et al. 1984). A problem that engages verbal skills uses a different side of the brain than one that engages performance IQ skills.

VIQ and PIQ subtests are administered in the following alternating order:

Verbal	Performance
1. Information	2. Picture completion
3. Similarities	4. Picture arrangement
5. Arithmetic	6. Block design
7. Vocabulary	8. Object assembly
9. Comprehension	10. Coding (or mazes)

The ten subtests taken together measure general intelligence in that they measure an individual's capacity to think rationally, act purposefully, and to deal effectively with the environment. They attempt to measure such things as long- and short-term memory, concentration, computational skills, verbal abstractions, awareness of and openness to one's culture and its norms, manual dexterity, visual/spatial acuity, and adaptability. However, there is no one-to-one relationship between the two subscales; they measure somewhat different domains of intelligence, with the performance scale providing an assessment for those whose family backgrounds do not promote verbal skills. Both subscales contribute about equally to an individual's full-scale IQ score.

Most sociological studies linking IQ to crime and delinquency have viewed IQ as a unit, correlating full-scale IQ with various measures of crime and delinquency. Such a conceptualization may obscure as much about the IQ/delinquency relationship as it reveals. Full-scale IQ (FIQ) is obtained by summing VIQ and PIQ scores and dividing by two. For example, an individual with a VIQ score of 100 and a PIQ score of 90 has an FIQ of $(100 + 90)/2 = 95$. The reason the use of FIQ might distort the IQ/delinquency relationship is that offenders tend to show a greater deficit in VIQ than in PIQ relative to the general population. Combining the two subscales to obtain FIQ makes the overall IQ mean scores for the general and delinquent populations somewhat more equal than they would otherwise be (Herrnstein 1989:3), so that the influence of cognitive variables on delinquency is underestimated.

Boys with low VIQ may be more prone to violence and aggression because they lack verbal skills that mediate between a stimulus and a response. Joseph (1982) has noted that the motor areas of the cortex mature earlier than the areas involved with thought processes, making for speedy responses to stimuli that are not mediated by thought processes on the part of infants and young children. As children mature there is increasing communication between the verbal and visual-spatial hemispheres of the brain; responses to stimuli are slowed while the left brain processes motor behavior initiated by the right brain. Initially, this is an after-the-fact process, but with increasing language acquisition and socialization, the child eventually is able to foresee a response before reacting. In Joseph's neuropsychological theory of the origin of thought (1982), he sees an ever-increasing engagement of the left hemisphere in the processing, organization, and (when needed) inhibition of emotional transmissions received from the right brain.

The efficiency with which the verbal qualities of the left hemisphere perform their interpretive and inhibitory task varies considerably from person to person, a variability apparently much influenced by early environmental experience. Joseph (1982:11-13) points out that there is stiff competition for synaptic connections within the infant's rapidly branching neurons and that the neurons that are activated most frequently are those that establish themselves firmly. To borrow metaphors from TA, established neuronal patterns function as "memory tapes" playing over and over in the head until they become a "life script" governing our interactions with others.

Children who have strong visual-spatial capabilities relative to their verbal capabilities may retain some of the unmediated rapidity of response to stimuli characteristic of the immature brain. As they grow older they retain their childhood priorities for instant pleasure and self-gratification without developing the "self-talk" necessary to generate discipline, responsibility, and a recognition of the rights of others. When a young child processes information this way we have a "brat" who slaps playmates and steals their toys. When a juvenile or adult uses similar cognitive processes we have a delinquent or a criminal who steals, assaults, robs, and rapes. The cognitive *processes* of the immature child and the delinquent or criminal are often the same, but the *content* of those cognitions becomes much more threatening as the person becomes older, stronger, and more ambitious in the pursuit of self-gratification.

Some researchers have linked low VIQ to levels of interpersonal maturity using the I-level ("I" for "interpersonal maturity") system (Andrew 1980). This system proposes that cognitive and personality integration follows a sequential pattern in normal human development and sets up seven I-levels, from level 1, the most basic, to level 7, the ideal. Criminals generally fall into levels 2 through 5, though level 5 is so rare that only levels 2 through 4 are usually used to assess delinquent and criminal subjects (Austin 1981:187).

Not surprisingly, interpersonal maturity varied positively with VIQ in Andrew's study (1980). Level 2 subjects, in whom the only system of cognitive reference appears to be themselves and their personal needs, had a mean VIQ of 78.7. Level 3 subjects, those who have internalized some social rules but use them to manipulate, had a mean VIQ of 90.4. Level 4 subjects, who tend to be neurotic and acting-out because of conflicts between personal needs and social rules that have been more strongly internalized than other I-level subjects, had a VIQ mean of 98.4. The differences were partly mediated by age, with younger children naturally being more cognitively immature. However, the effect (p .001) remained significant when controlling for age.

The main determinant of I-level appears to be verbal intelligence; Austin (1975) has suggested that the I-level system measures intelligence plus "moral orientation" more than social maturity (as measured by the Jesness Immaturity Scale). Intellectual maturity is probably a necessary, if not sufficient, condition for moral maturity. Moral orientation, of course, means moral reasoning, and moral reasoning means making decisions about what is acceptable behavior and what is not. A deficit in moral orientation also means a mental fixation on egocentric thinking and short-run hedonism, patterns of thought more congruent with brain development in infancy and early childhood than in the mature adult. What this suggests is that individuals with a deficit in left-brain VIQ relative to right-brain PIQ are likely to act out rather than think out. In a sense, then, violent and aggressive behavior is visual/spatial ability unregulated by verbal ability among individuals lacking in internal moral standards of conduct.

It was noted earlier that Andrew (1980) found VIQ to be related to interpersonal maturity using the I-level system. In an earlier study of 122 probationers, Andrew (1974) found that interpersonal maturity was even more closely related to the P > V discrepancy marker described in Chapter 3 than to VIQ. The most mature probationers (I-level 4) had a mean P > V discrepancy of 4.41 points, the I-level 3 probationers had a mean discrepancy of 7.33 points, and I-level 2s had a mean of 17.78. Low verbal intelligence alone cannot account for interpersonal immaturity; a high PIQ relative to VIQ also plays an important part.

It is clear that as criminal justice workers you will often have to deal with intellectually deficient individuals. By intellectual deficiency I do not mean mental retardation (variably defined, but usually related to IQs of 65 or below). Deficiency implies correctability; retardation connotes an impairment (possibly organic) of the ability to learn. Although mentally retarded individuals are overrepresented in the criminal justice system in comparison to their number in the general population (Lampert 1987), they are not likely to be on a probation and parole officer's caseload in relatively large numbers, as are clients with intellectual deficiencies. The latter have the mental capacity to commit crimes but not to forge a responsible lifestyle for themselves.

The link between IQ and criminal behavior has become a hot issue within sociological criminology, which had earlier tended to avoid the issue or even to consider it taboo (Gordon 1980), perhaps because mainstream sociology dislikes explanations having to do with individual differences (Hirschi & Hindelang 1977). It is considered particularly unfortunate to link individual differences to genetic factors. Without getting into the bitter issue of the nature and nurture of intelligence, it can be said that the most recent evidence from behavioral genetics suggests that 50 to 60 percent of the variance in IQ scores is attributable to genetic factors, leaving between 40 and 50 percent attributable to environmental and genetic/environmental interaction factors (Wolman 1985; Snyderman & Rothman 1988; Walsh 1991b). No matter what our natural intellectual endowment, it is stretched or suppressed by a host of environmental factors such as low birth weight, malnutrition, lack of stimulation, and abuse and neglect (Lewin 1975; Bouchard & Segal 1985).

Abuse and neglect appear to have a particularly deleterious effect on IQ. Children who were illegitimate, abused, and neglected had both the lowest average VIQ (83.02) and highest average PIQ (102.24) among four cross-classified groups of juvenile delinquents (Walsh 1990). These finding support the hypothesis developed in Chapter 3 that abuse and neglect affect the autonomic nervous system, leading to elevated PIQ scores relative to VIQ scores. A review of the literature by Salzinger and her colleagues (1991) found across various studies that abuse and neglect has a serious impact on IQ levels.

The Differential Detection Hypothesis

There is a "differential detection" hypothesis that states that lower IQ offenders are overrepresented in the criminal justice system because of their inability to avoid detection:

Case Study

Portrait of a Schizophrenic

Greg was a frail, good-looking man of twenty-four when I first met him. He had two prior convictions for misdemeanor vandalism and was now in my office convicted of felony vandalism. Greg had a nasty habit of throwing chunks of rock through plate glass windows.

He was extremely difficult to interview, for he manifested all the classic symptoms of the schizophrenic. He sat staring at me with flat affect, his hygiene was poor, and he didn't particularly care what I had to say to him. I was able to find out that his life revolved around the TV set, in front of which he spent practically every waking hour. He wasn't fussy about which programs he watched, but he was concerned that whatever channel it happened to be must not be changed. Each of his vandalism charges stemmed from arguments he had had with his mother or some other family member over changing channels. The upshot of those arguments was that his mother would throw him out of the house. When that occurred, Greg would proceed to the closest business establishment with a big glass window, put a brick through it, and sit down among the debris to await the arrival of the police. This tactic yielded him a place to sleep and another TV to stare at.

I took Greg to his home after the PSI interview because he had just been released from the county jail and was penniless. I also wanted to get a feel for his home environment. On meeting his mother, I soon formed an opinion of her as a dominating, egocentric, and manipulative shrew. She flatly informed me that the only reason that her son was welcome in her house was his $200 monthly disability check.

His four brothers were likewise unfriendly and cruel. Since Greg was much smaller than his brothers and a "wacko" to boot, he was a convenient target for their verbal and physical aggression. It seemed to me that rather than involving himself with those who rejected him and offered him no love, Greg had withdrawn into a semi-catatonic world of dials and plastic people. The characters on the screen could not rebuff him as real people could. I came to view his reactions to channel switching as an attempt to protect somehow the existence of those benign characters on the screen.

I learned that Greg was seeing a psychiatrist at a local center who was prescribing Thorazine for him. Unfortunately, family members never made it much of their business to make sure that Greg took his medication as directed. I was able to persuade his mother to request that his psychiatrist place him on Prolixin if medically advisable, arguing that for a small investment of her time (driving Greg to the center for his injection twice a month) she could enjoy a semblance of peace in the house. And, more important for her, she could be assured of the uninterrupted flow of his disability checks. I also suggested that to avoid future problems she might consider buying Greg his own TV set.

Greg's mother did both of these things, and peace reigned for about nine months. Greg reported at my office on time twice a month and was fairly agreeable. Visits to his home revealed to me that things were still the same in terms of the family's treatment of Greg. He was still picked on and rejected, even beaten, by other family members, even though his own behavior had improved rather remarkably.

Then I received a call from the mental health center informing me that Greg had missed his last two appointments with them. He was also a week late reporting to me. I decided to go to his home to find out what was going on. I was informed that two weeks prior to my visit Greg had gotten into a fight with his older brother and had stabbed him. Although the wound was superficial and the police had not been called, Greg panicked and fled from the house. I never heard from Greg again. Had he remained in my city, he would surely have been arrested again and I would have seen him. As far as I know, Greg is still out there somewhere among the hordes of loveless and rejected individuals who aimlessly wander the streets of our big cities. Greg's case is an example of how one's best efforts can sometimes come to less than an ideal ending. We have to accept failures as well as successes and learn from them both.

They are no more likely to commit crimes than are higher IQ individuals but are more likely to be caught. Although Hirschi and Hindelang (1977:583) concluded that the argument is "not supported by the available evidence," the argument persists.

Moffitt and Silva (1988) tested the differential detection hypothesis using a rather elegant research design. They obtained juvenile arrest and IQ data for every male born in New Zealand over a period of one year. They then divided these juveniles into three groups: (1) self-reported delinquents who actually had a juvenile record, (2) self-reported delinquents who were officially undetected, i.e., they were not known to the police, and (3) self-reported nondelinquents. All self-reports were cross-checked with police records for accuracy. It was found that the two delinquent groups (detected and undetected) did not significantly differ from one another on full-scale, verbal, or performance IQ, meaning that undetected delinquents were no "brighter" than their detected peers (detection is largely a matter of luck, community cooperation, and good policework, not the intelligence of offenders). Both delinquent groups, however, had significantly lower full-scale and verbal IQs than the nondelinquent group.

Table 15-1 Comparison of population norms on IQ with scores of a criminal sample

IQ Level	Descriptions and anticipations	Percentage of general population	Percentage of sample of felons
65 and below	Defective: Needs special education, can function in protected work situation	2.2	0.5
66-79	Borderline: Slow learner, can perform routine work under close supervision	6.7	13.3
80-90	Dull normal: Can function independently but needs vocational training	16.1	25.0
91-110	Normal: Can complete high school and some college-level work, has few vocational limitations	50.0	56.6
111-119	Bright: No limitations	16.1	2.4
120-127	Superior: No limitations	6.7	2.1
128 and above	Very superior: No limitations	2.2	0.5

*General population norms adapted from Wechsler, The Measurement of Adult Intelligence (Baltimore: Williams & Wilkins, 1944).

The two delinquent groups did not differ from the nondelinquent group on performance IQ, which once again underscores the superiority of PIQ relative to VIQ among offenders.

Working With the Intellectually Immature Client

Table 15-1 compares convicted adult male felons with the general population within seven IQ levels. The table, which represents the IQ levels of 376 individuals taken from presentence reports, suggests the distribution of IQ levels with which the criminal justice helper can expect to work. The mean IQ of this group is 93.5, higher than the ten-point gap (100 being the American mean IQ) Wilson and Herrnstein say is found consistently between offenders and nonoffenders (1985:159). However, the national mean includes the offender population, which means that if we excluded offenders in the calculation of the national mean it may be close to 103 (Herrnstein 1989:13).

The table is a comfort for those who believe in rehabilitation. Mindful of the limitations of the sample, what conclusions can we draw from it? It is clear that the great majority of crimes were committed by individuals with "normal" intelligence and that high intelligence (IQs over 110) is relatively incompatible with criminal activity (at least with the kind with which you will be most concerned as a corrections worker). Only 5 percent of our sample had IQs over 110, compared with 25 percent of the general population. At the other end of the scale, those with IQs less than the normal range were only slightly overrepresented in the sample, 38.3 percent as opposed to the 25 percent that we would expect if IQ and criminal activity were unrelated variables. With the possible exception of the "defectives," all the criminal clients in the sample had the intellectual capacity to be educable or trainable, and therefore to be taught to act responsibly.

How often does low intelligence appear in conjunction with a psychopathic personality? Some recent studies have found that psychopaths with low intelligence are significantly more violent than psychopaths functioning at higher intellectual levels (Heilbrun 1979; Heilbrun & Heilbrun 1985). An even more violent combination is the low-IQ psychopath with a history of severe love deprivation: comparing thirty-eight juvenile delinquents fitting this profile with 218 other delinquents, Walsh, Beyer, and Petee (1987) found that the former were 4.3 times more likely than the latter to have been convicted of at least one violent crime.

IQ does not represent in any total sense the limits of an individual's true problem-solving capacity. Any person's IQ score reflects a minimal not a maximal level of functioning. Many variables, among them motivation, test anxiety, attention span, cultural deprivation, and even the previous night's activities can reduce a test score. With a caring, involved, optimistic, and demanding helper, most clients can be taught to behave responsibly and motivated to make the best of their capacities. If you do not make this belief an integral part of your operational style, your talents might be better employed in another line of work.

The techniques of reality therapy are perhaps best suited to working with the intellectually deficient client. Its emphasis on specificity, concreteness, and taking one step at a time is tailor-made for clients who lack the talking and reasoning skills required for RET counseling or the analytical skills required to do structural analysis in TA. It is particularly important that you establish a warm supportive relationship with intellectually deficient clients because they operate primarily from an emotional rather than an intellectual frame of reference. But be careful that they do not become overly dependent on you.

There are no glaring difference between counseling intellectually deficient clients and other offenders. You may have to be more patient with them, pay special attention to balancing (not overtaxing) treatment efforts, be especially concrete and specific, and proceed very, very slowly.

Summary

You are likely to have at least one or two clients who have been diagnosed as schizophrenic on your caseload at any one time. The four As—autism, ambivalence, inappropriate affect, and loose associations—are used to identify schizophrenics. Schizophrenia can also be identified today by a PET scan, which reveals the brain's functioning rather than its structure.

At the physiological level, schizophrenia appears to be a function of an excess of chemical neurotransmitters, or perhaps of receptors for those neurotransmitters. Schizophrenics tend also to have been deprived of love in childhood.

Your job in dealing with schizophrenics is to monitor their medication and put them in touch with community agencies, such as sheltered workshops and specialized counseling services.

A high IQ is relatively incompatible with crime. The mentally deficient commit a slightly disproportionate amount of crime in comparison with those with normal IQs. Low intelligence coupled with a psychopathic personality is a combination highly associated with violence. The good news is that almost all the clients studied were educable or trainable. IQ tests measure only minimal, not maximal, functioning.

References and Suggested Readings

Andrew, J. 1974. Delinquency, the Wechsler P > V sign, and the I-level system. *Journal of Clinical Psychology* 30:331-335.

Andrew, J. 1980. Verbal IQ and the I-level classification system for delinquents. *Criminal Justice and Behavior* 7:193-202.

American Psychiatric Association. 1987. *Diagnostic and statistical manual of mental disorders* (3rd ed.-revised). Washington, D.C.: APA.

Applewhite, P. 1981. *Molecular gods: How molecules determine our behavior*. Englewood Cliffs, N.J.: Prentice-Hall.

Austin, R. 1975. Construct validity of I-level classification. *Criminal Justice and Behavior* 2:113-129.

Austin, R. 1981. I-level and the rehabilitation of delinquents. In *Correctional counseling and treatment*, edited by P. Kratcoski. Monterey, Cal.: Duxbury.

Bouchard, T., and N. Segal. 1985. Environment and IQ. In *Handbook of intelligence: Theories, measurements, and applications*, edited by B. Woolman. New York: Wiley.

Chase, T., P. Fedio, N. Foster, R. Brooks, G. Di Chiro, and L. Mansi. 1984. Wechsler Adult Intelligence Scale performance: Cortical localization of fluorodeoxyglucose F 18 positron emission tomography. *Archives of Neurology* 41:244-247.

Clare, A. 1979. *Psychiatry in dissent*. Philadelphia: Institute for the Study of Human Issues.

Duara, R., C. Grady, J. Haxby, D. Ingvar, L. Sokoloff, R. Margolin, R. Manning, N. Cultler, and S. Rapoport. 1984. Human brain glucose utilization and cognitive function in relation to age. *Annals of Neurology* 16:702-713.

Fincher, J. 1981. *The brain*. Washington, D.C.: U.S. News Books.

Freier, M. 1986. The biological bases of criminal behavior. In *Intervention strategies for chronic juvenile offenders*, edited by P. Greenwood. New York: Greenwood.

Gibbs, J. 1987. Symptoms of psychopathology among jail inmates: The effects of exposure to the jail environment. *Criminal Justice and Behavior* 14:288-310.

Glasser, W. 1975. *Reality therapy*. New York: Harper & Row.

Gordon, R. Reseach on IQ, race and delinquency: Taboo or not taboo? In *Taboos in criminology*, edited by E. Sagarin. Beverly Hills, Ca.: Sage.

Heilbrun, A. 1979. Psychopathy and violent crime. *Journal of Consulting and Clinical Psychology* 50:546-557.

Heilbrun, A., and M. Heilbrun. 1985. Psychopathy and dangerousness: A comparison, integration and extension of two psychopathic typologies. *British Journal of Clinical Psychology* 24:181-195.

Herrnstein, R. 1989. *Biology and crime*. National Institute of Justice Crime File, NCJ 97216. Washington, D.C.: U.S. Department of Justice.

Herrnstein, R. 1989. The individual offender. *Today's Delinquent* 8:5-35.

Hirschi, T., and M. Hindelang. 1977. Intelligence and delinquency: A revisionist review. *American Sociological Review* 42:571-587.

Hochstedler, E. 1987. Twice-cursed? The mentally disordered criminal defendant. *Criminal Justice and Behavior* 14:251-267.

Jeffery, C. 1980. Sociobiology and criminology: The long lean years of the unthinkable and the unmentionable. In *Taboos in criminology*, edited by E. Sagarin. Beverly Hills, Cal.: Sage.

Joseph, R. 1982. The neuropsychology of development: Hemispheric laterality, limbic language, and the origin of thought. *Journal of Clinical Psychology* 38:4-33.

Konner, M. 1982. *The tangled wing: Biological constraints on the human spirit*. New York: Holt, Rinehart & Winston.

Lampert, R. 1987. The mentally retarded offender in prison. *The Justice Professional* 2:60-70.

Lewin, R. 1975. Starved brains. *Psychology Today* (September).

Liebowitz, M. 1983. *The chemistry of love*. New York: Berkley Books.

Linn, R. 1982. Individual differences, prediction and differential prediction. In *Ability testing: Uses, consequences, and controversies*, edited by A. Wigdor and W. Garner. Washington, D.C.: National Academy Press.

Moffitt, T., and P. Silva. 1988. IQ and delinquency: A test of the differential detection hypothesis. *Journal of Abnormal Psychology* 97:330-333.

Salzinger, S., R. Feldman, M. Hammer, and M. Rosario. 1991. Risk for physical child abuse and the personal consequences for its victims. *Criminal Justice and Behavior* 18:64-81.

Seeman, P., and T. Lee. 1981. Chemical clues to schizophrenia. *Science News* 112 (November).

Snyderman, M., and S. Rothman. 1988. *The IQ controversy, the media, and public policy*. New Brunswick: Transaction Books.

U.S. Department of Health and Human Services. 1981. *Toward a national plan for the chronically mentally ill*. DHHS publication no. (ADM) 81-1077.

Walsh, A. 1990. Illegitimacy, child abuse and neglect, and cognitive development. *Journal of Genetic Psychology* 151:279-285.

Walsh, A. 1991a. *The science of love: Understanding love and its effects on mind and body*. Buffalo, N.Y.: Prometheus.

Walsh, A. 1991b. *Intellectual imbalance, love deprivation and violent delinquency: A biosocial perspective*. Springfield, Ill.: Charles C Thomas.

Walsh, A., J. Beyer, and T. Petee. 1987. Violent delinquency: An examination of psychopathic typologies. *Journal of Genetic Psychology* 148:385-392.

Wechsler, D. 1944. *The measurement of adult intelligence*. Baltimore: Williams and Wilkins.

Wilson, H., and C. Kneisl. 1983. *Psychiatric nursing*. Menlo Park, Cal.: Addison-Wesley.

Wolman, B. 1985. Intelligence and mental health. In *Handbook of intelligence: Theories, measurement, and applications*, edited by B. Wolman. New York: Wiley.

Chapter 16
The Juvenile Client

The logic of concentrating on treating the youngest of offenders is inescapable. There is almost universal agreement by crime experts of every persuasion that the roots of criminal behavior are often embedded in very early life. If past experience piles up around the offender in cumulative fashion, early roots . . . can soon grow too large to unearth.

Hans Toch

Legal Background

The juvenile probation system is different from the adult system. Juveniles are never called criminals even when they commit criminal acts. Juvenile acts that are forbidden by law are called delinquent acts. The term *delinquent* is from a Latin root that means "to leave undone." The connotation is that the juvenile delinquent has *not* done something that should have been done (behave lawfully) rather than done something forbidden. The difference is subtle, reflecting the rehabilitative rather than punitive thrust of American juvenile justice.

Juveniles enjoy, or depending on the perspective suffer, a special status in society and in its justice system. They are expected not to do a number of things adults have a right to do, such as smoke, drink, drive automobiles, leave home, and ignore the wishes of their parents. They are also expected to do a number of things that adults may ignore, such as attend school, obey curfews, and obey their parents. When juveniles violate one of these rules, they can be charged with a status offense—an act of commission or omission chargeable only to juveniles. Status offenses are the most common offenses in the juvenile system.

The special status of juveniles in the juvenile justice system rests on the concept of *parens patriae*, which literally means "father of his country" and in practice means that the state may take over the supervision of a child, substituting for the parents. Underlying this concept is the philosophy that if the child misbehaves, the parents are to blame, so the state may assume responsibility for the child, diagnose the problem, and take remedial action by (1) providing juvenile probation services with the child remaining in the parental home or (2) removing the child from the parental home to a state facility (detention center or group home).

All actions of the juvenile courts and their officers, in theory, are to be "in the best interests of the child." The juvenile courts do not hold trials, they have "hearings" or "adjudication hearings." The youth does not plead guilty or not guilty but "admits" or "denies" the charge. Instead of finding a youth guilty the court makes "a finding of fact" that he or she is or is not delinquent; delinquency is a condition requiring the intervention and care of the state. Instead of a presentence investigation report there is a "predisposition" or "social inquiry" report. Instead of sentencing the youth, the court "disposes" of the matter, seeking rehabilitation rather than punishment. But do not be misled by all these euphemisms into the belief that juveniles are not held responsible for their conduct.

Causality

Juvenile delinquency in the United States has been called a "growth industry" (Romig, Cleland & Romig 1989) and a "slow riot" (Curtis 1985). In 1989 1,744,818 juveniles were arrested for index offenses in this country—15.5 percent of total index arrests (FBI 1990). But delinquency is not unique to the United States; it is everywhere and at all times bemoaned—in his *Republic,* written 500 years before Christ, Plato soundly condemned the behavior of the youth of his time. But this does not diminish the urgency of the problem in the contemporary United States. It is unlikely that the youth in ancient Greece or anywhere else ran around drugged, wielding automatic weapons, and killing, raping, and robbing for fun, as happens all too often in American cities.

Of the factors alleged to cause antisocial behavior (see Chapters 3 and 4), some have special relevance to juvenile delinquency. Most of the juveniles in Curtis's "slow riot" (1985) do not become adult criminals (Boucher 1985), a fact that points toward unique aspects of youth that may increase the probability of antisocial behavior during this period but not necessarily later.

Psychological Factors

Among factors not previously discussed as possible causes of antisocial behavior are the psychosocial problems associated with adolescence, that sometimes confusing period between childhood and adulthood. In the United States, where individuals are kept in the dependent role of childhood longer than in most other nations, it is a particularly trying period. As Edwards and Nuckols (1991:25) dramatize it: "Statistically speaking, the United States is the most dangerous country on the planet for adolescents." In a television interview just after the Gulf War, Louis Sullivan, secretary of the Department of Health and Human Services, commented that more young people are killed on our urban streets every 100 hours than were killed in the 100 hours of the land phase of that war.

The strange, sometimes frightening, stage of life called adolescence begins at puberty, a period of profound biological change that generally occurs between the ages of eleven and eighteen for boys, nine and sixteen for girls. During puberty the body begins to produce sex hormones in larger quantities, leading to the greater visible differentiation of males and females.

Psychologically, adolescence has been considered everything from a normal developmental stage accompanied by—for about half of all teenagers—a few mild disturbances (Offer 1975) to a stage that is highly disturbing emotionally for almost all teenagers (Thornburg 1971). From a review of the literature, Udry (1990:2) lists the following typical changes for high-school-age adolescents: "They complete puberty, lower academic achievement values, increase values of independence, increase tolerance for violation of adult standards, decrease religiosity, decline in church attendance, increase reported alcohol and drug use, and increase sexual activity." Except for the completion of puberty, these changes are not likely to be welcomed by parents and other authority figures; they certainly represent a gap between biological and social maturity that must be bridged.

Psychologist Erik Erikson's *Eight Ages of Man* (1963) presents a model of human psychosocial development in which he identifies eight stages in the human life cycle in which individuals are confronted with new challenges and interactions within themselves and with their environment. In each stage crises can lead to opposite (positive or negative) personality outcomes depending on how the crises are resolved. In adolescence the two polar outcomes are *identity* versus *role confusion*. (In reality, of course, these outcomes are never either/or dichotomies. Most teenagers emerge from this stage situated somewhere on a continuum.)

During this stage young people start asking philosophical questions about themselves: "Who am I?" "What is my place?" "Where am I going?" "What does this or that person think of me?" They also start to form theories and ask questions about aspects of their environment that they formerly took for granted. Their surging hormones, abundant energies, and new questioning orientation make them impatient, action-oriented, and imbued with a sense of omnipotence. If, thanks to loving parents, they have been successful in navigating previous developmental states (*trust* versus *mistrust*, *autonomy* versus *doubt*, *initiative* versus *guilt*, and *industry* versus *inferiority*), they will emerge with a positive identity ("I'm okay, you're okay") and very little role confusion.

If mistrust, doubt, guilt, and inferiority were the outcomes of previous crises, role confusion is the likely outcome of adolescence. To seek out an identity teenagers will turn away from neglectful parents toward others in the same sorry boat as themselves. This is not a good strategy. The identity to be achieved in such groups is likely to be negative—"delinquent," "doper," "punk"—but a negative identity is better than no identity at all as long as it is accepted by the groups to which we belong.

Even youths from well-adjusted homes often conform more to their peers' expectations than to their parents' during adolescence. This is a normal part of growing up and finding one's own way in life. The trick is to find the right peers. Well-loved young people who are generally prosocial will seek the company of others like themselves. "Rejected and neglected children who do not find love and affection, as well as support and supervision, at home, often resort to groups outside the family; frequently these groups are of a deviant nature" (Trajanowicz & Morash 1983:90). About two-thirds of the children who run away from home do so in response to parental abuse (Hyde & Hyde 1985:2). To hold themselves together, rejected children, being unsure of themselves, often overidentify with the heroes of cliques and crowds or with the heroes the media provide for them.

Environmental Factors

As the authority of the family and religious and educational institutions diminishes in the United States, behavior, attitudes, and values come more and more under the influence of other forces. A good case could be made for the proposition that we have abrogated much of the responsibility for socializing our young to peer groups and to television, both of which represent immature, often antisocial, visions of reality. Groups have a morality of their own that is often radically different from the sum of their individual parts. Already unsure of identity and direction, juveniles in peer groups easily defer to the collective judgement. With standards submerged in the group, and with responsibility diffused among them, the manifestations of antisocial "group think," such as the brutal "wilding" of the Central Park jogger in 1989, can be horrifying.

Television, the other half of the socialization equation, provides our youth with standards of behavior. More than anything else, television models and sells greed, hedonism, impatience, and impulsiveness ("Buy this or that and you'll feel great and the boys/girls will love you. Do it now!"). Youngsters grow up seeing all kinds of complex problems solved in one hour (often by violent means) with six commercial breaks designed to sell us TV-land's version of the good life. Is it any wonder that kids become narcissistic, lower their thresholds for violence, become desensitized to the suffering of others, and have difficulty delaying gratification? If kids are watching television an average of 6.8 hours a day (Roberts & Bachen 1981), their highly impressionable minds must to be influenced by it.

Many movies and television shows seem to be produced by some malignant juvenocracy specifically to challenge traditional notions of decency and good character. Teachers are portrayed as helpless, bumbling idiots who are easily manipulated, intimidated, and outsmarted by crude (but "awesome") teenagers. Youths who study and behave respectably are characterized as "nerds" or "geeks" and are ostracized. Parents are "squares" and hypocrites (this, unfortunately, is all too often true) who indulge their own sexual and chemical appetites while condemning those of their children. The family warmth of Ozzie and Harriet, although smarmy and unrealistic, has been replaced as a family role model by the equally unrealistic but totally dysfunctional Bundy and Simpson families. In rap and heavy metal music, women are viewed as little more than sexual playthings whose favors, if not granted, may simply be taken. Obnoxious self-indulgence of all kinds is promoted, while sensitivity, responsibility, altruism, and other indications of decency and character are laughed at.

This is sometimes reinforced by those calling themselves moral relativists or situational ethicists, for whom there are no moral or ethical absolutes by which to govern social behavior. According to them, no one's system of values is inherently superior to anyone else's. The moral vacuum we have created has helped to produce approximately one million illegitimate children each year in the United States (Hanson, Myers & Ginsburg 1987), born to teens barely past menarche. The lack of proper mothering and social support (Crnic et al. 1984), increased risk of abuse and neglect (Walsh 1990), and diminished intellectual capabilities associated with such births (Sroufe 1979) eventually produce the thousands of gang members who infest our inner cities and bankrupt our hospitals' trauma centers.

Added to the effects of the breakdown of traditional morality must be the effects of poverty. Children from poor families who are supported by proper nurturing and a system of prosocial values do turn out well; poverty alone has never been an adequate explanation of antisocial behavior. But poverty today has taken on an insidious new form. Fagan (1990) predicts that high rates of juvenile violence are destined to persist, given the hardening of poverty in the 1980s. Black juveniles are particularly hurt by the hardening of poverty. Some social theorists consider that programs like affirmative action produce a black society bifurcated by class as the cream of the black culture is skimmed, leaving the rest locked into a permanent jobless underclass (Whitman et al. 1987; Norton 1987). A legacy of slavery and white racism (Norton 1987) combined with an excessive reliance on the legal and welfare systems to ameliorate disabilities (Loury 1987) has helped to create America's underclass.

Effective Supervision of the Juvenile Client

From a wide variety of sources, it appears that a child has at least nine needs for full psychosocial development. Love, though essential, is not enough. Although the primary responsibility for filling these needs rests with the parents, when a youth is placed in the care of the state it becomes partly the responsibility of the juvenile probation officer (JPO), the detention officer, or the group home counselor. The requirements present a minimal working model to help juvenile correctional workers understand their clients and meet their needs.

1. *Children need discipline*. The foundation for raising children to healthy and responsible adulthood is discipline. An undisciplined child is either smothered with unconditional love, making the child (with apologies to Carl Rogers) a spoiled brat who takes no responsibility for himself or herself, or is unloved, unruly, and probably will grow up to be an unconscionable adult. Discipline might be considered "applied love" (or "tough love," if you prefer).

Although there are components of punishment in discipline, the two are not synonymous. Often juvenile delinquents have suffered far more than their share of punishment, yet have received precious little discipline. Forcing children to follow rules by inflicting pain—hitting, punching, yelling, screaming, restraining, or other humiliation—is punishment. The family histories of delinquents reveal many arbitrary rules inconsistently applied. If mom or dad feels good on Friday (payday), the violation of rule X is perhaps overlooked. If they feel bad on Monday, the same violation is punished severely. No wonder the child, confused, comes to relate punishment more to parental mood than to rule violation. The child soon learns that getting caught rather than breaking rules is the thing to be avoided.

On the other hand, discipline "always starts with trying to teach children to follow reasonable rules through negotiation .... Discipline involves the sanctions of the loss of either freedom or privileges until the child is willing to negotiate" (Glasser 1984:197). Children must know the rules—what is expected of them. This does not mean that the household should be democratic in that the child's wishes are given equal status to those of the parents—children lack the maturity to be given such privileges. The concern should be the best interests of the child. There are few children who would not benefit from increased expectations for doing chores, being more courteous, and participating more in family and group functions. Living up to reasonable expectations gives children a sense of participation in common goals, a sense of accomplishment, a sense of being needed for one's contributions, and the beginnings of a success identity.

The child who violates expectations must be allowed to suffer the natural consequences. Although these sanctions should not be severe or designed to humiliate, they should be applied swiftly and with absolute certainty. Sanctions are punitive in the sense that the child does not welcome them, but when both the rules and the consequences of violating them have been agreed to before the violation occurs, the child retains a feeling of control that is absent where permissiveness alternates arbitrarily with punishment. Delinquents who lack this sense of control, Glasser asserts, should be "treated with strict but creative probation where they would learn to regain control of their lives" (1984:198).

2. *Children must learn to understand and accept their own selves.* The development of a realistic and positive self-concept is the goal of all interpersonal counseling. The JPO, in cooperation with the youth's family, teachers, and other interested parties, must help the juvenile client to accomplish this, making sure that concerned individuals are not working at cross purposes. Consistent discipline related to reasonable rules gives children structure, predictability, and the ability to think about an outcome in the abstract and then to select a behavior that will achieve it. This is called *self*-discipline. The sooner this scaffold of structure and predictability is in place, the sooner the youth can build a self-concept around it.

3. *Children must become aware of and understand their emotions and feelings.* This is the basis for a realistic sense of self and of self-control—the ability to select from a number of possibilities the appropriate response to a feeling. When children are aware of their feelings and understand them for what they are, they can respond to them more appropriately. A frustrated adolescent may yell, "I hate you," or "I could kill you"—immature labels for feelings that are not well-understood. It is to be hoped that what is meant is "I don't like what you've done," rather than "I hate you," and "I would very much like you to stop," rather than "I could kill you." Whenever a youth labels feelings inappropriately, these feelings should be explored in a patient, caring, and nonauthoritarian fashion. Even more than an adult client, the juvenile who perceives an attitude of "I know best" will shut down. You do "know best," but the youth must come to recognize that. The better youths relate to you, the sooner this will happen.

4. *Children must learn to understand the feelings and emotions of others.* Several studies have implicated a lack of empathy in delinquent behavior (Deardorff et al. 1975; Ellis 1982; Farrington 1989). Inappropriately socialized children live in egocentric worlds; they blame other people or circumstances for their antisocial behavior. A child who constantly feels angry, hostile, mean, and uncaring will assume that it is natural to feel that way and think everyone else feels that way too. In learning that this is not so, the child perceives alternatives and pays attention to positive role models who can exchange their caring, compassion, and understanding for the child's anger and hostility.

All children know when they have been hurt, and they do not like it. They must learn that other people have similar feelings that must be respected. Sometimes a lack of maturity prevents youths from realizing that a parent may be deeply hurt by their troublesome behavior. This is more often the ignorance of immaturity than the "I don't care" of malice. Empathy training in group sessions may stimulate this realization. Getting a youth enrolled in team sports, a church group, or an organization like 4-H or a Big Brother/Big Sister program goes a long way to show them that many people do care.

All communities contain their share of youngsters who are truly disadvantaged, physically and mentally. Delinquents supervised by a probation officer might well be assigned to help handicapped youngsters, perhaps wheeling chairbound youngsters around the local shopping mall or helping them to read. Handicapped youngsters would obviously benefit, and their delinquent helpers would achieve a measure of empathy with the truly disadvantaged and a feeling of accomplishment, community involvement, and enhanced self-esteem. As most of us know, it's often more rewarding to give than to receive, and research has shown that empathy training is useful in reducing aggressive behavior (Romig, Cleland & Romig 1989:131).

5. *Children must establish positive interpersonal relationships.* Juveniles and parents alike often blame "bad companions" for their troubles. The obvious answer is to forbid juvenile delinquents from associating with other juvenile delinquents—easier said than done. As with adolescent romantic relationships, to forbid is to drive the parties further into each other's arms (the "Romeo and Juliet" effect). We have to teach youths positive prosocial alternatives, discovering their prosocial interests and making them as exciting as making trouble. They have to learn to relate to more mature peers, to cooperate through teamwork, and to settle conflicts peacefully.

Sport is an excellent vehicle for teaching a youth teamwork, competence, and self-esteem through positive and constructive endeavors. Wakefield (1991) describes a low-cost athletic program for delinquents that had significant benefits for the participants. It was a running program staffed by volunteer coaches with running gear donated by local athletic stores. (It is surprising how generous businesses can be when asked for a good cause.) It resulted in increased pride in the runners—in both achievement and body image—as they covered increasing distances, felt greater group cohesion, and did less acting-out. Successfully completing a distance run brought the all-important approval of both peers and authority figures for socially acceptable behavior. Treating troubled youths means more than just sitting in an office trying to reason with them.

6. *Children must understand how to make choices and solve problems.* Everyone is constantly making choices and decisions; delinquents just make too many bad ones. To make positive choices one must know the remote as well as the immediate consequences of making one choice rather than another and have a sense of control that allows us to make relatively independent choices. When unloved and undisciplined youths turn to peer groups for affiliation and attention, the members, having had similar experiences, will all lack the ability to make positive decisions. Decisions within such a peer group will be made under antisocial pressure, on the basis of gut emotions unalloyed by any thought of remote consequences. The task of probation officers, like parents, is to achieve a sound balance between support for the youth's decision and insistence that it be a responsible one.

7. *Children need positive values and ideals with which to guide their lives.* Values are the core of society, the cement that holds it together, without which social life would be meaningless. Values have to be taught; children need to know what goals are worth striving for, what ideas are worthy of being preserved, what is important in life, and how to lead a good life. Some people view values like the Golden Rule, honor, and personal integrity as hopelessly old-fashioned and restrictive of personal liberty. On the contrary, values set us free by anchoring our lives in a meaningful sense of community. A child who never learns the value of values trudges through life caring for little else other than the immediate gratification of his or her selfish impulses.

Juvenile correctional workers must be role models for their clients, emphasizing in word and deed that positive prosocial values are indispensable. A little contemporary vernacular is fine, but stay away from delinquent slang that expresses antisocial values such as "nerd," "fink," "stoolie," "pigs," and "bad mutha." The use of such language by the correctional worker gilds it with an aura of legitimacy. This might be "identifying" with your clients, but the point of the whole process is to get them to identify with you and the prosocial values you represent.

8. *Children must learn to appreciate the value of education and work.* We all know the tremendous value of education and work, but preaching will never get the message over to delinquents. They have heard it all before and rejected it. Although many delinquents have attention deficit disorders and other learning disabilities, there is no reason why any healthy youth cannot master the typical American high school curriculum. But students need to know and understand *why* education is important and what it can do for them. Many a barely literate student athlete, much more interested in passing balls than tests, has been seen to knuckle down to study under "no pass, no play" rules. Youths who drop out of school in West Virginia cannot obtain a driver's license. Given the importance of driving to teenagers, no prizes are offered for guessing what has happened to West Virginia's dropout rate—it has declined substantially. That may be coercion (discipline), but everyone is coerced to some extent. People usually go to college not so much from an insatiable desire to acquire knowledge for its own sake but because they've made a contract with themselves to forego immediate gratification for the greater material rewards that education brings.

It's customary to think of police officers as "bustin' 'em" and probation officers as "trustin' 'em." But police officers and probation officers can work together along with school authorities to help troubled youths. For the past twenty-one years plainclothes police officers have been assigned to elementary and high schools in Boise as resource officers (Scheffer 1987). Because of the authority inherent in the police role, these officers can be more effective than school authorities in dealing with hostile and uncooperative youths and parents because they cannot be intimidated in the same way (Scheffer 1987:38-39). SROs are effective not only in detecting and deterring school crime, but also in counseling troubled youths:

> The interviews with students revealed a positive humanistic view of police and their role in society, a high degree of trust in the resource officer, and a clear indication that many students have altered their attitudes concerning wrongdoing as well as how they think about the functions and motives of the police (Scheffer 1987:85).

This is a heartening attitude from teenagers, many of whom have had little contact with caring police officers; they usually approach the police with fear, contempt, and disrespect. Turning kid's heads around about the most visible symbols of authority goes a long way toward turning their heads around about all authority. If your city has such a program, use this valuable resource to its fullest.

9. *Children need a sense of responsibility for their own actions and lives.* Responsibility means disciplined action—having chores to do around the house, doing schoolwork, occupying your time with meaningful activities, giving to others. It means having a positive self-concept around which you can organize your life to pursue meaningful, socially useful goals. It also means having the maturity to know when you are wrong and accepting the consequences without rancor. Even some law-abiding adults have problems with this, so be patient with your delinquent clients.

Community service and restitution go a long way toward developing a sense of responsibility in juvenile offenders. Repaying the community through work with a nonprofit organization can give the youth a sense of usefulness as a contributing member of the community. It also places the youth in the company of prosocial others who can give valuable lessons.

Thorvaldson (1980:22) views restitution as reparation ("repairing" damage done) performed for the sake of justice to the victim and to teach offenders moral values. In other words, the youth learns that you cannot get something for nothing. Sometimes restitution presents a problem for a youth too young for legal employment; in that case the court may order the parents or guardians to pay because they are financially and legally responsible for their children. Relatively mature offenders recognize restitution as right and see its reparative and rehabilitative intent; low-maturity offenders see it as punitive (Van Voorhis 1985). Your task is to convince all your clients who are ordered to pay restitution that it is the moral and responsible thing to do.

Adapting the Treatment to the Youth

Nothing works uniformly for everyone, particularly for juveniles in various stages of maturity and from various backgrounds. Subcultural delinquents who view the gang as an extension of the family are different from neurotic delinquents from fairly functional families, and both are different from sociopathic delinquents. There are many ways that delinquents could be classified for treatment purposes, far too many for exhaustive coverage here. Unless your department asks psychologists to test its youth and you are well-versed in translating the information from these tests into treatment action, you may be in danger of treating all your clients alike.

It is useful to know something about your clients' treatment potential. For instance, extroverts (people whose attention and interests are directed predominantly toward what is outside the self) condition less well than introverts (people who are predominantly inward-looking and introspective); praise motivates introverts and blame motivates extroverts (Nettler 1978:321); and extroverts do less well in school and are more likely to be delinquent than introverts (Wilson & Herrnstein 1985:62). Extroversion is also associated with sensation-seeking and hyporeactivity of the autonomic nervous system (Zuckerman, Eysenck & Eysenck 1978). Even in terms of this one dimension, extroversion/introversion, you would expect to follow different treatment strategies.

How do you know the level of maturity of your clients and whether they are introverts or extroverts? Edward Peoples describes the dynamics of I-level interviewing (1975), and there are other books and articles to help you sensitize yourself to this system. There are also scales that tap the concepts of sensation-seeking and introversion/extroversion. But otherwise you may be on your own. After two or three sessions with your clients you should have a good idea about their maturity levels and how they are situated along the introversion/extroversion continuum. Usually you will also have information that may serve as an adequate proxy for these intellectual and personality attributes: The Wechsler performance-verbal IQ profiles correlate highly with the I-level classification system (see Chapter 15), so much so that Andrew (1974) claims that these profiles may be more valuable than the I-level system itself in classifying juveniles into maturity levels and instituting treatment modalities. Moreover, a significant discrepancy in the direction of P > V is related to hyporeactive autonomic nervous system functioning (see Chapter 3), which in turn is associated with sensation-seeking and extroversion (Eysenck & Gudjonsson 1989:122-123).

Although the V > P intellectual profile (high maturity level/introvert) is rare among delinquent and criminal populations, a youth with such a profile who becomes seriously delinquent may be more psychologically disturbed than subcultural delinquents (Garth, Tennent & Pidduck 1971). V > P youths who do become delinquent are more seriously so than intellectually balanced (P = V) youths, but less so than P > V youths (Walsh, Petee & Beyer 1987). The implication is that while subcultural delinquents may be "normal" youths reacting to criminogenic environments, the delinquency of V > P youths may originate in psychological disturbance rather than in outside factors. It would be wise to have significantly V > P youths psychologically tested by a competent psychologist.

Of course, the Wechsler test is not a classification panacea. It should be interpreted with caution, and the help of a psychologist should be sought only if the subscale scores are significantly discrepant (twelve or more points). Even then, cognitive imbalance must be interpreted within an environmental context. In higher socioeconomic (SES) environments where resistance to crime is high, individual differences in physiology and neurology are likely to have greater impact on antisocial behavior than environmental factors. In lower SES environments where resistance to crime is low, the environment is likely to have more impact than individual differences (Nachshon & Denno 1987). Among juveniles from advantaged SES environments studied, all of the variance accounted for in violent delinquency was attributable to the P > V profile, with no variance being uniquely explained by environmental variables. Although juveniles from disadvantaged SES environments had a higher P > V mean score than advantaged juveniles, all of the explained variance in violent delinquency for them was attributable to the disabilities suffered in their environments (Walsh 1991). With so many factors to be considered, no wonder prediction and classification is such a tricky business.

Family Counseling

In juvenile probation work, unlike adult correctional work, there is the added difficulty of dealing with the youth's parents, who may confront you with as much resistance and hostility as the youth. If the youth comes from a negative family situation in which there is parental criminality and substance abuse, you will receive little voluntary cooperation. Parents who care little or not at all for the youth are not likely to understand why you should care and may consider you a sucker. Your home visits and telephone calls may be just another hassle they have to endure from "the Man." They may also be concerned that you might uncover negative aspects of the family's lifestyle (such as drug dealing or physical and sexual abuse) that may further incur the wrath of the authorities.

Even if the youth comes from a relatively healthy family, there may be parental hostility and resistance. Parents may feel threatened by your probing of the family dynamics. They may feel it an unwarranted intrusion into their private lives and perhaps an effort to pin the blame for their child's predicament on them. They may also seek to protect the youth from you, believing that he or she is a blameless victim of circumstances or the bad influence of friends. This is particularly devastating because the youth may come to view the relationship as "us against them" (he or she and the parents against you and probation services in general), defeating your efforts to help. Any feeling the youth has that he or she is being picked on is reinforced if "Mom and dad think so," too. Such parents are only enabling their children's delinquent behavior.

Nevertheless, the JPO needs and should insist on parental support. Parents must be made to understand that their responsibility is not diminished when their children are placed on probation; on the contrary, parental supervision is even more critical then. It is the parents, not the probation officer, who must handle day-to-day discipline in the home. Parents have to realize that their cooperation is of the utmost importance, and they should be supplied with guidelines for the direction this cooperation should take. The list should include such things as attending appointments with the JPO when requested, arranging transportation for their child's appointments, reporting violations of probation rules, enforcing consistent discipline, and working with their child on the conditions of probation, including family counseling.

The involvement of the family in the rehabilitative effort has been considered a must (Cobean & Power 1978). The youth is embedded in a family; if the family system is dysfunctional it is of little use concentrating on the youth, who is only a minor part of the whole. If the juvenile court is to function "in the best interests of the child," it must have jurisdiction over the family. The juvenile court has the authority to order parents, under pain of contempt of court, to receive counseling. This could take the form of simple parental effectiveness training (PET), in which parents are schooled in the art of parenting, or it could be designed to explore the family dynamics that are contributing to the youth's misbehavior.

Because the family is an interlocking system of complicated relationships, effective family counseling is more difficult than individual counseling. The maximum number of paired relationships in any family is equal to N (N - 1)/2, where N is the number of people in the family. If the Evans family consists of mother, father, and five children, the total number of possible paired relationships in that family is (7)(6)/2 = 21. And that's just the beginning. There are many other combinations of groups greater than two. These relationships may include everything from genuine love to genuine hatred, all within a single household. That is why family counseling should only be attempted by those who are specially trained.

Some well-funded jurisdictions have family crisis units directly responsible to the juvenile court (Janeksela 1981), but if your department lacks that luxury, you must be aware of counselors to whom you can refer the family. Even short-term family counseling—focusing on clarity of family communication, limit setting, contract negotiation, conflict resolution, and the presentation of alternative problem-solving strategies—has been shown to decrease delinquent behavior (Alexander & Parsons 1973). Similar programs also have positive effects on the prevention of younger sibling delinquency (Klein, Alexander & Parsons 1977). In other words, an improvement in family dynamics spills over to prevent delinquency in younger children who until the counseling took place were at risk of becoming delinquent.

Family intervention counseling is a valuable part of delinquency prevention and treatment. It is more realistic than individual counseling in a juvenile setting because it recognizes the context in which youths are immersed, and it enlists the treatment aid of more mature adults who are in full legal control of the youth. It often forces parents and children to engage in a dialogue they both want but do not know how to initiate themselves. Says the chief counselor of a family crisis center in Akron, Ohio:

> Our experience has shown that both the parents and the children who are referred to the center are pleading for help, and although they at first appear reluctant to become involved in family counseling and resist it, they eventually come around. The children, especially the girls, are trying to find a way to get along with their parents. Communication has broken down, the girl may want to tell her parents how she feels but cannot do so because opportunities are not available or she is afraid they won't understand. Often the acting-out behavior of these girls is a way of finally gaining their parents' attention. A setting which forces the parents and child to communicate is a welcome relief. (Quoted in Kratcoski & Kratcoski 1979:359).

Assessing the Youth's Needs

The first thing to do for a new juvenile client is to find out as much as you can about the youth. Table 16.1 is a suggested interview guide developed around the nine components for healthy psychosocial development to help you learn about the youth and his or her family and peers. Once you know something about the youth's needs, you will need a commitment from the family as well as the youth to cooperate with you in the rehabilitative effort. You then have to match the youth's needs with the resources in your community, making sure that you do not undertax or overtax the coping resources of the youth or the family.

A corrections professional in juvenile services has perhaps the most demanding and important job in the criminal justice field. As Hans Toch has said, the juvenile officer gets the individual at a crucial juncture, before criminal roots are too deeply embedded. If through your caring efforts you can wrench these roots from their criminogenic soil you have performed a great service both to the youth and to your community. Edwards and Nuckols offer a statement that all juvenile officers should engrave in their minds: "Working with high-risk children and adolescents is a long, long walk with many disappointments. It is important to know that no matter how horrible the environment, the fact remains that children respond to love, although it's a cliche, one person can make a difference in the life of a child" (1991:40).

Table 16-1 An assessment guide for juvenile delinquents and their needs

Personality and Maturity

Attitudes and Attributes

- What is your perception of the youth's self-worth?
- Does the youth often feel depressed, angry, or rejected?
- Does the youth lie and/or manipulate facts and situations?
- Does the youth accept the validity of society's value system?
- Does the youth express empathy toward others?
- What are the youth's full-scale, verbal, and performance IQ scores, and is there a discrepancy of 12 or more points between verbal and performance scores?
- Does the youth have any positive goals in life?

Behavior

- Do the youth's behavior patterns indicate age-appropriate maturity and sense of responsibility?
- Do the youth's behavior patterns indicate extroversion/introversion?
- Does the youth show the ability to defer gratification and control impulses?
- Does the youth show appropriate remorse for delinquent acts?
- Does the youth abuse alcohol/drugs and why (peer pressure, reduce inhibitions, kill emotional pain)?
- What is the youth's offense pattern (violent, sexual, stealing, related to substance abuse, status offenses), and does it evidence a pattern of increasing seriousness?
- Does the youth have any hobbies or engage in sports?
- Is the youth sexually active?

School Behavior and Attitudes

- How does the youth perform in school? Does the youth live up to potential as indicated by IQ scores and teachers' perceptions?
- Does the youth put adequate effort into studies?
- Does the youth have a learning disability that contributes to low self-esteem and school difficulties?
- What is the youth's attitude toward school and teachers?
- Does the youth have frequent absences (excused or unexcused)?
- Does the youth sufficiently appreciate the value of education?

Family Dynamics

- Does the youth feel attached to parents and siblings or feel rejected?
- What is the attitude of parents toward the youth?
- Is there evidence of abuse and neglect in the family?
- Do parents know the difference between punishment and discipline, and which do they use?
- Does the youth speak and behave differently when in the company of parents?
- What family stresses (financial, occupational, legal, emotional, and so forth) exist, and how are they being dealt with?
- Do parents and siblings model illegal and irresponsible behavior? Do parents encourage, support, and reinforce desired behavior?
- Do parents monitor school performance and take an active part in the youth's school interests?
- Do adequate communications skills exist in the family?
- Do parents expect too little or too much from the youth?

Peer Groups

- Does the youth associate with delinquent peers?
- Does the youth have any nondelinquent friends?
- Do the youth's peers model illegal behavior?
- How dependent on the peer group is the youth for support, attachment, acceptance, and direction?
- Has there been a recent drastic change in the youth's dress and appearance (tattoos, "uniforms," colors, hairstyle) suggesting a deepening integration into a gang subculture?
- What are the peer group's typical nondelinquent activities, and are they constructive or destructive?
- What was the peer influence (if any) on the current offense?

Summary

Working with juveniles presents special problems and opportunities. The official ideology of the juvenile court is frankly rehabilitative. It avoids many of the stigmatizing terms ("criminal," "defendant," "trial," "guilty," and so forth) used in the adult system.

With the realization that most delinquents do not become adult felons, certain psychological and environmental factors have been identified as possible causal factors in delinquency. Adolescence is a trying time for many youngsters, caught as they are in a "time warp" between childhood and adulthood. It is a time when they are trying to distance themselves from the authority of their parents and to find their own identities—often under the influence of the peer group and the entertainment media, both of which often model antisocial attitudes and behaviors. The "hardening" of poverty is also a factor in many of the worst manifestations of modern American delinquency.

The effective supervision of juveniles should emphasize the essential requirements for the healthy psychosocial development of youths, of which loving discipline is the first. This differs from punishment and lays a foundation for a responsible lifestyle. Other requirements are the youth's acceptance of self and of his or her emotions and feelings, understanding of the feelings of others, learning the process of making decisions and choices, problem solving, and establishing positive interpersonal relationships, as well as learning to recognize the value of values, education, and a responsible lifestyle.

In treating different individuals differently, two dimensions must be emphasized; maturity level and extroversion/introversion, using the Wechsler P > V test to form a preliminary impression of where the youth fits along these dimensions. Caution is advised in making interpretations; any interpretation should take the environmental context into account.

Family counseling is the most important component of a delinquent's treatment. Delinquency cannot be resolved until delinquency-generating factors in the family are confronted. Although many families are reluctant to accept counseling, they must; the JPO's task is to make sure that they come to appreciate its values. Many families and delinquents may actually welcome the opportunity to learn how to communicate more effectively.

Table 16-1 offers a guide for a needs assessment interview to help corrections workers get a sense of their clients and their environmental situation. Once the assessment is made, the next step is to match the youth's needs with the resources for help available in the community.

References and Suggested Readings

Alexander, J., and B. Parsons. 1973. Short-term behavioral intervention with delinquent families: Impact on family process and recidivism. *Journal of Abnormal Psychology* 81:219-225.

Andrew, J. 1974. Delinquency, the Wechsler PV sign, and the I-level system. *Journal of Clinical Psychology* 30:331-335.

Boucher, C. 1985. A child development perspective on the responsibility of juveniles. In *Criminal justice 85/86*, edited by J. Sullivan and J. Victor. Guilford, Conn.: Dushkin.

Cobean, S., and P. Power. 1978. The role of the family in the rehabilitation of the offender. *International Journal of Offender Therapy and Comparative Criminology* 22:29-38.

Curtis, L. 1985. *American violence and public policy*. New Haven, Conn.: Yale University Press.

Deardorff, P., A. Finch, P. Kendall, F. Lira, and V. Indrisana. Empathy and socialization in repeat offenders, first offenders, and normals. *Journal of Counseling and Psychology* 22:453-455.

Edwards, D., and C. Nuckols. Identifying kids at high risk. *Adolescent Counselor* 3:25-40.

Ellis, P. 1982. Empathy: A factor in antisocial behavior. *Journal of Abnormal Child Psychology* 10:123-134.

Erikson, E. 1963. *Childhood and society*. New York: Norton.

Perspectives from the Field

The Workaday World of a JPO

Grace J. Balazs

Balazs is a juvenile probation officer in Ada County, Idaho. A graduate of Boise State University in criminal justice, she formerly worked as a presentence investigator for Ada County's Fourth District felony court and as a co-counselor in a sexual abuse clinic.

If you want your typical day to be packed with action and challenges, if you are a JPO (juvenile probation officer) you've chosen the right profession. The pay is not exceptional, the stress is high, and time constraints abound. This is an eight-hour-a-day job that flies by in a matter of moments. There never seems to be enough time to attend to a demanding caseload, but you always seem to find it.

I guess that's one of the things I like about being a JPO; it's very exciting work with such variety in daily routine. My job entails everything from court appearances to field work to writing reports to monitoring and counseling "my" kids. A second reason, and probably most important, is that the work is extremely necessary, even if not always rewarding. I can think of nothing more worthwhile than making a contribution toward turning a troubled child's life around.

However, even worthwhile occupations can be tough and frustrating. As a JPO you run into many absurd situations that make you shake your head and wonder how children are able to endure. Within the last few weeks, for instance, I've had one seventeen-year-old girl who has already had three pregnancies and one fourteen-year-old girl who explained with relish, and perhaps a little pride, that she had been tested for the HIV virus! Most juveniles who come through "juvey" have already experienced traumas on a fairly regular basis. Many of these kids are survivors of dysfunctional families with a wide range of problems, anything from physical abuse and neglect to parents who enable their kids' delinquency by not providing them with behavioral boundaries.

I have a boy on probation who has experienced physical, mental, and chemical abuse for most of his life. This sixteen-year-old was abandoned by his mother at the age of four. He was raised by a "wicked stepmother" who didn't want him in her home and did all she could to deprive this youngster of love and affection. The boy's father had a serious alcohol problem, which interfered with employment and added to the family's stress. More stress led to more drinking and to more anger, which was directed at the boy. As a consequence, the boy became a user of chemicals himself, got into fights, had numerous problems in school, and constantly ran away from home. After being labeled a "worthless no-account," he was told that he was no longer welcome at home.

It seemed almost inevitable that this child would be turned over to the custody of the state; however, after some telephone investigation, I located his biological mother in another state. That was the easy part; the challenge was yet to come, for how do you attempt to reunite a relationship after twelve years? How does a child talk comfortably with a woman who abandoned him twelve years ago, when his only knowledge of her reflects a criminal record for drug abuse and prostitution? A lesson learned—you never assume anything. This woman, a recovering alcoholic, was turning her life around and had been steadily employed for four years. She was overjoyed at the prospect of seeing her son again. The "official" story was that she had abandoned her son; her story was that her husband had taken him from her because of her chemical abuse and that she didn't know how to go about getting him back.

Through an Interstate Compact (an agreement by one state to take over the supervision of another state's case) the boy was reunited with his mother after twelve years of no contact and with a headful of questions and misinformation. It appears to be a happy ending, but who knows what will happen in both their lives?

As a JPO I have to work with families to support their efforts to rehabilitate their children. Probably one of the most challenging tasks of the JPO is working with dysfunctional and difficult families. Such families are a problem because, even if the child is afforded the resources to help facilitate positive change, he or she must return to a family environment where our best efforts may be sabotaged.

Unlike dealing with adult offenders, where you need only to attend to the adults themselves, when dealing with juvenile delinquents you must face their parents as well. This is no easy task, for many are hostile toward the system, including the JPO. Many of them provide slim sources of strength, tough love, or guidance for their offspring. It's not uncommon for parents simply to want the court to lock their children up and to throw away the key. They may be angry and frustrated with their children, but this is no solution. Other parents will take the opposite stance, claiming that their child is without flaw of character and dispute the evidence against him or her. There are also parents who will fight and argue against every effort you make toward helping their child.

Every once in a while, some parents will take the initiative and seek help for their children. There are those who appreciate what you're doing, who will cooperate with your efforts, and perhaps even give you a "thanks." Such instances almost seem unnatural. I would have to say that many parents present the JPO with as much of a problem as the kids.

Consider a client I have who was molested by her "Uncle Jose" when she was six years old, whose father is a homosexual, and whose sister is brain-damaged as a result of being dropped on her head as an infant. This fourteen-year-old girl hates her mother for reasons she won't articulate, but she identifies her as the source of her troubles. The client is recovering from a major chemical dependency, but insists "I don't need counseling; I've worked it all out." I know this isn't true, and that it is imperative to work through feelings and issues and to establish new boundaries through counseling. She has lived with a series of foster families, and although she wears a fake smile, I really wonder what's going on in her mind and how psychologically sound she really is.

All case scenarios are not as interesting or challenging as those I've mentioned. Most of my clients are kids who have made a mistake and are pleasant to deal with. They will never see the inside of juvey again after their probation has expired. Although many of the kids I meet are able to creatively manipulate and twist the facts and some are cons in the making, I can honestly say that I haven't met a kid yet who I didn't believe had some saving quality. Only once have I had a client who made me so angry that I lost my "cool." At the next meeting, however, he was a pussycat, so I assume that I said something right to him to bring the relationship back to a working situation.

The agency here in Boise is a small community working for the best interests of the juvenile. We are a close-knit group, and the camaraderie I feel is one of the best experiences I've known. The prosecutor, public defender, judge, clerical staff, JPOs, intake staff, and detention staff are all fun and supportive people. I truly feel that I've found my niche in life. It is very rewarding for me in many ways, one of which is the gratification I receive from the knowledge that I am contributing to my clients' rehabilitation and to my community's protection.

References and Suggested Readings

Eysenck, H., and G. Gudjonsson. 1989. *The causes and cures of criminality*. New York: Plenum.

Fagan, J. 1990. Social and legal policy dimensions of violent juvenile crime. *Criminal Justice and Behavior* 17:93-133.

Farrington, D. 1989. Psychobiological factors in the explanation and reduction of juvenile delinquency: Genetics, intelligence, morality, and personality. *Today's Delinquent* 8:37-51.

Federal Bureau of Investigation. 1990. *Uniform crime reports.* Washington, D.C.: U. S. GPO.

Garth, D., G. Tennent, and R. Pidduck. 1971. Criminological characteristics of bright delinquents. *British Journal of Criminology* (July): 275-279.

Glasser, W. 1984. *Control theory: A new explanation of how we control our lives.* New York: Harper & Row.

Hanson, S., D. Myers, and A. Ginsberg. 1987. The role of responsibility and knowledge in reducing teenage out-of-wedlock childbearing. *Journal of Marriage and the Family* 49:241-256.

Hyde, M., and L. Hyde. 1985. *Missing children.* New York: Franklin Watts.

Janeksela, G. 1981. Mandatory parental involvement in the treatment of 'delinquent' youth. In *Correctional counseling and treatment*, edited by P. Kratcoski. Monterey, Cal.: Duxbury.

Klein, N., J. Alexander, and B. Parsons. 1977. Impact of family intervention systems on recidivism and sibling delinquency: A model of primary prevention and program evaluation. *Journal of Consulting and Clinical Psychology* 45:469-474.

Kratcoski, P., and L. Kratcoski. 1979. *Juvenile delinquency.* Englewood Cliffs, N.J.: Prentice-Hall.

Loury, G. 1987. The better path to black progress: Beyond civil rights. In *Social problems*, edited by L. Barnes. Guilford, Conn.: Dushkin.

Nachshon, I., and D. Denno. 1987. Violent behavior and cerebral hemisphere function. In *The causes of crime: New biological approaches*, edited by S. Mednick, T. Moffitt, and S. Sack. Cambridge: University of Cambridge Press.

Nettler, G. 1978. *Explaining crime.* New York: McGraw-Hill.

Norton, E. 1987. Restoring the traditional black family. In *Social problems*, edited by L. Barnes. Guilford, Conn.: Dushkin.

Offer, D. 1975. *From teenager to young manhood: A psychological study.* New York: Basic Books.

Peoples, E. 1975. The dynamics of I-level interviewing. In *Readings in correctional casework and counseling*, edited by E. Peoples. Pacific Palisades, Cal.: Goodyear.

Roberts, D., and Bachen. 1981. Mass communication effects. In *Annual review of psychology*, vol. 21, edited by M. Rosenzweig and L. Porter. Palo Alto, Cal.: Annual Reviews.

Romig, D., C. Cleland, and L. Romig. 1989. *Juvenile delinquency: Visionary approaches.* Columbus, Oh.: Merrill.

Scheffer, M. 1987. *Policing from the schoolhouse: Police-school liaison and resource officer programs.* Springfield, Ill.: Charles C Thomas.

Sroufe, A. 1979. The coherence of individual development: Early care, attachment, and subsequent developmental issues. *American Psychologist* 34:835-841.

Thornburg, H. 1971. *Contemporary adolescence.* Belmont, Cal.: Wadsworth.

Thorvaldson, S. 1980. Toward the definition of the reparative aim. In *Victims, offenders, and alternative sanctions*, edited by J. Hudson and B. Gallaway. Lexington, Mass.: Lexington Books.

Trajanowicz, R., and M. Morash. 1983. *Juvenile delinquency: Concepts and controls.* Englewood Cliffs, N.J.: Prentice-Hall.

Udry, J. 1990. Biosocial models of adolescent problem behaviors. *Social Biology* 37:1-10.

Van Voorhis, P. 1985. Restitution outcome and probationers' assessments of restitution. *Criminal Justice and Behavior* 12:259-287.

Wakefield, B. 1991. *Delinquency, exercise, and self-esteem: A look at a new program for high-risk youth.* Paper presented at the annual meeting of the Academy of Criminal Justice Sciences, Nashville, Tenn.

Walsh, A. 1990. Illegitimacy, child abuse and neglect, and cognitive development. *Journal of Genetic Psychology* 15:279-285.

Walsh, A. 1991. *Intellectual imbalance, love deprivation and violent delinquency: A biosocial perspective.* Springfield, Ill.: Charles C Thomas.

Walsh, A., T. Petee, and J. Beyer. 1987. Intellectual imbalance: Comparing high verbal and high performance IQ delinquents. *Criminal Justice and Behavior* 14:370-379.

Wilson, J., and R. Herrnstein. 1987. *Crime and human nature*. New York: Simon & Schuster.

Whitman, D., and J. Thornton. 1987. A nation apart. In *Social problems*, edited by L. Barnes. Guilford, Conn.: Dushkin.

Zuckerman, M., S. Eysenck, and H. Eysenck. 1978. Sensation-seeking in England and America: Crosscultural, age, and sex comparisons. *Journal of Consulting and Clinical Psychology* 46:139-149.

Chapter 17
The Female Client

Counselors of women must intervene with delicate balance. The goal is to help women adapt to transitions and resolve ambiguities in their own individual ways and according to their own values while also helping them move beyond where they are in order to become independent, autonomous human beings.

Nancy Schlossberg and Laura Kent

Differences in Male/Female Criminality

Across time, national boundaries, and types of crime, females commit far fewer crimes than males. From international crime data, Wilson and Herrnstein (1985:104) conclude that "Males are five to fifty times [depending on the country] more likely to be arrested as are females." Prostitution is the only crime in which females predominate; they are almost never arrested for other sex crimes such as child molestation (Steffensmeier 1980). For violent crimes the gap between the sexes is even wider. In 1988, 89 percent of all arrests for violent crimes and 76 percent of all arrests for property crimes in the United States were of males (Reid 1990:90). However, between 1975 and 1985, when the male arrest rate increased by 15 percent, the female arrest rate increased almost 30 percent, mainly for property offenses (Reid 1988:67).

Do these huge discrepancies in male/female crime accurately reflect actual sex differences in behavior, or something else? Some criminologists (e.g., Simon 1975) view the relationship between sex and crime as largely a function of differential reporting and differential application of formal arrests rather than actual differences in male and female criminality. In other words, there is a bias that disposes victims not to report crimes committed against them by women and a similar bias in the "chivalrous" criminal justice system that makes police officers less willing to arrest women and courts less willing to convict them.

To test this hypothesis, Hindelang (1979) compared Uniform Crime Report (UCR) data and National Victimization Survey (NVS) data for the years 1972 through 1976. He found that the official and self-reported rates of victimization accorded extremely well with one another, especially for violent crimes. The percentage of females arrested for simple assault as indicated by the UCR was identical with the NVS data at 14 percent. For robbery (UCR = 7 percent, NVS = 4 percent) and aggravated assault (UCR = 13 percent, NVS = 8 percent), official reporting was greater than survey reporting, a finding that runs directly contrary to the chivalry hypothesis. Hindelang's study suggests that arrest data are accurate with respect to the gender characteristics of offenders.

The Family Background of Female Offenders

Since female criminality is comparatively rare, it would seem to follow that females who become criminal are more atypical of their sex than are criminal males. Herrnstein (1989:20) says, "There are fewer female offenders than male, but they are more deviant [than nonoffending females] psychologically, both intellectually and in personality." The reasoning is that since females generally tend to be more conforming in their behavior than males, the criminal threshold is much higher for females than for males; it takes greater frequency or severity of the experiences typically related to criminal behavior to propel females over the line between deviance and nondeviance than it does for males.

The relatively few studies of female crime and delinquency tend to support the contention that female offenders come from more dysfunctional families than their male counterparts. Reige (1972) found female delinquents more sensitive to and more engaged in intrafamily conflicts than their nondelinquent siblings. Another study found that "There was more mother-adolescent conflict/hostility and a trend for more parental conflict/hostility in families of female delinquents than in the families of male delinquents" (Henggeler, Edwards & Borduin 1987:206). Studies of female prison inmates have found that they had been physically and sexually abused (either as children or by husbands and boyfriends) at three to four times the national rate (Chesney-Lind & Rodriguez 1983; Crawford 1988).

Summing up her study of 240 girls committed to the California Youth Authority, Rosenbaum (1989:38) states: "Not only did these girls suffer from their parents' broken marriages and multiple relationships, alcoholism, and mental illness, but they typically lacked the nurturing youth require." In a study of male and female adult sociopaths, Cloninger, Reich, and Guze (1975:20) found "many kinds of more frequent disruptive home experiences in female sociopaths compared to male sociopaths." Yet females are less sensitive than males to criminogenic factors in the environment that are located outside the family, such as poverty and peer influences (Wolkind & Rutter 1973; Cadoret 1982).

How do delinquent girls compare with boys in terms of intellectual imbalance? Of the seventy-four girls in the sample discussed in Chapter 3, forty-five (60.8 percent) were P = V, and twenty-nine (39.2 percent) were P > V imbalanced. None of the girls showed the V > P imbalanced profile, further emphasizing the atypicality of female delinquents. The fact that the P > V profile is overrepresented among female delinquents, with the V > P profile being completely absent, is further evidence that P > V is a marker of antisocial behavior and V > P is a marker of conforming behavior.

Causality

Structural

As with other sensitive areas of criminology, there is heated debate about the criminality gender gap. Some writers, citing the ideology that always seems to intrude into discussions of male/female differences in criminality (e.g., nature v. nurture, sexism, the role of the feminist movement), believe that the reluctance to explore the issue borders on the taboo (Henson 1980:67). The best approach is to admit that no single cause of crime exists. The issue is not one of nature versus nurture but of nature *via* nurture.

Early theories of female criminality were frankly sexist. Females were considered naturally loving and nurturing, so if they became criminal they were thought to be rebelling against their natural feminine roles and thus neurotic (Warren 1986:451). There is abundant evidence from many disciplines—anthropology, biology, chemistry, genetics, psychology, sociology, and so on—to show that females are indeed naturally more loving and nurturing than males (see Walsh 1991a for a compilation). What is sexist is to claim that female offenders are rebelling against their biological nature, and are therefore neurotic, when no such claims are made about male offenders.

As women enter the job market in greater numbers, opportunities for committing crime increase. Henson (1980:74) reports 47.9 percent and 49.2 percent increases in female arrests for embezzlement and fraud in a five-year period in which male arrests for the same crimes rose only 1.5 percent and 13.9 percent. The opportunities for greater involvement in the workforce for women and greater female crime are intimately related. Adler calls this "the dark side of the woman's liberation movement" and states that it has been used by those opposed to it as evidence of the undesirability of women's liberation (1980:150).

Joseph Weis disputes a link between feminism and female criminality: "The proposed relationship between 'liberation' and crime now seems more absurd than at face; after all, the woman's movement is dedicated to stopping and preventing the kinds of exploitation and victimization which comprise many criminal, as well as noncriminal, activities and relationships" (1982:164). Another argument against the liberation/crime thesis are findings that most female offenders do not share the goals and sentiments of the women's liberation movement (Giordano & Cernkovich 1979). Both arguments miss the point, for no matter what the stated goals of a movement are, all movements have unintended as well as intended consequences. Nor is it relevant whether or not the females who commit crimes support woman's liberation. As Henson puts it: "Feminism has given them the opportunities [to commit crimes] that they would not otherwise have had" (1980:74).

Biological

Increased opportunities may explain the increase in female property crime over the past few decades, but they have not resulted in a dramatic increase in female violent crime. Females still commit far fewer violent crimes than males, and their violent crimes are likely to be committed in self-defense against abuse or in a supportive role such as lookout or getaway driver (Wilson & Herrnstein 1985:123). Adler (1975:16) was puzzled at the large disparities between the sexes in the commission of violent offenses even while the gender gap for many property offenses is closing. As long as the commission of any crime is viewed simply as a function of differential opportunities, ignoring biological differences between the sexes, we will remain puzzled. The biological fact is that males are more "prepared" to do violence than females whether we look at young children, adolescents, or adults and regardless of the cultural context (Nettler 1978:84).

In her Presidential Address to the American Sociological Association, Alice Rossi admonished her colleagues to pay attention to the findings of the biological and neurological sciences to keep their theories about sex and gender viable (1984:4). This is particularly important if the sex difference we are attempting to understand is propensity for violence. We know that male and female brains have certain structural differences and are differentially sensitive to the steroid hormones that increase the probability of violence and aggression (Khan & Cataio 1984). Note that "There is little doubt that circulating levels of testosterone during the fetal stage have profound organizational effects on the brain of human and nonhuman primate males. These effects include an increased readiness to engage in aggressive behavior" (Olweus et al. 1988:268).

Hormones interact differently with male and female brains in areas sensitized—in utero—to be receptive to them. Both the androgens ("male" hormones) and estrogens ("female" hormones) act on the limbic system, the brain's emotional center, in areas that are structurally different in males and females. There testosterone (the major androgen) is transformed into sex-specific variations—estradiol in females, dihydrotestosterone in males.

Estradiol promotes nurturing behavior in females by lowering the threshold for firing the nerve fibers in the media preoptic hypothalamic area (Konner 1982:318). Testosterone, on the other hand, lowers the firing threshold of the amygdala, the area of the brain most associated with violence and aggression (Konner 1982:117).

Administering testosterone to animals of either sex increases fighting; administering estradiol reduces it. The male preoptic area responds to testosterone but not to estradiol, and the female preoptic area does not respond to testosterone (McEwen 1981:1307). It has been shown that castrated males (removing the gonadal source of testosterone production) become less aggressive and that estrogen (neutralizing the effects of testosterone) is fairly successful in treating aggressive sex criminals, though the treatment is not always legally permissible (Khan & Cataio 1984:105).

Using one hormonally based theory of female violence, Ellis and Austin conclude their study of female aggression in a correctional center by writing: "In the case of the woman who kills her husband, lover, child . . . this study suggests that it is important to ask: What was her menstrual condition at the time of the event?" (1971:395). The emotional ups and downs experienced by women during their menstrual cycle have had considerable research attention over the years. Cooke (1945) found that 84 percent of all reported violent crimes by women were committed during the paramenstruum period (four days prior to onset and four days into the menstrual period). From similar studies, it is estimated that 62 percent of violent crimes by women are committed during this period (Taylor 1984). If the female hormonal cycle had nothing to do with acts of violence such acts would be evenly distributed throughout the cycle rather than highly concentrated in one eight-day period.

Although the great majority of women deal readily with the mild mood swings associated with the monthly cycle, a small number experience deep mood changes that are difficult to control. Such women are said to suffer from premenstrual syndrome (PMS). The most usual theory about the causes of PMS is the progesterone deficiency theory. Women with PMS have lower levels of progesterone than non-PMS women, and treatment with progesterone alleviates the symptoms of PMS in most cases (Trunnell, Turner & Keye 1988). The calming effect of progesterone is evidenced in studies showing that females taking progesterone-dominant contraception pills report strong feelings of nurturance and affiliation and feel irritable and hostile when progesterone levels are low (Asso 1983:64).

During the paramenstruum period, progesterone levels drop almost to zero, estradiol levels drop to 50 percent of mid-cycle baseline measures, and testosterone remains relatively high at 82 percent of baseline (Utain 1980:32). Levels of norepinephrine (an "action" hormone) are also probably higher during this period (Asso 1983:142). Wilson (1981:36) speculates that the violence sometimes expressed by women who suffer extreme PMS occurs because these women are chemically more male-like at this time. There is support for this speculation. Barfield's (1976:71-73) review of the literature on the physiological fluctuations accompanying the menstrual cycle revealed premenstrual increases in metabolic rate and visual-spatial sensitivity and decreases in sensitivity to touch, sound, and smell. The characteristics that increase are those in which males normally excel; those that decrease are areas in which females normally excel. Wagenvoord and Bailey's review of gender differences in dreaming (1979:115) found that women's dreams tend to be friendlier, pleasanter, and far less violent than men's dreams, particularly at ovulation. However, during paramenstruum, many women report that their dreams are filled with hostility, anxiety, and frustration.

This does not mean that hormonal factors have a necessary connection with violence or that women are never violent absent hormonal influence. However, when a criminal justice worker has to deal with a consistently assaultive female, this is something to look into. All the counseling in the world will not change hormonal imbalance, but progesterone therapy is cheap, quick, and effective (see the Case Study).

Nor does it mean that sociocultural variables can be ignored. The effects of culture violence are obvious in Wolfgang's study of homicide in Philadelphia.

Case Study

"Dr. Jekyll and Ms. Hyde": Portrait of a Violent Woman

One of the most memorable cases I ever had was that of a well-educated thirty-year-old women who, all 5' 1" and 110 pounds of her, had gotten into a vicious fight with her husband. With the help of a butcher knife, which she embedded in his chest, she got the better of him. She then left the house, returning some minutes later to have another go at him. By that time her husband had staggered into a bedroom for his pistol, with which he shot her in the chest and shoulder. Both parties were taken to the hospital, he with a collapsed lung, she to have her right breast removed. She—I'll call her Jane—was arrested for aggravated assault.

Looking at Jane's record, it was clear that until the age of twenty-seven she was the picture of propriety and conformity, with only two traffic tickets on her rap sheet. After the age of twenty-seven her sheet began to resemble that of an aggressive psychopath, with assault after assault being recorded (including the present offense, there were ten). She had assaulted her parents several times, driven her car at police officers when they attempted to arrest her, chased a woman—whom she accused of having an affair with her husband—with an ice pick, and threatened her husband's employer with a gun. These attacks had grown in number and severity over the several months before the stabbing of her husband.

To all who knew her, it seemed as though this sweet and dedicated daughter, wife, and mother had been transformed overnight into a raging monster. She was only an occasional drinker, and her aggressive outbursts didn't coincide with her drinking, she did not use any kind of illicit substances, and her family couldn't identify any tension or stresses in her environment before the onset of her bizarre behavior. But she certainly had them now. The custody of her children had been awarded to her husband, her right breast had been shot off, and she was facing an aggravated assault sentence of four to twenty-five years in prison.

I conducted a PSI interview with Jane in the county jail. She was depressed but articulate and cooperative, and she didn't seem the least bit dangerous. Before going to jail, she had been placed in a psychiatric hospital for ten weeks. The staff had done the usual psychiatric workups and concluded that she was "rather severely maladjusted, extremely impulsive, and in dire need of psychiatric care." There was no attempt to explain Jane's apparent "Dr. Jekyll and Ms. Hyde" behavior or its abrupt onset at age twenty-seven. Instead, they had chosen to use adjectives to describe her emotional state at the time of the assaults (describing behavior does not explain it).

In a conclusion that was fully consistent with the diagnosis, the psychiatric team recommended "due process" (incarceration) with extensive psychiatric treatment. My initial reaction was to agree. But one thing she told me kept coming back to me. She told me her assaultive behavior always seemed to occur around the time of her menstrual period. She had mentioned this to her psychiatrist, but this was the late 1970s, the heyday of strict environmentalist explanations for all kinds of behavior, and he dismissed it as an "old wives tale." As it happened, I was studying for my comprehensive Ph.D. exams in criminology, and I was reading everything in sight about criminal behavior, especially European biological criminology. One of the things that intrigued me was a series of studies conducted by British psychiatrist Katharina Dalton and her colleagues. These studies strongly implicated premenstrual syndrome (PMS) in violent crime among women.

Further reading revealed that PMS had been successful as a defense in many European courts. I discussed these things with the sentencing judge, saying there might be a basis for medical treatment. He allowed me two extra weeks to complete the PSI, during which I was to seek out a physician to corroborate "this PMS stuff" and treat her. Although PMS is a well-known syndrome today, at that time many physicians agreed with Jane's psychiatrist that PMS is an old wives tale. Eventually I did find a psychiatrist who was biologically oriented and who prescribed progesterone hormone therapy for Jane. She remained in the county jail for two more months while the psychiatrist assessed the effectiveness of the treatment. Her behavior during that time was sufficiently good for the judge to take a chance with her and, much to the chagrin of her husband, she was released on probation.

While on probation, Jane received physical therapy for her arm, which had withered somewhat due to the effects of the gunshot wound, and continued with her progesterone treatments. She obtained employment and became reconciled with her parents. Although her husband retained custody of their children, Jane was allowed visitation rights. Not once during her four-year probation did Jane feel the urge to assault anyone. She was a very cooperative probationer.

Looking back on this case, I consider it a successful one from my point of view. However, from Jane's perspective it was something of a tragedy. Because of an accident of physiology, she lost her husband and the custody of her children, became estranged from her parents, had her right breast shot off, and was imprisoned in psychiatric wards and jails. Her unpleasant story might well have continued on the same track had I not been able to find a psychiatrist not afraid to go up against the conventional wisdom of the time. The simple administration of progesterone turned Mrs. Hyde back to the much more appealing Dr. Jekyll. It is a pity that it came so late.

Wolfgang (1958:55) found that although black males had a homicide rate four times that of black females, black females had a homicide rate three times that of white males. This study highlights both the biology of sex differences within groups (in both black and white communities males had a higher homicide rate) and the sociology of differences between groups (black females were more homicidal than white males). A more thorough examination of the biological bases of female criminality is found in Walsh (1991b).

Counseling Female Clients

Some readers may wonder why it is necessary to devote a separate chapter to the female offender: Aren't women people too, with the same motives and fragilities of men? Doesn't it 'ghettoize' females to treat them separately? Can't women benefit from the same kinds of counseling and treatment that men get? Resnik (1983:109) goes so far as to say that prison inmates should not be classified by sex because "sexual segregation does harm to the emerging, but still fragile, societal value of sexual equality." Some theorists believe that men and women should not be treated differently in counseling for much the same reasons (Spiegel 1979).

Although these arguments have some validity, women *are* different from men in certain respects that demand different (though not unequal) treatment. The American Psychological Association (APA) has set forth principles for the counseling of women. Those principles that apply to correctional settings are summarized and paraphrased from Corey (1986:341) below.

First, anyone counseling women should be sensitized to the biological, psychological, and social issues that have an impact on women. The counselor, says the APA, must be aware that models and treatment modalities developed for male clients may not apply to females. Naturally, females benefit from the skills of a warm and concerned counselor much as men do, but for women there are additional considerations.

Counselors must be sensitive to sexism in their language and behavior. Male counselors must be as professional with female clients as with male clients. Using terms like "honey" or "babe" sends messages that may not be received in the same spirit as they were sent: Women who are sensitive to the women's movement will take this as a sexist attempt to denigrate them; more traditional women may take it as a sexual come-on. In either case, you have damaged the professional relationship.

A power relationship exists between CJ worker and client; males supervising and counseling females should be aware of the possibility of sexual activity between counselor and client. This possibility must be avoided at all costs, and the male counselor must avoid giving female clients any impression of having more than a professional interest in them.

In Scott's long experience he found special and unique challenges in counseling female offenders. He writes that he never counseled a female criminal who had a healthy attitude about human relationships. This, he believes, is primarily because most female offenders have had negative experiences with males (1977:216). As a result, many such women may be hostile toward a male counselor, making him the target for past abuses. (This is not necessarily open hostility; it may be "passive aggressiveness.") However, Scott thinks a male counselor is preferable to a female counselor because female offenders must work through the relationship problem, which he considers to be the main obstacle to emotional health (1977:217).

Special Concerns of Women in Prison

No special efforts have been made to design separate prison classification systems for females (Clements 1986). Clements considers this "benign neglect" that reflects the reality that only about 4 percent of incarcerated individuals are women and that female inmates are less violent, more cooperative, and less likely to escape (1986:37-38). Female inmates do cause staff some trouble. Female inmates commit more disciplinary offenses than male inmates during the first year of incarceration, although these offenses are far less serious and may reflect less tolerance of female misbehavior on the part of correctional staff (Lindquist 1980).

Part of the reason that females may commit more disciplinary offenses is the abysmal state of the programs available for females in prison and the special pains of imprisonment they may feel (Pollock-Byrne 1990:3). Programs for women tend to be overwhelmingly sex-stereotyped, emphasizing clerical work, food service, and cosmetology or aimed at housekeeping skills such as cooking and sewing; few programs offer employable skills (Kratcoski & Babb 1990). These programs reinforce the social role and expectations of women as servants of others, their feelings of dependency, and their low self-esteem. Providing parental effectiveness training for women is not sexist; it simply reflects the fact that women do the vast majority of parenting and female offenders are not the best parents in the world.

Mothers in Jail

Adding to the normal pains of imprisonment is the fact that most female inmates have children under the age of eighteen. One study found that while only 20 percent of female inmates were currently married, 73 percent had children (Glick & Netto 1977). Vetter and Silverman describe the pains of imprisonment for inmate mothers:

> Imprisonment for the inmate mother has a twofold adverse effect. In addition to the emotional loss and pangs of separation suffered by the mother, she faces the prospect of endless worry over the care and custody of her children. . . . If there is no father or close relative to assume responsibility for looking after the children, the most likely result is that the children's care will be taken over by a social welfare agency and the children may be placed in a foster home or put up for adoption (1986:228).

In general, the male inmate does not suffer the same emotional pangs over separation from children; Scott (1977:219) says: "He walks away with ease—and at times, pride—from children he has fathered." The special concerns of inmate mothers should be always foremost in the minds of institutional counselors.

Unwed motherhood raises a particularly thorny problem for the correctional worker with female clients of childbearing age. Young women who consciously choose to bear illegitimate children without adequate means to support them or who irresponsibly fail to take proper precautions are in need of intensive counseling. Just as it's "cool" for many inner-city males to deal drugs and father numerous children, culturally it may be a mark of status for impoverished females to become mothers (Kondracke 1991:187). It has other benefits as well: A young woman lacking in love and affection now has her own child upon whom she can pour out her love and who has to love her in return. In other words, she is getting her love and worthwhileness needs met in the best way she knows how.

Some people will consider any efforts to try to change reproductive behavior an outrageous intrusion of privacy. But attempting to inculcate responsibility as it is defined by therapists such as Ellis and Glasser is not simply moralizing. It is on the face of it irresponsible to bring illegitimate children into dysfunctional environments. Among many unwed mothers there is much pride and love initially, but when the child begins to explore and put verbal demands on them, love gives way to "rather severe rejection" (Wilson & Herrnstein 1985:239). The effects of this rejection and other factors typically surrounding illegitimate birth among the poor are severe and criminogenic (Herrnstein 1989; Walsh 1990, 1991).

Without moralizing about sexual behavior, the correctional worker might point out the many disabilities of unwed motherhood. Many young women already know emotionally about them but lack the verbal skills to bring them fully to conscious realization. Here is where the correctional worker can help. These young women need alternative means to fulfill their needs for love and a sense of worth, and they need an understanding of how to think about the future for them and their offspring. If they become pregnant more because they do not take proper precautions than because they have a conscious desire to reproduce, a referral to a family planning agency for counseling and birth control devices may be in order. Community agencies offering parenting skills are also useful. Given the cultural pressures, you may not have much success, but you would be remiss if you did not try to encourage responsibility.

The Problem of Isolation

Female inmates are more isolated from the outside world than male inmates. Kratcoski and Babb's study of seven federal facilities found that 50 percent of female inmates never had visitors, compared with 25 percent of the men (1990:269). This may be because more male than female inmates are married and women are more likely to visit their men in prison or because women's facilities are more geographically isolated. The isolation of female inmates is particularly disturbing given that female self-esteem appears to be much more dependent on loving relationships than male self-esteem (Walsh & Balazs 1990). Moreover, "correctional experts agree that inmates who maintain contact with their spouses and families are likely to experience fewer adjustment problems than those who do not have family support" (Kratcoski & Babb 1990: 278). Correctional counselors and caseworkers should do what they can to compensate female inmates for their isolation from the outside world.

Positive Rehabilitative Prospects

So far, all seems negative. As a group, female criminals have suffered more abuse and neglect than male criminals; they appear to be more atypical of their sex than males are of theirs; if imprisoned, they seem to adjust less well initially, have fewer programs to occupy their time, and have emotional problems because of separation from children and other loved ones. Is there any hope for female offenders? Yes: Females possess many attributes that make them better candidates for rehabilitation than males.

First, females in general tend to possess more of the attributes that contribute to a prosocial lifestyle, such as empathy and altruism, than males. Studies of large numbers of twin pairs have shown that females of all ages are inherently more altruistic than males (Rushton et al. 1986), a difference attributed to the influence of genes on sex hormone secretion patterns. There is also evidence of a greater decency among women in interpersonal relationship patterns in institutions. In male prisons, rape and brutality are rife, with rape being used to humiliate and dominate as much as to relieve sexual tension. Coerced sexuality in female prisons is rare. Female inmates tend to form close emotional relationships, get "married," and form "families," but in women's prisons "much of what has been described as prison homosexuality does not even include a sexual relationship. Rather, the women involved receive the

Perspectives from the Field

The Special Challenge of the Female Offender

Cyndee J. Heyrend

After a career in a variety of criminal justice positions, Heyrend became the superintendent of the Boise Community Work Center for women in 1988. The Work Center functions as a halfway house providing a safe, secure, and humane environment that promotes respect and dignity for inmates and staff while recognizing the need to provide programs that specifically address women's issues. This facility is the first in Idaho committed to providing a comprehensive program for the needs of female offenders and served as the model for Idaho's new women's prison to be opened in 1993.

The Idaho Department of Corrections has challenged itself to not only redesign our female offender program, but also, through a National Institute of Corrections grant, to develop a new risk and needs classification instrument designed specifically for the female offender, thus acknowledging that prior male measurement tools served little benefit when applied to the female offender. Once recognizing that the female offender is cut from a different cloth than the male, it offers a unique opportunity for professionals in our field to increase their repertoire of counseling and security abilities.

In dealing with the female offender, one of the most compelling issues and differences between the male and female is the "processing" of information. The male inmate appears to have been socialized and trained to more easily accept a monosyllabic answer. However, the female offender demands processing and dialogue of any given situation. This necessitates a staff that is open to explaining the reasons for a "no"; the reasons for policies and procedures, rules and regulations, or referrals. In an institution, if the staff does not take the time to give the offender these explanations, you can pretty well bet that within a course of one hour, you will not have just one upset, disgruntled, or frustrated woman, but an entire tier.

Female offenders tend to be very literal. Besides extended explanations, simple verbal comments by staff members can upset or defuse a situation dramatically. Emotional issues of women are close to the surface and can be triggered at any given time by an external variable. Therefore, prior to making a judgment or answering a question, it is paramount that the staff member assess the situation and the female's emotional and cognitive level and endeavor to determine the ramifications of their interaction.

For the male staff members, this type of interaction becomes even more complex. Knowing that a great percentage of female offenders are dealing with codependency issues and a strong probability of prior abuse by male family members, training necessary for male staff members becomes a critical issue. Training must include progressive and active approaches to determine a healthy role model plus provide training in the subtleties of manipulation that these women have used with males to survive.

When a woman enters a correctional institution, the staff must be prepared to deal with her complexities. Anger management and stress reduction programs must be developed to resolve bitterness, anxiety over the loss of her children, shame, and the fear of the future. The staff must be alert to the physical health of the woman, gynecological status, prenatal and postpartum care, birth control, and of course the AIDS virus. We also place an emphasis on the sensitive issues of physical and sexual abuse or domestic violence. It is important to remember that the majority of female offenders, like men, are alcohol and substance abusers and should receive appropriate programming. Additionally, a well-balanced mental health treatment program must be devised to maintain the appropriate security concerns, primarily because female offenders become more self-abusive rather than destructive toward the facility or staff.

Realizing that the female offender will most likely become the sole support of her family and children, programming must address educational and vocational training. Placement in these programs is emphasized as part of their return to the community. Resocialization at an improved level financially is as important as improvement emotionally. More recognition should be placed on female offenders' individualized program plan to include parenting skills, child development, and educational programs. Facilities should include a parent-child visitation room and a children's playroom to provide training for both mother and child in a supervised program.

From my experience in dealing with offenders of both sexes, I can say that the female offender is more complex and demanding. Working with female offenders, therefore, requires great attention and appropriate decision making. It focuses on creativity and demands changes of a predominating male system. Interaction is more intense with female offenders but allows the greatest possible opportunity for change. It necessitates knowledge of the offender and knowledge of the community so that the transition from incarceration to resocialization may be accomplished.

The future for female offenders will be determined by the professional staff that have the cognizance, dedication, and realization that the female offender is different and deserves specific programs to answer her long-unaddressed needs.

---

affection and attention they need in a dyad with sexual connotations" (Pollock-Byrne 1990:144).

Second, females get very little peer support for their criminality. Males do receive some psychic rewards (a "rep")—destructive though they may be—from like-minded others, but such psychic rewards are not forthcoming for females. Women get no accolades for being tough and street-smart as men do. Consequently, females are less comfortable with a deviant identity, less committed to criminal values, and psychologically more motivated to change their behavior (Warren 1986).

Third, female offenders appear to have better intellectual skills than male offenders. Within the I-level classification system (see Chapter 15), female offenders tend to show higher maturity levels than male offenders (Warren 1986). A study of all male and female inmates in North Carolina (Joesting, Jones & Joesting 1975) found that female inmates had a significantly higher mean IQ (100.5) than male inmates (85.5), and males scored significantly higher on all except three of the MMPI subscales indicative of psychological and characterological problems. In no instance was the female mean significantly higher than the male mean.

Such studies can be safely generalized to all female offenders because they reflect male/female differences typically found among nonoffender samples as well. It is fairly well-established that the female brain matures earlier than the male brain, that girls talk earlier than boys, that there are fewer mentally retarded females than mentally retarded males, and, in general, females of all ages do better than males on standardized tests of verbal skills (Romig, Cleland & Romig 1989:63). It follows that most females will be better candidates for counseling methods that emphasize cognitive skills, such as RET. In other words, they seem to be in a better position intellectually than male offenders to use information about themselves and their situations to change and become prosocial and independent. You can help them to do this if you understand the special disabilities and stresses suffered by women in a society that still affords them second-class status.

Summary

Although some women can be as dangerous and as criminal as men, women in general are much less crime-prone, though increasing participation in the workforce is giving them increasing opportunities to commit crimes like forgery and embezzlement. While female rates of economic crimes are increasing faster than male rates, they are still much lower.

Females who become criminal have usually suffered a greater frequency or intensity of many of the negative environmental factors said to increase the probability of criminal activity than male criminals: more physical, sexual, and psychological abuse; more parental substance abuse; more parental neglect; and poorer homes or homes more likely to be broken. It appears that women have a higher threshold against antisocial behavior than men.

There have not been dramatic increases in rates of female violence. Greater nonviolence among women is probably attributable to hormonal factors. When the female hormonal balance is upset, as it is for the few women who suffer from extreme PMS, the tendency to become violent increases. These women can be treated effectively with progesterone. (This obviously does not mean that all, or even most, female violence is attributable to PMS—or that all, or even most, women who suffer from PMS will be violent.)

Females appear to have greater adjustment problems than men when incarcerated. Unwed motherhood, the lack of meaningful programs, and a greater sense of isolation from the outside world are the reasons. The disabilities of unwed motherhood, both for the mother and her child, will require special attention from the criminal justice worker.

On the positive side, female offenders may be better candidates for rehabilitation than male offenders. Females are less comfortable with a deviant lifestyle, are more altruistic, and have higher maturity levels and higher IQs than male offenders. Thus, although women suffer greater social disabilities than men and are less well-served by the criminal justice system on the whole, their personal characteristics afford them greater rehabilitative potential.

References and Suggested Readings

Adler, F. 1975. *Sisters in crime.* New York: McGraw-Hill.

Adler, F. 1980. The interaction between women's emancipation and female criminality: A cross-cultural perspective. In *Women, crime, and justice*, edited by S. Datesman and K. Scarpitti. New York: Oxford University Press.

Asso, D. 1983. *The real menstrual cycle.* New York: Wiley.

Barfield, A. 1976. Biological influences on sex differences in behavior. In *Sex differences: Social and biological perspectives,* edited by M. Teitelbaum. Garden City, N.Y.: Anchor.

Cadoret, R. 1982. Genotype-environmental interaction in antisocial behavior. *Psychological Medicine* 12:235-239.

Cloninger, C., T. Reich, and S. Guze. 1975. The multifactorial model of disease transmission: II. Sex differences in the familial transmission of sociopathy (antisocial personality). *British Journal of Psychiatry* 127:11-22.

Cooke, W. 1945. The differential psychology of American women. *American Journal of Obstetrics and Gynecology* 49:457-472.

Chesney-Lind, M., and N. Rodriguez. 1983. Women under lock and key: A view from the inside. *Prison Journal* 63:47-65.

Clements, C. 1986. *Offender needs assessment.* College Park, Md.: American Correctional Association.

Corey, G. 1986. *Theory and practice in counseling and psychotherapy,* 3rd ed. Monterey, Cal.: Brooks/Cole.

Crawford, J. 1988. *Tabulation of a nationwide survey of female offenders.* College Park, Md.: American Correctional Association.

Ellis, D., and P. Austin. 1971. Menstruation and aggressive behavior in a correctional center for women. *Journal of Criminal Law, Criminology, and Police Science* 62:388-395.

Giordano, P., and S. Cernkovitch. 1979. On complicating the relationship between liberation and delinquency. *Social Problems* 26:467-481.

Glick, R., and V. Neto. 1977. *National study of women's correctional programs.* Washington, D.C.: U. S. GPO.

Henson, S. 1982. Female as totem, female as taboo: An inquiry into the freedom to make connections. In *Taboos in criminology*, edited by E. Sagarin. Beverly Hills, Cal.: Sage.

Henggeler, S., J. Edwards, and C. Borduin. 1987. The family relations of female juvenile delinquents. *Journal of Abnormal Child Psychology* 15:199-209.

Herrnstein, R. 1989. The individual offender. *Today's Delinquent* 8:5-35.

Hindelang, M. 1979. Sex differences in criminal activity. *Social Problems* 27:143-154.

Joesting, J., N. Jones, and R. Joesting. 1975. Male and female inmates' differences on MMPI scales and revised Beta IQ. *Psychological Reports* 37:471-474.

Khan, A., and A. Cataio. 1984. *Men and women in biological perspective: A review of the literature*. New York: Praeger.

Kondracke, M. 1991. The two black Americas. In *Sociology 91/92*, edited by K. Finsterbusch. Guilford, Conn.: Dushkin.

Konner, M. 1982. *The tangled wing: Biological constraints on the human spirit*. New York: Holt, Rinehart and Winston.

Kratcoski, P., and S. Babb. 1990. Adjustment of older inmates: An analysis of institutional structure and gender. *Journal of Contemporary Criminal Justice* 6:264-281.

Lindquist, C. 1980. Prison discipline and the female offender. *Journal of Offender Counseling, Services & Rehabilitation* 4:305-318.

McEwan, B. 1981. Neural gonadal steroid actions. *Science* 211:1303-1311.

Nettler, G. 1978. *Explaining crime*. New York: McGraw-Hill.

Olweus, D., A. Mattson, D. Schalling, and H. Low. 1988. Circulating testosterone levels and aggression in adolescent males: A causal analysis. *Psychosomatic Medicine* 50:261-272.

Pollock-Byrne, J. 1990. *Women, prison, and crime*. Pacific Grove, Cal: Brooks/Cole.

Reid, S. 1988. *Crime and criminology*, 5th ed. New York: Holt, Rinehart and Winston.

Reige, M. 1972. Parental affection and juvenile delinquency in girls. *British Journal of Criminology* 12:55-73.

Resnik, J. 1983. Should prisoners be classified by sex? In *Criminal corrections: Ideals and realities*, edited by J. Doig. Lexington, Mass.: Lexington Books.

Romig, D., C. Cleland, and L. Romig. 1989. *Juvenile delinquency: Visionary approaches*. Columbus, Oh.: Merrill.

Rosenbaum, J. 1989. Family dysfunction and female delinquency. *Crime and Delinquency* 35:31-41.

Rossi, A. 1984. Gender and parenthood (American Sociological Association 1983 Presidential Address). *American Sociological Review* 49:1-19.

Rushton, J., D. Falker, M. Neale, D. Nias, and H. Eysenck. 1986. Altruism and aggression: The heritability of individual differences. *Journal of Personality and Individual Differences* 6:1192-1198.

Simon, R. 1975. *Women, crime, and criminology*. London: Routledge and Kegan Paul.

Spiegel, S. 1979. Separate principles for counseling of women: A new form of sexism. *Counseling Psychologist* 8:49-50.

Steffensmeier, D. 1980. Sex differences in patterns of adult crime, 1965-1977: A review and assessment. *Social Forces* 58:1080-1108.

Scott, E. 1977. Women criminals: Therapy with female offenders. *International Journal of Offender Therapy and Comparative Criminology* 21:208-220.

Taylor, L. 1984. *Born to crime*. Westport, Conn.: Greenwood.

Trunnel, E., C. Turner, and W. Keye. 1988. A comparison of the psychological and hormonal factors in women with and without premenstrual syndrome. *Journal of Abnormal Psychology* 97:429-436.

Utain, W. 1980. *Menopause in modern perspectives*. New York: Appleton-Century-Crofts.

Vetter, H., and I. Silverman. 1986. *Criminology and crime: An introduction*. New York: Harper & Row.

Wagenvoord, J., and P. Bailey. 1979. *Women: A book for men*. New York: Avon.

Walsh, A. 1990. Illegitimacy, child abuse and neglect, and cognitive development. *Journal of Genetic Psychology* 151:279-285.

Walsh, A. 1991a. *The science of love: Understanding love and its effects on mind and body*. Buffalo, N.Y.: Prometheus.

Walsh, A. 1991b. *Intellectual imbalance, love deprivation and violent delinquency: A biosocial perspective*. Springfield, Ill.: Charles C Thomas.

Walsh, A., and G. Balazs. 1990. Love, sex, and self-esteem. *Free Inquiry in Creative Sociology* 18:37-41.

Warren, M. 1986. The female offender. In *Psychology of crime and criminal justice*, edited by H. Toch. Prospect Heights, Ill.: Waveland.

Weis, J. 1982. The invention of the new female criminal. In *Contemporary criminology*, edited by L. Savitz and N. Johnson. New York: Wiley.

Wilson, G. *Love and instinct*. New York: Quill.

Wilson, J., and R. Herrnstein, R. 1985. *Crime and human nature*. New York: Simon and Schuster.

Wolfgang, M. 1958. *Patterns in criminal homicide*. Philadelphia: University of Pennsylvania Press.

Wolkind, S., and M. Rutter. 1973. Children who have been 'in care'—an epidemiological study. *Journal of Child Psychology and Psychiatry* 14:97-105.

Chapter 18
The Older Offender

Grace J. Balazs

If society has little place for the elderly man/woman in general, it has even less place for the elderly prisoner or ex-convict.

Delores Golden

The Scope of the Problem

The older criminal offender has received relatively little attention in the criminal justice system or in the criminological literature. "Criminological gerontology is highly neglected, if not completely nonexistent" (Krause & Schafer 1971:3). This neglect is probably due to the fact that there are relatively few elderly criminal justice clients. However, we can expect an increase in older offenders as the American population ages. In 1989, 26 percent of the American population was at least fifty years of age, with the figure expected to rise to 33 percent by the year 2010 (Kratcoski & Babb 1990:264).

In society generally, the term "elderly" is usually reserved for those who have achieved senior citizen status, which comes at age sixty-five. But age is relative, and in prisons anyone over the age of thirty is

---

Balazs, a graduate of Boise State University with a degree in criminal justice, is a juvenile probation officer for Ada County, Idaho. She formerly worked as a presentence investigator for the Ada County adult felony courts and as a co-facilitator for a sexual offender program in Boise. Balazs has conducted research on the elderly offender and has published in the area of self-esteem.

considered "old" (Chaiklin & Fultz 1985:26). Alston points out that the literature on the "older offender" includes forty-year-olds as well as sixty-five-year olds and adds that these discrepant definitions make generalizations difficult (1986:214).

Only 12 percent of the inmates of U.S. prisons are fifty or older (U.S. Department of Justice 1989), though the number of elderly in the prison population is rising at a faster rate than other age groups (Carroll 1989). Moreover, criminal justice administrators are reluctant to allocate scarce funds for special programs for offenders who present them with few supervision problems, "as we have found from research on female offenders, small numbers and the designation of an offender group as a 'nonproblem' may lead to lack of agency attention" (McCarthy & Langworthy 1987:8).

In 1984, people sixty-five and over accounted for only 4 percent of arrests (Steffensmeier 1989). Of course, the age distribution of the population must be taken into account: in 1986 Americans over sixty-five accounted for only 12 percent of the total population (Alston 1986:155), so the elderly are still very much underrepresented among criminal justice clients (Wilson & Herrnstein 1985:129). However, there is evidence that elderly criminal activity has been steadily increasing over the past few decades (Shichor 1984). Alston's analysis of arrest rates between 1972 and 1982 showed that the percentage of index crime arrests has risen more dramatically for the over-sixty-fives than for any other age category—although she cautions that this must be interpreted in light of their much lower base rates (1986:128-129).

Causes of Elderly Crime

For older offenders with long criminal histories, the social or personal situations that first moved them in criminal directions presumably still influence them today. They may be successful career criminals who continue to receive psychic and financial rewards from crime, which they prefer to those they might receive from leading a straight life. Since most criminals "mature" out of crime by the time they are forty (Jolin & Gibbons 1987), offenders who continue the criminal lifestyle past this age must either be successful criminals or immature individuals who lack the insight to engage in the midlife reassessment that most of us, criminal or not, go through.

But what about offenders who enter the criminal justice system for the first time at an advanced age? Why, after presumably leading a conventional life, do they commit crimes for the first time long after most criminals have stopped? From a biological perspective, it has been suggested that a chronic brain syndrome associated with age may lead to loss of inhibitions against illegal sexual behavior, such as exhibitionism and child molesting, and against aggression (Rodstein 1975). But this explanation would explain only a very small proportion of older criminal behavior. Abnormal brain functioning secondary to old age (e.g., Alzheimer's Disease) is far less common than many people think and typically begins around age seventy (Twining 1988:28).

Turning to psychology, Weigand and Burger (1979) see many of the frustrations of old age—poverty, loss of occupational status, and boredom—combined with situational factors such as loneliness and liquor create opportunities for sexual acting-out or violence. Shichor and Korbin (1978) locate the problem in a declining range of personal contacts, which may lead to emotional intensity and conflict.

MMPI profiles of older prison inmates show them to be less psychopathic than younger inmates, but much more neurotic (Panton 1976/1977). Commenting on these profiles, Panton states: "They appeared to have limited ability to cope with emotional stress and appeared to have difficulty in personal adaptability and resourcefulness" (1976/1977:207). Any or all of the causal factors identified by Weigand and Burger may have contributed to the sudden onset of criminal behavior. The spontaneity and impulsiveness of the crimes of the older first offender (Geotting 1983) also point to the possibility that the infirmities of age played an important role.

Not that there is a geriatric crime wave in this country: Very few older people are arrested for the major index offenses (murder, rape, and robbery). However, a surprisingly large proportion of older, particularly first, offenders, are incarcerated for committing violent offenses (Teller & Howell 1981; Chaiklin and Fultz 1985). More than 85 percent of elderly arrests in 1984 were for either alcohol-related offenses such as driving while intoxicated (mostly males) or petty thievery (mostly females) (Steffensmeier 1989:299).

Maturing Out of Crime

Why are the elderly, even the elderly who were formerly criminals, less crime-prone than the young? Is it that crime is a physical occupation requiring strength and stamina—attributes that decline with age—so criminals desist from crime when they can no longer cut the mustard? As appealing as this simple explanation may be, it misses the mark. Maximum endurance can be maintained into the mid-thirties, strength usually does not peak until the late thirties to early forties, and the coordination of a fifty-year-old man is about on a par with a twenty-five-year-old's (Donnelly et al., 1991:80). Most criminals withdraw from crime before forty—long before any normal person becomes enfeebled (Jolin & Gibbons 1987:240).

A more plausible physiological explanation for declining crime among the elderly is that monoamine oxidase (MAO) levels increase and testosterone levels decrease with age. MAO is an enzyme that removes neurotransmitters by oxidation after they have performed their excitator tasks. Among males, MAO is at its lowest level and testosterone at its highest in the late teens and early twenties and declines steadily thereafter (Mawson & Mawson 1977). Low levels of MAO are associated with sensation-seeking, aggressiveness, and antisocial behavior (Coursey, Buchsbaum & Murphy 1979), as are high levels of testosterone (Rushton et al. 1986). Changes in the balance of these two substances will bring a decline in the kinds of behavior they are associated with.

Steffensmeier offers a more social and psychological perspective:

> The elderly are likely to experience changes in role expectations and in their aspirations and goals, so that they no longer strive for the same level of material fulfillment and recognition that they sought when younger. In effect, the major sources of reinforcement for criminal behavior—money, sex, status, intense and lasting hostility toward others, and antisocial peer pressure—are absent or relatively weak in old age (1989:305).

The physiological and social-psychological explanations complement each other. We would expect to witness a reduction in the kinds of behavior Steffensmeier mentions on the basis of hormonal changes alone, but along with these changes there is also a growing psychological maturity, more opportunities to develop ties with the conventional world, more reasonable (scaled-down) ambitions, and an increase in conservatism (Jolin & Gibbons 1987:243).

The Elderly Behind Bars

There is some minimal evidence that older offenders, all other things being equal, are treated more leniently than their younger counterparts and that the general public expects this to be so (McCarthy & Langsworthy 1987:10). For instance, Hucker (1984) found that older male sex offenders were less likely to be sent to prison than younger offenders (1 percent versus 27 percent), but were also less likely to receive counseling (33 percent versus 50 percent). Of course, the criminal justice system has limits to its sentencing flexibility for the elderly who violate societal rules and regulations. The elderly do not expand these limits merely because of their age and the perplexities that accompany the aging individual.

The number of inmates over fifty-five in American prisons has topped 20,000, and the number over eighty-five is 400 (Carroll 1989). Males constitute 80 percent of geriatric inmates (Alston 1986:214), and the older prison population is doubling every four years (Carroll 1989). Does this mean that there is a geriatric crime wave after all? Chaneles thinks not:

> Several broad social and psychological trends have combined to produce the greying of our prisons. They include the overall aging of our population, combined with an ever faster-rising level of expectations among older people; a 'get tough' policy that has resulted

> in longer mandatory sentences; and increased normalization of life inside prison (1987:47).

Thus, much of the increase in the rate of old-age inmates can be attributed to their growth as a proportion of the population. Not only are the numbers of elderly increasing in society, they are enjoying more health and vigor due to improved medical intervention and a social emphasis on wellness and staying in shape. The elderly are retiring from legitimate occupations later than they used to and are enjoying increased opportunity to enter new careers. It follows that if opportunities for extending legitimate opportunities are increasing, so are opportunities for illegal activities.

Regardless of the crimes that put them in prison, the management of the elderly is an issue that correctional institutions must learn to deal with. The prison milieu adds to physical and psychological woes and to the confusion and disorder of the truly geriatric individual. On the other hand, the elderly are not generally a management problem, are generally cooperative with the prison staff, get along well with other inmates, and accumulate significantly lower numbers of disciplinary write-ups than youthful and middle-aged inmates (Goetting 1983:299).

Prison Programs for the Elderly

Public representatives and correctional leaders are hard-pressed to support programs designed specifically for the incarcerated elderly. Such tailor-made programs are low on the hierarchy of priorities in a system in which the bulk of the clientele are young men (Alston 1986:219). The expense of medical care and maintenance of the older inmate constitutes a severe strain on the correctional budget quite apart from any nonessential geriatric services. According to Carroll, it costs an average of $69,000 per year to incarcerate a man over fifty-five years of age—about three times the average for younger offenders (1989:70).

Many do feel that prison programs for the elderly are necessary; Chaiklin and Fultz write:

> The emphasis in most correctional training and placement programs often has been on youthful offenders. As an unfortunate consequence, older offenders experience proportionately greater hardship in the civilian labor force. There is an obvious need for special programs emphasizing job placement and community-based treatment to aid older offenders (1985:27).

One serious problem with the lack of programs for the elderly is that it can hurt their chances of parole. As is well-known, participation in prison programs goes a long way toward positive parole decisions for inmates (Alston 1986:219). Of course, this is not a problem for older offenders who are fit and enjoy good health, but basketball and boxing are programs that do not appeal to the older population either inside or outside prison walls. Additionally, older offenders are not particularly motivated to participate in vocational-type programs because they feel that they have "done their time" in the workforce already (Goetting 1983:298).

The elderly are not currently seen as constituting a unique group, as are women and juveniles, though this is changing. Once upon a time, neither women nor juveniles were treated differently from male offenders either, but as we began to realize their unique situations we began to deal with them differently. Perhaps we shall at some point view the older offender as a unique population. As Krajick has written: "They're a corrections problem, they're a parole problem, they're a welfare problem, they're a mental health problem, and no one takes care of them" (1979:36).

Psychological Aspects of Incarceration

Being sentenced to prison is a traumatic experience, especially for the older first offender. The elderly are supposed to be wise, serene, and to have reached a point in their lives at which they can expect respect and deference from the young. But older inmates find themselves in an environment in which they are constantly ordered around by young correctional officers and "constantly hustled and cheated by younger inmates" (Chaneles 1987:51). The natural need to evaluate oneself as one ages must be felt even more intensely for the incarcerated geriatric offender whose life has been turned upside down.

Erik Erikson best described this process of self-evaluation in his "eight ages of man" model of socialization (Yablonsky & Haskell 1986:122-124): After individuals have proceeded through several stages of life in which they have to establish new basic orientations to the self and to the social world, they are confronted with conceptualizing their entire lives and being. Erikson calls this the life-stage of "*ego identity* versus *despair*." Here, individuals find a sense of resignation and perhaps wisdom from the circumstances of their lives, or they find only disgust or bitter resentment. The prison environment can obviously have a substantial effect on how older offenders resolve this final life-stage.

As Panton said (1976/1977), older criminals are more likely to be neurotic than psychotic or psychopathic. Their psychological problems arise from loneliness, lack of self-esteem, and medical disabilities such as Alzheimer's disease. Chaiklin and Fultz (1985) found that half the older inmates they studied had IQs below 90, and 25 percent were receiving psychiatric treatment: "A comprehensive workup on this group would show that their mental health is as poor as their physical health. They survive because, in its own way, prison provides a supportive and structured life" (1985:29).

Inabilities, such as decreased stamina and strength, the inability to endure discomfort, and fatigue and memory loss are additional handicaps of the elderly. Health problems, such as arthritis, strokes, infections, imbalanced blood chemistries, and insufficient and improper medication, are daily concerns (Chaiklin & Fultz 1985). The inability to deal with such problems may plunge them further into depression and despair. On the other hand, Goetting (1983:295) found several studies that show older inmates reporting only slightly less life satisfaction than senior citizens in free society. This could be because they have learned to have fewer expectations about themselves and their lot in life.

Supervising the Older Client on Probation or Parole

Most older offenders, like most other convicted offenders, are given a suspended sentence and placed on probation (Robin 1990:505). There are at least four offenders under community supervision for every one in prison (McCarthy & Langsworthy 1987:9). In general, probation and parole departments find no difficulty in supervising the older offender (McCarthy & Langsworthy 1987:18). The elderly do not cause much trouble and are often placed on inactive supervision status (mailed-in reports). However, at times the geriatric offender is truly senile, causing a different kind of problem for a probation or parole officer.

Most are on probation or parole for crimes against the person, primarily sexual crimes such as child molestation, and many are granted probation for crimes that probably would have resulted in incarceration for younger offenders (McCarthy & Langsworthy 1987; Shichor 1988). Older female offenders constituted about one-fourth of the clients studied and were convicted primarily of welfare fraud. About two-thirds of the elderly clients never finished high school, and more than half were unemployed and had income below the poverty level.

Although most older clients present few supervision problems, there are certain aspects of their supervision that the criminal justice worker should be aware of. Foremost is the need to be on guard against negative or preconceived stereotypical attitudes toward them based on their age ("ageism"). As in any other instance of bias based on visible characteristics, such as sex or race, harboring age bias severely limits a counselor's effectiveness. Avoiding ageism, as well as sexism and racism, does not mean that you ignore real basic differences. Rather, these "isms" reflect attitudes that go beyond what the data warrant to assert an inferiority, usually considered inherent, in the class of people identified. In other words, be aware of the limiting factors involved with advanced age, but by no means assume that advanced age automatically limits clients in their activities (some sixty-five-year-olds are physically and mentally fitter than some twenty-five-year-olds), their attitudes toward change, or their ability to do so.

Active listening is particularly important with elderly clients. You will need to take more time with them because decreased speed in processing information is one of the universal facts of aging (Twining 1988:49). Although the verbal skills of elderly clients are little affected, they need more time to process what *you* are

Case Study

The Older Inmate: A View From the Inside

"Frank James" is a sixty-three-year-old inmate at the Idaho State Correctional Institution. He began his incarceration in August 1987 for the sexual abuse of his fifteen-year-old stepdaughter, for which he is serving a sentence of five to ten years. Frank believes that because of his age and poor health he is serving a life sentence. Frank has severe emphysema, for which he needs an oxygen supply day and night. He does not berate the court for his incarceration, but questions the severity of his sentence given his lack of previous convictions.

Frank is a personable gentleman; he is quiet and courteous and does not appear to be disturbed in his present environment. His social history reflects only a tenth-grade education, and he admits that he has a bad conduct discharge from the Army. He has been married five times, with the longest marriage lasting nine years and the shortest lasting just over one year. He is presently unmarried and has no communication with any of his ex-wives or his nine children. His victim is living in a foster home in another state, and he resents the fact that he was not consulted on this matter.

He is presently in denial of the offense. He stated that he had told his daughter that if the occasion should arise where he was confronted with such an accusation he would simply deny the charge. Frank is currently involved in a sex offender therapy group. He states that he knows that the psychologist thinks that he is lying and that no progress will be made until he admits the offense, but he remains consistent in his denial.

Frank was asked to describe his world as he sees it as an older offender. One of the first things he said was that most offenders do not have a support system of individuals on the outside. This is even more evident for the elderly, whether they are incarcerated or not. Many times good families neglect their elderly members for many different reasons. This is unfortunate but true, and he identifies himself as one of those neglected individuals. His sole contact is his ninety-one-year-old mother, who lives in Nebraska and is seriously ill.

Frank says that he functions quite well in prison and gets along with both older and younger inmates. He finds that the prison provides adequate accommodations for his medical needs, although he states that it is often a "hassle" to obtain medical care. He states that at times the hassle is not worth the effort to seek it out. He sees a doctor in prison much less often than he did on the outside. He spent thirty days in the hospital before being sent to prison while the institution made arrangements for his health care.

Frank has taken the attitude of "live and let live" at the institution. He cooperates with prison officials and does not pry into the business of other offenders. He has also not let the prison environment affect his state of mind. He says that he feels much the same as he did on the outside and that he functions in much the same way. He states that he has not suffered from any periods of depression, although he acknowledges that this is unusual for the older offender.

Frank is housed with a group of fifteen to twenty individuals who range from sixty to eighty years old. Their age does not exclude these men from associating with other inmates at the institution, but many just seek to be left alone to serve out their sentence. TV and cards are popular pastimes among these men. Frank has not explored the entire facility, choosing to restrict himself to his cellblock. He chooses to take his meals in his cellblock because this is more convenient for him in terms of mobility and personal comfort. He seldom finds it necessary to visit the commissary; he receives no money from outside the prison that would allow him to make purchases there. He does not feel deprived, however, and feels that his needs are adequately met without his having to supplement them.

Frank does not think that it is necessary to have correctional institutions designed specifically for the elderly, especially not if the purpose is to separate them from younger offenders. He feels that younger inmates have a positive effect on the older inmates because morale is usually higher among the older men when free association is permitted. Mixing with the younger men, says Frank, is uplifting and provides the older offender with mental and physical stimulation. He also feels that older offenders act as a "stabilizing influence" on the "younger bucks" inside the walls. This mixture of ages is the closest thing the inmates have to a community atmosphere, the likes of which many of these men may not see for some time. However, Frank says that the prison environment "can get you down quick enough" in one way or another.

Frank's time is pretty much his own, with his day beginning when he chooses. Breakfast is served at 7 a.m., but he rarely gets up that early. Instead, he asks for his breakfast to be brought to the cellblock around 9 a.m., after he's up and about. His day is not demanding. He functions at his own pace because many of the prison's activities are of no interest to him, with the exception of working with leather. He seems quite proud of the fact that he has learned to work leather into many practical articles. These articles cannot be put up for sale at the prison site or in the community. He is disappointed about this, stating that it would be nice to have some extra cash created by the motivation that comes from his sense of accomplishment. This hobby is the only pastime that adds variety to his day. The rest is routine: get up, watch TV, cards, meals, lights out. Although lights are out officially at 10 p.m., he reads until 1:30 a.m, thanks to the individual lights in each room.

Frank stated several times that his routine does not vary much from what it was at home. He was relatively inactive then, with limited employment because of his disability. The lack of privacy is the single thing that bothers him most, "but what can be done about that in a place like this when one is under continual guard?" He does not care much for his cellmate either, but goes with the flow and does not make an issue about something he cannot change. He does not want to cause trouble, stating that it is better to work together and avoid controversy so that the correctional officers don't lock down the cellblock.

Frank James will continue to serve his time with little change in his routine until his five years are up. He says that he has little to worry about inside or outside the institution. He has no personal obligations outside the prison that require his attention. He plans to live in Nebraska with his mother when he is released, if she is still alive. If not, he is familiar with the services available through the housing authorities, food programs, welfare, and Medicare to adequately sustain him for the rest of his life.

---

saying, so your normal rate of speech may present a problem for them. They also may be reluctant to ask you to repeat what you have said, so you must anticipate this need for them. If you do not, you may be faced with a lot of miscommunication and confusion.

Also, be aware of the possibility of some hearing loss among truly elderly clients, many of whom may not be able to afford corrective devices. If this is the case, you will have to increase the tone of your speech somewhat—without giving the impression that you are shouting at your clients. Elderly people are more prone to anxiety than the young (Twining 1988:51), so be careful that your efforts to make yourself heard do not reflect themselves in agitated looks or a barking tone. Many older people try to cover up hearing loss by pretending to hear because they fear ageist reactions from others. Such people have been found to have significantly more negative self-concepts than older people who realistically accept their impairment (Blackwell & Levey 1987).

Some elderly clients play on hearing loss even when their hearing is not impaired, using it as an excuse for infractions or claiming that it caused them to misunderstand a situation or instruction or to make a bad decision based on misperceived information (Shichor 1988:171). Do not add to the negative self-concepts of bluffers by ridiculing them when you point out their bluffs, but neither should you let hearing impairment be an excuse for not following instructions. Simply point out that there is no need to engage in such behavior, that you fully understand and accept their impairment, and that you do not mind repeating yourself at any time. Make sure they also know that it is their responsibility to be sure that they have understood your instructions correctly.

Older people quite rightly feel that they have achieved a stage in life that entitles them to special respect. Many elderly clients have an especially low opinion of themselves for having acquired a criminal label. Along with this loss of self-respect, imagine how embarrassing it must be to have a great part of their lives controlled by an officer who is, in all likelihood, half their age. Never condescend to your older clients by talking down to them as if they are children, although extra patience may sometimes be required when dealing with those who have impaired cognitive functioning. Unless requested to do otherwise, always show your respect by referring to your older clients as "Mr.," "Mrs.," "Ms.," or any such title they may prefer. While it is necessary to respect the dignity of all clients, it is especially necessary to respect the dignity of those who have reached their "golden years."

The imprisoned older offender's reentry into the community can be quite confusing for them, a time filled with anxiety, embarrassment, and a mixture of excitement and depression (Studt 1973:43). (The readjustment problem was dramatically presented in a movie, *Tough Guys,* which featured two wise old cons played by Kirk Douglas and Burt Lancaster who were released after thirty years inside into a world that bewildered them.) If parolees have no support from friends and significant others, such as family members, their reassimilation into the community can be painful. This is true for parolees of any age, but particularly for elderly parolees: "Many have lost or outlived their families. They may have no homes or job skills. Who hires an older person anyway, much less and ex-con? They have no savings or medical insurance, and may not know how to take advantage of welfare programs" (1989:70).

The ability of the older offender to function outside the criminal justice system is of great concern. Being set free with next to no resources poses a threat especially for those individuals who have become dependent on the institution. It may be a natural impulse to want to go that extra mile for an older person, but you must not let them transfer their dependency on the institution onto you. As with your other clients, do things *with* them rather than *for* them. Elderly individuals must learn to draw on physical and mental reserves, which do not come easily to them any more. The parole agent must be aware of resources in the community that may ease the older parolee's transition into a world that may be quite different from the one left behind years before.

Alcoholism and problem drinking are a particular problem among older criminal justice clients (McCarthy & Langsworthy 1987). Increasing age leads to an increasing likelihood of alcohol abuse among the elderly who suffer from social isolation, bereavement, ill health, low self-esteem, and the side effects of medication (Fishman 1988:65-66). Many older people take to drinking because it serves as a substitute for what they have lost, replacing lost friends, dulling the psychic pains of bereavement and the physical pains of ill health, and temporarily bolstering self-esteem.

Fishman (1988:66) believes that problem drinking among the elderly is not best treated in mainstream alcoholism programs, particularly if the problem drinking is of recent onset, situational, and related to the problems of old age. He feels that they are best treated through counseling and increased social involvement with age peers, where the prognosis for successful treatment is good for late-onset elderly problem drinkers. Fishman's message to correctional workers is that narrow and uniform approaches to alcohol treatment will not suffice and that you must be sensitive to the special needs of special classes of clients.

Another aspect of ageism is the notion that "you can't teach old dogs new tricks." While older individuals do tend to resist change more than younger individuals, it is wrong to assume that older people cannot develop new components of their lives if enough motivation is generated. You just need a bit more flexibility in your approach. As Twining (1988:177) puts it: "It is no good having a few standard solutions to problems and then just picking the one that seems to fit best. This might not work too badly for younger people, but it is no good for people who are older." Whatever your solutions might be, above all treat your older clients with the dignity they especially deserve.

Summary

Until quite recently little attention was paid to older offenders. They are much underrepresented in the criminal population and thus have been considered a nonproblem. However, the proportion of elderly citizens under some form of correctional supervision is rising as our society ages.

The word "elderly" has been defined differently in different studies. Given the youthful nature of our criminal population, anyone over thirty is considered old in prison, but here we have defined the lower limit at fifty. The reasons why, after a lifetime of noncriminal behavior, so many older offenders commit crime can range from the biological impairments sometimes accompanying old age to the social and psychological problems of the elderly.

The elderly behind bars are not a behavioral problem. Probably for this reason (like female inmates), there are few programs designed specifically for them. The main problem the elderly present for institutional corrections is financial: Because of their health problems, it costs about $69,000 a year to maintain a person who is fifty-five or older in prison.

Perhaps partly because of this, many older offenders are diverted into community corrections. They present relatively few supervision problems, except for problem drinking and hearing impairment. It is important to treat older clients with respect and dignity—while also holding them accountable.

References and Suggested Readings

Alston, L. 1986. *Crime and older Americans.* Springfield, Ill.: Charles C Thomas.

Blackwell, D., and L. Levy. 1986. Hearing impairment, self-concept, and morale among the elderly. *Free Inquiry in Creative Sociology* 15:21-26.

Carroll, G. 1989. Growing old behind bars. *Newsweek* (20 November).

Chaneles, S. 1987. Growing old behind bars. *Psychology Today* (October): 47-51.

Chaiklin, H., and L. Fultz. 1985. The service needs of older offenders. *Justice Professional* 1:26-33.

Coursey, R., M. Buchsbaum, and D. Murphy. 1979. L. platelet MAO activity and evoked potentials in the identification of subjects biologically at risk for psychiatric disorders. *British Journal of Psychiatry* 134:372-381.

Donnelly, S., J. Kane, M. Thigpen, and D. Thigpen. 1991. It's coming back to me now. *Time* (22 April): 78-80.

Fishman, R. 1986. *Alcohol and alcoholism.* New York: Chelsea House.

Goetting, A. 1983. The elderly in prisons: Issues and perspectives. *Journal of Research in Crime and Delinquency* 20:291-309.

Hucker, S. 1984. Psychiatric aspects of crime in old age. In *Elderly criminals,* edited by E. Newman et al. Cambridge, Mass.: Oelgeschlager, Gunn, and Hain.

Jolin, A., and D. Gibbons. 1987. Age patterns in criminal involvement. *International Journal of Offender Therapy and Comparative Criminology* 31:237-260.

Krajick, K. 1979. Growing old in prison. *Corrections Magazine* (March): 33-39.

Kratcoski, P., and S. Babb. 1990. Adjustment of older inmates: An analysis of institutional structure and gender. *Journal of Contemporary Criminal Justice* 6:264-281.

Krause, E., and S. Schafer. 1971. *Prisoners of age,* Final report to the National Institute of Mental Health. Washington, D.C.: NIMH.

Mawson, A., and C. Mawson. 1977. Psychopathy and arousal: A new interpretation of the psychophysiological literature. *Biological Psychiatry* 12:49-73.

McCarthy, B., and R. Langsworthy, R. 1987. Older offenders on probation and parole. *Journal of Offender Counseling, Services & Rehabilitation* 12:7-25.

Panton, J. 1976/77. Personality characteristics of aged inmates within a state prison population. *Offender Rehabilitation* 1:207.

Robin, G. 1990. *Introduction to the criminal justice system.* New York: Harper & Row.

Rodstein, M. 1975. Crime and the elderly: The criminals. *Journal of the American Medical Association* 234:639.

Rushton, J., D. Fulker, M. Neale, D. Nias, and H. Eysenck. 1986. Altruism and aggression: The heritability of individual differences. *Journal of Personality and Social Psychology* 50:1192-1198.

Shichor, D. 1984. The extent and nature of lawbreaking by the elderly: A review of arrest statistics. In *Elderly criminals,* edited by E. Newman, D. Newman, and M. Gerwitz. Cambridge, Mass.: Oelgeschlager, Gunn, and Hain.

Shichor, D. 1988. An exploratory study of elderly probationers. *International Journal of Offender Therapy and Comparative Criminology* 32:163-174.

Shichor, D., and S. Korbin. 1978. Note: Criminal behavior among the elderly. *Gerontologist* 19:213-218.

Steffensmeier, D. 1989. The invention of the 'new' senior citizen criminal. *Research on Aging* 9:281-311.

Studt, E. 1973. Reintegration from the parolee's perspective. In *Reintegration of the offender into the community.* Washington, D.C.: National Institute of Law Enforcement and Criminal Justice.

Teller, F., and R. Howell. 1981. The older prisoner: Criminal and psychological characteristics. *Criminology* 18:549-555.

Twining, C. 1988. *Helping older people: A psychological approach.* New York: Wiley.

U.S. Department of Justice. 1989. *Monday morning highlights.* Washington, D.C.: U.S. Department of Justice, Federal Bureau of Prisons.

Weigand, N., and J. Burger. 1979. The elderly offender and parole. *Prison Journal* 59:48-57.

Wilson, J., and R. Hernnstein. 1985. *Crime and human nature.* New York: Simon and Schuster.

Yablonsky, L., and M. Haskell. 1980. *Juvenile delinquency.* New York: Harper & Row.

Chapter 19
Community Agencies and Volunteers as Treatment Resources

Corrections personnel must do more to discover how community and societal resources can be brought to bear on the problems of offenders, bearing in mind that the community is the corrective aspect of the correctional process . . . what helps the offender protects the community.

Louis Radelet

Community Resources

Individual and group counseling of clients is not always enough. Often the process of changing offending behavior requires not as much intensive counseling to reconstruct faulty thinking and attitudes as the accurate assessment of offenders' needs and the knowledge of how to go about helping them.

Attempting to move your clients toward more responsible lifestyles is a difficult burden that you need not bear alone. Corrections is a community problem; you are in partnership with community-supported agencies in the rehabilitative endeavor. Probation and parole departments do not have the resources to provide for all the needs of their clients. As Carlson and Parks explain:

> It is the task of the probation [and parole] officer to assess the service needs of the probationer [or parolee], locate the social service agency which addresses those needs as its primary function, to refer the probationer [parolee] to the appropriate agency, and to follow up referrals to make sure that the

probationer [parolee] actually received the services. (1979:120).

Carlson and Parks (1979:121) even assert that the relationships of criminal justice workers with community service agencies are more important than their relationships with their clients; they see criminal justice workers more as brokers of community services than as counselors. More practically, the broker and counselor roles should probably have equal importance.

Unfortunately, many criminal justice workers are unaware of the help available in the community to their clients and to themselves. To make proper use of community agencies, you must understand their functions before you need them. Only with this knowledge can you make the appropriate referral for a specific need. Mangrum says that the corrections worker's ability to provide extended and effective services to clients will be proportional to the scope of his or her knowledge of resources in the community (1975:258). This kind of knowledge, though helpful in the supervision of all criminal justice clients, is particularly important for parolees who must be integrated back into the community after long absences. Here is a brief overview of the community resource agencies available in most cities.

Mental Health Centers

The mental health center is the resource with which the criminal justice worker is most familiar. Most jurisdictions have a diagnostic and treatment center specifically for criminal justice clients, staffed by social workers, psychologists, and psychiatrists. They do competency testing, presentence evaluations, and postsentencing and parole testing and treatment, and usually also offer specialized individual, group, and family counseling.

In addition to court-related centers, there are general mental health centers, which may be preferable for some clients because they are not part of the criminal justice system. In any case, you must learn to recognize symptoms of mental illness and specific diagnostic and treatment needs best dealt with by a mental health professional. Never underestimate client symptoms that suggest serious mental problems. You may be wrong, but err on the side of caution: Refer.

Substance Abuse Resources

Substance abuse resources, which can be either private or public agencies, include hospitals, chapters of Alcoholics Anonymous, Volunteers of America, methadone centers, halfway houses, and residential centers, some designed specifically for criminal justice clients. Veterans Administration hospitals provide excellent inpatient substance abuse treatment free of charge for those who are eligible. Health insurance often covers the cost of drug and alcohol treatment. Clients who are working often overlook their insurance benefits—as do probation officers.

Educational and Vocational Guidance

Since most convicted criminals tend to be unemployed high school dropouts, education and vocational training should be high on the list of client needs. Community high schools offer free GED preparation classes, as well as some vocational training for minimal fees. One drawback of GED classes at local high schools is that the teaching methods are traditional. The group is taught without much attention to individual levels of ability. Some Departments of Correction have set up their own GED programs that allow students to proceed at their own pace. It is a good idea for all probation and parole departments. Money to employ a part-time teacher need not come from tight departmental budgets; small grants from local churches and other concerned organizations are usually available.

The Bureau of Vocational Rehabilitation, a particularly useful agency, offers many opportunities for vocational testing and training. Since this program operates within the prison system as well as in the community, it is sensitive to the special needs of criminal justice clients. It has counselors who can assist clients with job interviewing and other work-related skills.

State employment agencies duplicate many of the same functions, with somewhat less success, but they do have lists of currently available employment. In this age of technology, however, many of the jobs on the employment office's ever-decreasing job list require special vocational preparation.

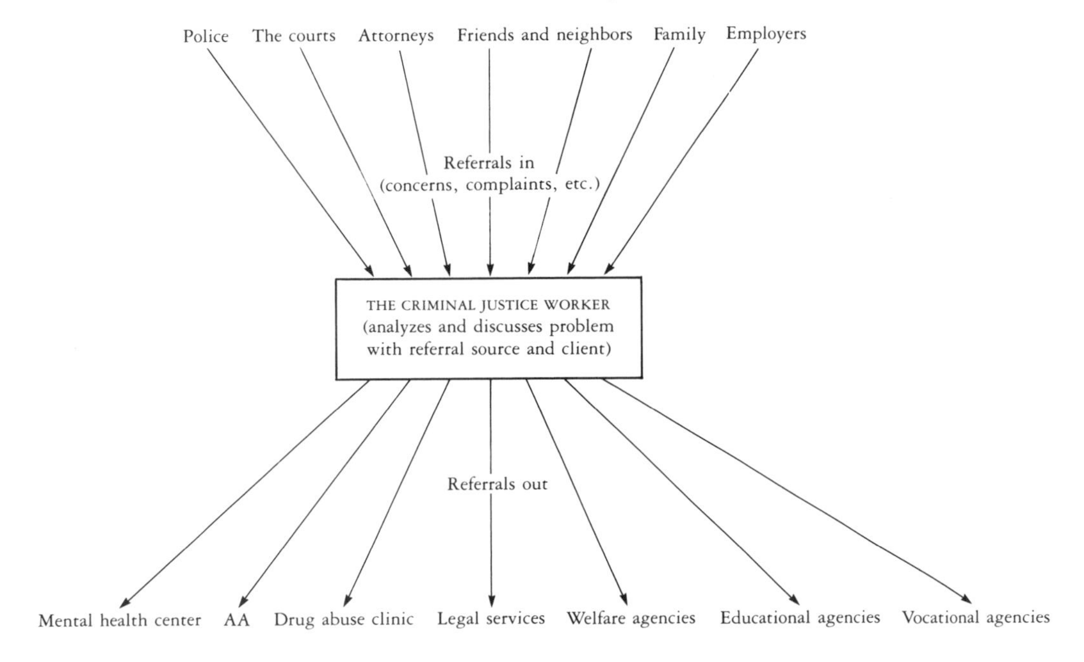

Figure 19-1 Flowchart of in and out referrals

Welfare Agencies

Welfare departments administer federal, state, and local welfare programs. Most criminal justice clients are better acquainted with "the welfare" than their officers are, but many are not aware of the range of programs available. In addition to general relief and food stamps, this agency administers among other programs aid to the disabled, medical assistance, aid to the aged, and family counseling. It is useful for probation and parole officers to get to know someone at the welfare department who will expedite matters when the need for client assistance is acute, as when a homeless and penniless client has been released from jail or prison or a young man has been thrown out of his family home with only the clothes on his back.

Most communities have an agency that specializes in finding accommodations for the homeless. In cooperation with the welfare department, it may give clients and their families permanent or temporary accommodation. It can also help provide homemaking skills, such as family planning and budgeting. Temporary shelter can be found at religious and secular missions. These places offer meals, counseling, and companionship as well as accommodations.

In and Out Referrals

You will not always be able to determine your clients' needs and problem areas by yourself. Quite often other agencies—the police, courts, prosecutors, ministers, neighbors, family members, and concerned citizens—will provide information regarding your clients' needs and problems. Your task is to act as a broker, matching the concern referred to you with the appropriate action. Often this will be a referral of your own to another specialized agency. Figure 19-1 is a flowchart illustrating the in-and-out-flow of referrals.

Volunteers

Volunteer Speakers Programs

Some years ago, a probation department in Toledo, Ohio, instituted a successful program aimed at helping clients deal with various problems of living. The pro-

Week #	Subject	Speaker or source
1	Job opportunities and employment aids	Employment bureau
	Finding and keeping a job	Local employers
	Social Security benefits	Social Security Administration
	Unions and employment	Union representative
2	Sensible spending and budgeting	Financial counselor
	Sensible borrowing	Credit Union representative
	Insurance needs	Insurance representative
	Your welfare department	County welfare department
3	The family	Family counselor
	Human relationships	Human relations counselor
	Responsible citizenship	Leaders in civic affairs
	Veteran's benefits	Veterans Administration
4	Personal health	State and county health departments
	Alcohol and drug abuse	AA and NA members
	Educational and vocational opportunities	Bureau of Vocational Rehabilitation
	Mental health and general assistance agencies	Mental health and Community Chest professionals

Table 19-2 Community resource information speakers' program

gram, which is designed to prepare inmates for release into the community. It is based on the recognition that much recidivism can be traced to an inability to cope with what most of us would consider relatively mundane problems. Inability to cope was in turn traced to simple ignorance rather than lack of native ability or debilitating mental health problems. The Citizens' Volunteer Speakers' Bureau was the answer; it gives probationers much-needed guidance on matters of daily living. Each volunteer—and many are willing to serve—was a specialist.

The program first identifies clients with simple problems of living and asks them to agree to attend a four-week cycle (two nights per week) of informal "resource information" talks. Insistence on attendance may be counterproductive, but it is a good idea to imply that you will view their attendance positively as indicating their desire to help themselves. Typical topics and sources of speakers are presented in Table 19-2.

The program was never formally evaluated for its effectiveness, but the consensus was that it was extremely helpful to clients and to officers, who learned a great deal about community resources. Formal evaluation of the Texas Pre-Release Program found that it significantly reduced recidivism (Clark 1975:240).

Volunteer Officers in Corrections

The practice of probation began with unpaid nonprofessional volunteers, and to a lesser extent so did parole (Scheier 1974). Volunteers can be a tremendous aid to the professional probation and parole officer, doing far more than filing cases and licking stamps. I began my career in probation as a volunteer before accepting a paid position. With proper screening for suitability, initial and ongoing training, and proper matching with clients, volunteers can be a most useful addition to any community corrections program.

The successful volunteer program must be well-planned and must have the support of the professional staff. As McCarthy and McCarthy (1984:377) say: "Poor staff-volunteer relations are a frequent cause of program failure," and "Positive staff-volunteer relations are essential for program success." The professional staff may view volunteers as "amateurs" sticking their noses into areas in which they have no expertise. A good training program for volunteers and education for the professionals about the positive things that volunteers can do can take care of any staff-volunteer relationship problem.

When staff-volunteer relationships are good, professional staff are quite positive about volunteer involvement:

> Overall, officers were quite pleased with the quality of volunteers' performance. Their ratings suggested satisfaction with VIC [Volunteers in Corrections] service in every activity included in this assessment. While all of the areas examined received average performance ratings of "good" or better, officers were particularly pleased with volunteer services directly delivered to clients (e.g., high ratings for operation of treatment programs and counseling), as well as volunteers' direct interactions with officers regarding client progress. (Lucas 1987:73).

What kind of person is a volunteer? "Typically, the volunteer is a sensitive and concerned individual with maturity and control over his or her own life. The volunteer relates well to others and is usually a warm and caring person capable of giving and receiving love" (Henningsen 1981:119).

In other words, the volunteer's self must be every bit as "together" as the professional. If volunteers are to be used efficiently and meaningfully by professionals, they have to be very much like professionals. A non-caring, nonloving, and immature dilettante is of no use to either you or your clients. If such a person manages to slip through the selection net, he or she will not stay long, but can do a lot of damage in the meantime.

What can you as a professional corrections worker expect to gain from the services of volunteers? According to Scheier (1974), the answer is amplification of services and diversification of services. The volunteer frees the professional worker from dealing with less problematic cases so that he or she can increases meaningful contact time with more needy clients. Clients often accept volunteers more readily than professionals because they see volunteers as less threatening. Some may also view volunteers as more concerned precisely because they receive no remuneration for their time and services. (See Shields, Chapman, and Wingard [1983] for other benefits.)

Volunteers can be especially well-accepted if you match clients and volunteers carefully. For example, an older "nurturing parent" volunteer could be matched with a young offender who has lacked for caring elders. Another client might be more comfortable with a same age and sex peer volunteer who could serve as a role model. Table 19-3 shows the matching criteria employed in a highly successful volunteer probation officer program in Lincoln, Nebraska. Notice that the importance of a criterion varies according to the type of client/volunteer relationship desired. For example, if an adult role model relationship is desired, matching for ethnicity is "essential"; if a friend/companion relationship is desired, ethnic matching is seen as "very useful"; but it is only "useful" if a supervisory or counseling relationship is desired. In contrast, counseling skills are essential if a counseling relationship is desired but only "useful" in any of the other three kinds of relationships. The chart may prove valuable to you in matching clients with volunteers.

With respect to the diversification of services, Scheier (1974:263) cites one report that a court system made use of fifty different skills brought to it by citizen volunteers. Volunteers can provide clients with everything from spiritual guidance to jogging classes, valuable services that most certainly could not have been supplied by the professional staff. As for the benefit to the department, one retired volunteer with my department put in as much time as any of the paid staff for about ten years. He supervised

Perspectives from the Field

Volunteer Probation Work

Dr. Stephen B. McConnell

Dr. McConnell is professor of sociology at the University of Toledo specializing in criminology and social stratification. He began as a volunteer probation officer with Lucas County adult offenders in 1983. Dr. McConnell also has worked in a large California prison.

Many things are too important to be left to the professionals: defense to the Pentagon, medicine to the M.D.s, law to legislators and lawyers. If any truth lies in this observation, there may well be a point for volunteerism in criminal justice, for after all, an array of professional personnel implements correctional policy.

Whatever value volunteer probation officers (VPOs) have, it has minimally to do with saving a jurisdiction money or sparing regular staff even bigger caseloads. The central contribution of VPOs derives from the inclusion of ordinary citizens—civic-minded ones—in the operation of justice proceedings. The professionalism of full-time staff is leavened with the innocence of volunteers.

There is a well-documented tendency for police officers to develop cynicism as an occupational necessity. Similarly, though to a much lesser extent, probation officers can develop a less-than-sanguine view of offenders and rehabilitation. Volunteers who have value systems and understandings built outside the criminal justice system, for whom criminal cases have not become routinized affairs, can—and occasionally do—challenge the orthodoxy of the prevailing professional views and ideology. In short, volunteers can ask fresh questions, even provide new insights that do not occur to veteran professionals.

So much of corrections work pivots on anticipating which offenders will or will not repeat crime. Predicting human behavior is a crapshoot at best—especially predicting criminal recidivism. Some psychologists would have us believe that prediction is a science, but the fact is otherwise. Nobody has a monopoly on predicting what another will do postconviction/postprobation or parole. On this count, the VPO whose mature understanding of behavior stems from coping with life itself is on equal footing with the professionals.

The justice system involves a number of somewhat technical and arcane practices that obscure the reality of criminal justice. Informed volunteers can demystify and demythologize the system for a public for which such matters are remote and alien. Likewise, volunteers can step beyond the "trained incapacities" (the inability to see beyond the taken-for-granted realities imposed by professional role socialization) of professionals-as-professionals.

The motivations of volunteers in criminal justice are broad. College students are amassing experience to ease their transition into paid positions on graduation. Older volunteers have more altruistic and diverse motivations. In my own case, the motivation is twofold: I had been teaching in the city for over a decade and wanted to repay in some fashion the community from which I extract a living. Equally important, I wanted to gain some hands-on experience with offenders, for it is nearly twenty years since I worked in the field. I knew how direct experience contributes so much to the rethinking and refining of the theoretical ideas I teach in my criminology and corrections classes. In brief, I saw the chance to volunteer as a means of keeping fresh in the classroom.

Being a VPO requires a host of qualifications too numerous to recount here. Certainly one learns to listen with the third ear to detect what clients are saying indirectly (or trying to conceal) rather than saying directly.

And since serving as a VPO involves making recommendations, even giving direct orders to clients about intimate aspects of their lives, it behooves the VPO to know as much as he or she can about society. (For this reason, sociology continues to be a valuable study for people in correctional work.) At the broadest level, the VPO comes to see how the U.S. economic system of capitalism creates a permanent underclass from which the huge majority of garden-variety criminal justice clients come. The VPO also comes to realize how the occupational structure works—how, for example, a drop in the unemployment rate increases the likelihood of clients' getting minimum wage jobs in, say, the fast food or motel industries.

As well, the VPO comes to understand the components of community organization. This information covers everything from local agencies that may be able to help a poor or alcoholic or drug-addicted client to the subtleties of the operation of the courts, the police department, and the prosecutor's office.

Thus, for a person to be effective as a VPO, there is a great deal of information to be absorbed. This information can then be passed on to clients for their benefit, and it enables the VPO to understand clients' behavior in a realistic context.

A cautionary note is in order. Corrections work is not for the fainthearted volunteer. Nor is it for people who demand 100 percent success. Criminal justice clients can be difficult to work with and on occasion are outright hostile. Not all clients make good on probation or parole: some do commit new offenses and are sent to, or back to, prison. The VPO adapts to the idea that whatever he or she does or doesn't do, much of the eventual outcome for a client lies effectively beyond his or her control. Respect the fact that clients are responsible for their own destinies. Maybe it's fair to say that working as a VPO lends a certain humility to one's perspective.

Table 19-3 Matching clients with volunteers by type of relationship

Volunteer/ client match	Relationship desired by usefulness of match			
	Adult role model	Friend/companion	Supervisor	Counselor
Ethnicity	Essential	Very useful	Useful	Useful
Sex	Essential	Essential	Irrelevant	Irrelevant
Age	Essential	Essential	Useful	Irrelevant
Education	Very useful	Very useful	Irrelevant	Irrelevant
Community contacts	Useful	Useful	Very useful	Irrelevant
Interests	Very useful	Essential	Irrelevant	Irrelevant
Social class	Very useful	Very useful	Irrelevant	Very useful
Counseling skills	Useful	Useful	Useful	Essential

Adapted from Richard Ku, *The Volunteer Probation Counselor Program,* Lincoln, Nebraska (Washington, D.C.: U.S. GPO, 1975) p. 48.

all of the department's welfare fraud cases, as well as a number of other volunteers.

Although not all corrections agencies can expect to find a similar volunteer, they are remiss not to recognize the tremendous variety of skills available in any community. To use volunteers effectively and efficiently not only magnifies the efforts of professional workers, but also greatly assists in the rehabilitation of clients. Isn't that what it's all about?

A word of warning: You have to make quite sure that clients are not manipulating volunteers and that volunteers are holding clients responsible for living up to their conditions of supervision. Problems arise if volunteers are not screened for suitability, if they are not adequately trained, or if they are not matched well with clients. You retain the responsibility for monitoring the client's progress. Thus, volunteers should submit monthly progress reports on each of the clients they supervise for you. Volunteers expect and appreciate this. They need the feedback in order to improve their services to clients and to feel that they are being taken seriously.

Summary

Numerous specialized agencies in the community can help clients with their day-to-day problems. Your task is to recognize client problem areas and to make referrals to appropriate agencies if the problems are not within your area of expertise. You will be acting as a broker matching clients with agencies.

You can also give your clients and yourself much-needed information by organizing a community resource information speakers' program, to be run periodically to accommodate new clients. Many clients find themselves in trouble simply because they do not have access to information about the kind of help that exists in the community. Speakers' programs have proven helpful to clients and corrections workers alike.

Another valuable resource is the desire of many individuals in the community to be useful. These people can be fruitfully incorporated into the correctional enterprise as volunteers. Probation and parole volunteers amplify and diversify services to criminal justice clients. Volunteers must be screened, trained, and matched carefully with clients. Their performance should be monitored by the professional worker to make sure that they are holding clients responsible and that they are not being manipulated by clients.

References and Recommended Readings

Carlson, E., and E. Parks. 1979. *Critical issues in adult probation: Issues in probation management.* Washington, D.C.: U.S. GPO.

Exercises in Using Community Resources

1. Nearly all communities have a clearinghouse for information about resources available to help the unfortunate. Identify the needs of a client on whom you have written a PSI report and match them with agencies that would be appropriate in theory; then find out if your community has an agency that can in fact deal with your client's problem. If not, what would your second-best referral or plan of action be?
2. Devise a resource information speakers' program based on the needs of criminal justice clients as you perceive them. What resources not discussed in this chapter do you think clients would find useful?
3. Find out if the community corrections agencies located in your community have volunteer programs. If so, call and ask them what criteria they use for volunteer selection, the training offered to volunteers, and whether they attempt to match volunteers with clients. What do professionals consider the most useful attribute for a prospective volunteer?

Clark, J. 1975. The Texas pre-release program. In *Correctional classification and treatment,* edited by L. Hippchen. Cincinnati, Oh.: Anderson.

Henningsen, R. 1981. *Probation and parole*. New York: Harcourt Brace Jovanovich.

Lucas, W. 1987. Staff perceptions of volunteers in a correctional program. *Journal of Crime and Justice* 10:63-78.

Mangrum, C. 1975. *The professional practitioner in probation.* Springfield, Ill.: Charles C Thomas.

Scheier, I. 1974. The professional and the volunteer in probation: An emerging relationship. In *Corrections in the community,* edited by G. Killinger and P. Cromwell, Jr. St. Paul, Minn.: West.

Shields, P., C. Chapman, and D. Wingard. 1983. Using volunteers in adult probation. *Federal Probation* 47:57-64.

Epilogue

The professional application of the knowledge, tools, and techniques presented in this book will assist you in helping those unfortunates whose lives you touch as a corrections worker. It is an awesome responsibility to be charged with helping, befriending, and rectifying the attitudes and behaviors of another human being. Never cease examining and improving yourself or learning everything you can about your profession. Make wise use of the community resources available to aid you.

But the most important person in the rehabilitative effort will always be the client. Do not fall into the trap of doing things for and to clients; do things *with* them. Foster client responsibility through self-reliance. It is fine if clients lean on you a little—but only if they lean in order to lift themselves up to responsibility.

The experienced worker may be excused for asking how all these concepts, suggestions, and techniques can be realistically put to work given the constraints imposed by time and large caseloads. The judicious management of caseloads requires organization and a thorough knowledge of the clients. This is best accomplished by proper client classification based on presentence investigation information. Proper classification and risk and needs assessment enable the officer to determine which clients need the most attention. Many clients on the average caseload require little, if any, treatment beyond occasional reporting and the monitoring of daily arrest sheets. These low-risk/low-needs clients are often "situational" offenders whose trip through the system is enough to teach them the errors of their ways. The time you save by having minimal contact with these clients can be put to good use with more problematic offenders. Knowledge and proper use of community resources (and of the skills and motivations of volunteers) will strengthen your efforts. There is always enough time for organized, efficient, and caring criminal justice workers to do the job. Done well, few vocations are more psychologically rewarding and uplifting.

Appendix A

SOCIAL HISTORY QUESTIONNAIRE ______________________________

Prior to your next appearance in court for final disposition, the Adult Probation Department must complete a presentence investigation for the judge. This presentence investigation includes information about your background that the judge will take into consideration when deciding whether to place you on probation or not. Please completely fill out this questionnaire, and if you have any questions concerning the questionnaire, feel free to ask. The information that you provide will be confidential in that only the Probation Department and the judge will be allowed to see it. Upon completion of this questionnaire, please return it to the person who gave it to you.

GENERAL INFORMATION:

FULL NAME:______________________________

PRESENT ADDRESS:______________________________

TELEPHONE #:______________________________

PLACE OF BIRTH:______________________________

DATE OF BIRTH:______________________________

SOCIAL SECURITY NO.:______________________________

SOCIAL HISTORY QUESTIONNAIRE (continued)

FAMILY:

Please list the members of your family, including parents, brothers, sisters, spouse, and children.

NAME	RELATIONSHIP	AGE	ADDRESS
PARENTS:			
BROTHERS & SISTERS:			
WIFE/HUSBAND:			
CHILDREN:			

Have you ever been married before? Yes / No

Date of wedding:

Date of divorce:

SOCIAL HISTORY QUESTIONNAIRE (continued)

EDUCATION:

Please list what schools you have attended (elementary, secondary, college, and job training programs).

SCHOOL	DATES ATTENDED	HIGHEST GRADE COMPLETED

EMPLOYMENT:

Please list in order your job history. If employed at the present time, please note where and the name of your supervisor.

EMPLOYER	ADDRESS	DATE STARTED	DATE LEFT	REASON

Spouse's Current Employer:

MILITARY HISTORY:

Please note the following information:

Branch of Service:____________________

Date of Entry:____________________

Date of Discharge:____________________

Type of Discharge:____________________

Location of Service:____________________

____

HEALTH:

Please make a statement as to your general state of health. Do you have any medical problems, are you under a doctor's care, or are you on medication? Please note below:

PRIOR RECORD: **BIR #** **FBI #**

If you have been arrested before, either as a juvenile or adult, please list these arrests. Also, please note what happened in court after these arrests. Please note if you have been on probation or parole before, or if you are under any supervision at the present time.

SOCIAL HISTORY QUESTIONNAIRE (continued)

Please fill in the following list of information:

1. Housing costs: Weekly:______________________ or monthly: ______________________

2. Food costs: Weekly: ______________________ or monthly: ______________________

3. Approximate Monthly Cost of Utilities:

A. Telephone: ______________________
B. Gas: ______________________
C. Water: ______________________
D. Electric: ______________________

4. Loan Payments:

A.

B.

C.

D.

E.

5. Other Miscellaneous Costs:

A.

B.

C.

D.

E.

SOCIAL HISTORY QUESTIONNAIRE (continued)

Print in your own words a statement concerning the offense. What did you do, when, who was involved, why, did you repay the victim?, etc.

CLIENT MANAGEMENT CLASSIFICATION ASSESSMENT INSTRUMENT

The purpose of CMC is to provide the probation professional with an efficient and effective case management system. CMC includes procedures for developing individualized strategies for the quality supervision of adult offenders. This process is accomplished through the completion of the three system components: an assessment procedure, a supervision planning process, and supervision according to one of five distinct strategies, depending on individualized case needs. It is not to be used with juveniles nor for any other than its stated purpose.

CMC INSTRUCTIONS

There are four parts to the CMC assessment instrument. Whenever possible, the following sequence (A to D) should be followed.

A. Attitude interview (45 items)
B. Objective history (11 items)
C. Behavioral observations (8 items)
D. Officer impressions of contributing factors (7 items)

The Attitude Section

Column One:
A SEMI-STRUCTURED INTERVIEW with suggested questions has been developed to elicit attitude information about the offense, the offender's background, and about present plans and problems. The average interview takes about forty-five minutes and the scoring about five minutes.

Use a **natural, open** conversational style of interviewing that is comfortable for both you and the probationer. If the probationer presents some important or interesting information requiring follow-up, feel free to do so before returning to the structured sequence. While stressing free-flowing communication, some structuring is required to ensure the reliability and validity of the instrument. Therefore, make every effort to **preserve the meaning of the questions** when transposing them into your own words.

In the interview, each section is introduced by one or two open-ended questions, which are intended to encourage discussion on a particular subject. If the information needed to score the items is not obtained from the open-ended questions, one or two specific questions are provided for each item. If those questions fail to elicit the needed information, continue to inquire with increasingly direct questions unless you see the word **-STOP-**. **"-STOP-"** means to discontinue inquiry (except to repeat or clarify a misunderstood question).

For some items, "a" and "b" questions are included. If the "b" question is asterisked (*), always ask it unless the answer to the "a" makes the "b" questions meaningless (e.g., "no" to question 10a). If question "b" is not asterisked, ask it if the needed information was not elicited from question "a."

Column Two:
THE ITEM OBJECTIVES AND RESPONSES are listed in column two. Many times the suggested questions will approach the item objective in an indirect manner in order to elicit the most valid response.

Column Three:
A SCORING GUIDE is included to provide criteria and assistance in scoring ambiguous responses. When scoring, you must choose only one alternative for each item. If you cannot choose an alternative, do not rate the item.

Attitudes About Offense

Could you tell me about the offense that got you into trouble?

QUESTIONS	RESPONSES	SCORING GUIDE
1a. How did you get involved in this offense?	1. Motivation for committing the offense (a) emotional motivation (e.g., anger, sex offense, etc.)	1. a. -Using drugs -Assault (not for robbery)
1b. (If denied) What did the police say that you did?	(b) material (monetary) motivation	b. -Prostitution -Car theft (except for joy riding) -Selling drugs (including to support a habit)
	(c) both emotional and material motivation	c. -Stealing from parents for revenge -Stealing primarily for peer acceptance -Man who won't pay alimony primarily because he's angry with his ex-wife
2a. How did you decide to commit the offense? 2b. Could you tell me more about the circumstances that led up to the offense?	2. Acceptance of responsibility for current offense (a) admits committing the offense and doesn't attempt excuses (b) admits committing the offense but emphasizes excuses (e.g., drinking, influence by friends, family problems, etc.) (c) denies committing the offense	2. a. Explains circumstances but takes responsibility b. Blames circumstances and does not take responsibility c. Probationers who deny any significant aspect of the offense are scored "c" (e.g., the probationer admits that he helped to jimmy a car window but denies responsibility for removing valuables because his friends removed them).

QUESTIONS	RESPONSES	SCORING GUIDE
3a. Looking back at the offense, what is your general feeling about it? -STOP-	3. Expression of guilt about current offense (a) expresses guilt feelings or spontaneous empathy toward victim (b) expresses superficial or no guilt (c) victimless crime	3. a. Probationer must feel some personal shame and regret (not just verbalization to impress the officer). b. -"I feel bad because now I have a record." -"People are disappointed in me." (Indicates some regret but not necessarily guilt.) -"I know it was wrong." (Emphasis is on having done wrong, but not on feeling bad because one has done wrong.) c. -Using drugs -Sexual activities between consenting adults

Offense pattern

I'd like to talk to you about your prior offenses. Have you been in trouble before? (Obtain a *complete* picture of probationer's offense style, including current offense, when scoring items 5-8.)

QUESTIONS	RESPONSES	SCORING GUIDE
4a. What prior offenses have you been convicted of? *4b. Were you ever in trouble as a juvenile?(List on grid below)	4. Offense and severity (a) no prior offenses (Skip items 5, 6, 7, and 8.) (b) mainly misdemeanors (c) no constant pattern (d) mainly felonies	4-8. Include juvenile and serious traffic offenses (e.g., drunk driving). Don't count dismissals. 4. Use only prior offenses. b. Should not be used if probationer has more than two serious felonies. (Use choice "c" or "d.") d. Over 50% of probationer's offenses are felonies.

QUESTIONS	RESPONSES	SCORING GUIDE
5a. Have you ever been armed or hurt someone during these offenses? *5b. Did you ever threaten anyone?	5. Was probationer ever involved in an offense where he (she) was armed, assaultive, or threatened injury to someone? (a) yes (b) no	5-8. Use current and prior offense factors to score 5-8.
6a. How did you decide to commit these offenses? 6b. Did you plan these offenses beforehand? (Discuss offenses individually until a clear pattern emerges).	6. Offenses were *generally* (a) planned (b) no consistent pattern (c) impulsive	6. Officer's judgement based on all factors. a. -Exhibitionist who drives around in a car looking for a girl to whom to expose himself. b. -Person who decides to commit an offense, then drinks to build courage. c. -Exhibitionist who is driving to work, suddenly sees a girl, and pulls over and exposes himself. -Person gets drunk and into a bar fight.
7. Were you drinking or on drugs when you committed this offense?	7. Percent of offenses committed while drinking or on drugs (a) never (b) 50% or less (c) over 50%	7. Count offenses where there was *any* chemical use regardless of whether person was intoxicated or not.
8. Did you do the offense alone or with others?	8. Offenses were *generally* committed (a) alone (b) no consistent pattern (c) with accomplices	

CMC (continued)

Offense	(Item 4) Fel./Misd.	(Item 5) Assaultive?	Circumstances of Offense	(Item 6) Planned?	(Item 7) Chemicals?	(Item 8) Accomplices?

School and Vocational Adjustment

Now, I'd like to find out some things about your background. Let's begin with school. How did you like school?

QUESTIONS	RESPONSES	SCORING GUIDE
9. What was your favorite subject in school? -STOP-	9. Favorite subject (a) vocational (b) academic (c) gym (d) no favorite subject	9. a. -Business course. b. -Music or art.
10a. Did you have a favorite teacher in high school? 10b. What did you like about him (her)?	10. Attitude toward teachers (a) no favorite teacher (b) teacher chosen because of certain qualities that the probationer admired (c) teacher chosen because of close personal relationship with the teacher	10. b. -"She would help kids." c. -"She would help me."

QUESTIONS	RESPONSES	SCORING GUIDE
11a. How far did you go in school? 11b. Did you have any problems with schoolwork? (If probationer did not graduate from high school, find out why not.)	11. Probationer's school performance (a) no problems (b) learning problems (difficulty performing schoolwork) (c) lack of interest, behavior, or other problems	11. a. Don't use for probationer who didn't complete high school. b. For probationer whose learning problems result from a lack of capacity (not just from lack of interest or behavioral problems). If probationer has both a lack of capacity *and* behavioral problems, score "b." Lack of capacity takes precedence when scoring.
12. Now, I'd like to know about your work history. What kinds of jobs have you had? (Find out actual job responsibilities. Use grid on next page.)	12. Primary vocation (a) unskilled labor (b) semi-skilled (c) skilled labor or white collar (d) no employment history (homemaker) (Skip 13 & 14) (e) student or recent graduate (Skip 13 & 14)	12. a. -Average person could do job without training. -Probationer's been in the job market for over six months, but has no employment history. (Also score items 13 and 14.) c. Job requires some training and/or experience. d. For homemaker, use prior vocational history, if any. If none, check "d" and skip items 13 and 14. e. Probationer was recently (within six months) a student and hasn't had the opportunity to establish an employment pattern. (Skip items 13 and 14.)

CMC (continued)

QUESTIONS	RESPONSES	SCORING GUIDE
13a. How long did you work on your most recent job? 13b. How long between that job and your previous job? (Start with most recent job and go backwards, until a clear pattern emerges. Use grid for 12 - 14.)	13. Percent of working life where probationer was employed full-time (a) over 90% (b) over 50% to 90% (c) 50% or less	13. "Working Life..." i.e., time period society would expect one to be working. Subtract time in school, institutions, etc.
14a. What was your reason for leaving your most recent job? 14b. Have you had any trouble getting jobs?	14. Primary vocational problem (a) none (Can be used only if item 13 is scored "a.") (b) problems due to lack of skills or capacity (c) attitude or other problems	14. a. Don't use "a" if working less than 90% c. -"Because of my drinking problem."

(Item 12) (Start with most recent) Jobs and Job Responsibilities	(Item 13a) Duration	(Item 14a) Reason for Leaving
(Item 13b) Unemployment Interval		
(Item 13b) Unemployment Interval		
(Item 13b) Unemployment Interval		

QUESTIONS	RESPONSES	SCORING GUIDE
15a. Where do you live now? 15b. Have you moved around much? (Deal with time period after probationer turned 18.)	15. Living stability background (a) essentially stable living arrangements (b) some unstable periods (c) essentially unstable living arrangements	15. Consider what is stable for the probationer's age group.
16a. Have you had any trouble supporting yourself or received welfare? 16b. (If applicable) How did you support yourself when you were unemployed?	16. History of being self-supporting (a) probationer has usually been self-supporting (b) probationer has had several periods where he (she) wasn't self-supporting (c) probationer has essentially not been self-supporting	16. Illegal activities and welfare are not counted as self-supporting. For probationer who has not had the opportunity to support her/himself (e.g., homemaker or person living with relative), estimate the likelihood of (her) his being able to support (her) himself.

FAMILY ATTITUDES

Now I'd like to know about your childhood. Can you tell me what it was like?

QUESTIONS	RESPONSES	SCORING GUIDE
17a. How do (did) you get along with your father? 17b. How do you feel about your father?	17. Present feelings toward father (a) close (b) mixed or neutral (c) hostile	17. In multi-father families, use the person whom the probationer identifies as father. b. -"We get along" (without implication of closeness)
18a. If you did something wrong as a teenager, how did your father handle it? 18b. What kind of discipline did he use?	18. Type of discipline father used (during probationer's teenage years) (a) verbal or privilege withdrawal (b) permissive (generally let probationer do as he (she) pleased) (c) physical	18. If the probationer didn't live with father or father figure during at least part of his (her) adolescent years, do not rate item 18. b. -"He always left it to mom."
19a. How do (did) you get along with your mother? 19b. How do you feel about your mother?	19. Present feelings towards mother (a) close (b) mixed or neutral (c) hostile	19. In multi-mother families, use the person whom the probationer identifies as mother. b. -"We get along" (without implication of closeness).
20a. If you did something wrong as a teenager, how did your mother handle it? 20b. What kind of discipline did she use?	20. Type of discipline mother used (during probationer's teenage years) (a) verbal or privilege withdrawal (b) permissive (generally let probationer do as he (she) pleased) (c) physical	20. If the probationer didn't live with mother or mother figure during at least part of his (her) adolescent years, do not rate item 20. b. -"She always left it to Dad."

QUESTIONS	RESPONSES	SCORING GUIDE
21a. Were you ever abused by either of your parents? 21b. Did either of them ever go over-board on the punishment? -STOP-	21. Was probationer ever physically abused by a bio-logical, step, or adoptive parent? (a) yes (b) no	21. Item 21 should be based on facts described and not whether the client felt abused. a. -cuts on face -severe body bruises -sexual abuse -locked in closet or starved for unusual periods of time
22a. How would your parents have described you as a child (before you were a teenager)? *22b. Did both of your parents see you the same way?	22. Parental view of probationer (prior to adolescence) (a) good child (b) problem child (c) parents differed	22. a. -No special problems. -"Like anybody else." b. -"My parents were always complaining about me." -Seen as "strange kid."
23. How would you describe yourself as a child (before you were a teenager)?	23. As a child, probationer describes self as (a) good child (normal or average) (b) problem child	23. Accept what the probationer says even if his (her) behavior does not match his (her) perception. (Examples from item 22 apply here.)
24a. How do you get along with your brothers and sisters? 24b. How do you feel about them?	24. General feelings toward siblings (a) close (b) neutral or mixed (c) hostile (d) no siblings	24. Include half-siblings; exclude step-siblings. b. -"Like some, not others."
25. Would you describe your early childhood (before you were a teenager) as happy or unhappy? -STOP-	25. General attitude toward childhood (a) happy (b) not happy	25. Accept the probationer's view.

QUESTIONS	RESPONSES	SCORING GUIDE
26. If you could change anything about your childhood, what would you change?	26. Satisfaction with childhood (a) basically satisfied (would change little) (b) dissatisfied with material aspect (c) dissatisfied with self, family, or emotional climate	26. c. -"I should've gone to school."
27. Can you describe your father's personality? (If answer is unclear, ask probationer to describe another person he (she) knows well.)	27. Probationer's description of personality (a) multi-faceted (b) superficial (e.g., "good," "bad," "nice," etc.)	27. The focus of this item is the *complexity* with which the probationer views people. The ability to describe attributes, or explain the reasons for behavior, is being measured. "Superficial" indicates a lack of capacity to perceive depth in personality and not just an evasion of the question. One or two complex statements are sufficient for an "a" score. a. -"Ambitious and honest." -"Sensitive to others." -"Dad was strict because that is the way he was brought up." b. -"No good drunk" (with no further explanation). -"Kind." -"Don't know."

Interpersonal Relations

Let's talk about your friends. Do you spend much time with them?

QUESTIONS	RESPONSES	SCORING GUIDE
28a. What are your friends (associates) like? *28b. Have any of them been in trouble with the law? (If probationer has no current associates, use prior associates.)	28. Probationer's associates are (a) essentially non-criminal (b) mixed (c) mostly criminal	28. Don't count marijuana use (alone) as criminal. a. Don't use "a" if probationer committed offense(s) with accomplices.
29a. How do you get along with your friends? *29b. How do they act toward you?	29. In interaction with friends, probationer is (a) used by others (b) withdrawn (c) other problems (d) normal	29. This item should be based on *officer's judgement* of the quality of the probationer's interactions. If the officer thinks the probationer is used by friends even though the probationer thinks he (she) gets along "ok," check choice "a."
30a. Do you have a closest friend? *30b. What do you like best about him (her)? -STOP-	30. Description of probationer's relationship with his (her) closest friend (a) talk (share feelings) or help each other (b) do things together (less emphasis on talking or sharing feelings) (c) has none	30. a. -"We do things for each other." -"We're like brothers." b. -"He's a hunter too."
31. Are you satisfied with the way you get along with people?	31. Satisfaction with interpersonal relationships (a) feels satisfied (b) feels dissatisfied	31. Accept the probationer's statement.

QUESTIONS	RESPONSES	SCORING GUIDE
32. In general, do you tend to trust or to mistrust people? -STOP-	32. General outlook toward others (a) basically trusting (b) mixed or complex view (c) basically mistrusting	32. b. A complex view of people (e.g., trusts in some situations and not in others) -"I trust people too much." -"It takes a while to get to know them."
33a. Can you tell me about your relationships with women (men)? *33b. Do you generally go out with a lot of women (men) or date the same person for long periods?	33. Probationer's opposite sex relationship pattern generally is (a) long-term (over six months) or serious relationships (b) short- and long-term relationships (c) short-term, less emotionally involved relationships, or little dating experience	33. c. Short-term relationships with no solid commitments to persons of the opposite sex
34. In your relationship with your wife/girlfriend (husband/boyfriend), who tends to make the decisions?	34. In opposite sex interactions, probationer generally (a) dominates (b) is average or adequate (c) is nonassertive or dominated	34. *Officer's judgement:* Do not accept the probationer's response without exploring his (her) relationships or seeing how some specific decisions are made (e.g., who decides what to do or with whom to socialize; who controls the money).

Feelings

Now, I'd like to ask you about your feelings. Have you had any problems handling your feelings?

QUESTIONS	RESPONSES	SCORING GUIDE
35. Do you consider yourself to be a nervous (or anxious) person? -STOP-	35. Does probationer view self as a nervous person? (a) yes (b) no	35. Accept the probationer's statement. a. -"I worry a lot." -"I'm hyperactive."
36a. What kind of things get you depressed? 36b. What do you do when you're feeling depressed? (If denies, find out how he (she) keeps from getting depressed.)	36. What does probationer do when feeling depressed? (a) seeks someone to talk to, or tries to figure it out (b) seeks an activity to distract self (c) drinks or uses drugs (d) isolates self	36. b. -"Forget about them." -"Watch T.V." d. -"I pray." -"I go to sleep."
37a. Have you ever thought seriously about hurting or killing yourself? 37b. (If probationer says yes to above) Have you ever tried it?	37. Self-destructive behavior (a) never seriously contemplated suicide (b) has had definite thoughts of suicide (c) has attempted it	37. c. Requires overt action that resulted in self-harm or clear intent toward suicide.
38a. What do you do when you are feeling angry with people? 38b. Have you ever hurt anybody when you were angry?	38. In handling anger, probationer (a) is physically aggressive (b) avoids expression to others or has trouble expressing anger appropriately (c) responds appropriately	38. Based on all sources of reliable information (e.g., offense history) and not just on probationer's statement: Physically aggressive problems should take precedence in scoring. If probationer says, "I leave," find out if/how he (she) deals with the anger later. b. -"I break things."

QUESTIONS	RESPONSES	SCORING GUIDE
39a. Can you describe your personality? 39b. What do you like and what do you dislike about yourself? -STOP-	39. In describing self, probationer (a) emphasizes strength (b) emphasizes inadequacy (probationer tends to downgrade self) (c) can't describe self	39. If the probationer gives both positive and negative statements about (him) herself, *choose the one emphasized most.* If the positive and negative have equal emphasis, choose the first response given. c. Choice "c" is designed to identify the probationer who is incapable of showing *insight* or *complexity* into (him) herself; e.g., "I'm okay" (and can't elaborate); "I'm nice"; "I get into too much trouble"; etc.
40. (No questions asked. Rate your impression of probationer's openness in discussing feelings.)	40. Openness in discussing feelings (a) discusses as openly as able (b) is evasive or superficial	40. a. If the officer felt that the probationer was fairly straightforward in talking about his (her) feelings. b. If the officer thought the probationer was evasive or superficial.

Plans and Problems

QUESTIONS	RESPONSES	SCORING GUIDE
41. Aside from your legal problems, what is the biggest problem in your life right now? -STOP-	41. What does the probationer view as his (her) most important problem area right now? (a) personal (b) relationships (c) vocational-educational (including employment) (d) financial (e) no big problems presently (Score item 42 as "a")	41. a. Probationer names several important problems -Drinking or drugs -"Get my head together." b. -"Get things straightened our with my fiancee." -"Try to get along better with my parents."
42. How do you expect this problem (from item 41) to work out?	42. Attitude toward solving problems (a) optimistic; expects to succeed (Include 41. e) (b) unclear (c) pessimistic; expects to fail	42. a. -"O.K., because I've got a better paying job." b. -"O.K., I hope." -"I'll be O.K. if I get a better paying job." c. Probationer is pessimistic about outcome or can't figure out a solution.
43a. What goals do you have for the future? *43b. What are your plans for achieving your goals? -STOP-	43. Future plans (a) short-term goals (most goals can be fulfilled within about six months) or no goals (b) unrealistic goals (c) realistic, long-term goals (most goals are well-developed and extend beyond six months)	43. a. -"Just live day to day." Poorly developed goals with no plans for achieving them b. -Strange, way-out, or impossible-to-achieve goals c. Probationer is able to (1) set a goal within the realm of possibility and (2) list the steps necessary to achieve the goal.

QUESTIONS	RESPONSES	SCORING GUIDE
44. (No question asked. Rate the item based on follow-through on jobs, education, training programs, treatment programs, etc., based on all sources.)	44. Probationer usually sticks with, or completes, things he (she) begins. (a) yes (b) no	44. Compare to the average probationer.
45a. How will being on probation affect your life? 45b. What do you expect to get from being on probation? -STOP-	45. Probationer's general expectations about supervision (a) no effect (b) monetary, counseling, or program help (c) hopes supervision will keep him (her) out of trouble (d) negative expectations (e) mixed or unclear expectations	

Objective Background Items

Instructions: Ask direct questions to obtain the following information.

QUESTIONS / **SCORING GUIDE**

Legal History

1. Age of earliest court appearance:
   (a) 14 or younger
   (b) 15-17
   (c) 18-22
   (d) 23 or older

46. Include juvenile offenses and serious traffic offenses (e.g., drunk driving, hit and run). Exclude divorce, custody proceedings, etc.

2. Number of prior offenses:
   (a) none
   (b) 1-3
   (c) 4-7
   (d) 8 or more

47. Exclude the probationer's present offense in rating this item. Include juvenile and serious traffic offenses.

3. Number of commitments to state or federal correctional institutions:
   (a) none
   (b) 1
   (c) 2 or more

48. Include juvenile commitments.

4. Time spent under probation or parole supervision:
   (a) none
   (b) 1 year or less
   (c) over 1 year; up to 3 years
   (d) over 3 years

49. Include juvenile supervision.
   a. Use "a" for new probationer.

Medical History

5. (Circle all applicable choices.)
   (a) frequent headaches, back, or stomach problems
   (b) serious head injuries
   (c) prior psychiatric hospitalization
   (d) outpatient psychotherapy
   (e) none of the above

50. a. Vague complaints not diagnosed by a physician
   b. Skull fractures
   Head injuries that required treatment (beyond X-ray)
   d. Professional inpatient or outpatient drug/alcohol treatment

QUESTIONS | **SCORING GUIDE**

School History

6. Highest grade completed:
   (a) 9th or below
   (b) 10th to 12th
   (c) high school graduate (exclude GED)
   (d) some post-high school training leading toward a degree

7. Did probationer ever receive special education or remedial help in school?
   (a) yes
   (b) no

52. Include special programs for learning deficiencies (rather than behavior problems). Do not include English-as-a-second-language.

Family History

8. Probationer was raised primarily by:
   (a) intact biological family
   (b) other

53. Choice "a" requires *both natural parents* in an intact home until probationer reached about 16 years of age.

9. Did either parent have a history of (Circle all applicable choices):
   (a) being on welfare
   (b) criminal behavior
   (c) psychiatric hospitalization
   (d) suicide attempts
   (e) drinking problems
   (f) none of the above

54. Includes step and adoptive parents.

10. Have siblings (including half- and step-siblings) ever been arrested?
   (a) none
   (b) some
   (c) most
   (d) not applicable

Marital Status

11. Currently probationer is:
   (a) single (never married)
   (b) single (separated or divorced)
   (c) married (including common-law)

——— END INTERVIEW ———

CMC (continued)

Behavioral Patterns

Instructions: Rate the following behaviors as observed during the interview. Use (b) for the average probationer. Use (a) and (c) for distinct exceptions to the average.

1. **Grooming and Dress**

   (a) Below Average (b) Average (c) Above Average

2. **Self-confidence**

   (a) Lacks Confidence (b) Average (c) Overly Confident

3. **Attention Span**

   (a) Easily Distractable (b) Average (c) Very Attentive

4. **Comprehension**

   (a) Below Average (b) Average (c) Above Average

5. **Thought Processes**

   (a) Sluggish (b) Average (c) Driven (Accelerated)

6. **Affect**

   (a) Depressed (b) Average (c) Elated

7. **Self-disclosure**

   (a) Evasive (b) Average (c) Very Open

8. **Cooperation**

   (a) Negativistic (b) Average (d) Eager to Please

Impressions

Instructions: On the continuum below, rate the significance of each factor with regard to the probationer. Did (does) this problem contribute to the probationer's legal difficulties? At least one item must be rated a "1" and at least one item must be rated a "5."

A. SOCIAL INADEQUACY

Socially inept. Unable to perceive the motives and concerns of others. Unable to survive in society and care for self.	(1) (2) (3) (4) (5)	Socially adept. Able to assert self and to perceive the motives and concerns of others. Able to survive in society and care for self.	*Do not merely rate performance on social situations. Rate ABILITY.*

B. VOCATIONAL INADEQUACY

Lacks the capacity to obtain and maintain relatively permanent and reasonably paying employment.	(1) (2) (3) (4) (5)	Has the capacity to obtain and maintain relatively permanent and reasonably paying employment.	*Do not merely rate job performance. Rate CAPACITY.*

C. CRIMINAL ORIENTATION

Criminal behavior is an acceptable and common part of the probationer's life and s/he attempts to live off crime without trying to make it in a pro-social way.	(1) (2) (3) (4) (5)	Criminal behavior is not an acceptable nor common part of his/her life, nor does s/he attempt to live off of crime without trying to make it in a pro-social way.	*Do not merely rate the frequency of offenses. Rate VALUES and ORIENTATION.*

D. EMOTIONAL FACTORS

Emotional problems (e.g., chemical dependency, sex, fear, depression, low self-esteem, anxiety, self-destructiveness) contributed highly to the offense (pattern).	(1) (2) (3) (4) (5)	Emotional factors did not contribute significantly to the offense (pattern).

E. FAMILY HISTORY PROBLEMS

Parental family problems in childhood and adolescence contributed significantly to the offense (pattern).	(1) (2) (3) (4) (5)	Parental family problems of childhood and adolescence did not contribute significantly to the offense (pattern).	

F. ISOLATED SITUATIONAL (TEMPORARY CIRCUMSTANCES)

Unusual or temporary circumstances in the probationer's life, which are unlikely to be repeated, contributed significantly to the offense.	(1) (2) (3) (4) (5)	Offense is not a result of unusual or temporary circumstances (i.e., offense is part of a continuing pattern).	*Do not merely rate infrequency of offenses. Rate OVERALL PATTERN.*

G. INTERPERSONAL MANIPULATION

Uses, controls, and/or manipulates others to gain his/her own ends with little regard for the welfare of others.	(1) (2) (3) (4) (5)	Misuse of others, manipulation, and control did not contribute significantly to offense (pattern).	

CMC (continued) ______________________________

Supervision Planning

STEP 1: FORCE FIELD ANALYSIS: Using all resources available, identify the strengths/resources and problems/weaknesses, if any, that pertain to each area in reference to the probationer and his (her) primary environment.

Area	Rank	Strength/Resource	Problem/Weakness	Rank
Present offense				
Offense pattern				
Correctional history				
Education				
Mental ability				
Employment record				
Vocational skills				
Finances				
Residential stability				
Family history				
Interpersonal skills				
Companions				
Intimate relationships				
Emotional stability				
Drugs & alcohol				
Plans & goals				
Probation expectations				
Sexual behavior				
Health				
Values & attitudes				

STEP 2: PRIORITIZATION: Apply the following criteria to the above in order to rank the four most important areas relative to the probationer's legal difficulties: the relative strength, the alterability, the relative speed with which change can occur, and the interdependency with other areas.

CMC (continued) ______________________________

STEP 3: TENTATIVE SUPERVISION PLAN: Using the priority areas from step B, "pencil in" tentative goals, objectives, and action plans. Use Supervision Guidelines as a resource.

1. Problem Statement: ______________________________

____

Long-range Goal: ______________________________

____

Short-range Objectives: ______________________________

______________________________ Date Achieved: ______________

____

______________________________ Date Achieved: ______________

____

Probationer Action Plan: ______________________________

____

____

____

____

____

Officer/Referral Action Plan: ______________________________

____

____

____

2. Problem Statement: ______________________________

____

Long-range Goal: ______________________________

____

Short-range Objectives: ______________________________

______________________________ Date Achieved: ______________

____

______________________________ Date Achieved: ______________

Probationer Action Plan: ______________________________

____

____

____

____

____

Officer/Referral Action Plan: ______________________________

____

____

STEP 4: FINAL PLAN: Negotiate the above with the probationer and modify accordingly.

REASSESSMENT PLAN: Revise at routine intervals or when special circumstances so indicate.

1. Problem Statement: ______

   Long-range Goal: ______

   Short-range Objectives: ______

   ______ Date Achieved: ______

   ______ Date Achieved: ______

   Probationer Action Plan: ______

   Officer/Referral Action Plan ______

2. Problem Statement: ______

   Long-range Goal: ______

   Short-range Objectives: ______

   ______ Date Achieved: ______

   ______ Date Achieved: ______

   Probationer Action Plan: ______

   Officer/Referral Action Plan: ______

FELONY SENTENCING WORKSHEET ________________

Defendant's Name: ______________________ Case No. ______________

OFFENSE RATING

1. Degree of Offense

Assess points for the one most serious offense or its equivalent for which offender is being sentenced, as follows: 1st degree felony = 4 points; 2nd degree felony = 3 points; 3rd degree felony = 2 points; 4th degree felony = 1 point. ______

2. Multiple Offenses

Assess 2 points if one or more of the following applies: (A) offender is being sentenced for two or more offenses committed in different incidents; (B) offender is currently under a misdemeanor or felony sentence imposed by any court; or (C) present offense was committed while offender on probation or parole. ______

3. Actual or Potential Harm

Assess 2 points if one or more of the following applies: (A) serious physical harm to a person was caused; (B) property damage or loss of $300 or more was caused; (C) there was a high risk of any such harm, damage, or loss, though not caused, (D) the gain or potential gain from theft offense(s) was $300 or more, or (E) dangerous ordnance or a deadly weapon was actually used in the incident, or its use was attempted or threatened. ______

4. Culpability

Assess 2 points if one or more of the following applies: (A) offender was engaging in continuing criminal activity as a source of income or livelihood, (B) offense was part of a continuing conspiracy to which offender was party, or (C) offense included shocking and deliberate cruelty in which offender participated or acquiesced. ______

5. Mitigation

Deduct 1 point for each of the following, as applicable: (A) there was substantial provocation, justification or excuse for offense; (B) victim induced or facilitated offense, (C) offense was committed in the heat of anger, and (D) the property damaged, lost, or stolen was restored or recovered without significant cost to the victim. ______

NET TOTAL = OFFENSE RATING ______

OFFENDER RATING

1. Prior Convictions

Assess 2 points for each verified prior felony conviction, any jurisdiction. Count adjudications of delinquency for felony as convictions. ______

Assess 1 point for each verified prior misdemeanor conviction, and jurisdiction. Count adjudications of delinquency for misdemeanor as convictions. Do not count traffic or intoxication offenses or disorderly conduct, disturbing the peace, or equivalent offenses. ______

2. Repeat Offenses

Assess 2 points if present offense is offense of violence, sex offense, theft offense, or drug abuse offense, and offender has one or more prior convictions for same type of offense. ______

3. Prison Commitments

Assess 2 points if offender was committed on one or more occasions to a penitentiary, reformatory, or equivalent institution in any jurisdiction. Count commitments to state youth commission or similar commitments in other jurisdictions. ______

4. Parole and Similar Violations

Assess 2 points if one or more of the following applies: (A) offender has previously had probation or parole for misdemeanor or felony revoked; (B) present offense committed while offender on probation or parole, (C) present offense committed while offender free on bail; or (D) present offense committed while offender in custody. ______

5. Credits

Deduct 1 point for each of the following as applicable: (A) offender has voluntarily made bona fide, realistic arrangements for at least partial restitution; (B) offender was age 25 or older at time of first felony conviction; (C) offender has been substantially law-abiding for at least 3 years; and (D) offender lives with his or her spouse or minor children or both and is either a breadwinner for the family or, if there are minor children, a housewife. ______

NET TOTAL = OFFENDER RATING ______

FELONY SENTENCING WORKSHEET (continued) ______

Indicated Sentence

Circle the box on the chart where the offense and offender ratings determined on the previous page intersect. This indicates a normal sentencing package. If the indicated sentence appears too severe or too lenient for the particular case, do not hesitate to vary from the indicated sentence. In that event, however, list the reasons for the variance in the space provided on the next page.

OFFENSE RATING	OFFENDER RATING 0 - 2	3 - 5	6 - 8	9 - 11	12 OR MORE
6 OR MORE	Impose one of three lowest minimum terms. No probation.	Impose one of three highest minimum terms. No probation.	Impose one of three highest minimum terms. No probation.	Impose one of two highest minimum terms. Make at least part of multiple sentences consecutive. No probation.	Impose highest minimum term. Make at least part of multiple sentences consecutive. No probation.
5	Impose one of three lowest minimum terms. Some form of probation indicated only with special mitigation.	Impose one of three lowest minimum terms. No probation.	Impose one of three highest minimum terms. No probation.	Impose one of three highest minimum terms. No probation.	Impose one of two highest minimum terms. Make at least part of multiple sentences consecutive. No probation.
4	Impose one of two lowest minimum terms. Some form of probation indicated.	Impose one of three lowest minimum terms. Some form of probation indicated only with special mitigation.	Impose one of three lowest minimum terms. No probation.	Impose one of three highest minimum terms. No probation.	Impose one of three highest minimum terms. No probation.
3	Impose one of two lowest minimum terms. Some form of probation indicated.	Impose one of two lowest minimum terms. Some form of probation indicated.	Impose one of three lowest minimum terms. Some form of probation indicated only with special mitigation.	Impose one of three lowest minimum terms. No probation.	Impose one of three highest minimum terms. No probation.
0 - 2	Impose lowest minimum term. Some form of probation indicated.	Impose one of two lowest minimum terms. Some form of probation indicated.	Impose one of two lowest minimum terms. Some form of probation indicated.	Impose one of three lowest minimum terms. Some form of probation indicated only with special mitigation.	Impose one of three lowest minimum terms. No probation.

PROBATION AVAILABILITY

Sometimes the preceding chart will indicate probation when it is forbidden by law in the particular case. Before recommending or imposing sentence in any case, consult the statutes for probationability and check the boxes below if applicable.

☐ **OFFENDER IS A REPEAT OFFENDER OR A DANGEROUS OFFENDER.** See RC 2929.01 for definitions. Probation for drug treatment permitted in limited cases under RC 2951.04 (B) (3).

☐ **OFFENSE IS NON-PROBATIONAL PER SE.** Indicates aggravated murder, murder, rape, felonious sexual penetration, any offense committed while armed with a firearm or dangerous ordnance, and any offense in which a sentence of "actual incarceration" is required.

SENTENCE IMPOSED; VARIANCES

ACTUAL SENTENCE IMPOSED

Term imposed each count, and fine if any

____

____

____

____

☐ Committed to serve sentence.

☐ Committed but shock probation possible.

☐ Other probation granted (describe)

____

____

REASONS FOR VARIANCE

If the actual sentence imposed varies from the disposition indicated on the chart in any respect, state the reasons for the variance.

____

____

____

____

____

____

____

____

CLIENT RISK AND NEED ASSESSMENT SURVEY

DEPARTMENT OF CORRECTIONS
DIVISION OF PROBATION & PAROLE

Client No. ______________________ Client Name: ______________________
Officer No. ______________________

CLIENT RISK ASSESSMENT

Instructions: Enter numerical rating in box at right.

1. TOTAL NUMBER OF PRIOR FELONY CONVICTIONS:
(include juvenile adjudications, if known):
a. None. .... Enter 0
b. One .... Enter 2
c. Two or more .... Enter 4
☐

2. PRIOR NUMBER OF PROBATION/PAROLE SUPERVISION PERIODS:
(include juvenile, if known):
a. None .... Enter 0
b. One or more .... Enter 4
☐

3. PRIOR PROBATION/PAROLE REVOCATIONS:
(adult only)
a. None .... Enter 0
b. One or more .... Enter 4
☐

4. AGE AT FIRST KNOWN CONVICTION OR ADJUDICATION:
(include juvenile, if known)
a. 24 years or older .... Enter 0
b. 20 through 23 years .... Enter 2
c. 19 years or younger.................... Enter 4
☐

5. HISTORY OF ALCOHOL ABUSE:
a. No history of abuse .... Enter 0
b. Occasional or prior abuse .... Enter 2
c. Frequent current abuse.................... Enter 4
☐

6. HISTORY OF OTHER SUBSTANCE ABUSE:
(prior to incarceration for parolees):
a. No history of abuse .... Enter 0
b. Occasional or prior abuse .... Enter 1
c. Frequent current abuse.................... Enter 2
☐

CLIENT RISK AND NEED ASSESSMENT SURVEY (continued)

7. AMOUNT OF TIME EMPLOYED IN LAST 12 MONTHS:

(prior to incarceration for parolees; based on 35-hr. week):

a. 7 months or more .... Enter 0

b. 4 months through 6 months .... Enter 1

c. Less than 4 months .... Enter 2

d. Not applicable .... Enter 0

☐

8. AGENT IMPRESSION OF OFFENDER'S ATTITUDE:

a. Motivated to change; receptive to assistance .... Enter 0

b. Dependent or unwilling to accept responsibility .... Enter 3

c. Rationalizes behavior, negative; not motivated to change .... Enter 5

☐

9. RECORD OF CONVICTION FOR SELECTED OFFENSES:

(include current offense; add categories and enter total):

a. None of the following .... Enter 0

b. Burglary, Theft, Auto Theft, Robbery .... Add 2

c. Forgery, Deceptive Practices (Fraud, Bad Check, Drugs) .... Add 3

☐

10. ASSAULTIVE OFFENSES:

Crimes against persons, which include use of weapon, physical force, threat of force, all sex crimes, and vehicular homicide.

Yes/No (circle one)

Total Score (Range: 0-34): ☐

CLIENT RISK AND NEED ASSESSMENT SURVEY (continued) ____________________

CLIENT NEED ASSESSMENT

Instructions: Enter numerical rating in box at right.

1. ACADEMIC/VOCATIONAL SKILLS:

a. High school or above skill level .... Enter 0
b. Has vocational training, additional not needed/desired .... Enter 1
c. Has some skills; additional needed/desired .... Enter 3
d. No skills; training needed .... Enter 5

☐

2. EMPLOYMENT:

a. Satisfactory employment for 1 year or longer .... Enter 0
b. Employed; no difficulties reported; or homemaker, student, retired, or disabled and unable to work .... Enter 1
c. Part-time, seasonal, unstable employment or needs additional employment; unemployed, but has a skill .... Enter 4
d. Unemployed & virtually unemployable; needs training .... Enter 7

☐

3. FINANCIAL STATUS:

a. Longstanding pattern of self-sufficiency .... Enter 0
b. No current difficulties .... Enter 1
c. Situational or minor difficulties .... Enter 4
d. Severe difficulties .... Enter 6

☐

4. LIVING ARRANGEMENTS (within last six months):

a. Stable and supportive relationships with family or others in living group .... Enter 0
b. Client lives alone or independently within another household .... Enter 1
c. Client experiencing occasional, moderate interpersonal problems within living group ..... Enter 4
d. Client experiencing frequent and serious interpersonal problems within living group....... Enter 6

☐

5. EMOTIONAL STABILITY:

a. No symptoms of instability .... Enter 1
b. Symptoms limit, but do not prohibit adequate functioning .... Enter 5
c. Symptoms prohibit adequate functioning .... Enter 8

☐

6. ALCOHOL USAGE (Current):

a. No interference with functioning .... Enter 1
b. Occasional abuse; some disruption of functioning; may need treatment .... Enter 4
c. Frequent substance abuse; serious disruption; needs treatment .... Enter 7

☐

7. OTHER SUBSTANCE USAGE (Current):

a. No interference with functioning .... Enter 1
b. Occasional substance abuse, some disruption of functioning; may need treatment............ Enter 4
c. Frequent substance abuse; serious disruption; needs treatment .... Enter 6

☐

CLIENT RISK AND NEED ASSESSMENT SURVEY (continued)

8. REASONING/INTELLECTUAL ABILITY:

a. Able to function independently .... Enter 1
b. Some need for assistance; potential for adequate adjustment .... Enter 4
c. Deficiencies suggest limited ability to function independently .... Enter 7

☐

9. HEALTH

a. Sound physical health, seldom ill .... Enter 1
b. Handicap or illness interferes with functioning on a recurring basis .... Enter 2
c. Serious handicap or chronic illness; needs frequent medical care .... Enter 3

☐

10. AGENT'S IMPRESSION OF CLIENT'S NEEDS:

a. None .... Enter 0
b. Low .... Enter 1
c. Moderate .... Enter 4
d. High .... Enter 6

☐

Total Score (Range 5-61)

SCORING AND OVERRIDE

Instructions: Check appropriate block.

SCORE-BASED SUPERVISION LEVEL: ☐ Maximum ☐ Medium ☐ Minimum

Check if there is an override: ☐ Explain: ____________________

____

FINAL CATEGORY OF SUPERVISION: ☐ Maximum ☐ Medium ☐ Minimum

APPROVED:____________________

(Supervisor Signature and Date) Agent

Date Supervision Level Assigned: MONTH: DAY: YEAR:

RISK ASSESSMENT SCORING GUIDE

This scale emphasizes behavior while on supervision. The reassessment is based on behavior since the last classification form was completed.

1. Total number of prior felony convictions (include juvenile adjudications if known).

   A. Do not count present offense. The item refers to prior convictions.
   B. Multiple convictions are counted as separate offenses.
   C. For juveniles, this includes only behavior that would be a felony if committed by an adult.

2. Prior number of probation/parole supervision periods (include juvenile, if known).

   A. Revocation hearings that result in a continuance are not counted as a new period of probation/parole.
   B. For juvenile records count only those periods of probation that follow an actual adjudication.
   C. Note: The officer needs only one prior probation/parole in order to move client out of the 0 category. It is not necessary to know the total number of revocations that may have occurred.

3. Prior probation/parole revocations - (adult only)

   A. Disposition of the court or board must be revocation, even though the client may later be reinstated or immediately granted a new parole/probation.

4. Age at first known conviction or adjudication, include juvenile if known.

   A. Convictions may be for a felony or misdemeanor.
   B. Exclude routine traffic, such as: speeding, stop sign, parking violations, etc. Include convictions for DUI, Reckless Driving, Careless Driving, etc.
   C. For juvenile, include only those instances where a person has actually been adjudicated for a crime they could be convicted of if they were an adult.

5. History of alcohol abuse.

   A. This item should be interpreted to mean "in the last 36 months."
   B. The officer is not to make a judgment based simply on number of drinks consumed per day or information of that nature; rather, does the client's drinking interfere with his/her ability to function and meet day-to-day demands. Indications of problems in this area would thus include such things as arriving for work late due to a hangover, frequent drunken quarrels at home or work, excessive expenditure on alcohol, etc. Alcohol-related arrests should generally be coded as indications of serious problems.

C. Probationers/parolees being supervised for a crime such as DUI Manslaughter should automatically be scored as 4.

6. History of other substance abuse.

A. The officer should interpret this item to mean "in the last 36 months." The scoring of this item is similar to that of the alcohol item with one difference. The officer must bear in mind that drug usage may, in itself, be a violation of the law and thus is much more threatening to the client's remaining out of legal trouble. The officer should be attuned to other problems stemming from legal drug use as well. In this regard, prescriptions that the client has should be scrutinized in terms of both frequency and duration of usage.

7. Amount of time employed in the last 12 months (prior to any incarceration based on a 35-hour week).

A. A person will receive a 0 in this category if he has been employed for seven or more months, averaging at least 35 hours per week during the last 12 months.

A person will receive a score of 1 if he has been employed four to six months, averaging a 35-hour week during the last 12 months.

A client will receive a 2 if he has been employed less than four months throughout the past twelve months.

B. Part-time employment should be averaged. If a client has been employed for the past twelve months working 20 hours per week, he would receive a score of 1.

C. Students are scored non-applicable, even though they may have been working part-time. Use non-applicable if in the officer's judgment, there are valid reasons why the client could not have been employed, as in situations of extended illness, disability, or are retired and receiving a monthly retirement check.

8. Current Living Situation: This area can only be determined after a home visit has been conducted.

A. A person will receive a 0 in this category if his present living situation is stable. There must be an adequate income and no serious family disturbances such as fights that require law enforcement or outside parties to calm the incident. Takes pride in the appearance of his/her residence.

B. A person will receive a 3 if there is an inadequate income in the home, occasional serious argument, which may require outside assistance to calm, and/or cluttered living area.

C. A person will receive a 5 if any of the following conditions exist: (1) there is little, if any, income coming into the home; (2) there are fights that require law enforcement assistance to calm; (3) there is separation or divorce; (4) there is a dirty, cluttered home; (5) child protective has investigated abuse or neglect or any other serious incident that creates disorganization or stress.

9. Agent's impression of offender's attitude.

A. This term is inherently subjective. The officer will find scoring easier if he/she focuses on the phrase "motivated to change." Does this client recognize the need for change, and does he/she accept the responsibility for change? Are there any indications that he/she is beginning to make initial behavior changes? The difference between a score of 3 or 5 would be the client's motivation to change.

10. Record of conviction for selected offenses (include current offense—add categories and enter total).

A. This category includes convictions, felony or misdemeanant, during the past five years.

B. The only possible answers are 0, 2, 3, or 5. If the item does not apply, enter 0. The only way to receive 5 points is to have at least one offense that receives 2 points plus one that receives 3 points.

11. Violent or assaultive offenses within the last five years.

A. This category receives no points. If yes is checked, the client may be classified maximum regardless of the number of points acquired.

B. If a client was committed to a treatment for custody, exclude the time spent in those facilities as part of the last five years, unless the client was convicted for a new offense.

C. For parolees, count assaultive offenses occurring five years prior to incarceration.

D. An assaultive offense is defined as an offense against a person that involves the use of a weapon, physical force or threat of force, all forcible felonies, and all sex crimes.

E. The current offense is counted if it is assaultive.

NEEDS ASSESSMENT SCORING GUIDE

INTRODUCTION

The needs assessment form has been constructed to provide a standardized information base from which programs may be developed. Its purpose is to serve as a tool in making objective classification decisions.

The items and scores on the instrument are based on agent's time required to deal with the various problem areas and levels. The basic idea behind the scoring of each item is the same: to what extent, if any, is the client's ability to function in the day-to-day world impaired. The needs assessment instrument differs from the risk assessment instrument in that both positive and negative points are awarded.

The form is designed to indicate areas of programming need and to distinguish among those clients who definitely need programming, those that may require some programming, and those who need no programming in each designated area. The needs assessment form has not been designed to make classification a more rigid, mechanical, or routine process, nor is its purpose to eliminate client input. In those areas where programming is definitely needed or may be needed, the agent should discuss with the client the various program options and the nature of each program. After reviewing the needed programming and the options available, the probation/parole officer should formulate a supervision plan.

The usefulness of the needs assessment instrument is largely dependent on the quality of information relied upon.

The goal of the needs assessment instrument is to eliminate subjectivity and the personal interpretation from the classification decision-making process. The new classification process will consist of decisions based on objective criteria. It is believed that this process will be beneficial to both the probation and parole officer who must justify their decisions and to clients being classified who demand fairness.

1. ACADEMIC AND VOCATIONAL SKILLS

The item focuses on functional skills rather than actual academic credentials. Therefore, a skilled craftsman may receive zero even though he or she may have little formal education. The individual's ability to make his or her way in the world is an important consideration. College, high school diploma, or G.E.D. may not be enough—ability must be shown.

(a) High school or above skill level (demonstrates ability)...Enter 1
(b) Has vocational training; additional not needed/desired (adequate skills)...........................Enter 1
(c) Has some skills; additional needed/desired, low skill level, may have high school diploma or G.E.D. but demonstrates difficulty reading and writing. Real difficulty filling out written reports or job applications. Has ability to do better...Enter 3
(d) No skills; training needed, minimal-retarded, special education classes or unable to read, write, or do simple mathematical computations...Enter 5

2. EMPLOYMENT

The probation/parole officer must look beyond simple employment/unemployment in rating the item. Underemployment should be taken into account as should "unsatisfactory" employment. An example of "unsatisfactory" employment would be a client with a serious alcohol problem and repeated alcohol-related offenses who is employed as a bartender. In order to score this item, the probation/parole officer must establish a firm employment chronology. While attempting to do so, the agent should be particularly sensitive to gaps in employment.

(a) Satisfactory employment for one year or longer, likes the job, salary sufficient to pay for basic needs, education or vocational background. .... Enter 0
(b) Employed; no difficulties reported, or homemaker, student, retired, or disabled and unable to work, chance for upward advancement with current employer. .... Enter 1
(c) Part-time, seasonal, unstable employment and needs additional employment; unemployed, but has a skill, job has no future. .... Enter 4
(d) Unemployed and virtually unemployable; needs training, large gaps in employment, culturally handicapped, self-employment highly questionable. .... Enter 7

3. FINANCIAL STATUS

Does the client have the skills to handle the simple financial responsibilities of everyday life such as maintaining a checking account and preparing a personal budget?

(a) Long-standing pattern of self-sufficiency, well-off. .... Enter 0
(b) No current difficulties, providing—not overextending, no serious indebtedness. .... Enter 1
(c) Situational or minor difficulties, employed but not making it, difficulty in paying court obligations, overextending, difficulty paying bills. .... Enter 4
(d) Severe difficulties, welfare, can't pay court obligations, bankruptcy. .... Enter 6

4. LIVING ARRANGEMENTS (Within the last six months)

(a) Stable and supportive relationship with family or other living group, marriage intact—no history of separation; both parents together, no prior criminal record for other family member, good attitude toward spouse/parents. .... Enter 0
(b) Client lives alone or independently within another household, relatively stable, getting along, no noticeable problems. .... Enter 1
(c) Client experiencing occasional, moderate interpersonal problems with living group, disorganized, recognize problems exist, motivated to change. .... Enter 4
(d) Client exhibiting frequent and serious interpersonal problems within living group, children removed, recently separated or divorced (within two years); history of bad marriage; extensive prior criminal records of family members; sexual abuse; lack of control; abusive drinking; domestic violence. .... Enter 6

5. EMOTIONAL STABILITY

Guides for the probation/parole officer in regard to this item are as follows: Does the client deal with anger appropriately? Does he/she exhibit excessive anxiety or become immobilized by stress? Ability to cope with day-to-day life situations is a concern here. The 5 score would be used for a neurotic client, with 8 reserved for those with psychotic characteristics.

(a) No symptoms of instability; no apparent stress, well-adjusted .... Enter 1
(b) Symptoms limit, but do not prohibit adequate functioning; neurotic, mild symptoms of depression, anxiety, or acting out, occasional abuse of alcohol or other drugs .... Enter 5
(c) Symptoms prohibit adequate functioning; psychotic, severe symptoms of depression, anxiety, or acting out, frequent use of alcohol or other drugs; suicidal .... Enter 8

6. ALCOHOL USAGE (Current)

As on the risk assessment instrument, "interference with functioning" is the key here. Parole/probation officers are to avoid moral judgments regarding alcohol use and focus instead on the role of alcohol in the client's life. Alcohol-related driving offenses receive a 7.

(a) No interference with functioning, no alcohol abuse.. Enter 1
(b) Occasional abuse; some disruption of functioning; may need treatment; gets "drunk" by own definition twice a month or more; some disruption in functioning when drinking (whether or not "drunk") with family, work, socially, etc. Minor alcohol-related offenses .... Enter 4
(c) Frequent abuse; serious disruption; needs treatment; drinks regularly although never or rarely gets "drunk"; has withdrawal symptoms if stops drinking; has physical symptoms of alcoholism; memory lapse, blackouts, passing out; serious disfunction at work; absenteeism, fired, fights with co-workers or other supervisors or customers; with family, becomes violent, neglectful, abusive toward spouse, children, parents, can't pay bills, separation occurrence; past driving record involving alcohol; present offense or any arrests within the past five years involving alcohol before or during .... Enter 7

7. OTHER SUBSTANCE ABUSE (Current)

The scoring of this item is to be accomplished in the same manner as the "drug usage" item in the risk assessment instrument. A 4 score would apply to clients convicted of marijuana possession while the 6 would refer to present involvement with the drug.

(a) No interference with functioning, no abuse.. Enter 1
(b) Occasional substance abuse; some disruption of functioning; may need treatment; convicted of marijuana possession, but no longer using.. Enter 4
(c) Frequent substance abuse; serious disruption; needs treatment; addiction or recent use of marijuana, narcotics, medication as not prescribed; conviction for possession or intent to deliver; deals in selling of drugs.. Enter 6

8. REASONING/INTELLECTUAL ATTITUDE

This item looks at organic cognitive capacity as opposed to emotional ability, hence the problem level relates to the possibility of retardation. Is the client mentally alert or able to function effectively?

(a) Able to function independently; appears to be average intelligence. Can comprehend what is being said in normal conversation. Can read and comprehend rules of probation/parole .... Enter 1

(b) Some need for assistance; potential for adequate adjustment; has difficulty in completing forms without assistance; has difficulty understanding written or verbal communication; has difficulty using or reading a clock, ruler, calendar, dictionary; has difficulty in following directions; emphasis on difficulty in comprehension ....Enter 4

(c) Deficiencies suggest limited ability to function independently; borderline mental retardation; client cannot function independently; client receives SSI benefits for reason due to developmental disabilities; client is employed in shelter work house ....Enter 7

9. HEALTH

The probation/parole officer should take mental health into account (particularly in the case of the substance abuser), as well as the presence of physical handicaps. Alcoholism or drug abuse is automatically 2 points.

(a) Sound physical health; seldom ill; no problems. ....Enter 1

(b) Handicap or illness interferes with functioning on a reoccurring basis; client may have a condition that restricts employment, requires occasional medical attention (high blood pressure, heart condition, epilepsy, missing limb, back problems, etc.) ....Enter 2

(c) Serious handicap or chronic illnesses; needs frequent medical care; client has a condition that severely restricts employment and program participation. He/she requires frequent medical attention and may be on medication (blindness, serious heart conditions, terminal illness, deafness, paralysis, etc.) ....Enter 3

10. AGENT'S IMPRESSION OF CLIENT'S NEEDS

This is designed to accommodate the agent's subjective impressions.

(a) None. ....Enter 0
(b) Low ....Enter 1
(c) Moderate...Enter 4
(d) High..Enter 6

Appendix B

PRINCIPLES OF CLASSIFICATION

The foundation of classification is a system—the organized and established procedure for combining an interdependent group of events into a unified whole. A system entails the coming together of all components to produce a product: classification. The type of system that exists will determine the type of classification that exists. The *process* by which classification is effected is an integral part of the product. If the process (embodied in the policy and procedure manual) changes, then the classification decisions will change.

Any classification system must operate on the basis of valid principles; those presented below describe the factors necessary for a classification system to exist (Solomon 1980). (In addition, the 14 principles listed below make up the criteria for a classification system assessment tool for evaluating basic system functioning. Specific methods for use of the principles as an assessment tool are discussed in Section 5, *Prison Classification: A Model Systems Approach.*) It is important to note that the following principles must apply to the *entire* prison system, including women and youthful offender institutions and programs.

1. There must be a clear definition of goals and objectives of the total correctional system.

Traditionally, security and custody have been the primary goals and objectives of correctional systems. While most also have rehabilitation as a goal, it is secondary to security and custody, as the latter comprise the primary public mandate to corrections. Humane care and treatment, however, should be integral to all systems.

Prior to attempting to design a classification process or other system-wide program, the Department of Corrections must be very clear as to its own goals and objectives (its function, purpose, and priorities). These should be realistic and understandable to both staff and inmates.

Within these goals, a classification system can be developed to sort those inmates whose identified needs fall within the agency's objectives. Only after conceptualizing its own goals can a correctional system develop a rational classification process.

2. There must be detailed written procedures and policies governing the classification process.

An essential component for a classification decision-making model is a policy statement that sets forth the Department of Corrections' goals, objectives, and purposes for the new classification system. For example, when developing its new classification system in 1979, the Minnesota Department of Corrections based the system on eight departmental "principles" regrading classification. These principles, in order of importance to Minnesota's Department of Corrections, are:

- Minimize risk to the public
- Minimize risk to other inmates and institution staff
- Minimize breaches of security
- Minimize system risk
- Minimize security levels
- Maximize fairness (similar offenders treated in a similar manner)
- Maximize the objective and quantitative nature of all classification criteria
- Maximize inmate understanding of the classification system and inmate participation in program decisions

Policies such as Minnesota's should be included in a comprehensive departmental classification policy manual. The American Correctional Association (ACA) Manual of Standards for Adult Correctional Institutions (1977) calls "essential" (Standard No. 4373) a ". . . classification manual containing all the classification policies and detailed procedures for implementing policies; this manual is made available to all staff involved with classification and is reviewed at least annually and updated as necessary."* The manual must be written clearly and concisely and *must* be understood by classification personnel. The policies contained in the manual should deal with such classification issues as:

- Initial inmate classification and reclassification
- Instructions regarding the makeup of classification committees, units, and teams and the full responsibilities of each
- Definitions of various committees' responsibilities for custody, employment, and vocational/program assignments
- Instructions concerning potential changes in an inmate's program
- Procedures relating to inmate transfer from one program to another and from one institution to another
- Content of the classification interview
- Method of documentation of decisions made

Since classification policies must be dynamic, constantly subject to change and revision as the classification process is continuously evaluated, the classification manual should be prepared in such a manner as to provide for easy update. (An important caution here is that the length of the manual is not necessarily correlated with its quality.)

3. The classification process must provide for the collection of complete, high-quality, verified, standardized data.

The classification system must define the data needed and the format in which it is to be collected and analyzed. High-quality, standardized data is essential to a valid statistical base for classification decision making and for correlation of prediction and need factors.

Complete and verified data permits:

- Equitable determinations based on particular factors of individual cases
- Similar decisions among individual classification analysts on roughly comparable cases
- Quantitative analysis of trends in classification decision making for individual facilities or the Department of Corrections as a whole

Through its technical assistance projects, NIC has found that the quantity and quality of offender data (criminal history, personal and family background, etc.) available to teams when the classification decision must be made are frequently less than adequate, and sometimes entirely unusable. Forms often are incomplete, some data collected are of questionable relevance, and much information is subject to broad interpretation because of its qualitative (narrative) nature.

---

*This standard has since been superseded by Standard 3-4282, which states: "Written policy, procedure, and practice provide for a written inmate classification plan. The plan specifies the objectives of the classification system and methods for achieving them, and it provides a monitoring and evaluation mechanism to determine whether the objectives are being met. The plan is reviewed at least annually and updated as needed." Standards for Adult Correctional Institutions, Third edition, 1990.

In many of the systems studied, NIC found that no specific guidelines were given to field staff regarding the collection of offender background data necessary for a valid classification decision. Without specific and objective guidelines, field staff are not likely to prepare reports sufficiently comprehensive and reliable to be used in an empirically valid statistical analysis.

4. Measurement and testing instruments used in the classification decision-making process must be valid, reliable, and objective.

The numerous legal grievances filed by inmates in recent years charging that classification decision-making processes are discriminatory, biased, or invalid point up the necessity to ensure that any tests administered to inmates have been validated for reliability as predictors of custody and/or program needs. In addition, correctional departments must be able to demonstrate that the testing processes are objective, logical, and fundamentally fair and are designed to meet the needs of both the inmates and the institution. By the same token, tests designed for other purposes should not be used to classify inmates (I.Q. tests, personality inventories).

In mid-1979, NIC sponsored a national survey of screening and classification processes, which assessed the current state-of-the-art in the design and utilization of classification instruments for decision making (American Justice Institute 1979). The survey found that correctional agencies have been shifting from subjective judgments to standardized instruments for classification decision making. The instruments being used are printed forms containing a fixed set of weighted criteria that provide an overall offender summary score. Considerations of this score in the process assists the classification team in making more uniform and consistent decisions that are less subject to legal challenge. (North Carolina and Minnesota submitted their instruments for legal review prior to implementation.) In some states, the forms are used both for custody and needs decision making.

5. There must be explicit policy statements structuring and checking the discretionary decision-making powers of classification team staff.

A corrections department must establish clear guidelines governing the discretionary decision-making powers of classification team staff. Otherwise, the department leaves itself open to allegations of unfairness, arbitrariness, and bias.

Discretionary powers of classification staff remain unstructured in too many systems. One example of the resultant problems was provided by a state corrections department in a grant application to NIC: "There is a very broad range of subjective and informal criteria used by those responsible for the classification of inmates; each person involved in the classification process has internalized his own set of significant variables, has established the relative importance of each of these variables according to his own value scale, and applies these standards in the classification decision on a case-by-case basis.

While discretion cannot and should not be completely eliminated, steps can be taken to designate boundaries within which classification decisions will be made, thus eliminating too broad discretionary power of individuals. A system in which the classification processes, rules, policies, findings, and reasons are open to scrutiny can further serve to check discretion.

Structuring and checking discretion is the responsibility of the Department of Corrections' central office. This responsibility is carried out by:

- Direction and supervision of the classification process by high-level central office personnel
- Establishment of procedures for interinstitutional transfer, including review by central office staff and an appeal procedure and administrative review of difficult cases
- Establishment of procedures for central office monitoring and evaluation of the classification process to ensure that it is operating according to policy
- Establishment of procedures for consideration of mitigating or aggravating factors in decision making
- Initiation of policy pertaining to classification, inmate programs/treatment, and casework, including a classification manual
- Selection, training, and supervision of counselors and other classification staff members

6. There must be provision for screening and further evaluating inmates who are management problems and those who have special needs.

This necessary function, also the responsibility of the Department of Corrections' central office, must be included in any model classification system.

Inmates who are management problems and require special considerations in placement and programming fall into several categories:

- Those who require protection and separation because they may be in danger from other inmates
- Those who, by reason of their offense, criminal record, or institutional behavior require particularly close supervision
- Those who received unusual publicity because of the nature of their crime, arrest, or trial or who were involved in criminal activities of a sophisticated nature, such as organized crime

The most dangerous inmates must be separated from the less violent individuals; thus, the classification process, by necessity, needs to include procedures to determine which inmates are potentially dangerous, such as those who have a history of assaultive or predatory behavior.

In addition to screening and further evaluating inmates who are management problems, the correctional system's central office must provide for inmates who have special needs. Those individuals who, through effective screening, are shown to require special program assignments and monitoring include, but are not limited to, the aged and infirm, the mentally ill and retarded, and those with special medical problems.

7. There must be provisions to match offenders with programs; these provisions must be consistent with risk classification needs.

This process involves the establishment of clear, operational definitions of the various types of offenders and available institutional programs. But risk as well as need factors must be considered when decisions are being made.

Thus, NIC recommends that the classification process be directed toward:

- Identifying and evaluating the factors underlying each inmate's needs
- Recommending programs and activities for inmates according to their *specific* needs and the availability of resources

- Developing and recording the necessary data to support services and long-range program planning

To fulfill these tasks, it is necessary to identify and utilize *all* programs that are available to each individual inmate. This function can be accomplished through a systematic classification of the offender and subsequent development of a program plan specifically designed for him/her.

8. There must be provision to classify each inmate at the least restrictive custody level.

This model classification system component targets the prevalent problem of overclassification. Eliminating overclassification is among the most significant objectives of new classification systems being designed and implemented in Minnesota, Tennessee, New York, and other states.

The first step involved here is developing specific criteria for differential custody assignments. Equally crucial is the second step of ensuring that both staff and inmates are aware of these criteria.

NIC recommends that clearly understandable custody definitions and supervision guidelines be applied system-wide. At a minimum, definitions should be given for (1) the traditional levels of custody—maximum, close, medium, and community and (2) the different uses of segregation (especially disciplinary segregation). A basic premise is that every inmate should be in the lowest custody believed suitable for adequate supervision and warranted by his/her behavior.

9. There must be provision to involve the inmate in the classification process.

Each new inmate should be provided with a copy of the custody criteria; a written explanation of the classification process; and a written explanation of the health care, employment, vocational training, education, transfer, and special programs available, including the selection criteria for each.

In addition, the correctional system should provide for classification teams at each institution so the inmate can participate in the classification decision-making process. ACA standard No. 4374 [Standard 3-4284, Third edition, 1990] calls for "maximum involvement of . . . the inmate in classification reviews." The inmate should be present except, perhaps, during deliberations of the classification team.

10. There must be provisions for systematic, periodic reclassification hearings.

Providing for reclassification on a regularly scheduled basis is another "essential" standard (No. 4376)[Standard 3-4287, Third edition, 1990] recommended by the ACA. Periodic review and reclassification is a cornerstone of any model classification system.

In reporting on its study of the classification process at the Tennessee Department of Corrections, NIC suggested the adoption of the following reclassification guidelines:

- Review/reclassification within two weeks following the inmate's transfer from another institution within the system
- Review every three months for inmates serving terms of 18 months or less
- Review every six months for inmates serving terms of 18 months and one day to five years
- Annual review for inmates serving terms of five years of more (NIC now recommends review every six months.)

If suitable manpower is available, reviews can be conducted on a more frequent basis. Optimally, inmates should be permitted to initiate reviews of their progress, status, and programming (ACA "important" Standard No. 4379)[Standard 3-4290, Third edition, 1990].

11. The classification process must be efficient and economically sound.

An empirically based classification system should enable the Department of Corrections to handle large numbers of offenders efficiently through a grouping process based on needs and risk. This can be accomplished by using modern technology to assist in the storage, correlation, and retrieval of data, although use of a computer should not be essential.

An efficient, economically sound classification system also makes effective use of other components of the criminal justice system, as well as social service agencies, for the provisions of offender data (such as information obtained for pre-sentence reports).

The development of a model classification system should involve cooperating with other agencies to devise a standard reporting format for offender information, preferably one that elicits quantitative data insofar as possible.

12. There must be provisions to continuously evaluate and improve the classification process.

Any true process continuously strives to improve itself through feedback, evaluation, and action to correct deficiencies. Thus, the model classification system, if it is to be effective, must be able to continuously improve to meet the changing needs of the inmate population and the correctional system as a whole. It must be responsive to emerging knowledge and professional understanding of the classification process. The system must also be responsive to staff and inmate input.

13. Classification procedures must be consistent with constitutional requisites.

The central office must keep abreast of litigation applicable to its jurisdiction in order to ensure the continued legality of its classification policies, procedures, and decisions. Most state Departments of Correction have a legal section that can be of assistance in this area.

14. There must be an opportunity to gain input from administration and line staff when undertaking development of a classification system.

In summary, the hallmark of classification is *the non-capricious assignment of individuals*. In order to accomplish equity in custody, security, program and treatment determination, and placement, a system reflecting the above principles must exist. Furthermore, it must be utilized.

A basic tenet to classification takes the idea of non-capricious placement a step further. As stated earlier, classification seeks to determine the placement of individuals in accord with their various correctional needs. Each of these outcomes may be accomplished separately, but it is only when they are combined into a comprehensive process that strives for equity and objectivity that we define it as classification. Since equity and objectivity are goals, principles and procedures should be employed that reflect these aims.

INITIAL INMATE CLASSIFICATION

Custody

Name:______________________________ Number:______________

Last First MI

Classification Caseworker:______________________ Date:______________

1. HISTORY OF INSTITUTIONAL VIOLENCE Score:______

(Jail of Prison, code most serious within last five years)

None 0

Assault and battery not involving use of a weapon or resulting in serious injury 3

Assault and battery involving use of a weapon and/or resulting in serious injury or death 7

2. SEVERITY OF CURRENT OFFENSE Score:______

(Refer to the *Severity of Offense Scale* on p. 303. Score the most serious offense if there are multiple convictions.)

Low 0

Low moderate 1

Moderate 2

High 4

Highest 6

3. PRIOR ASSAULTIVE OFFENSE HISTORY Score:______

(Score the most severe in inmate's history. Refer to the *Severity of Offense Scale*.)

None, low, or low moderate 0

Moderate 2

High 4

Highest 6

4. ESCAPE HISTORY (Rate last 3 years of incarceration) Score:______

No escapes or attempts (or no prior incarcerations) 0

An escape or attempt from minimum or community custody, no actual or threatened violence:

Over 1 year ago 1

Within the last year 3

An escape or attempt from medium, or above custody, or an escape from minimum or community custody with actual or threatened violence:

Over 1 year ago 5

Within the last year 7

CLOSE CUSTODY SCORE (Add items 1 through 4) ☐

(If score is 10 or above, inmate should be assigned to close custody. If score is under 10, complete items 5 through 8 and use medium/minimum scale.)

5. ALCOHOL/DRUG ABUSE Score:_____

None 0
Abuse causing occasional legal and social adjustment problems 1
Serious abuse, serious disruption of functioning 3

6. CURRENT DETAINER Score:_____

None 0
Misdemeanor detainer 1
Extradition initiated - misdemeanor 3
Felony detainer 4
Extradition initiated - felony 6

7. PRIOR FELONY CONVICTIONS Score:_____

None 0
One 2
Two or more 4

8. STABILITY FACTORS Score:_____

(Check appropriate box(s) and combine for score.)
Age 26 or over .... -2
High school diploma or GED received .... -1
Employed or attending school (full or part-time) for six months or longer at time of arrest .... -1

MINIMUM/MEDIUM SCORE (Add items 1 through 8.) **Total Score:**_____

MEDIUM/MINIMUM SCALE:

Medium Custody 7-22
Minimum Custody .... 6 or less

Severity of Offense Scale

(From Massachusetts Superior Court Sentencing Guidelines Project, 1979)

6 POINTS:

- Armed assault in a dwelling
- Armed robbery while masked
- Armed robbery
- Arson in a dwelling place, night, occupied
- Burglary, being armed
- Kidnapping to extort
- Murder*
- Rape
- Robbery
- Stealing by confining or putting in fear

5 POINTS:

- Extortion
- Incest
- Kidnapping
- Manslaughter
- Mayhem

4 POINTS:

- Arson (Note: not Arson as listed above)
- Breaking and entering, nighttime
- Burglary, not being armed
- Burning to defraud
- Burning insured property
- Burning real property
- Carrying a firearm+
- Common receiver
- Indecent A&B child under 14
- Mfg., dist., or poss. with intent to dist., Class A&B

3 POINTS:

- Assault and battery to collect a loan
- Assault and battery with a dangerous weapon
- Assault with intent to murder, maim
- Assault with intent to rob while being armed
- Attempt to murder by poisoning
- Breaking and entering in the daytime

Attempt or accessory before the fact of an offense receives the same score as the substantive offense.

*Score only if prior offense.

+If present offense, score only if *not* most serious offense.

INITIAL INMATE CLASSIFICATION (continued)

Assessment of Needs

NAME:______________________________ NUMBER:____________________
Last First MI

CLASSIFICATION CHAIRMAN:______________________________

DATE:____________________

TEST SCORES:

I.Q.:__________
Reading:_______
Math:_________

NEEDS ASSESSMENT: Select the answer that best describes the inmate.

HEALTH: Code:________

1. Sound physical health, seldom ill.
2. Handicap or illness that interferes with functioning on a recurring basis.
3. Serious handicap or chronic illness, needs frequent medical care.

INTELLECTUAL ABILITY: Code:________

1. Normal intellectual ability, able to function independently.
2. Mild retardation, some need for assistance.
3. Moderate retardation, independent functioning severely limited.

BEHAVIORAL/EMOTIONAL PROBLEMS: Code:________

1. Exhibits appropriate emotional responses.
2. Symptoms limit adequate functioning, requires counseling, may require medication.
3. Symptoms prohibit adequate functioning, requires significant intervention, may require medication or separate housing.

ALCOHOL ABUSE: Code:________

1. No alcohol problem.
2. Occasional abuse, some disruption of functioning.
3. Frequent abuse, serious disruption, needs treatment.

INITIAL INMATE CLASSIFICATION (continued)

DRUG ABUSE: Code:________

1. No drug problem.
2. Occasional abuse, some disruption of functioning.
3. Frequent abuse, serious disruption, needs treatment.

EDUCATIONAL STATUS: Code:________

1. Has high school diploma or GED.
2. Some deficits, but potential for high school diploma or GED.
3. Major deficits in math and/or reading, needs remedial programs.

VOCATIONAL STATUS: Code:________

1. Has sufficient skills to obtain and hold satisfactory employment.
2. Minimal skill level, needs enhancement.
3. Virtually unemployable, needs training.

INITIAL INMATE CLASSIFICATION (continued) ______________________________

Initial Classification Summary

1. Override Considerations Code:______

- Custody Classification

1. None
2. Inmate Needs Protection
3. Temporary Placement-Pending Investigation
4. Temporary Placement-Punitive Isolation
5. Temporary Placement-Suicide Threat
6. Other, Specify:

____

____

2. Custody Level Assignment: Code:______

1. Community
2. Minimum
3. Medium
4. Close
5. Maximum
6. Protective Custody
7. Other, Specify:

____

____

____

3. Facility Assignment: Code:______

4. Program Recommendations
(In order of priority)

	Program Code	Enrollment Code*
______________________	_____	_____
______________________	_____	_____
______________________	_____	_____
______________________	_____	_____

Score:______

I.Q.______

Score:______ Reading:______

Math:______

Code:______

Score:______

Code:______

Score:______

Score:______

Code:______

☐

Code:______

Score:______ Code:______

5. Work Recommendations:

	Work Code	Inmate Skills	Skill Code
____________	____	____________	____
____________	____	____________	____
____________	____	____________	____
____________	____	____________	____
____________	____	____________	____

Score:______ Code:______

Score:______ Code:______

Score:______

TOTAL SCORE:______

*Enrollment Code
Program available = 1
Program currently at capacity/unavailable = 2
Program needed but does not exist at required custody level = 3
Inmate refuses program = 4

CORRECTIONAL ADJUSTMENT CHECKLIST (CACL) ____________

Name and number of inmate:____________

Name of person completing this checklist: ____________

Your position:____________ Date completed:____________

Instructions: Please indicate which of the following behaviors this inmate exhibits. If the behavior describes the inmate, circle the "1." If it does not, circle the "O." *Please complete every item.*

0	1	1. Worried, anxious
0	1	2. Tries, but cannot seem to follow directions
0	1	3. Tense, unable to relax
0	1	4. Socially withdrawn
0	1	5. Continually asks for help from staff
0	1	6. Gets along with the hoods
0	1	7. Seems to take no pleasure in anything
0	1	8. Jittery, jumpy; seems afraid
0	1	9. Uses leisure time to cause trouble
0	1	10. Continually uses profane language; curses and swears
0	1	11. Easily upset
0	1	12. Sluggish and drowsy
0	1	13. Cannot be trusted at all
0	1	14. Moody, brooding
0	1	15. Needs constant supervision
0	1	16. Victimizes weaker inmates
0	1	17. Seems dull and unintelligent
0	1	18. Is an agitator about race
0	1	19. Continually tries to con staff
0	1	20. Impulsive; unpredictable
0	1	21. Afraid of other inmates
0	1	22. Seems to seek excitement
0	1	23. Never seems happy
0	1	24. Doesn't trust staff
0	1	25. Passive; easily led

CORRECTIONAL ADJUSTMENT CHECKLIST (continued)

0	1	26. Talks aggressively to other inmates
0	1	27. Accepts no blame for any of his troubles
0	1	28. Continually complains; accuses staff of unfairness
0	1	29. Daydreams; seems to be mentally off in space
0	1	30. Talks aggressively to staff
0	1	31. Has a quick temper
0	1	32. Obviously holds grudges; seeks to "get even"
0	1	33. Inattentive; seems preoccupied
0	1	34. Attempts to play staff against one another
0	1	35. Passively resistant; has to be forced to participate
0	1	36. Tries to form a clique
0	1	37. Openly defies regulations and rules
0	1	38. Often sad and depressed
0	1	39. Stirs up trouble among inmates
0	1	40. Aids or abets others in breaking the rules
0	1	41. Considers himself unjustly confined

Source: Herbert C. Quay, Ph.D.

RAW SCORE FORM: CORRECTIONAL ADJUSTMENT CHECKLIST (CACL) ____

Name and number of inmate:______________________________

Name of person completing this checklist:______________________________

Your position:______________________ Date completed:______________________

Instructions: For each "1" circled on the Correctional Adjustment Checklist, place a checkmark on the line corresponding to the item number. Add the checkmarks to obtain the Raw Score for each group.

Group I	Group II	Group IV	Group V
			1. _____
		2. _____	3. _____
		4. _____	5. _____
6. _____		7. _____	8. _____
9. _____			
10. _____			11. _____
		12. _____	
13. _____		14. _____	
15. _____			
16. _____		17. _____	
18. _____	19. _____		
20. _____			21. _____
22. _____		23. _____	
	24. _____	25. _____	
26. _____			
27. _____	28. _____	29. _____	
30. _____			
31._____			
32._____		33. _____	
	34. _____	35. _____	
36. _____			
37. _____			38. _____
39. _____			
40. _____	41._____		
Total (Raw Score): _______	_______	_______	_______

Source: Herbert C. Quay, Ph.D

CHECKLIST FOR THE ANALYSIS OF LIFE HISTORY RECORDS OF ADULT OFFENDERS (CALH) ____________

Name and number of inmate:______________________________

Name of person completing this checklist:______________________________

Your position:____________________ Date started: ____________________

Instructions: Circle each behavior trait that describes this inmate's life history.

1. Has few, if any, friends
2. Thrill-seeking
3. Preoccupied; "dreamy"
4. Uncontrollable as a child
5. Has expressed guilt over offense
6. Expresses need for self-improvement
7. Socially withdrawn
8. Weak, indecisive, easily led
9. Previous local, state, or federal incarceration
10. Tough, defiant
11. Irregular work history (if not a student)
12. Noted not to be responsive to counseling
13. Gives impression of ineptness, incompetence in managing everyday problems in living
14. Supported wife and children
15. Claims offense was motivated by family problems
16. Close ties with criminal elements
17. Depressed, morose
18. Physically aggressive (strongarm, assault, reckless homicide, attempted murder, mugging, etc.)
19. Apprehension likely due to "stupid" behavior on the part of the offender
20. Single marriage
21. Expresses feelings of inadequacy, worthlessness
22. Difficulties in the public schools
23. Suffered financial reverses prior to commission of offense for which incarcerated
24. Passive, submissive
25. Bravado, braggart
26. Guiltless; blames others
27. Expresses lack of concern for others

Source: Herbert C. Quay, Ph.D

RAW SCORE FORM: LIFE HISTORY CHECKLIST (CALH) ____________________

Name and number of inmate: ____

Name of person completing this checklist: ____________________________________

Your position: ______________________ Date completed: ________________

Instructions: For each item circled on the Checklist for the Analysis of Life History Records of Adult Offenders, place a checkmark on the line corresponding to the item number. Add the checkmarks to obtain the Raw Score for each group.

	Group		
	I	III	IV
			1. ______
	2. ______		
			3. ______
	4. ______		
		5. ______	
		6. ______	
			7. ______
			8. ______
	9. ______		
	10. ______		
	11. ______		
	12. ______		13. ______
		14. ______	
		15. ______	
	16. ______		17. ______
	18. ______		19. ______
		20. ______	
			21. ______
	22. ______	23. ______	
			24. ______
	25. ______		
	26. ______		
	27. ______		
Total (Raw Score):	__________	__________	__________

Source: Herbert C. Quay, Ph.D.

RAW SCORE TO NORMALIZED T-SCORE CONVERSIONS FOR CORRECTIONAL ADJUSTMENT CHECKLIST (CACL)

Scale I		Scale II		Scale IV		Scale V	
Raw score	T-score	Raw score	T-score	Raw score	T-score	Raw score	T-score
0	41	0	44	0	40	0	39
1	49	1	54	1	47	1	46
2	53	2	59	2	51	2	50
3	56	3	62	3	54	3	54
4	58	4	65	4	56	4	57
5	59	5	70	5	59	5	61
6	60			6	61	6	65
7	61			7	63	7	71
8	62			8	65		
9	63			9	69		
10	64			10	73		
11	65			11	78		
12	66						
13	67						
14	68						
15	69						
16	71						
17	73						
18	76						

RAW SCORE TO NORMALIZED T-SCORE CONVERSIONS FOR LIFE HISTORY CHECKLIST (CALH)

Scale I		Scale III		Scale IV	
Raw score	T-score	Raw score	T-score	Raw score	T-score
0	35	0	39	0	39
1	43	1	47	1	47
2	47	2	52	2	53
3	51	3	58	3	58
4	55	4	64	4	62
5	58	5	70	5	66
6	61	6	76	6	70
7	64			7	74
8	67			8	82
9	71			9	90
10	75				
11	82				

CLASSIFICATION PROFILE FOR ADULT OFFENDERS ____________________

Name and number of inmate: ____________________

Name of person completing this profile: ____________________

Your position: ____________________ Date: ____________________

	Scale	Raw Score	T-score
1. Correctional Adjustment Checklist (CACL)	I	______	______
	II	______	______
	IV	______	______
	V	______	______
Checklist for the Analysis of Life History Records (CALH)	I	______	______
	III	______	______
	IV	______	______

	Scale	CACL T-score		CALH T-score			Final T-score
2. Combined Scores	I	______	+	______	÷ 2	=	______
	II	______				=	______
	III			______		=	______
	IV	______	+	______	÷ 2	=	______
	V	______				=	______

3. Assignment

_____ Group I
_____ Group II
_____ Group III
_____ Group IV
_____ Group V

CLASSIFICATION PROFILE FOR ADULT OFFENDERS (continued)

Instructions:

1. Transfer Totals from Raw Score forms onto appropriate Raw Score lines.
   Using the appropriate conversion table, convert each Raw Score to a T-score.
   - If two CACLS are used per inmate, convert all Raw Scores to T-scores; then add the T-scores obtained for each scale and divide the sum by 2.
2. List the final CACL and CALH T-scores on the appropriate lines in the Combined Scores section.
   - For Scales I and IV, add the T-scores and divide by 2.
3. Use the highest Final T-score to make the final assignment.
   If the two scores are tied, use the following tie-breaker rules:
   - If Group I and Group II are tied for highest,
     —and there is one housing unit for *both* groups, assign to Heavy.
     —and there is one housing unit for *each* group, assign for the best balance or use of available housing.
   - If Group IV and Group V are tied for highest,
     —and there is one housing unit for both groups, assign to Light.
     —and there is one housing unit for each group, assign for the best balance or use of available housing.
   - If Group I *or* Group II are tied with any other group, assign to Heavy.
   - If Group IV *or* Group V are tied with Group III, assign to Light.

(Note: Before using any tie-breaker rules, recheck all scoring and calculations.)

Appendix C

TERMS ASSOCIATED WITH ALCOHOL AND DRUG ADDICTION

AA Alcoholics Anonymous

alcoholic paranoia a delusional system suffered by some alcoholics; feelings of being persecuted and plotted against

alkie alcoholic

acid LSD

acid head user of LSD

angel dust PCP

bad trip unpleasant experience after taking a drug

bag or baggie small packet of drugs, usually marijuana

barbs barbiturates

big D LSD

big chief mescaline, a hallucinogen

black beauties black capsule containing caffeine and phenylopropanolamine, often sold as speed

black tar about 50% pure heroin: looks like a chunk of tar

blaze LSD or acid

blackout temporary loss of memory from drinking alcohol

bummer unpleasant experience after taking a drug; not as unpleasant as a bad trip

buzz minor degree of euphoria after taking a drug

chasing the dragon smoking cocaine

coke cocaine

connection drug peddler

confabulation pseudomemory associated with alcoholism; the person reminisces about things that never occurred

cook up a pill to smoke opium

cooker spoon used for dissolving heroin over a flame

crack ready-to-smoke, freebased cocaine (also known as *rock*)

crash to come down hard from a drug experience

crystal methamphetamine

cut to adulterate drugs with another substance such as milk-sugar

detox detoxification, the process of ridding the body of toxicants

dexie Dexedrine, a stimulant

double trouble Tuinal, a sedative

downers all kinds of depressants—alcohol, barbiturates, etc.

dried out withdrawn from alcohol or drugs

drivers amphetamines

DTs delirium tremens, extreme bodily tremors experienced by alcoholics withdrawing from alcohol; often accompanied by terrifying hallucinations

dynamite a mixture of heroin and cocaine

fix a dose or shot of a narcotic

flash a sudden euphoria after the injection of heroin or methamphetamine

freak out a temporary psychotic reaction after using hallucinogens

freebase process of freeing cocaine from its "cut." Purifying and smoking cocaine

fruit salad taking a mixture of different kinds of pills, often with alcohol as a chaser

hash hashish, most potent source of THC, pure resin of the cannabis plant

high under the influence of drugs

hit dose of drugs or drag on a marijuana cigarette

hooked addicted

horse heroin

jolly beans amphetamines

joint marijuana cigarette

junkie narcotic addict

key short for kilo, 2.2 pounds of any drug

kick break the drug habit

lid street measure of marijuana; makes about 40 joints

lude methaqualone, a depressant drug

TERMS ASSOCIATED WITH ALCOHOL AND DRUG ADDICTION (continued)

mainlining injecting drugs directly into the veins

Mexican brown high-grade marijuana from Mexico

microdot small round pill of LSD

pep pills amphetamines

pink ladies Seconal, a barbiturate drug

pot marijuana; ***hay, grass, weed, reefer, tea, maggies,*** and ***Mary Jane*** are all street synonyms

red devils, or reds Seconal, a barbiturate drug

roach clip any device used to hold a marijuana cigarette

rush warm euphoric feeling after injecting heroin

rush Amyl/Butyl/Nitrate, an inhalant that produces a hallucinogenic effect

scag heroin

score buy drugs

shroom psilocybin mushroom, a hallucinogen

seccy Seconal, a barbiturate

shakes beginning stages of DTs

shoot up inject drugs

shooting gallery place to shoot up drugs

snow cocaine

stoned under the influence of drugs

STP a synthetic hallucinogen: "serenity, tranquility, peace"

THC tetrahydrocannabinol, the active ingredient in hashish and marijuana

tracks collapsed veins from frequent drug injections

trip an experience with a hallucinogenic drug

wasted heavily under the influence of alcohol or drugs

water pipe pipe used to smoke drugs

Wernicke-Korsakoff syndrome a condition associated with alcoholism and thought to be due to extreme Vitamin B deficiency. The syndrome is characterized by amnesia, distortion of memory, and disorientation of time and place. Sometimes called *Korsakoff psychosis.*

wet brain neurological condition of a long-term alcoholic; sometimes used inaccurately as a synonym for Wernicke-Korsakoff syndrome

wired high, especially on methamphetamine

THE MICHIGAN ALCOHOLISM SCREENING TEST

Points		Yes	No
	0. Do you enjoy a drink now and then?	____	____
(2)	*1. Do you feel that you are a normal drinker? (By normal we mean you drink less than or as much as other people.)	____	____
(2)	2. Have you ever awakened the morning after drinking the night before and found that you could not remember a part of the evening?	____	____
(1)	3. Does your wife, husband, parent, or other near relative ever worry or complain about your drinking?	____	____
(2)	*4. Can you stop drinking without a struggle after two drinks?	____	____
(1)	5. Do you ever feel guilty about your drinking?	____	____
(2)	*6. Do friends or relatives think you are a normal drinker?	____	____
(2)	*7. Are you able to stop drinking when you want to?	____	____
(5)	8. Have you ever attended a meeting of Alcoholics Anonymous (AA)?	____	____
(1)	9. Have you ever gotten into physical fights when drinking?	____	____
(2)	10. Has your drinking ever created problems between you and your wife, husband, parent, or other relative?	____	____
(2)	11. Has your wife, husband, or another family member ever gone to anyone for help about your drinking?	____	____
(2)	12. Have you ever lost friends because of your drinking?	____	____
(2)	13. Have you ever gotten into trouble at work or school because of drinking?	____	____
(2)	14. Have you ever lost a job because of drinking?	____	____
(2)	15. Have you ever neglected your obligations, your family, or your work for two or more days in a row because you were drinking?	____	____

THE MICHIGAN ALCOHOLISM SCREENING TEST (continued)

Points		Yes	No
(1)	16. Do you drink before noon fairly often?	____	____
(2)	17. Have you ever been told you have liver trouble? Cirrhosis?	____	____
(2)	**18. After heavy drinking have you ever had delirium tremens (DTs) or severe shaking or heard voices or seen things that really weren't there?	____	____
(5)	19. Have you ever gone to anyone for help about your drinking?	____	____
(5)	20. Have you ever been in the hospital because of drinking?	____	____
(2)	21. Have you ever been a patient at a psychiatric hospital or on a psychiatric ward of a general hospital where drinking was part of the problem that resulted in hospitalization?	____	____
(2)	22. Have you ever been seen at a psychiatric or mental health clinic or gone to any doctor, social worker, or clergyman for help with an emotional problem, where drinking was part of the problem?	____	____
(2)	***23. Have you ever been arrested for drunk driving, driving while intoxicated, or driving under the influence of alcoholic beverages? (If yes, how many times? ____)	____	____
(2)	***24. Have you ever been arrested, or taken into custody, even for a few hours, because of other drunk behavior? (If yes, how many times? ____)	____	____

Scoring system: In general, five points or more would place the subject in an alcoholic category, four points would be suggestive of alcoholism, and three points or less would indicate that the subject was not alcoholic.

*Alcoholic response is negative.
**Five points for delirium tremens.
***Two points for each arrest.

Source: M.L. Selzer, 1971-1980.

Index